THE LOST WORLD OF ITALIAN AMERICAN RADICALISM

THE LOST WORLD OF ITALIAN AMERICAN RADICALISM

Politics, Labor, and Culture

Edited by
Philip V. Cannistraro
and Gerald Meyer

Italian and Italian American Studies
Spencer M. Di Scala, Series Adviser

Westport, Connecticut
London

Library of Congress Cataloging-in-Publication Data

The lost world of Italian American radicalism : politics, labor, and culture / edited by
    Philip Cannistraro and Gerald Meyer.
        p. cm. — (Italian and Italian American studies, ISSN 1530-7263)
    Includes bibliographical references and index.
    ISBN 0-275-97891-5 (alk. paper) — ISBN 0-275-97892-3 (pbk. : alk. paper)
    1. Italian Americans—Politics and government.   2. Working class—United
States—History.   3. Radicalism—United States—History.   4. Italian American
literature—History and criticism.   I. Cannistraro, Philip V., 1942–   II. Meyer,
Gerald, 1940–   III. Series.
E184.I8L83   2003
320.53'089'51073—dc21   2003051072

British Library Cataloguing in Publication Data is available.

Library of Congress Catalog Card Number: 2003051072
ISBN: 0-275-97891-5
        0-275-97892-3 (pbk.)
ISSN: 1530-7263

First published in 2003

Praeger Publishers, 88 Post Road West, Westport, CT 06881
An imprint of Greenwood Publishing Group, Inc.
www.praeger.com

Printed in the United States of America

The paper used in this book complies with the
Permanent Paper Standard issued by the National
Information Standards Organization (Z39.48–1984).

10 9 8 7 6 5 4 3 2 1

Copyright Acknowledgments

Every reasonable effort has been made to trace the owners of copyrighted materials in
this book, but in some instances this has proven impossible. The editors and the publisher will be glad to receive information leading to more-complete acknowledgments in
subsequent printings of the book and in the meantime extend their apologies for any
omissions.

Excerpts from Gary Mormino, *The Immigrant World of Ybor City: Italians and Their Latin
Neighbors in Tampa* (Gainesville: University Presses of Florida, 1998), pp. 143–64,
reprinted with permission of the University Presses of Florida.

Extracts from Maria Mazziotti Gillan, "The Coming of Age of Paterson," *In Defense of
Mumia,* and "Growing up Italian," *Taking Back My Name,* reprinted with permission.

Contents

Part II: Politics

Part III: Culture

Foreword

The conservative image of Italian Americans contrasts stridently with the strong radical tradition found in Italy. This book, edited by Philip V. Cannistraro and Gerald Meyer, helps provide an explanation for this seeming discrepancy by showing that Italian Americans do indeed have a vibrant, radical past. What emerges from their research and that of the other authors represented in this work is that the disappearance of radicalism from Italian American history was no happenstance but the deliberate result of an "erasure." Moreover, the book explodes a number of stereotypes—for example, by demonstrating that the radicalization of most immigrants began in southern Italy, before they came to the United States, and by showing how southern Italian radicalism adapted to the conditions it found in the New World.

The book closely follows the elements of this adaptation by examining the interrelationship between Italian radicalism and the existing social and political conditions in the United States at the time of the great migration. In accomplishing this task, the authors make an important contribution to Italian American scholarship by rejecting commonplace explanations, such as the contention that Italian immigrants attempted to replicate their villages in the "Little Italies." This discussion is intimately bound up with other social issues, such as the role of the Catholic Church. The editors reach an interesting and countercurrent conclusion on this point by maintaining that Italian Americans remained substantially immune to the political influence of the Church.

An important aspect of this book is its comparative approach to history, emphasizing similarities and differences in the scale of difficulties faced by Italian Americans and other immigrant groups. The authors also make skillful use of data on voting patterns to demonstrate that Italian Americans today do not fit the conservative mold in which they are generally placed.

The editors have put together a wide-ranging book that covers the entire Italian American radical experience. Its chapters include the present, discussing Italian American radicals of the 1960s, the role of women, and gay and lesbian aspects of Italian American life. In addition, it has an important cultural and literary dimension that shows how Italian American novelists and other writers are finally coming into their own. Philip Cannistraro and Gerald Meyer have recaptured the most important elements of a tradition that may have been "lost" but not forsaken.

Spencer M. Di Scala
Series Adviser, Italian and
Italian American Studies

Acknowledgments

The editors wish to acknowledge those friends and colleagues who have contributed to the making of this volume. A great debt of thanks goes to Dr. Joseph V. Scelsa, vice president for Institutional Development at Queens College/CUNY and dean of the John D. Calandra Italian American Institute, whose enthusiastic support for the conference on Italian American radicalism held in 1997 under the aegis of the Calandra Institute was an act of courage and foresight. This book has been made possible as a result of that successful experience. For their support of this conference, thanks are also owed to Frances Horowitz, president of the CUNY Graduate Center, and David Nasaw, director of the CUNY Center for the Humanities. Maria Fosco, Rosaria Musco, and the other staff members of the Calandra Institute gave generously of their talents and time to make this a groundbreaking event.

We wish to express our gratitude to Professor Nunzio Pernicone of Drexel University, who read and corrected the introduction and put his unparalleled knowledge of Italian American radicalism at the disposal of the editors. Gil Fagiani, Jennifer Guglielmo, Ron Ilardo, Joseph Sciorra, and Rudolph Vecoli provided helpful information, and Paola Sensi-Isolani and Salvatore Salerno read and commented on portions of the volume. David A. Hacker helped with research.

To all, our sincere thanks.

PVC
GM

Introduction
Italian American Radicalism: An Interpretive History

Philip V. Cannistraro and Gerald Meyer

> I am suffering because I am a radical and indeed I am a radical; I have suf-
> fered because I was an Italian, and indeed I am an Italian.
>
> Bartolomeo Vanzetti

On March 4, 1912, in the midst of the famous Bread and Roses strike in
Lawrence, Massachusetts—a major industrial strike in the United States, involving workers from an array of ethnic backgrounds[1]—a young girl named Cammella
Teoli, daughter of Italian immigrant parents, sat before a congressional committee
in Washington, D.C., testifying about working conditions in the factories of
Lawrence, where she lived. Cammella explained that when she was 13, she had
worked for a short time in the textile mills, until one day her hair got caught in a
machine—she was scalped, and spent seven months in a hospital. In the visitors'
gallery that day was the wife of President William Howard Taft, who, like the rest
of the audience, was moved by the powerful testimony of the teenage girl.[2]

Newspapers across the country carried Cammella's story on their front pages.
Her testimony prompted a federal investigation of factory conditions and added
a human face to the strikers. Sixty-four years later, after Cammella had died, Paul
Cowan, a reporter for the *Village Voice*, tracked down her daughter in a suburb of
Lawrence. He was stunned to discover that Cammella's daughter, whom he
called Mathilda, knew nothing at all about Cammella Teoli's political past—
nothing about her trip to Washington, nothing about Mrs. William Howard
Taft's presence, nothing about the sensational impact her mother had made on
the nation's conscience. The Cammella Teoli her children knew was just a mill
hand with an odd bald spot on her head, a sweet, silent lady who bought and
cooked the traditional eels on Christmas Eve, who rarely missed a Sunday mass.
She had been submerged by the immigrants' reluctance to discuss their heroic
past. She had never once mentioned the trip to Washington, which must have
been the proudest moment of her life. When Mathilda read her mother's testimony in the official transcript of the hearings, she exclaimed, "Now I have a
past. Now my son has a history."[3]

It is this sense of a lost history—indeed, of a lost world—that the historian A. William Salomone had in mind when he wrote more than a quarter of a century ago of the urgency of documenting the story of Italian American radicalism before its traces disappeared with the passing of the first generation of immigrants. "Unless this is done quickly, soon," he predicted, "we will witness the vanishing of truly precious parts of both Italian and American history. For those complicated and fascinating little worlds of Italian-American radicalism . . . that struggled to survive within the larger worlds of alternatively predominant conservatism and liberalism will otherwise surely go under, submerged, to become only legendary remembrances of strange things past."[4]

For most Americans, Italian American radicalism is an oxymoron. The media portray Italian Americans as anti-intellectual thugs or sentimental types, who fight a lot while eating dinner together and managing to perpetuate large families.[5] This image is powerfully reinforced by endless Hollywood and television depictions of the Mafia as integral to the Italian American family and community life, representations that must surely count as one of the most insidious cultural assaults against an ethnic group in American society. The most recent example of this distorted picture is the extraordinarily popular television series *The Sopranos*, which a coalition of Italian American organizations has condemned for "defaming and assassinating the cultural character of Americans of Italian descent."[6] What has been at times lost in the focus on combating the *mafioso* stereotype is the pernicious effects—if not intentions—of representations of Italian Americans as reflexive conservatives who are hostile to political, racial, ethnic, and sexual minorities.[7] One consequence of these emanations from the dominant culture is that the ideas of Italian Americans—if any are present at all—are restricted to mundane notions that reinforce this picturesque world. Whatever else may be its effects, nothing in this picture, which is reproduced with countless variations, allows for the presence of radical ideas or activities.

For most Italian Americans, the experiences of grandparents and parents are replete with deafening silences that are the product in part of the fears and taboos that drove many first-generation immigrants to bury aspects of their past that seemed to make them somehow too Italian and not sufficiently American. These silences are also in part a result of the discomfort of children who find their ancestors' beliefs embarrassing or alien to their own values. The lost world of Italian American radicalism is perhaps the most profound of such zones of silence. Within the ethnic community, few have ventured to remember or ask about that part of their history that deviated from the norms of the dominant society. Perhaps this process of jettisoning community segments that do not comfortably fit within the parameters of political respectability as defined by American society is an understandable result of remembered discrimination and the unrelenting defamation of the Italian American community. However benign the motivations behind them, these efforts to sanitize the history of Italian Americans serve to reinforce the stereotypes that increase the community's vulnerability. For example, the marginalization—or outright omission—of East Harlem's radical congressman Vito Marcantonio from the Italian American experience has until recently had the effect of excising a major civil rights leader and spokesperson for minorities from a group that, however unfairly, has been widely viewed as racist.

What is at stake is both historical accuracy and Italian American self-perception. It is therefore more reprehensible that opinion within the field of Italian American studies has validated this truncated rendition of the Italian American experience. Richard Gambino's influential survey, *Blood of My Blood*, for example, excludes any mention of the two most important representatives of Italian American radicalism, Carlo Tresca and Vito Marcantonio, and rejects the notion that Italian Americans had any interest in politics or ideology.[8] An especially distorted element contributing to the omission of radicalism from the Italian American picture has been the all-encompassing application of the idea of "amoral familism," which argues that southern Italians were not capable of collective action and obscures or dismisses manifestations of southern Italian history that contradict its tenets.[9] Today, scholars of immigrant radicalism reject this view: "Rural Europeans," noted Donna R. Gabaccia, "were neither apathetic nor unfamiliar with the principles of collective action in their homelands."[10]

As an area of study, Italian American radicalism is a relatively recent development.[11] In November 1972, the American Italian Historical Association titled its fifth annual conference "Italian American Radicalism: Old World Origins and New World Developments." However, as Rudolph J. Vecoli observed about that first organized effort to address the subject, "it proved difficult to enlist contributors who could address themselves to the various phases of Italian American involvement in radicalism. While everyone had heard of Arturo Giovannitti and Carlo Tresca, of Lawrence and Paterson, there had been little research in depth on these and related subjects. . . . Italian American radicalism, we have learned, is yet another neglected aspect of the Italian experience in America."[12] The conference, which focused on anarchism and the Sacco and Vanzetti case, omitted studies of Italians in World War I and in the socialist or the communist movements, as well as more-recent manifestations of radicalism, such as the civil rights, women's, or gay and lesbian movements.

Twenty-five years later, in May 1997, the John D. Calandra Italian American Institute of Queens College, City University of New York (CUNY), organized a conference titled "The Lost World of Italian American Radicalism," at which more than sixty scholars working in both the social sciences and cultural areas documented that, from the inception of the Great Migration in 1880 to the present, leading figures and segments of the Italian American community—at times larger and more influential than at others—have been radical. The sixteen essays that appear in this volume are based on the most important papers delivered at this groundbreaking event.

The term *radical* in everyday parlance has become almost interchangeable with the term *extremism*. Here, however, *radical* is used in the same sense as the radical, that is, the root of a number. In this sense, radical signifies individuals or movements that seek to get at the causes rather than the symptoms of political, economic, and social conditions. The term was first used in this way to describe the Levellers and others who, during the seventeenth-century English Revolution advocated reform beyond the boundaries of purely religious and political questions to social and economic areas. However, it was the Jacobins of the French Revolution who came to embody the modern idea of political and social "radicalism." In the nineteenth century, the word was applied to those who wanted to expand the franchise, and it was especially associated with anticlerical republicanism, as well as with movements aimed at democratic change. More recently, parties in France, Italy, Argentina, and Chile that use the term *radical* in their names have espoused a wide range of social and political reforms.

Within the specific context of the Italian American experience, the concept of "radical" was generally expressed by the term *sovversivo*, or subversive, a designation that Italian authorities had used from the 1860s until the fall of Fascism to describe leftist radicals, and by which the radicals themselves preferred to be called.[13] The word *radical* as we use it in this volume includes those individuals, movements, and ideologies that have sought a more equitable redistribution of wealth or political power. Cultural production intended to advance or sustain these redistributive efforts, or that is oppositional to the dominant norms, falls within this definition. In this sense, "radical" is a term linked to the political Left. Liberalism (unlike classical liberalism), which has supported trade unions and government intervention to regulate, ameliorate, and to some extent redistribute, is also included within this definition. Current movements to empower traditionally marginalized groups and to reduce domination based on ethnicity, gender, race, and sexual orientation also are, by this definition, inherently radical.

The Sacco and Vanzetti case, no doubt the best-known event associated with Italian American radicalism, has generated significant research, especially by Paul Avrich and Nunzio Pernicone, about anarchism in the Italian American community.[14] Rudolph Vecoli has also produced a steady stream of work pointing toward a vision of the Italian American experience that includes its full spectrum of ideological and organizational responses.[15] Three biographies of Vito Marcantonio and one of Carlo Tresca (limited in its treatment of Tresca's radical activities and focusing on his murder) have placed these major figures of Italian American radicalism before a larger public.[16] No existing work, however, has assembled the various shades and types of radicalism—anarchism, syndicalism, socialism, and communism, as well as less easily ideologically defined movements for radical democracy—that have functioned, and at times flourished, within the Italian American community.[17]

In a classic early work on Italian emigration, Robert Foerster wrote that "emigration . . . implies a readiness to sever (or loosen) patriotic ties. It is simpler and may seem surer than revolution; it is more satisfactory for the individual. . . . But it is also the method of the miserable man whose patriotic or civic ties, being slender, are easily sundered—whose fatherland is whatever country will give him his bread."[18] Today we know that this simplistic view of Italian loyalties, and of the relationship between radicalism and migration, is both inaccurate and inadequate. As Donna Gabaccia has posed the issue, it is necessary "to view the lost world of Italian American radicalism not as a world unto itself with its own internal debates—worthy as these are—but rather as one important dimension of a global history of population movements out of Italy."[19]

Both domestic American history and transnational developments have contributed significantly to the shaping of Italian American radicalism, and Italian American radicalism in the United States has responded in an ongoing way to Italian circumstances. From the late nineteenth century, Italian anarchists and socialists in the United States had developed and maintained through correspondence, newspapers, and publications a network of regular contacts with comrades in Europe; the trans-Atlantic connection continued throughout the twentieth century as syndicalists, communists, and anti-Fascists made use of the same kinds of transnational connections. It is possible, in fact, to speak of a "radical chain migration" operating in both directions across the Atlantic—Italy supplied a continuing influx of radicals and ideas to the Little Italies, and in turn the radical elements in these communities often raised money for and supported causes back home.[20] The impact of radical movements on the Italian American community and the wider society has varied depending on a number of factors, not the least of which has been the prevailing political climates in the United States and in Italy. The history, and, therefore, the periodization, of Italian American radicalism does not, however, entirely correspond to the general trajectory of radicalism in either country, or for that matter to patterns within other American immigrant communities.

The Sacco-Vanzetti case stands as a talisman for both the limits and the possibilities of a historical understanding of the *sovversivi*. It has, on the one hand, contributed to an interpretation of Italian American radicalism that presents August 23, 1927—the date of Nicola Sacco and Bartolomeo Vanzetti's deaths—as "the end of the road of Italian-American radicalism."[21] This view fails to acknowledge that anarchism was almost everywhere a first-generation phenomenon.[22] A broader perspective suggests the inadequacy of this view and points to the tragedy instead as a crossroads: thus, after attending a huge protest rally in New York's Union Square on the night of the executions, the young writer Pietro Di Donato joined the Communist Party.[23]

We propose, therefore, a periodization for the history of Italian American radicalism as follows: (1) 1880–1917. During the great wave of immigration, radicalism—in the forms of anarchism, socialism, and syndicalism—had accompanied migration from Italy and was partially transformed by experiences in the United States, where it became widespread throughout the Italian American community. (2) 1917–1931. During World War I and the postwar period, along with the entire U.S. Left, Italian American radicalism sharply declined under the impact of systematic government repression. With Mussolini's rise to power in Italy in 1922, the Left redirected much of its energy toward the anti-Fascist struggle, continually challenging, and in some instances successfully contesting, the Fascist hegemony within the community. (3) 1932–1945. The Great Depression gave impetus to the New Deal and the organization of the working class, which after 1935 engendered an Italian American contingent of the Popular Front, where socialism and communism supplanted anarchism and syndicalism as the dominant ideologies. (4) 1946–1961. In the post–World War II period, along with the entire American Left, Italian American radicalism was suppressed by a combination of circumstances lethal to radicalism—widespread prosperity and attendant assimilation in tandem with the political repression that accompanied domestic cold war politics. (5) 1962 to the present. Although the Italian American community (along with much of American society) moved to the center and to the Right, individual Italian Americans provided leadership in the student and civil rights movements and later in the movements for women's rights and gay and lesbian rights.

* * *

In 1850, a mere 853 Italians lived in New York City, a number that by 1870 had increased only to 2,800. Between 1876 and 1880 as few as 13,000 Italians had entered U.S. ports.[24] However, the great migration to the United States from 1880 to 1920 brought 35 million so-called New Immigrants from eastern and southern Europe to the United States. Approximately five million of these immigrants were from Italy, who constituted the largest nationality. Like the other New Immigrants, they were not Protestant and did not speak English. Moreover, when compared to the earlier immigrants from northwestern Europe, they maintained customs and lifestyles that the dominant Anglo-Saxon culture regarded as exotic and dangerous.

Among all the new immigrant nationalities, the Italians had the most difficult adjustment. Their occupational and social patterns were the least adaptable to their new environment; and, unlike the Jews, for example, they had no sizable group of previously arrived compatriots to provide services and advocate for them.[25] The Italian immigrants received the least hospitality and experienced the most-insistent and pervasive hostility. It has become increasingly clear that American officials accepted notions of southern Italian racial inferiority that had been propagated by anthropologists in Italy itself. Consequently, Italians were frequently not thought of as "white,"[26] and naturalization certificates issued by the U.S. Immigration and Naturalization Bureau used "South Italian" as an officially separate racial designation from Italians in general.[27]

Eighty percent of the five million Italians who entered the United States between 1880 and 1920 emigrated from the *mezzogiorno*, where already-woeful social and economic conditions had deteriorated after unification. The bulk of these emigrants derived from the most oppressed class, the *contadini*, land-poor peasants who generally did not own sufficient land to maintain their own families and who consequently had to resort to hiring themselves out to large landowners. The *contadini* lived in isolated agrotowns, often under semifeudal social and economic conditions, where they endured a host of disabilities, including restricted access to education, subsistence income, inadequate nutrition, and poor health.[28] The other southern Italian immigrants to the United States, with remarkably few exceptions, were *artigiani*, who—despite their higher rates of literacy and some genuine independence from the control of the nobility, large landowners, and their agents—lived lives not greatly different from the peasant masses. The Risorgimento's success in uniting Italy had not alleviated exploitation, implemented the construction of schools and roads, or brought about social reforms so desperately needed by southerners. At the same time, the Catholic Church remained enmeshed in a system that bore the worst characteristics of both feudalism and capitalism. Among the *contadini*, and especially the *artigiani*, these conditions led to a general rejection of liberalism and, at least among the men, an endemic anticlericalism.

Social and economic inequality, combined with the failure of both secular and religious authority to win the allegiance of the *contadini* and the *artigiani*, created an ideal milieu for radicalism. In the first decades after the unification of Italy, anarchism inspired centers of radical activity in north-central Italy as well as in Naples and Sicily. In contrast with its vast following in central and northern Italy, by 1919 the Socialist Party attracted no more than 10 percent of the vote in the South. These electoral statistics, however, enormously underestimate the extent of radicalism in southern Italy. In part, this is due to the insistence on identifying radicalism with the urban proletariat, an attitude that socialist leaders of the reformist variety generally encouraged. Nowhere else in Europe were socialism and unionism so prevalent among agricultural workers.[29] Between 1889 and 1893, the Sicilian Fasci dei Lavoratori—a socialist movement that began in the cities among workers and artisans but eventually included *contadini*, *mezzadri* (sharecroppers), and *braccianti* (day laborers)—boasted more than 300,000 activists. The uprising of the Fasci in 1893–94 resulted in direct action and land seizures and led Prime Minister Francesco Crispi to send some 40,000 troops to the island. The government reaction proved to be the prelude to a six-year-long period of repression.[30] The Partito Popolare, established in 1919 by the Sicilian priest Don Luigi Sturzo, was meant to counter the attractions of anarchism and socialism among the *contadini* while embracing agrarian reform and social legislation. Once organized, however, the *contadini*, who enthusiastically filled its ranks, moved the party much further left than its clerical sponsors had intended, to the point that it demanded the division of the *latifondi* and even participated in land seizures.[31]

When the Southern Italians boarded ships headed for the United States, they did not leave their vision of a radically reordered society behind them.[32] Donna Gabaccia's research established that contrary to the proposition that the southern Italian exodus represented an alternative to radicalism, Sicilian "emigrants came from precisely those towns and those backgrounds where labor militancy enjoyed its greatest appeal . . . and the most militant towns had the highest average migration rates."[33]

In the United States, there has been a close association between immigrant status and radicalism. "The main day-to-day role of the Left among immigrant groups," notes Paul Buhle, "had long been to legitimate a quasi-national solidarity within the groups, and to balance it with class interests. Thus the free thinkers, socialists, Wobblies, and later Communists among the immigrant radicals of the various ethnicities not only participated in community development, they frequently had played a major part in creating the immigrant communities and continually giving them new shape."[34] Salvatore Salerno's study of the Industrial Workers of the World (IWW) shows that, despite its reputation as a "native" American expression of radicalism, the foreign born comprised a majority of its membership.[35] After its founding in 1901 the Socialist Party, under the leadership of German-born Victor Berger, opposed the growing numbers of New Immigrants in the United States. Indeed, the states where it garnered the highest percentage of the electorate—Oklahoma, Nevada, Montana, Washington, California, and Idaho—contained relatively few recent immigrants.[36] By 1919, however, most members of the Socialist Party were immigrants and its foreign-language federations provided a majority of its membership.[37] Consequently, the loci of its much-diminished strength centered around cities and districts (for example, Milwaukee; Reading, Pennsylvania; and the Brownsville section of Brooklyn) populated by those who were a part of, or close to, the first-generation immigrant cultures. Throughout the 1920s, 90 percent of the membership of the Communist Party was foreign born. It was not until the late 1930s that as many as one-half of its membership was American born, and most of this cohort was second-generation American.[38]

The persistence of the immigrant experience within the Italian American community made it an ideal environment for radicalism. Second-generation Italian Americans (that is, those who had at least one parent born in Italy) did not outnumber first-generation Italians until 1915. Remarkably, it was not until 1953 that the third generation (those whose parents were born in America but who had at least one grandparent born in Italy) exceeded second-generation Italian Americans, and the third and later generations outnumbered the combined total of the first- and second-generation some years later.[39]

Even less often recognized, however, is that thousands of Italian immigrants, including Sacco and Vanzetti, did not bring their radicalism with them to the United States, but were radicalized by their experiences in the United States. The Italian emigrants to the United States were the most proletarianized of any European nationality. A survey of the leading occupations of Italian fathers of children born in New York City in 1916 revealed that 50.4 percent were laborers and that the next four largest categories were *artigiani*: tailors (5.4 percent), barbers (5.3 percent), shoemakers (2.9 percent), and carpenters (2.1 percent). Only a miniscule 1.2 percent and .7 percent were listed as "professional" and "clerical," respectively, on the birth certificates of their children.[40] Annual statistics compiled by Italian sources showed that from 1901 to 1910, the percentage of unskilled workers emigrating from Italy to the United States ranged from a low of 75 to a high of 90 percent.[41] This concentration in low-paying, insecure occupations was not solely a first-generation phenomenon. Upward mobility remained painfully slow within the Italian American community. Furthermore, many of the gains that had been made were lost during the Great Depression, because unemployment was most severe in exactly those areas of the economy with the highest concentrations of Italian Americans. In New York City in 1934, manual workers (who had comprised 35 percent of the workforce) represented 50 percent of all workers on relief, and more than 18 percent of construction workers were receiving relief. By 1940, the situation had changed little: more than 31 percent of construction workers were still unemployed, and 27 percent of musicians (a predominantly Italian profession) were unemployed.[42] Similarly, in the early 1930s, the district where most Italians in Philadelphia lived had the highest unemployment rates in the city, and one-third of all heads of Philadelphia families who applied for relief were of Italian origin.[43] It is likely that during the Great Depression, Italian Americans had the highest rates of unemployment of any European ethnic group.

The general occupational profile of the Italian immigrants and most of their children corresponded to those sectors of the population most prone to radicalism. What so intensified this potential was the treatment of Italians as an inferior caste. The Quota Act of 1921 and the Immigration Act of 1924 established the national-origins quota system, which limited the annual entry of immigrants to only 2 percent of each foreign-born group residing in the United States in 1890, that is, *before* the mass of Italians had begun to arrive. Although these laws affected all groups of New Immigrants, they were directed against the two largest and most stigmatized of these nationalities—Jews and Italians. Conversely, these laws greatly favored immigrants from northeastern Europe, the bulk of whom had arrived before 1890. Indeed, the annual quotas of the ethnic groups deriving from northeastern Europe were so large that they were seldom filled. These discriminatory immigration laws, which remained in force until 1965, served as a de facto legal codification of the Americanization movement, which was intended to replace as quickly as possible the original immigrant cultures—and especially the languages—with Anglo-Saxon culture and English. Americanization's implicit message insisted upon the inferiority of all other cultures and languages.[44] Although Jews, Slavs, and such other smaller groups as Armenians and Greeks were subject to the same laws and nativist hostility, the effects of this treatment were greatest on the Italians because they were the most economically vulnerable. They did not, as in the case of the Jews, benefit from the support of a cohort of prosperous and influential co-nationals who had arrived earlier; nor did they, as in the case of the Slavic nationalities, have the advantage of being defended by a national church.

The Roman Catholic Church proved to be a major bulwark against the radicalization of the working class in the United States.[45] Initially, the Church opposed all measures designed to alleviate the workers' plight. In his 1864 encyclical *Quanta cura* (which contains the "syllabus of errors") Pope Pius IX anathematized religious toleration, freedom of the press, socialism, and rationalism, and denied that the pope either could or should come to terms with "progress, liberalism, and modern civilization." Abandoning this obscurantist approach, Pope Leo XIII in 1891 promulgated his *Rerum novarum*, which conceded that property should be more equitably divided and that workers had the right to form unions.[46] This encyclical enunciated the Catholic Church's determination to directly compete with the Socialist parties for the allegiance of the workers by establishing political organizations and trade unions. In response to the Russian Revolution, the Church moved toward a more religion-based opposition when, for example, it propagated the cults of Our Lady of Fatima and Saint Joseph the Worker. Despite the Catholic Church's newfound interest in the plight of the workers, it was absent from the front lines of unionism and worker movements. A well-known case in point is that of Father Mariano Milanese of Lawrence, Massachusetts, who opposed the general strike from his pulpit.[47]

In local communities, radicals were generally the only people competing with the priests for the allegiance of Italian immigrants. Especially after the signing of the Lateran Accords in 1929 between Pius XI and Mussolini, the Catholic Church in the Italian American community forged alliances with Fascist diplomatic representatives and with the *prominenti* who ruled the Little Italies. Together they worked to promote Italian nationalist sentiment and to combat radicalism.[48] Later still, the Church also formed organizations such as the Association of Catholic Trade Unionists, which helped lead and execute raids on the left-wing unions in the Congress of Industrial Organizations (CIO).[49] In the post–World War II era, the Catholic Church, under the leadership of the cardinal of New York City's diocese, Francis Spellman, fused hypernationalism and religious symbolism into an increasingly militant anti-Communism that became the central theme of the American Catholic hierarchy.[50]

Italian Americans as a whole, at least until the domestic cold war became entrenched, remained relatively immune to Catholic social and political ideology in general and its antiradical message in particular. Illustrating the persistence of these attitudes were the much lower percentages of Italian American children who attended parochial schools when compared to other Catholic ethnic groups.[51] Anticlericalism, which originated in Italy, partially reflected Old World grievances. In Chicopee, Kansas, coal miners greeted priests with a volley of rocks and rotten vegetables, and in Barre, Vermont, stoneworkers drove an Italian priest out of town.[52] The opposition of Catholic priests to immigrant radicalism acted as a spur to leaders like Carlo Tresca, who persistently fought the influence of the Church in the Little Italies.[53] On at least two occasions—in Natick-Providence, Rhode Island, in 1936 and in Cleveland, Ohio, in 1940—Italian parishioners openly opposed the close relationship between their local churches and Fascism.[54]

The efforts of the American Catholic Church to standardize the religious behavior of the waves of Catholic immigrants[55] meant in practice the imposition of Irish Catholicism. This version of Catholicism contrasted with southern-Italian Catholicism, which was concrete, emotional, and communal.[56] The high-handed and abusive treatment of Italian Catholics by the American Church when they arrived in the United States is encapsulated by the history of Italian Harlem's Our Lady of Mount Carmel Church, which opened its doors in 1884. Italian craftsmen, who lived in the community, literally built the edifice with their own hands after returning from their backbreaking labors. However, after the completion of the church, the Italians were consigned to worship in the basement. Despite the fact that more than 90 percent of the baptisms were performed for the infants of Italian immigrants, it was not until 1919 that an Italian priest became its pastor. In 1903, Pope Leo XIII awarded a set of golden crowns to adorn the Madonna and the infant Jesus and declared the church a basilica (a designation shared with only one other church in the United States). Nonetheless, the statue of Our Lady of Mount Carmel was not moved from the basement to the church proper until 1923.[57]

No matter the degree of hostility from the hierarchy, clergy, or fellow Catholics, conversion to Protestantism was not an option for most Italians. Although some prominent Italian Americans—including Arturo Giovannitti and Leonard Covello—became Protestant, by 1916 only approximately 1 percent of Italian Americans had converted to Protestantism.[58] Therefore, in ways similar to those of the Jewish community, where conversion to Christianity occurred only rarely, radicalism provided an alternative to religion—a *weltanschauung*: a teleology, a community, and a culture.

The overwhelming majority of Italian Americans settled in Little Italies, which were subject to the same degree of defamation as the Italians themselves. Throughout the United States from 1910 until 1950, Italians had the greatest degree of residential segregation of any foreign-born nationality.[59] One study showed that in 1910 Milwaukee's Italians were found to have "the highest rate of [residential] isolation ever recorded for an ethnic group."[60] A survey of New York City's Italian American population based on the 1930 Census (which only counted first- and second-generation Italian Americans as "Italian") revealed that overwhelmingly its 1,070,355 Italian residents (who comprised one-fourth of the total of first- and second-generation Italians in the United States) lived together in 39 areas where from 30 to 90 percent of the population was of Italian origin.[61] These communities were generally divided within themselves based on the place of origin of their residents, so that in Italian Harlem on East 112th Street lived people from Bari, and on East 107th Street people from Sarno near Naples, as well as Sicilians from Santiago.[62] The fragmentation of these communities was exacerbated by the absence of unifying institutions. Leonard Covello complained that the Little Italies were not communities at all, but "galaxies of similarly organized families."[63] Nonetheless, they invariably boasted all the requirements of an urban village, including at least one Italian church (Italian Harlem had four Italian parishes), where some of the religious services were conducted in Italian and church bulletins were published in Italian. No less important, these churches looked like Italian churches, which meant among other things that they were populated with numerous multicolored statues of local saints and various manifestations of Mary. The *feste*, which brought together all the aspects of Italian popular religious practice, which were originally sponsored by *congregazióni* (regionally based mutual-aid societies), over time became more directly tied to the Italian churches. In these *colonie italiane* the immigrants and their children could shop at *latticini* and *salumerie* and buy fresh bread each morning from innumerable *panetterie*—in New York City alone in 1940 could be found 10,000 Italian grocery stores and 2,000 bakeries. Little Italies were almost invariably built next to sites of employment (indeed, many were mixed residential, commercial, and industrial districts) or had good access to public transportation.

These Little Italies served as the immigrants' major defense against the injuries of pervasive anti-Italian sentiment.[64] The fact that Italian immigrants to Latin America did not form Little Italies suggests that it was primarily the effects of discrimination, not the instinct to replicate the southern Italian villages, that determined residential patterns in the United States. Faced with adverse circumstances, immigrants in Little Italies had recourse to their traditional ways of life, particularly the extended family clan and the re-creation of the familiar social patterns of their southern Italian hometowns. Although commentators on the Italian American experience have underscored the conservative consequences of these survival strategies, what has gone largely unnoticed is that this same set of circumstances also contained a potential for the maintenance of radicalism brought from Italy, as well as the incubation of radicalism here. Moreover, the communities had the effect of insulating their residents from Americanization, which everywhere functioned as a decidedly deradicalizing process.[65] The possibility of this group of poor, working-class people becoming radical greatly increased because of the overlapping of occupational and residential identities. By sharing the same communities, these people sensed the commonality of their lives, which enabled them to conceive of challenging their employers and in some cases the underlying assumptions of capitalism. As Vecoli has pointed out, Little Italies created situations where at least "for a time . . . their dual identities as proletarians and as Italians were congruent sources of solidarity."[66]

Italian American radicals developed distinct cultures and an alternate societies that reflected their own values and were designed to provide the immigrant community with a substitute for religion and the hegemonic culture sustained by the *prominenti*. On Sundays, attendance at lectures or cultural events substituted for attendance at Mass. Radicals established worker holidays and memorial days to replace nationalistic and religious holidays. Instead of celebrating Christmas or the Fourth of July, they would commemorate May Day and November 11, the date of the Haymarket anarchists' execution.[67]

Radical culture expressed itself through a wide variety of institutions—from newspapers, orchestras, and choral groups to theaters, libraries, and schools. However, the Italian-language radical press was without question the major vehicle for the dissemination and perpetuation of the culture of the *sovversivi*. A comparison of the circulations of radical and mainstream Italian newspapers in New York in the 1920s reveals that perhaps as much as one-third of the city's Italian-language circulation fell in the radical category. This in turn reflects two related facts: that although the illiteracy of Italian immigrants in general has been exaggerated, literacy was considerably higher among radicals. "Radicalism and illiteracy," noted social reformer Antonio Stella, "usually do not go together."[68] The radical press not only linked comrades throughout the country and across the Atlantic, but also conveyed an entire world of culture as well as politics to its readers. Commented *Il Proletario* in 1902, "the book and the newspaper are the most potent means to hasten the triumph of workers' rights."[69] Indeed, newspapers contained not only political information, editorials, and general news, but also poetry and installments of plays and novels, as well as announcements about lectures, music, and theatrical performances. The radical movement constantly organized fund-raising events, especially picnics, to support its newspapers, which represented the most important radical institution. These fund-raising activities, in turn, helped integrate and sustain the communities.

Italian radicalism also spawned a rich artistic and literary culture, with sculpture and illustrations by Onorio Ruotolo, sculpture by Attilio Piccirilli, and drawings and caricatures by Fort Velona. One of the most important cultural institutions created by the radicals was the Leonardo Da Vinci Art School (New York), founded by Ruotolo and Piccirilli in 1923. Until its demise in 1941, the school—which, as expressed by Ruotolo, "diffuses among the children of workers, the light of art"[70]—provided artistic instruction for immigrants of all backgrounds.[71] In the early decades of the twentieth century, Arturo Giovannitti, whose influence reached into mainstream literary publications, was the most original radical poet. Women's poetic voices were represented by syndicalist Bellalma Forzata Spezia, who ran a small publishing house in West Hoboken; Rosa Zagnoni Marinoni, the "poet laureate of the Ozarks"; and anarchist Virgilia D'Andrea, who died as a young woman in the mid-1930s. The best-known radical author was Pietro Di Donato, whose powerful *Christ in Concrete* (1939) conveyed an authority and genuineness that made him a widely recognized "proletarian" author.[72]

Italian radicals also sustained a vibrant theatrical culture from the turn of the century, and the innumerable theaters they filled put on plays by Italian and Italian immigrant writers such as Pietro Gori and Giovannitti, as well as more-famous works, such as Emile Zola's *Therese Raquin* and Ibsen's *Doll House*. In Antonio Maiori's theater, anarchist papers were sold during intermission, and Riccardo Cordiferro (pen name for Alessandro Sisca) wrote and acted in plays with a socialist message. Salvatore Abbamonte's dramatic group put on "evenings of social propaganda" known as "red evenings" (*serate rosse*) in New York, and La Filodrammatica dell'Unione Socialista presented benefits for *Il Proletario*.[73]

Radicalism of all varieties affirmed the indigenous cultures of its members and sought to use these cultures to build a multicultural movement. At least in the United States, where radicalism offered only slight chances for realization of its beliefs and exposed its adherents to substantial losses and risks, the fellowship and culture of radical communities represented major compensations. Indeed, these same cultural events that sustained radical politics also had the potential of replacing political activity and becoming an end in themselves. Although we know something of the cultural norms and activities of Italian American anarchism,[74] much less work has been done to re-create similar developments within the Italian American socialist and communist communities.

The earliest Italian American "radical community" flourished in Ybor City, a section of Tampa, Florida, where Italians joined already-established Cuban and Spaniard radicals who worked in the cigar industry. From 1890 until 1950, the three nationalities established a remarkable set of interrelated institutions that sustained what was probably the longest-standing radical community in the United States. Together they launched and fought the 1910 strike in Tampa, in which Italians participated.[75] Gary Mormino has noted that "What was most extraordinary, a 'Latin' identity evolved, a culture which bonded Italians, Cubans (white and black), and Spaniards around commonly-held values: working class solidarity, international brotherhood, and distrust of institutions, chiefly the Catholic Church." At the epicenter of this phenomenal community stood *los lectores*, who read radical novels and newspapers to the cigar workers from elevated lecterns. In this way, the Italians learned radical theory and had access to a wider world.[76] Radicals of every ideological tendency formed *circoli* based on ideological predilection, debating clubs, libraries, and speaking societies. For several days in February 1900, Errico Malatesta, speaking in both Spanish and Italian, filled to capacity Tampa's halls. The hegemony of the Left in this community is suggested by the total absence of a commercial Italian-language newspaper.[77] Ybor City survived over a long period of time, despite the constant danger of Ku Klux Klan terrorism, because it succeeded in making the transition from anarchism to socialism and communism. This allowed it to maintain connections to larger causes (for example, support for the Spanish Republic) and survive periods of repression. This radical tradition persisted. Henry Wallace, during his 1948 presidential campaign as the Progressive Party candidate, spoke to integrated rallies in Ybor City, whose election districts were among the 30 within the United States that awarded him a plurality.[78]

Ybor City remained the most integral and elaborate radical Italian community, but it was not unique. In large cities, specific neighborhoods were home to Italian radicals for decades. In New York, wrote Nunzio Pernicone, "the district of Manhattan that extended from 8th to 23rd Street and Fifth Avenue to Second Avenue, with Union Square Park as its epicenter, contained the headquarters of numerous radical organizations and labor unions and their newspapers: the Rand School, the Italian Chamber of Labor, the Amalgamated Clothing Workers Union, Local 48 of the International Ladies Garment Workers Union, Tresca's *Il Martello*, the Communist *Il Lavoratore*, and the anti-Fascist *Il Nuovo Mondo*."[79] San Francisco spawned a radicalized Italian–Spanish community that formed a special Latin branch of the IWW. Unlike its analogue in Tampa, where it was the other way around, here the Italians were the senior partner: Spanish articles appeared in radical Italian-language newspapers. In San Francisco, syndicalism prevailed, and there were few signs of support for Luigi Galleani's anti-organizational anarchism. The power of radicalism within this community was demonstrated by instances of solidarity across class lines, where the Italian-language commercial press, owned by and reflecting the views of the *prominenti*, sided with the Italian workers and even with the radicals when they were arrested during free-speech fights.[80] Italian Harlem, which provided the major electoral base for congressmen Fiorello La Guardia (1922–1932) and Vito Marcantonio (1934–1959), was yet another radicalized community. Wallace in 1948 garnered 21 percent of Italian Harlem's vote, and in 1950 more than one out of four voted for W. E. B. Du Bois, when he ran for senator on the American Labor Party line.[81]

The radical community of Barre, Vermont, was based on granite workers from Carrara, some of whom had emigrated after an insurrection in the Lunigiana region resulted in the imposition of martial law. In Barre, their militancy led to strike activity that mobilized the workers and maintained their solidarity through music and the display of red flags. Barre was one of the communities to which the Lawrence strikers sent their children for the duration of the strike.[82] From 1903, when it was launched, until 1912, Galleani's incendiary weekly, *Cronaca Sovversiva*, which despite its limited circulation had an influence wherever Italian anarchists congregated, was published in Barre (and later, from 1912 to 1918, in Lynn, Massachusetts). This small and isolated community was hit very hard by the postwar deportations, which, among others, ensnared Galleani. In 1922, after the demise of *Cronaca Sovversiva*, Galleani's disciples launched *L'Adunata dei Refrattari* in New York, which was edited for most of its existence by Raffaele Schiavina (alias Max Sartin or Bruno), who had been deported in 1919 along with Galleani but managed to reenter the United States clandestinely.[83]

Women played important roles in the formation and sustaining of these and other oppositional communities in the early decades of immigration. "Contrary to popular impression," observes Pernicone, "there was a considerable number of women in the radical movement, although not always in positions of high visibility and influence." Women sustained family cultures that nurtured and perpetuated radicalism and, as Jennifer Guglielmo has argued, "formulated strategies of resistance and survival that called into question systems of power and authority within their families, communities, and the larger society."[84] Women were generally attracted to currents of anarchism that favored an organized worker movement—the most important female Italian American anarchist figure was undoubtedly Virgilia D'Andrea, who followed her lover Armando Borghi to the United States in the late 1920s. Women generally favored participation in more-practical efforts aimed at organizing within the communities and workplaces rather than conspiring to carry out heroic acts. There are numerous examples of women's activism in the IWW and in building unions of every imaginable political orientation, but they were generally absent among the Galleanisti. The latter's focus on individual acts, which often involved violence, were incompatible with women's socialization, which stressed cooperation. Angela Bambace is the best known among hundreds of Italian American women union organizers. Italian women played an especially large role in the Lawrence general strike of 1912, during which they "finally broke open the strike" by sending their children to be cared for by Italian families in New York City and elsewhere.[85]

Almost from the inception of the great migration until the intervention of the United States in World War I, Italian immigrants played a decisive role in the American working class movements wherever they settled. They prominently participated in the widespread industrial warfare of this period and provided impetus to major strike actions. However, what has been endlessly disseminated since the Dillingham Commission report of 1911 is the stigmatized representation of Italians-as-strikebreakers rather than their far more consequential involvement and leadership in these trade union insurgencies. The commission's findings were intended to demonstrate not only that Italians in general were unsuited to American circumstances, but also to show the difference between northern Italians—39.8 percent of whom were unionized—and their southern compatriots, less than 11 percent of whom were union members. What the commission failed to point out, however, was that southern Italian immigrants were widely represented throughout the radical movement.[86]

The 1912 Lawrence strike, perhaps more than any other labor conflict, inspired the Italian American working class and especially its radical contingent.[87] Although the importance of Italians in this event has been acknowledged, there has been a tendency to underplay the leadership role of Joseph Ettor (who generally is not identified as Italian), Arturo Giovannitti, and Carlo Tresca. Moreover, many accounts of this major event in the history of the American working class fail to recognize the Italians as the most important and militant of the ethnic groups in Lawrence.[88]

Aside from the events in Lawrence, Italians played a central part in strikes across the country before World War I. These included the Mesabi Iron Range strikes of 1907 and 1916, the bitter Westmoreland, Pennsylvania, mining strike of 1910, the Ludlow strike of 1914, and the anthracite coal strike in eastern Pennsylvania, of 1916.[89] Textile strikes, which involved large numbers of Italians, often turned violent. Examples are the Paterson, New Jersey, silk workers' strikes of 1902 and 1913 and the 1910 strike in New York, which represented a turning point in the unionization of that industry.[90] In New York City, Italian immigrants provided both the mass base and the leadership for the longshoremen's strikes of 1907 and 1919. These strikes, both of which were carried out in opposition to the leadership of the International Longshoremen's Association, took on the character of rebellions, which spilled over into the Little Italies. During the first strike, Italians marched across the Brooklyn Bridge waving a number of different flags, including the red flag, in a successful effort to "pull out" the predominantly Irish longshoremen working on Manhattan's docks. The 1919 strike, the largest to date, involved 150,000 workers, many of whom engaged in pitched battles with strikebreakers.[91] The year 1919 also saw the founding of Local 89 of the International Ladies' Garment Workers' Union (ILGWU), as well as strikes in Seattle and Lawrence in which Italians played crucial roles.[92]

To a degree and span of time unique among all the immigrant nationalities, anarchism was the dominant radical ideological tendency among the Italians. Of the five hundred anarchist newspapers published in the United States in a dozen or more languages between 1870 and 1940, Italians produced about one hundred. The earliest Italian anarchist newspaper in America of which we have information—*L'Anarchico* of New York—appeared in 1885. Francesco Saverio Merlino, who arrived in 1892, spread the movement among early immigrants on the East Coast. The poet Pietro Gori popularized anarchist doctrine during a year-long tour of Italian communities in 1895–1896 and founded *La Questione Sociale* in Paterson, New Jersey. Other anarchists seeking to escape the government reaction in Italy arrived in the 1890s, including Giuseppe Ciancabilla, Malatesta, and Galleani. Malatesta represented the most important of the so-called organizational anarchists, who wanted to form a revolutionary workers' movement. Galleani, on the other hand, was the leading anti-organizational anarchist who advocated direct action, including terrorist violence, and eschewed both political parties and labor unions. Galleani's brand of anarchist-communism attracted a circle of Italian immigrant radicals that included Nicola Sacco and Bartolomeo Vanzetti.[93]

Even in this period, anarchism was not the sole form of radicalism within the Italian community. The first Italian socialists came to the United States perhaps as early as the 1880s,[94] and by the 1890s their local groups in New York, Chicago, and elsewhere adhered to Daniel De Leon's Socialist Labor Party. The autonomous Italian Socialist Federation (FSI)—founded in 1902–1903 under the leadership of Giacinto Menotti Serrati (who between 1902 and 1904 edited its weekly newspaper *Il Proletario*, which began publishing in 1896)—coalesced a large number of Italian labor and radical groups. It attempted to establish a movement that simultaneously was developing in Italy and combined mutual aid societies, cooperatives, and unions. The FSI eventually boasted 80 sections with more than one thousand members. The circulation of *Il Proletario* (edited by Tresca from 1904 to 1906) eventually reached 5,600. The disparate character of its constituent organizations makes the FSI difficult to categorize ideologically. A split widened between those who wanted to pursue a political strategy through the Socialist Party of America and the syndicalists, who believed that only workers in industrial unions were capable of destroying capitalism. In 1908, the syndicalists became a majority in the FSI, and three years later the organization declared revolutionary syndicalism its official ideology and joined forces with the IWW. In 1910, a smaller social democratic group, also calling itself the Italian Socialist Federation, was founded within the Socialist Party of America and claimed a membership of five hundred. This group, centered in Chicago and led by Giuseppe Bertelli and Arturo Caroti, argued that immigrants should become citizens, vote, and become part of the mainstream socialist movement in the United States.[95]

From his arrival in the United States in 1904 until his murder on the streets of New York on January 11, 1943, Carlo Tresca helped to define the very contours of the history of the Italian American Left.[96] An electrifying orator and unsurpassable agitator, he played major roles in most of the important strike actions—Lawrence, in 1912; Patterson, in 1913; the Mesabi Range strike, 1916, and many others—involving Italian workers Although his attitude toward, and connection to, first the Socialist Party and then the Communist Party alternated from cooperation to intense hostility (at the time of his death, he had become a dedicated anti-Communist), he can best be categorized as an anarcho-syndicalist. Tresca is best remembered as the editor of *Il Martello,* a hard-hitting weekly that was published from 1917 until three years after his death. Despite its limited circulation (which peaked at 10,500 in 1924), its consistent opposition to Fascism in Italy and its supporters in the United States greatly encouraged anti-Fascists everywhere and earned Tresca the undying enmity of the Fascists.[97]

The great industrial rebellions and near civil wars in which the first generation participated and often provided leadership, were not repeated by the second generation. This had more to do with changes—both political and economic—in the United States than with the process of Americanization. The bloody repression of the general strikes in Paterson, Passaic, and Gastonia, North Carolina, all dampened the fires of the class struggle. Nothing like the great strike wave of 1919 took place until the sit-down strikes of 1935.

From 1917 to 1920, during a systematic government crackdown on radicals (the most famous manifestation of which was the notorious Palmer Raids), about three thousand aliens underwent deportation proceedings, and eight hundred, including many Italians, were actually deported.[98] Galleani, arguably the most important anarchist in the United States, was deported in 1919; he died in Italy in 1931, shortly after being released from prison. Starting with the Alien-Sedition Acts, the periodic attempts to suppress the Left that punctuate U.S. history relentlessly targeted the foreign born as subversive. After 1893, foreign-born radicals began living at great risk in the United States. On the grounds that deportation was an administrative and not a criminal proceeding, the Supreme Court endorsed the federal government's "absolute" right to deport aliens and to deny the accused the procedural guarantees enshrined in the Constitution.[99] Although from 1922 until 1943, deportation of radicals to Italy generally meant long-term incarceration in Mussolini's prisons, at all times it resulted in permanent separation from family, including American-born spouses and children. Despite the draconian consequences of deportation, the government adopted the position that deportation was an exercise of the sovereign state's right to determine who shall reside within its borders.[100] From the Trading with the Enemy Act of 1917, to the Alien Registration Act of 1940 and the Walter-McCarran Act of 1952, the targeting of resident aliens for deportation and even the denaturalization of foreign-born American citizens constricted the scope of the political activities of these communities and had the effect of causing them to turn inward.

Italian American radicalism was weakened in 1917 when the United States joined with Italy and her allies in World War I. The German Americans suddenly found themselves the target of intense hostility, and for the first time Italians were not at the bottom of the ethnic totem pole. The U.S. government encouraged support for the war in the Little Italies and other ethnic communities, where the patriotic fervor made radicals and their opposition to the war anathema; perhaps as many as 300,000 Italian Americans joined the U.S. armed forces, and 65,000 returned to Italy to fight. In 1915, when Italy entered the war, journalist Agostino De Biasi launched the important journal *Il Carroccio* in New York as a patriotic organ of Italian opinion, and founded the first Fascio di Combattimento there in 1921. For some radical Italians in the United States, as for Benito Mussolini in Italy, Italian intervention in the war had provoked a crisis of conscience as their leftism collided with their patriotic sentiments. This was the case for Edmondo Rossoni (who had been editor of *Il Proletario*), Filippo Bocchini, Aldo Tarabella, Domenico Trombetta, Ottavio Dinale, and other socialists and syndicalists, all of whom broke with their comrades and turned fervently pro-war. In the postwar period they became Fascists, either in the United States or in Italy. The radical cultural journal *Il Fuoco* switched from an antiwar to a pro-war position when activist–poet Giovannitti, one of its two editors, left the magazine in the hands of sculptor–illustrator Onorio Ruotolo. After the war, Italian Americans did not experience the widespread revulsion against the war that fueled leftist insurgencies throughout Italy in 1919. Instead, much of the Italian American community became obsessed with Italian irredentism and resentment about Italy's having been "cheated" out of the fruits of victory by its own allies at the Paris Peace Conference—sentiments that contributed to Fascism's growing influence.[101]

A Fascist movement, replete with Blackshirt squads, made its presence felt in the Little Italies even before Mussolini came to power in Italy.[102] True, Fascists remained a small but vocal minority, but millions of Italian immigrants looked to Mussolini as a source of pride in a society that had consistently denigrated them. Adherence to Fascism, Covello pointed out, was a reaction of "a human group upon which the stigma of inferiority had been fastened." Covello's insight, with which other anti-Fascists agreed,[103] is supported by the contrasting experience in that period with the Italian immigrant communities in Europe and Argentina, which for the most part sided with the Left and were generally anti-Fascist. Since then, scholars such as John Diggins have demonstrated the accuracy of Vecoli's observation that "ethnic nationalism [served] as a shield against intensified Nativist assault."[104]

By the mid-1920s, the struggle against Fascism had begun to reshape the special contours of Italian American radicalism. At times, the appeal of Fascism dramatically reduced the size and influence of the Left within the Italian American community; indeed, the Italian American Fascists and Mussolini's consular agents managed to spread the notion within the community that radicalism was anti-American but that Fascism was very much within the mainstream of American values of home, family, religion, and law and order.[105] Anti-Fascism, on the other hand, was inherently a project of the Left, which briefly prefigured elements—as well as many of the tensions—of an incipient popular front. For one thing, the anti-Fascist movement entailed a struggle against the *prominenti*, who overwhelmingly supported Fascism, thereby politicizing the class struggle within the community. It also connected anti-Fascism to the full spectrum of Italian American radical ideologies, from the anarchists, socialists, and Communists to radical Republicans, both within the United States and internationally.[106]

Although they agreed on the necessity of combating Fascism, the various strains of radicalism rarely coalesced around a common strategy for accomplishing this goal. This became evident when the first major anti-Fascist organization, the Anti-Fascist Alliance of North America (AFANA), founded in 1923, quickly disintegrated as a result of intractable differences, mainly between the Communists and the Socialist-led labor unions. Tresca, leader of the *Martello* group, and the Communists led by Vittorio Vidali, secretary of the Communist Party's Italian branch, however, did manage to forge a temporary alliance in 1925 that resurrected AFANA. Together, with significant effect, they waged a campaign against local Blackshirts and visiting Fascist emissaries. AFANA's daily newspaper, *Il Nuovo Mondo,* whose circulation reached almost thirty thousand in the late 1920s, significantly contributed to the anti-Fascist cause.[107]

The major base for anti-Fascist activism was the Italian American unions, especially Italian Locals 48 and 89 of the ILGWU, founded in 1916 and 1919, respectively. Luigi Antonini—the president of Local 89, which boasted forty thousand members at its height in the 1930s, and a first vice president of the ILGWU—became a prominent figure in New York City's anti-Fascist community. The ILGWU-sponsored *Giustizia,* the Italian-language edition of *Justice,* the union's weekly (which was also published in Yiddish), reached out to its membership and the wider Italian community through Italian-language radio programs; Antonini allocated union funds to support AFANA (until the socialists withdrew in 1926), *Il Nuovo Mondo,* and other initiatives.[108]

Despite his initial support for the Russian Revolution, from the mid-1920s, Antonini's politics combined a socialist identity with relentless anti-Communism. In 1935, following the lead of the ILGWU leadership, Antonini left the Socialist Party when Norman Thomas (whom they considered too leftist) became its leader. Antonini then participated in the formation of the Social Democratic Federation, which formed the nucleus for the ILGWU'S leading role in the founding of New York's American Labor Party (ALP). When the Left wing, led by Marcantonio, gained leadership of the ALP in 1944, Antonini, together with ILGWU president David Dubinsky, exited the ALP and helped to establish the Liberal Party. Significantly, while the Left-led ALP maintained, and even expanded, its Italian American following (including, presumably, many members of the ILGWU), Italian Americans were conspicuously absent from the Liberal Party.[109] During World War II, with the goal of excluding the Communists from Italy's postwar government, Antonini, in concert with "pre-Pearl Harbor Fascists" such as Generoso Pope, struggled to keep the Communists and their sympathizers out of the anti-Fascist Mazzini Society and such organizations as the Italian American Victory Council and the American Committee for Italian Democracy.[110]

The Amalgamated Clothing Workers of America (ACWA) represented another important center for Italian American anti-Fascism. Its newspaper, *Il Lavoro*, took an anti-Fascist stance, and its staff included many leading Italian American anti-Fascists, such as Augusto and Frank Bellanca and Joseph Catalonotti.[111]

In 1935, the initiation of the Popular Front, which proposed that revolutionary goals be replaced by a defense of social democracy against Fascist advances, seemed for a while to resolve the internecine struggles among some of the Left tendencies. Nevertheless, Trotskyists and anarchists continued to insist that Fascism could only be defeated through the revolutionary replacement of capitalism. These doctrinal disagreements played themselves out in practice in Spain, where the Communists, following the position laid down by the Soviet Union, united with Socialists and radical Republicans in a Popular Front government intent on implementing social programs, distributing land to the peasants, and disestablishing the Catholic Church.[112]

The defeat of the Spanish Republic and the attendant suppression of the last mass anarchist movement had profound effects on Italian American radicalism. Italian American support for Francisco Franco was strong, and less than three hundred joined the Abraham Lincoln Brigade or the Brigata Garibaldi. Nevertheless, in the second half of the 1930s, the dominant form of Italian American radicalism became Popular Frontism. Anarchism and Trotskyism, which rejected the Popular Front, had no organized presence within the Italian American community. Indeed, anarchism rapidly ceased to be a significant political factor, and the militant anti-Communism of Tresca, arguably the single most important figure of Italian American radicalism, contributed to his political isolation and declining influence.[113] Membership in the two Italian Socialist federations had declined steadily in the 1920s.[114] Antonini and other officers of the ILGWU were the only prominent Italian American representatives of anti-Communist social democracy.[115]

As expressed by the Left New Deal, the Popular Front's growing power substantially ended the marginalized status of the radicals within the Italian American community. Ultimately, hundreds of thousands of Italian Americans came into its orbit as participants in the CIO and the political coalitions that, among other accomplishments, contributed to the election of Fiorello La Guardia.[116] Some Italian American socialists, including Girolamo Valenti, followed the lead of Europe-based Pietro Nenni and, reversing their earlier enmity for the Communists, supported the Popular Front. In fact, Valenti's newspaper *La Stampa Libera* (transformed in 1939 into *La Parola*), became the organ of the "United Front of Italian Socialists and Communists of New York."[117] Unaffiliated socialists like Valenti and those around the ACWU tended to accept the Popular Front, which in practice brought them into political alliances and organizations led by Communists and their sympathizers.

The presence of Communism in the Italian American community was less than in other ethnic communities—by 1928, the Italian Communist Federation numbered about one thousand members. Nonetheless, as the only Italian radicals to increase their strength in the 1930s, they represented a small-but-genuine force that merits the attention of those who wish to comprehend the course of Italian American radicalism.[118] Between 1937 and 1939, *Il Popolo*, a paper that revolved around Vito Marcantonio's leadership, also supported Communist positions. In 1939, the Communist Party founded *L'Unità del Popolo*, (which succeeded *Il Lavoratore* and *L'Unità Operaia*), an eight-page weekly, whose circulation never exceeded ten thousand. In its first years, *L'Unità del Popolo* was edited by Maria Testa and Gino Bardi. Support for the Party's Italian-language press came from the Garibaldi-American Fraternal Society (the Italian section of the International Workers Order, a fraternal organization closely linked to the Communist Party), which in 1947 had nearly eleven thousand members organized into 150 lodges.[119]

The Communist Party's Italian American membership and influence, however, were not limited to its Italian-language section. The ideological assumptions of the Popular Front attracted either as members or sympathizers a number of cultural figures, such as Pietro Di Donato, Ralph Fasanella, Carl Marzani, and Jerre Mangione. It is not without significance that the first candidate openly running as a Communist for an important elective office was Peter Cacchione, who was elected under the then prevailing system of proportional representation to three successive terms (1941, 1943, and 1945) to the New York City Council. Perhaps most importantly, the mass organizations that the Communist Party led (such as the ALP and the left-wing CIO unions) were able to function and even thrive in the Italian communities.[120]

Italian American radicalism continued to be a transnational phenomenon in the interwar period. The defeat of the Left in Italy by the Blackshirts meant that Italian American radicalism was continually reinvigorated by an influx of *fuorusciti*, as the anti-Fascist exiles were called.[121] Vidali, secretary to the Communist Party's Italian branch and editor of its organ, *Il Lavoratore*, had arrived in New York as a stowaway in 1923, and socialist militant Vincenzo Vacirca, who served as editor of *Il Nuovo Mondo*, came the following year. Both became active in AFANA.[122] Max Ascoli, the first president of the Mazzini Society and later the editor of the influential liberal magazine, *The Reporter*, arrived in 1931. Gaetano Salvemini, the anti-Fascist historian and the founding spirit behind the Mazzini Society, took a permanent position at Harvard University in 1933 after making several earlier lecture tours in the United States.[123]

Among Italian Americans, the efforts of these extraordinary individuals were far outweighed by the growing prestige of the Fascist regime. Especially because of the support by the *prominenti*, Fascism dominated the infrastructure of the community. Despite the temporary secession of the New York lodges brought about by La Guardia and New York State Senator Salvatore Cotillo, the 1,100 lodges of the Order of the Sons of Italy in America became pro-Fascist. After the signing of the Lateran Pact in 1929, which recognized the sovereignty of the pope over the Vatican, the Italian national parishes became, in the words of Salvemini, "transmission belts" for Fascist propaganda, with priests like Father Joseph Cafuzzi of Our Lady of Mount Carmel in the Bronx, and Father Alfonso Archese of the Church of Sacred Hearts of Jesus and Mary in Brooklyn, promoting the cooperation of religion and Fascism. Of the 126 Italian-language newspapers in 1923, only eight were critical of Fascism. Generoso Pope, the publisher of *Il Progresso Italo-Americano* (which boasted a daily circulation of over 100,000) and several other papers, became the leading propagandist for Fascism in the United States.[124]

The fall of France reinforced the anti-Fascist ranks with hundreds of leading *fuorusciti* who, fleeing the Nazi onslaught, made their way to the United States. They constituted the core of the Mazzini Society's membership, which was founded in the fall of 1939 by Salvemini, Ascoli, and other exiles as a center-leftist (but non-Communist) anti-Fascist organization. Although numerically small (it had about one thousand members), the society published a sophisticated weekly newspaper, *Nazioni Unite*, and boasted among its supporters some of the most-prestigious figures of the anti-Fascist opposition, including Carlo Sforza, Don Luigi Sturzo, and Arturo Toscanini. Its principal goals were to break the hold of pro-Fascist propaganda on the Italian Americans and to work for a postwar democratic Italy freed from Fascism, the monarchy, and the Vatican.[125]

After Pearl Harbor, virtually the entire class of *prominenti* was in crisis as they scurried to return their medals to Mussolini and denounce Fascism. Within a year and a half, most made common cause with the anti-Fascists and stopped their war against the radicals. However, the coup against Mussolini in the summer of 1943, followed by the king's armistice with the Allies in September, freed them to become Italian "patriots" once again. Thereafter they tried to regain control of Italian policy from the radicals and began to oppose Communist influence in the Italian American community as they sought to shape the postwar Italian government.[126]

On the eve of World War II, Italian Americans, who numbered over six million, constituted the largest ethnic group deriving from the New Immigrants. They counted the greatest number of aliens, more than 600,000, and the largest number of foreign born.[127] The declaration of war by Italy on the United States on December 11, 1941, led to the tagging of all unnaturalized Italian Americans—including the newly arrived anti-Fascists—as "aliens of enemy nationality," who were then subject to registration and various restrictions, such as the need to apply for permission to travel outside their hometowns, and the denial of the right to own cameras, firearms, and shortwave radios. Although President

Roosevelt approved the lifting of this stigma (Italians were the only group removed from the enemy alien list before the end of the war), on Columbus Day 1942, considerable damage was inflicted on the morale and integrity of the Italian American community.[128]

At the outbreak of World War II, the Italian Americans were overwhelmingly working class, and 88 percent lived in urban areas, where the Little Italies were still very much intact. They were culturally distinct and subject to defamation and discrimination. However, the war greatly accelerated Italian American acculturation. Italian American men and women enlisted in the armed forces in staggering numbers—perhaps as many as 200,000 from New York alone. There, they were integrated with young people from other ethnic groups as well as those whose family origins predated the great migrations to America. Having traveled to distant places or even having been stationed in different states loosened their ties to their communities This general phenomenon is illustrated by the 40 percent decrease in broadcasting in immigrant languages between 1942 and 1948. In the postwar period, encouraged by G. I. benefits, second-generation Italian Americans moved in large numbers out of the cities and into the suburbs, abandoning not only their old neighborhoods but much of their past as well.[129]

Along with Communism, Socialism, and the leftist Populism of the New Deal, Italian American radicalism was dismantled in a political repression that constituted the domestic expression of the international cold war. In 1947, along with some three hundred other organizations, the International Workers Order and the American Committee for the Foreign Born were placed on the attorney general's list of subversive organizations. Membership in these organizations—past or present—or simply the membership of family members, provided sufficient cause for dismissal from government jobs or jobs where private businesses had been awarded government contracts. Worse yet, association with these organizations and/or reading *L'Unità del Popolo* could be used as cause for deportation. Anarchist Armando Borghi, who had come to the United States in 1928, was deported to Italy as early as 1945. Michael Salerno, the editor of *L'Unità del Popolo*, was deported in 1951, and in 1954 the State of New York seized the insurance funds of the International Workers Order.[130] Within the community, the Catholic Church, veterans' organizations, and the popular press propagated the notion that patriotism and Americanism were synonymous with anti-Communism. The effects of this comprehensive repression destroyed the infrastructure of radicalism in the Italian American community—and encouraged the erasure of its memory. Parents and other relatives withheld their stories of involvement in the Left or only told part of what was to be told.

The transnational character of Italian American radicalism continued into the McCarthy era. Luigi Antonini worked with the "pre-Pearl Harbor" *prominenti* in a massive effort to rebuild Italy and prevent the Communists from coming to political power. Antonini himself went to Italy to help in the creation of a non-Communist trade union movement.[131] In 1948, Generoso Pope, with the support of the Roman Catholic Church, organized a massive letter-writing cam-

paign by Italian Americans in the United States to relatives in Italy for the purpose of encouraging them to vote against the Communist Party. Vincent Impellittieri not only supported the 1948 effort but pursued his own vigorous
anti-Communist campaign as mayor of New York.[132] Many of the Mazzini Society exiles returned to Italy, some to take part in the early postwar governments,
as did those who were deported or fled in advance of anticipated deportations.
Some of these individuals went on to play important roles in the postwar political reconstruction of Italy.

Immigrant radicalism barely survived into the postwar era. The radical press,
which had been the mainstay of the Italian American Left, eventually disappeared: Il Proletario, Il Martello, and La Parola each ceased publication in 1946
and L'Unità del Popolo in 1951, a victim of McCarthyism. Yet, Controcorrente, the
anarchist paper edited by Aldino Felicani, appeared until 1967, L'Adunata until
1971, and Egidio Clemente's socialist La Parola del Popolo lasted into the 1980s.
After having been defeated in 1950 by a coalition candidate of the Democratic,
Republican, and Liberal parties, at 51 years of age, Marcantonio fell dead in
1954. Some of the old-timers survived past the McCarthy period but began to die
off one after another—Valenti in 1958, Giovannitti in 1959, Fort Velona in
1965, Ruotolo in 1966, Felicani in 1967, Borghi and Antonini both in 1968. A
handful lived on into comparatively recent times: the communist Vidali died in
Italy in 1983 and the socialist Clemente in Chicago in the mid-1980s, but two
anarchists of the old school lived to a ripe age—Raffaele Schiavina passed away
in Utah in 1987 and Valerio Isca in New York in 1995.

Just as the generation of immigrant radicalism was dying out, Fiorello La
Guardia, the reform mayor of New York, became a leading champion of leftist
causes. A forceful progressive while serving in the House of Representatives in
1922–1932, La Guardia had moved steadily to the Left during the 1940s. In the
two years after his last term as mayor ended in 1945, when he was no longer
encumbered by electoral alliances, his political activities grew remarkably radical. In addition to maintaining his ALP registration, La Guardia wrote a weekly
column for the left-wing daily PM, in which he opposed both the Truman Plan
and the president's Loyalty Oath program while giving glowing reports of Tito's
Yugoslavia and sympathetic descriptions of the Soviet Union's reconstruction
efforts. Other columns supported a national health program, price controls, and
public housing. La Guardia died in 1947, before having had the opportunity, as
was widely expected, to run in 1948 as the vice presidential candidate on Henry
Wallace's Progressive Party ticket.[133]

In the immediate postwar period, singer Frank Sinatra sustained a brief but
intense involvement with the Left that led the FBI to dub him a "communist
sympathizer." Between 1944 and 1948, he was a sponsor of, contributor to, or
speaker for a score of leftist organizations, including the Joint Anti-Fascist
Refugee Committee, the Free Italy Society, the American Crusade to End
Lynching, and the Independent Citizen Committee of the Arts, Sciences, and
Professions. His singing of "The House I Live In" (1945), and his starring role in

the documentary of that name, tied him to the movement for a racially and ethnically pluralistic America. After an intense red-baiting campaign led by newspaper columnist Walter Winchell, Sinatra began severing his ties with the Left. In 1948, he joined Jimmy Durante and Joe DiMaggio in the campaign to help defeat the Communist Party in the Italian elections.[134]

Despite the long history of Italian American radicalism, and the examples of such prominent figures as La Guardia and Sinatra, it has become a widely held assumption that the political sentiments of post–World War II Italian Americans range from politically conservative to reactionary. "The prevailing judgment among social scientists," observed Scimecca and Femminella, "is that Italian-Americans are a basically conservative ethnic group."[135] Nevertheless, Italian American politicians have for many years built up a widespread tradition of liberalism that has deep roots in the Italian ethnic experience. Indeed, the most-prominent Italian American political figures range from liberal to very liberal; moreover, with the exception of the Jews, Italian American voting patterns are no less liberal—and in some instances more so—than other European national groups.

The list of nationally prominent Italian American liberals is long. John Pastore, who was born of Italian immigrant parents in Providence, Rhode Island, was the first Italian American to be elected governor (1946) and to sit in the Senate (1950). In the Senate, he fought to erase the racist character of U.S. immigration laws, and played important roles in the passage of the Nuclear Non-Proliferation Treaty of 1963, the Civil Rights Act of 1964, and the Public Broadcasting Act of 1969. A major figure of the Democratic Party's liberal wing, he was long remembered for his nominating speech for Lyndon B. Johnson at the Democratic presidential convention, when he denounced Senator Barry Goldwater as a captive of "reactionaries and extremists."[136] Mario Cuomo served as three-time governor of New York, from 1982 to 1994. He represented the most prominent American office holder who opposed capital punishment and favored the establishment of a universal health care program. His speech at the 1984 Democratic presidential convention enunciated the underlying premises of Left New Dealism.[137] Peter Rodino served in Congress for 20 consecutive terms, from 1948 to 1988. One of the most-influential legislators in the House of Representatives, he sided with the liberal wing of the Democratic Party on all major issues, including civil rights, the right to abortion, and opposition to prayer in the public schools. A testament to his progressive credentials was the absence of any challenger in his district, which centered around Newark, New Jersey's North Ward, even after it experienced a dramatic decease in the number of Italian Americans and a great increase in African Americans.[138] Geraldine Ferraro was a three-term Congresswoman and 1984 vice presidential candidate, who consistently upheld the liberal agenda and incurred the wrath of the Catholic Church for her forthright advocacy of abortion rights. Despite her very active role in building and supporting Italian American organizations, when her family came under attack during the presidential campaign for alleged links to organized crime, she was disappointed with "many of the leaders in our community [who] seemed ready to remain silent and let others shape events."[139]

On the national level, Italian American voting patterns do not reveal the conservatism so often ascribed to the community. Alfred E. Smith's 1928 presidential campaign, which dramatically swung all the non-Protestant nationalities into the Democratic Party's ranks, caused Italian Americans to increase their Democratic vote from 48 percent in 1924 to 77 percent in 1928.[140] In 1936, among ethnic and racial groups in urban areas, only Jews voted in larger percentages (91 percent) than Italian Americans (88 percent) for Franklin Delano Roosevelt. In tandem with Roosevelt's smaller pluralities from his unprecedented landslide in 1936, the Italian American vote for the president in 1940 decreased to 75 percent, which was equal to the percentage of Roosevelt's Irish American vote, although less than the 89 percent tally for Jews.[141]

These figures indicate that far too much has been made of the "desertion" of Italian Americans from the ranks of the New Deal coalition as a response to Roosevelt's characterization in 1940 of Mussolini's invasion of France as a "stab in the back." A closer look at the 1940 presidential voting returns indicates that the percentage of Italian American men who shifted their vote from Roosevelt to Wendell Wilkie approximated the percentage of this shift among all male voters.[142] Moreover, Roosevelt's slippage among Italian Americans to 64 percent in 1944 was not anomalous: although his vote increased still further among Jews and African Americans, it also decreased among other ethnic groups.

In the postwar period, the movement of Italian Americans away from Democratic Party affiliation and liberalism and toward the Republican Party and conservatism did not occur until after the 1948 election, and it has been essentially in the same range as other Catholic ethnic groups. For example, a detailed study of the voting patterns in Elmira, New York, for the 1948 presidential election shows that of all the ethnic groups—including Jews and African Americans— Italian Americans voted in the smallest percentages for the Republican candidate. Indeed, from 1928 until today, in the United States the great divide in voting behavior is not among racial and ethnic groups but between "ethnics" and white native-born Protestant voters, who overwhelmingly vote Republican, regardless of class.[143] In 1968, 67 percent of Italian Americans voted Democratic in the presidential election, and in the 1972 presidential election, despite the widespread reaction against George McGovern's guaranteed-income proposal, 63 percent continued to vote Democratic.[144] Even during the Reagan landslide of 1984, when 57 percent of Italian Americans voted Republican, this was only slightly higher than his overall 55 percent of the Catholic vote but far less than the 73 percent white Protestant vote.[145]

Although the history of Italian American liberal leadership and voting patterns may seem somewhat removed from the "lost world" of radicalism, it does point to a continuing tradition of progressive politics that did not entirely disappear with the first generation of immigrants but has gone equally unrecognized. No one, for example, has yet to connect the social and political movements of the 1960s and 1970s with Italian Americans.[146] Indeed, these movements have generally been portrayed as middle class phenomena which elicited opposition from "white ethnics" in general and very much from Italian Americans in particular. The leadership of two Italian Americans—Mario Savio and Father James Groppi—suggest the need to reexamine this assumption. The radicalism of Fr. Groppi and Savio was tied to their Italian American experience or identity. Both melded their Catholic culture to these movements and infused their political activities with an Italian American sense of family and community.[147]

Fr. Groppi was arguably the most important white civil rights leader of this period. From 1965 to 1975, he provided leadership for a unique mass movement in the African American community of Milwaukee, Wisconsin, that succeeded in having open-housing laws passed in Milwaukee and in surrounding communities. In 1967, the editors of the Associated Press newspapers, and radio and television station member affiliates, voted him the most important religious figure for that year. Yet, his name has all but disappeared from the histories of the Civil Rights movement and the Italian American experience.[148]

Mario Savio, a product of a working-class Italian American family, became politically active when in 1963 he transferred from Manhattan College (an Irish Christian Brothers institution) to Queens College. He continued these activities when he enrolled at the University of California, Berkeley. After participating in the Mississippi Summer Project in 1964, as coordinator of the Berkeley chapter of the Friends of the Student Non-violent Movement, he brought the Civil Rights movement to the North. When the college administration attempted to curtail the student movement's activities on campus, Savio led a vast demonstration that gave birth to the Berkeley Free Speech movement and helped inaugurate the confrontational tactics and moralistic approach of the movements that characterized the 1960s.

In more recent years, Italian American radicalism has become increasingly identified with issues of identity politics. In 1992, a group of Italian Americans in New York City active in social justice causes founded Italian Americans for a Multicultural United States (IAMUS), an organization initially devoted to countering the place of Christopher Columbus in Italian American mythology. Since then, IAMUS has sponsored a number of other events celebrating the history of radicalism in the ethnic community.[149]

The new radicalism has been most closely associated with women's issues and gay and lesbian identity, movements that had their origins in the student activism and Civil Rights movements. The Caffe Cino in Greenwich Village, an important center for experimental theater in the early 1960s, was perhaps the first Italian American site to be associated with the gay rights activism of that era. But as gay and lesbian Italian Americans emerged out of the shadows of nonexistence in the 1970s and 1980s—Gay and Lesbian Italians was founded in New York in 1985[150]—many began an interior journey to interrogate the meaning of their joint identities, a journey that eventually expressed itself through a growing body of literature. The forces against which gay and lesbian Italian Americans have struggled seem not terribly far removed from those their immigrant ancestors faced: "We have deviated substantially," explained a group of such writers from California just last year, "from *la via vecchia,* the ways of the old, the much revered traditions by which we were raised. . . . We are also shunned by the Catholic Church, and often develop an awareness about our sexuality steeped in a climate of repression, fear, and homophobia within the family."[151]

The radicalism of Italian American feminists and gays and lesbians identifies patriarchy and homophobia as the enemy. As Edvige Giunta notes in speaking of women as public intellectuals, "Over the last two decades, Italian American women writers have begun to transform 'silence' into 'language and action.' In breaching the boundary between traditionally private and public spaces, authors such as Louise DeSalvo, Helen Barolini, Mary Cappello, Nancy Caronia, Rosette Capotorto, Maria Mazziotti Gillan, Rose Romano, and Sandra M. Gilbert, to mention just a few, have given form to untold stories and utterance to unspoken words."[152] Italian American gay, lesbian, and feminist writers explore and reveal sexual and gender identity not in abstract terms but rather ground their work specifically in the consequences of their Italian American heritage. In this way, they break many of the "silences" that have long surrounded sexuality and private forms of oppression in families as well as in the larger community. "The root of Italian American radicalism in the literature of the late twentieth century," Mary Jo Bona explains, "goes back to the family, is unceasingly about the family, as it struggles with the complexities of its own ethnicity and the divergent paths that children of families take regarding how they are going to live and whom they are going to love."[153] Whether it be Robert Ferro's *The Family of Max Desir* (1983), Carole Maso's *The Art Lover* (1990), Rose Romano's *The Wop Factor* (1994), or Louise DeSalvo's *Vertigo* (1996), Italian American writers seek the sources of identity in their families as well as in their ethnicity. By the simple act of self-definition, Italian American women and gay and lesbian authors stake out what in some ways is the most radical territory of all.

The transnational nature of radicalism continues to reveal itself. In recent years third- and fourth-generation Italian Americans, moved in part by a rekindling of ethnic pride and a consequent desire to trace family roots, have "rediscovered" Italy. It remains to be seen whether this rediscovery will affect the political consciousness of Italian Americans—Italy has a much more highly politicized society than the United States, and the Left traditions that have played such a powerful role in shaping contemporary Italy stand in sharp contrast to the marginalization of the Left in American political culture. It is hardly conceivable, for example, that most Americans would accept the fundamental notion proclaimed in the opening article of the postwar Italian constitution—that Italy is "a democratic republic founded on labor." And of course since World War II, while the United States went through its McCarthyistic trauma and beyond, the Italian people have regularly elected a variety of socialist and communist members to its Chamber of Deputies and as mayors of its principal cities, and until fairly recently made the Communist Party the second-largest political party in the country. Nowhere is this perhaps more evident than by contrasting the programmatic differences between Italian and American conservatives—the Italian Right, for example, supports unions, a strong central government, public schools, the protection of secular values, and government control of natural resources, as well as free and universal health care, all of which the American Right opposes. Perhaps Italy has lessons yet to teach its overseas descendants. Here in the United States, the maintenance of an Italian identity associates Italian Americans with the concerns of other cultural minorities and distances them from the values associated with the dominant Anglo-Saxon culture, which has only conservative consequences. Logically, this translates into opposition to restrictions on immigration and opposition to English-only laws and support for those parts of a Left agenda that reinforce family and community functioning, such as, universal day care, access to medical treatment, and so on.[154]

* * *

The history of Italian American radicalism has shown that class politics and identity politics are not opposites; in fact, class and ethnicity more often than not appear, in some fashion or other, together. Historically, Lipset and Marks point out, "When ethnicity and class coincided or overlapped, conflict in the workplace could be intensified."[155] What happens politically—in terms of both ideology and activity—with an individual or group often depends on the nature of the interaction between class position and identity based on culture, religion, gender, or sexual orientation.

Much of the explanation about why "there is no socialism in America" has been ascribed to the ethnic diversity of its working class.[156] Ethnic groups in this paradigm serve to "maintain the solidity of American society and avoid class consciousness and class conflict."[157] There are, however, any number of problems with this assumption. If the heterogeneity of the working class blunted working-class consciousness and impeded working-class solidarity, then how can we explain the opposition of the Right to the expression of non-Anglo-Saxon languages and cultures? If maintenance of ethnic identity benefited the Right, why would nativism be a constant part of its ideological armature? Why would the Right advocate restrictions on immigration? Furthermore, how could we explain the extraordinary concentration of Leftism among first- and second-generation ethnic Americans of non-Anglo-Saxon backgrounds, its gradual disappearance from the third and fourth generations, and its virtual absence among workers from "old stock" white Protestant backgrounds?

Although the mass base of radical movements was comprised of immigrants (and to a somewhat lesser degree their children) who were generally organized according to their separate nationalities, these organizations, and especially the Socialist Party, viewed ethnic and racial differences as transitory phenomena without political significance—and this in stark contrast to the organization of their members into nationality groups themselves. In the 1930s, however, the Communist Party began to insist that all non-Anglo-Saxon national groups were oppressed minorities because they were subjected to coercive acculturation and denied the right to maintain and develop their own cultures. Politically this translated into a defense of their rights to cultural expression alongside an insistent advocacy for, and defense of, the immigrants' legal rights and protection from discrimination. This political paradigm encouraged the social organization of the nationalities within their own communities and their unification within the CIO and around common cultural and leisure activities. According to the Communists, therefore, ethnicity was a more or less permanent feature of American society that deserved to be celebrated.[158] This position was popularized by Louis Adamic, whose books and articles achieved a vast circulation.[159] One measure of the favorable response to the Communist Party's position was the development of Communist-led fraternal organizations based on nationality, fourteen of which coalesced into the International Workers Order, whose membership peaked in 1947 at 184,000 members organized into 2,500 lodges, and almost thirty foreign-language newspapers, which in 1940 reached a combined circulation of over 400,000.[160] Italian Fascism did in fact promote *Italianità*, but it did so on the basis that Italians Americans were "Italians abroad," that is, they were part of a diaspora whose participants owed their allegiance to the "mother country." This position conflicted with the desires of some Italians and other immigrant groups to have full citizenship in the United States along with the right to maintain an identity based on their country of origin.

Although Italian Americans have begun to rediscover their Italian roots, there are signs that they have also begun to find renewed interest in their immigrant radical past. In addition to the 1997 conference "The Lost World of Italian American Radicalism," sponsored by the Calandra Institute, Fieri National has spearheaded a campaign to restore the memory and reputation of Vito Marcantonio. This effort culminated in "Vito Marcantonio: A Recognition and Celebration," a program held on November 12, 1998, at New York University. It attracted more than four hundred people and was cosponsored by the American Italian Historical Association, the Calandra Institute, and Il Circolo Italiano of New York University, and endorsed by 70 other organizations, most of which were Italian American. One outcome of this event is the reprinting of *I Vote My Conscience* (1956), the collection of Marcantonio's speeches and writings, edited by Annette Rubinstein.[161] Also, from October 11, 1999, to February 20, 2000, the New York Historical Society hosted *The Italians of New York: Five Centuries of Struggle and Achievement*, an exhibition sponsored by the Calandra Institute featuring political and cultural radicals prominently among its themes. Significantly, none of the many published reviews or the thousands of comments of the attendees recorded in the guest books, questioned or criticized their inclusion.[162]

What meaning lies in this reawakening? What if any lessons can the Italian American community draw from the history of its own radicalism, and more important, how can its radical past help guide the Italian American agenda for the twenty-first century? The answer lies perhaps in a reconsideration of the differing roles of the two forms of leadership that have always marked Italian American history—the _prominenti_ and the _sovversivi_.

The _prominenti_ have made the campaign against the Mafia stereotype their own special preserve since 1931, yet after more than seventy years of protests Italian Americans have never been more widely or more pervasively vilified by that image than they are today. Why has this effort to defend the ethnic community failed so completely? Throughout the Italian American experience, the _prominenti_ have consistently endorsed a closely linked agenda of patriotism and Americanization, which has essentially meant supporting the coercive efforts of American society designed to strip Italian immigrants and their descendants of their history, culture, and identity. The dual focus of _prominentismo_ has always been to promote the separate interests of a particular elite rather than of the community as a whole, and to stress what Italian Americans are not. Their one effort to encourage identification with the _patria_, namely by supporting Mussolini's Fascist regime, resulted during World War II in one of the most serious episodes of defamation the Italian community ever experienced. Americanization, the anti-Mafia campaign, and support for Fascist Italy constituted the core of the project advanced by Generoso Pope, the archetypical _prominente_, from as far back as the late 1920s. Recent discussions about recreating an "Italy lobby" among Italian Americans have, ironically, deliberately looked back to Pope, who invented the pro-Mussolini lobby on the basis of presumed obligations owed by immigrants to their mother country.

Although radical activism was essentially class based, its goals were aimed at benefiting the social and economic interests of the vast majority of Italian immigrants and their American-born family members. Moreover, the radicals politicized Italian ethnicity and made it an integral part of their militancy, so that the _sovversivi_ historically stood squarely against Americanization and in defense of the cultural rights of the entire community. It was the old-time radicals, not the _prominenti_, who understood the link between the material and the spiritual aspects of Italian American identity, and their example may yet serve the interests of the community.

NOTES

1. Only 14 percent of Lawrence's 85,000 residents were native born of native parents; almost half had been born abroad: nearly 8,000 in Canada, about 6,500 in Italy, 6,000 in Ireland, 4,000 in the Russian Empire (including Poland), and 2,000 in the Turkish Empire.

2. "Congressmen Hear Strikers' Children," _New York Times_, 5 March 1912. Sources give at least three versions of Teoli's first name; we use Cammella, the spelling in the original _New York Times_ article.

3. Quoted from Paul Cowan, introduction to _Lawrence 1912: The Bread and Roses Strike_, by William Cahn (New York: Pilgrim Press, 1982), 5. One of the editors of this book (and coauthor of this essay) experienced much the same revelation as Cammella

Teoli's daughter: a colleague, Jennifer Guglielmo, found a letter to the editor of the Communist newspaper *L'Unità del Popolo* written by Filippo Cannistraro, Philip Cannistraro's grandfather, on April 4, 1943. Subsequently, the other editor of this volume, Gerald Meyer, found Filippo's name in the April 16, 1949, issue on the list of contributors for *L'Unità*'s annual May Day appeal. After making inquiries of relatives, Cannistraro discovered that Filippo—who in old age read *Il Progresso Italo-Americano*—had attended meetings of Communist organizations in the Bronx and had organized a letter-writing campaign against Mussolini during World War II.

4. A. William Salomone, "The Italian Anarchists in America: Comment and Historical Reflection," in *Italian American Radicalism: Old World Origins and New World Developments*, ed. Rudolph Vecoli, Proceedings of the Fifth Annual Conference of the American Italian Historical Association (Staten Island, N.Y.: American Italian Historical Association, 1972), 42.

5. Annette Wheeler Cafarelli, "No Butter on Our Bread: Anti-Intellectual Stereotyping of Italian Americans," *VIA* 7 (spring 1996): 39–47. Giovanna Capone, Denise Leto, and Tommi Mecca proclaimed, "We are tired of the stereotypical portrayals of Italian/Sicilian men as violent Mafiosi and Italian women as glamorous bombshells or long-suffering martyrs." *Hey Paesan! Writings by Lesbians and Gay Men of Italian Descent* (Oakland, Calif.: Three Guineas Press, 1999), 1.

6. George de Stefano, "Ungood Fellas," *The Nation*, February 2000, 31.

7. For an example of how this stereotype was used in defeating an Italian American political candidate, see Peter Vellon, "Immigrant Son: Mario Procaccino and the Rise of Conservative Politics in Late 1960s New York City," *Italian American Review* 7 (spring/summer 1999): 117–36. On the use of the Mafia stigma against Geraldine Ferraro when she ran for vice president, see Maria Lisella, review of *Framing a Life: A Family Memoir*, by Geraldine Ferraro, *Italian American Review* (winter 2000): 141.

8. Richard Gambino, *Blood of My Blood: The Dilemma of the Italian-Americans* (New York: Guernica, 1997; first published in 1974), 327. Elsewhere, Gambino has repeated this idea: "The masses of Italian immigrants . . . had little use for politics and almost none for abstract ideologies." See Richard Gambino, review of *La Storia: Five Centuries of the Italian American Experience*, by Jerre Mangione and Ben Morreale, *Italian Americana*, fall/winter 1993, 120.

9. The concept was first made popular by Edward Banfield's *The Moral Basis of a Backward Society* (New York: Macmillan, 1958). For criticisms of the Banfield argument, see Louis J. Gesualdi, "A Documentation of Criticisms Concerning Amoral Familism," in *The Family and Community Life of Italian Americans*, ed. Richard N. Juliani, Proceedings of the Thirteenth Annual Conference of the American Italian Historical Association (Toronto: Multicultural History Society of Ontario, 1983), 129–32. Familism can illuminate the southern Italian social structure and values and their adaptation to host societies, but the idea must be used with caution. For a heuristic use of this concept, see Leonard Covello, *The Social Mores of the Southern Italo-American School Child: A Study of the Southern Italian Family Mores and Their Effects on the School Situation in Italy and America* (Leiden, The Netherlands: E. J. Brill, 1967).

10. Donna R. Gabaccia, *Militants and Migrants: Rural Sicilians Become American Workers* (New Brunswick, N.J.: Rutgers University Press, 1988), 16.

11. For examples of early works dealing with Italian American radicalism, see Mario De Ciampis, "Storia del movimento socialista rivoluzionario italiano," *La Parola del Popolo* 9 (December 1958–January 1959): 136–63; Grazia Dorè, *La democrazia italiana e l'emigrazione*

in America (Brescia, Italy: Morcelliana, 1964); Grazia Dorè, "Socialismo italiano negli Stati Uniti," *Rassegna di Politica e di Storia* 14 (January–March, 1968): 1–6, 33–40, 114–19; Edwin Fenton, *Immigrants and Unions, A Case Study: Italians and American Labor, 1870–1920* (New York: Arno Press, 1975); Anna Maria Martellone, "Per una storia della sinistra italiana negli Stati Uniti: Riformismo e sindacalismo, 1880–1911," in *Il Movimento migratorio italiano dall'unità nazionale ai giorni nostri*, ed. Franca Assante, (Geneva: Droz, 1976), 181–95; Paul Buhle, "Italian American Radicals and Labor in Rhode Island, 1905–1930," *Radical History* 17 (spring 1978): 121–51; George E. Pozzetta, ed., *Pane e Lavoro: The Italian American Working Class*, Proceedings of the Eleventh Annual Conference of the American Italian Historical Association (Toronto: Multicultural History Society of Ontario, 1980).

12. Rudolph Vecoli, ed., preface to *Italian American Radicalism*, iv.

13. Nunzio Pernicone, "Italian Immigrant Radicalism in New York," in *The Italians of New York: Five Centuries of Struggle and Achievement*, ed. Philip V. Cannistraro (New York: John Calandra Italian American Institute and the New York Historical Society, 1999), 77–90.

14. Nunzio Pernicone, *Italian Anarchism, 1864–1892* (Princeton, N.J.: Princeton University Press, 1993); Pernicone, "Carlo Tresca: Life and Death of a Revolutionary," in *Italian Americans: The Search of a Usable Past*, ed. Richard N. Juliani and Philip V. Cannistraro (Staten Island, N.Y.: American Italian Historical Association, 1989), 216–35; Pernicone, "Luigi Galleani and Italian Anarchist Terrorism in the United States," *Studi Emigrazione* (September 1993): 469–89; Pernicone, "Carlo Tresca and the Sacco-Vanzetti Case," *Journal of American History* 66 (December 1979): 535–47; see also his "War among the Italian Anarchists: The Galleanisti's Campaign against Carlo Tresca," chapter 2 of this book. The best study of the anarchist context for the Sacco-Vanzetti case is Paul Avrich, *Sacco and Vanzetti: The Anarchist Background* (Princeton, N.J.: Princeton University Press, 1991). See also *Sacco-Vanzetti: Developments and Reconsiderations—1979* (Boston: Trustees of the Public Library of the City of Boston, 1982). For a basic bibliography on the Sacco-Vanzetti case in general, see Gil Fagiani, "Remember! Justice Crucified: A Synopsis, Chronology, and Selective Bibliography of the Sacco and Vanzetti Case," *Differentia* 8–9 (spring/autumn 1999): 253–67. The letters of Sacco and Vanzetti, originally published in 1928, have been reprinted as *The Letters of Sacco and Vanzetti*, ed. Marion Denman Frankfurter and Gardner Jackson (New York: Penguin Books, 1997).

15. Rudolph J. Vecoli, "Italian American Workers, 1880–1920: Padrone Slaves or Primitive Rebels?" in *Perspectives in Italian Immigration and Ethnicity*, ed. Silvano M. Tomasi (New York: Center for Migration Studies, 1977), 25–49; Vecoli, "The Italian Immigrants in the United States Labor Movement from 1880 to 1920," in *Gli italiani fuori d'Italia. Gli emigrati italiani nei movimenti operai dei paesi d'adozioine 1880–1940*, ed. Bruno Bezza (Milan: Angeli, 1983), 257–306; Vecoli, "Italian American Workers, 1880–1920," in *New Perspectives in Italian Immigration and Ethnicity*, ed. Lydio F. Tomasi (New York: Center for Migration Studies, 1985), 88–112; Vecoli, "Italian Immigrants and Working Class Movements in the United States: A Personal Reflection on Class and Ethnicity," *Journal of the Canadian Historical Association* (1993): 193–205; Vecoli, " 'Free Country': The American Republic Viewed by the Italian Left, 1880–1920," in *In the Shadow of Liberty: Immigrants, Workers, and Citizens in the American Republic, 1880–1920*, ed. Marianne Debouzy (Saint-Denis, France: Presses Universitaires de Vincennes, 1988), 23–44; and Vecoli, "The Making and Un-Making of an Italian Working Class in the United States, 1915–1945," chapter 1 of this book.

16. Alan Schaffer, *Vito Marcantonio: Radical in Congress* (Syracuse, N.Y.: Syracuse University Press, 1966); Salvatore La Gumina, *Vito Marcantonio: The People's Politician* (Dubuque, Iowa: Kendall/Hunt, 1969); and Gerald Meyer, *Vito Marcantonio: Radical Politician* (Albany: State University of New York Press, 1989). See also Annette T. Rubinstein, ed., *I Vote My Conscience: Debates, Speeches and Writings of Vito Marcantonio, 1935–1950* (New York: Marcantonio Memorial Fund, 1956) and Dorothy Gallagher, *All the Right Enemies: The Life and Murder of Carlo Tresca* (New York: Penguin Books, 1989). Nunzio Pernicone is writing an in-depth biography of Tresca as an Italian immigrant radical.

17. Surveys of Italian American history have been limited and highly selective in their treatment of radicalism. The earliest is no doubt Michael Musmanno, *The Story of the Italians in America* (Garden City, N.Y.: Doubleday, 1965). The fact that there is no discussion of radicalism or strike activity, no mention of Marcantonio, and that Sacco and Vanzetti are never identified as anarchists, is all the more startling given that as a young attorney Musmanno was a member of the Sacco-Vanzetti defense team. Alexander DeConde's *Half Bitter, Half Sweet: An Excursion into Italian-American History* (New York: Charles Scribner's Sons, 1971) addresses the subject briefly. Erik Amfitheatrof's *Children of Columbus: An Informal History of the Italians in the New World* (Boston: Little, Brown, 1973) contains a chapter on the Lawrence strike and an adequate discussion of the Sacco-Vanzetti case, Tresca, and similar matters. See also Luciano Iorizzo and Salvatore Mondello, *The Italian Americans* (New York: Twayne, 1971) and Humbert Nelli, *From Immigrants to Ethnics: The Italian Americans* (New York: Oxford University Press, 1983). The most recent survey, Mangione and Morreale's, *La Storia*, includes a chapter ("The Road to Sacco and Vanzetti") that outlines the activities of radicals in the immigrant communities as well as profiles of Tresca and Marcantonio. Nonetheless, there is no Italian equivalent to Irving Howe's *The World of Our Fathers* (New York: Schocken Books, 1976) that places the radical strains within the general context of the community, a lacuna which the editors hope this book to some degree addresses.

18. Robert F. Foerster, *The Italian Emigration of Our Times* (Cambridge: Harvard University Press, 1919), 102.

19. Donna R. Gabaccia, "Lost and Found: Italian American Radicalism in Global Perspective," conclusion of this book.

20. Perhaps the first scholarly work to pose the notion of "transnationalism" before the term came into general use was Ernesto Ragionieri, "Italiani all'estero ed emigrazione di lavoratori italiani: Un tema di storia del movimento operaio," *Belfagor* 17 (November 1962): 641–69. Randolph Bourne, a pioneer of cultural pluralism, coined the term, which he spelled *trans-nationalism*. See Leslie Vaughan, *Randolph Bourne and the Politics of Cultural Radicalism* (Lawrence: University Press of Kansas, 1997), 1, and Bourne, "Toward a Trans-national America," *Atlantic Monthly,* July 1916. See also George E. Pozzetta and Bruno Ramirez, *The Italian Diaspora across the Globe* (Ontario: Multicultural History Society of Ontario, 1992); Donna R. Gabaccia and Fraser Ottanelli, "Diaspora or International Proletariat?" *Diaspora* 6, no. 1 (1997): 61–83; Gabaccia and Ottanelli, *For Us There Are No Frontiers: Italian Labor Migration and the Making of Multi-Ethnic Nations* (forthcoming, University of Illinois Press).

21. Michael Topp, "The Italian-American Left: Transnationalism and the Quest for Unity," in *The Immigrant Left in the United States,* ed. Paul Buhle and Dan Georgakas (Albany: State University of New York Press, 1996), 142.

22. Paul Avrich, *Anarchist Portraits* (Princeton, N.J.: Princeton University Press, 1988), 180. See also David DeLeon, *The American as Anarchist: Reflections on Indigenous*

Radicalism (Baltimore: Johns Hopkins University Press, 1978), 85–101; George Carey, "The Vessel, the Deed, and the Idea: Anarchists in Paterson, NJ, 1895–1908," *Antipode* (1979): 46–58; Carey, "*La Questione Sociale*: An Anarchist Newspaper in Paterson, New Jersey (1895–1908)," in Tomasi, *New Perspectives*, 289–97.

23. Michael Esposito, "The Evolution of Pietro di Donato's Perception of Italian Americans," in *The Italian Americans through the Generations*, ed. Rocco Caporale (Staten Island, N.Y.: American Italian Historical Association), 176–84. Donato participated in the fourth congress of the Communist-led League of American Writers in June 1940. See "In Defense of Culture," *L'Unità del Popolo*, 3 May 1941.

24. Philip V. Cannistraro, "The Italians of New York: An Historical Overview," in Cannistraro, *Italians of New York*, 3; Frederick Binder and David Reimers, *All the Nations under Heaven: An Ethnic and Racial History of New York City* (New York: Columbia University Press, 1995), 135; Gianfausto Rosoli, ed., *Un secolo di emigrazione italiana, 1866–1976* (Rome: Centro Studi Emigrazione, 1978), 353.

25. For a comparative study of Jewish and Italian social and economic mobility, see Thomas Kessner, *The Golden Door: Italian and Jewish Immigrant Mobility in New York City, 1880–1915* (New York: Oxford University Press, 1977). Kessner argues that the Italians' illiteracy, lack of skills, and short-range ambitions limited their mobility.

26. On "whiteness" see especially David R. Roediger, *The Wages of Whiteness: Race and the Making of the American Working Class* (London: Verso, 1991); Noel Ignatiev, *How the Irish Became White* (New York: Routledge, 1995); Matthew Frye Jacobsen, *Whiteness of a Different Color: European Immigrants and the Alchemy of Race* (Cambridge, Mass.: Harvard University Press, 1998). On the Italians see David Richards, *Italian American: The Racializing of an Ethnic Group* (New York: New York University Press, 1999), 158–212; Jennifer Guglielmo and Salvatore Salerno, eds., *Are Italians White?* (New York: Routledge, 2003).

27. The Dillingham Commission, for example, cited the authority of such figures as Giuseppe Sergi and Cesare Lombroso in categorizing southern Italians low on a racial hierarchy. See Peter R. D'Agostino, "Craniums, Criminals, and the 'Cursed Race': Italian Anthropology in American Racial Thought" (unpublished paper), and Vito Teti, *La razza maledetta: Origini del pregiudizio antimeridionale* (Rome: Manifestolibri, 1993).

28. The literature on the so-called "Southern Question" in Italian history has expanded greatly in recent years. Among the older works, see Rosario Villari, ed., *Il sud nella storia d'Italia* (Bari: Laterza, 1963). For examples of newer approaches, see Jane Schneider, ed., *Italy's Southern Question: Orientalism in Our Country* (Oxford/New York: Berg, 1998); John Dickie, *Darkest Italy: The Nation and Stereotypes of the Mezzogiorno, 1860–1999* (New York: St. Martin's Press, 1999); Nancy Riall, "Which Road to the South: Revisionists Revisit the Mezzogiorno," *Journal of Modern Italian Stidues* 1 (2000): 89–100; Robert Lumley and Jonathan Morris, eds., *The New History of the Italian South: The Mezzogiorno Revisited* (Exeter, England: University of Exeter Press, 1997).

29. On the labor movement in Italy, see Joseph La Palombara, *The Italian Labor Movement: Problems and Prospects* (Ithaca, N.Y.: Cornell University Press, 1957); Daniel L. Horowitz, *The Italian Labor Movement* (Cambridge, Mass.: Harvard University Press, 1963); Maurice F. Neufeld, *Italy: School for Awakening Countries* (Ithaca: New York State School of Industrial and Labor Relations, Cornell University, 1961); Humbert Gualtieri, *The Labor Movement in Italy* (New York, 1946); Richard Hostetter, *The Italian Socialist Movement, Its Origins* (New York, 1958); and Nunzio Pernicone, "The Italian Labor Movement," in *Modern Italy: A Topical History*, ed. Edward R. Tannenbaum and Emiliana P. Noether (New York: New York University Press, 1974), 197–227.

30. Bruno Cartosio, "Sicilian Radicals in Two Worlds," in Debouzy, *Shadow of Liberty*. The classic literature on the Sicilian *Fasci* includes "I Fasci Siciliani," special issue of *Movimento Operaio* 6 (November–December 1954): 801–1111; Salvatore F. Romano, *Storia dei Fasci siciliani* (Bari, Italy: Laterza, 1959); Francesco Renda, *I Fasci Siciliani 1892–94* (Turin, Italy: Einaudi, 1977); and Massimo S. Ganci, *I Fasci dei Lavoratori* (Caltanissetta and Rome: Sciascia Editore, 1977). On the government repressions of radical movements in Italy, see Umberto Levra, *Il colpo di stato della borghesia: La crisi politica di fine secolo in Italia 1896/1900* (Milan: Feltrinelli, 1975). In post–World War II Italy, the Communist Party (PCI) had been consistently stronger in the predominantly agricultural region of central Italy than in the highly industrialized North. In 1963, the *mezzadri* in central Italy was the class that regularly gave the PCI the highest percent of the vote (47 percent); in the South the largest bloc of PCI members were *contadini* and *braccianti*. See Sidney Tarrow, *Peasant Communism in Southern Italy* (New Haven, Conn.: Yale University Press, 1967), 131, 135–36, 205.

31. See Gabriele De Rosa, *Storia del Partito Popolare* (Bari, Italy: Laterza, 1958); Richard A. Webster, *The Cross and the Fasces* (Stanford, Calif.: Stanford University Press, 1960); Francesco Piva and Francesco Malgeri, *Vita di Luigi Sturzo* (Rome: Cinque Lune, 1976).

32. Anthony Mansueto, "Blessed Are the Meek: Religion and Socialism in Italian American History," in *The Melting Pot and Beyond: Italian Americans in the Year 2000*, ed. Jerome Krase (Staten Island, N.Y.: American Italian Historical Association, 1987), 125.

33. Donna R. Gabaccia, "Neither Padrone Slaves nor Primitive Rebels: Sicilians on Two Continents," in *"Struggle a Hard Battle": Essays on Working Class Immigrants*, ed. Dick Hoerder (De Kalb: Northern Illinois University Press, 1986), 104–5. For a more extended study of the phenomenon, see her *Militants and Migrants*. Early studies on the relationship between political militancy and emigration include John S. MacDonald, "Agricultural Organization, Migration, and Labor Militancy in Rural Italy," *Economic History Review*, 2d ser., 16 (1963): 61–75; John and Leatrice MacDonald, "Italy's Rural Social Structure and Emigration," *Occidente* 12 (1956): 437–56; and "Chain Migration, Ethnic Neighborhood Formation and Social Networks," *Milbank Fund Quarterly* 42 (January 1964): 82–91.

34. Paul Buhle, *A Dreamer's Paradise Lost: Louis Fraina/Lewis Corey (1892–1953) and the Decline of Radicalism in the United States* (Atlantic Highlands, N.J.: Humanities Press, 1995), 70.

35. Salvatore Salerno, *Red November, Black November: Culture and Community in the Industrial Workers of the World* (Albany: State University of New York Press, 1989), 10. On the IWW, see also early studies by Melvyn Dubofsky, *We Shall Be All: A History of the I.W.W.* (New York: Quadrangle, 1969); Philip S. Foner, *History of the Labor Movement in the United States*, vol. 4, *The Industrial Workers of the World, 1905–1917* (New York: International Publishers, 1965); and Michael M. Topp, *Those without a Country: The Political Culture of Italian American Syndicalists* (Minneapolis: University of Minnesota Press, 2001).

36. James Weinstein, *The Decline of Socialism in America, 1912–1925* (New Brunswick, N.J.: Rutgers University Press, 1983), 24, 182.

37. Seymour Martin Lipset and Gary Marks, *It Didn't Happen Here: Why Socialism Failed in the United States* (New York and London: W. W. Norton, 2000), 143–44.

38. Harvey Klehr and John Haynes, *The American Communist Movement: Storming Heaven Itself* (New York: Twayne, 1992), 18–19, 73–74; Irving Howe and Lewis Coser, *The American Communist Party: A Critical History* (New York: Praeger, 1962); Nathan

Glazer, *The Social Basis of American Communism* (New York: Harcourt, Brace, and World, 1961), 221.

39. Richard Alba, *Italian Americans: Twilight of Ethnicity* (New York: Prentice Hall, 1985), 47.

40. John D'Alesandre, *Occupational Trends of Italians in New York City* (New York: Casa Italiana Educational Bureau, 1935), 5, 7. The U.S. Census Bureau defined "Italian fathers" as those having at least one parent born in Italy.

41. Silvano Tomasi, *Piety and Power: The Role of the Italian Parishes in the New York Metropolitan Area, 1880–1930* (New York: Center for Migration Studies, 1975), 25. In 1903, the commissioner of immigration categorized southern Italian immigrants as professionals, 551; tradesmen, 24,895; and laborers (including farmers) 118,751; see Andrew Rolle, *The American Italians: Their History and Culture* (Belmont, Calif.: Wadsworth, 1972), 96. In 1900, one-third of New Jersey's Italian males were either self-employed or were skilled workers; see Michael A. La Sorte, "Immigrant Occupations: A Comparison," in Juliani and Cannistraro, *Italian Americans*, 90.

42. Ronald Bayor, *Neighbors in Conflict: The Irish, Germans, Jews, and Italians of New York City, 1919–1941* (Baltimore: Johns Hopkins University Press, 1978), 10–13.

43. Stefano Luconi, "Italianness in the Depression Years," in *From Paesani to White Ethnics: The Italian Experience in Philadelphia* (State University of New York Press, forthcoming).

44. For the text of the Quota Act of May 19, 1924, see Michael Lemay and Elliott R. Barkan, eds., *U.S. Immigration and Naturalization Laws and Issues* (Westport, Conn.: Greenwood Press, 1999), 133–35. For the text of the Immigration Act of May 26, 1924 (the Johnson-Reed Act), see pp. 148–51. The quota system and the Americanization movement sent a message to workers who were "native born of native stock," especially if they were Protestant or, to a lesser extent, Catholics from northeastern Europe, that they—unlike the Jews, Italians, and Slavs—were real Americans. This in large measure accounted for (1) the predominance of the foreign born and their children and the absence of "old-stock" Americans on the Left, and (2) the far greater likelihood of "ethnics" to vote for the Democratic Party than their Anglo-Saxon Protestant class counterparts.

45. Lipset and Marks, *It Didn't Happen Here*, 147–54.

46. Christopher Seton-Watson, *Italy from Liberation to Fascism, 1870–1925* (London: Methuen, 1967), 10–12, 53–61.

47. Christopher M. Sturba, "The Education of an Italian Priest in America: Father Mariano Milanese and the Holy Rosary Parish of Lawrence, Massachusetts, 1902–1935," *Italian American Review* (winter 2000): 21–50.

48. Peter R. D'Agostino, "The Scalabrini Fathers, the Italian Emigrant Church, and Ethnic Nationalism in America," *Religion and American Culture* 7, no. 1 (winter 1997): 121–59. See also D'Agostino's *The Contest for Italy in America: Explorations in Catholic Ideology, 1848–1940* (forthcoming, University of North Carolina Press).

49. Paul Douglas Seaton, "The Catholic Church and the Congress of Industrial Organizations: The Case of the Association of Catholic Trade Unionists, 1937–1950" (Ph.D. diss., Rutgers University, 1975).

50. Kathleen Gefell Centola, "The American Catholic Church and Anti-Communism, 1945–1960: An Interpretive Framework and Case Studies" (Ph.D. diss., State University of New York, Albany, 1984), 12–13; John Cooney, *The American Pope: The Life and Times of Francis Cardinal Spellman* (New York: Times Books, 1984).

51. Virginia Yans-McLoughlin, *Family and Community: Italians of Buffalo, 1880–1930* (Ithaca, N.Y.: Cornell University Press, 1971), 227. Yans-McLoughlin notes, "Like most of their countrymen, the Italians in Buffalo had an aversion to parochial education."

52. Mangione and Morreale, *La Storia*, 329. On immigrant anticlericalism see Rudolph J. Vecoli, "Prelates and Peasants," *Journal of Social History* 2 (spring 1969): 217–68.

53. Pernicone, "Carlo Tresca: Life and Death," 218.

54. Peter R. D'Agostino, "The Triad of Roman Authority: Fascism, the Vatican, and Italian Religious Clergy in the Italian Emigrant Church," *Journal of American Ethnic History* 17 (spring 1998): 3–37; D'Agostino, " 'Fascist Transmission Belts' or Episcopal Advisors? Italian Consuls and American Catholicism in the 1930s," Cushwa Center for the Study of American Catholicism: *Working Paper Series* 24, no. 3 (spring 1997): 1–37.

55. Rudolph J. Vecoli, "Cult and Occult in Italian-American Culture," in *Immigrants and Religion in Urban America*, ed. Randall Miller and Thomas Marzik (Philadelphia: Temple University, 1975), 41.

56. Ibid., 52.

57. Domenico Pistella, *The Crowning of a Queen* (New York: Eugene Printing Service, 1954), 68, 105, 118, 128; Robert Anthony Orsi, *The Madonna of 115th Street: Faith and Community in East Harlem, 1889–1950* (New Haven, Conn.: Yale University Press), 19, 54.

58. For statistics on Italian American Protestantism, see Tomasi, *Piety and Power*, 146, 155. The Waldensians, who despite fierce persecution had maintained their Protestantism since the High Middle Ages, were among the earliest Italian settlers in the United States. Rolle, *The American Italians*, 15, 72. As a child, La Guardia's parents, who were of mixed religious backgrounds (the husband Catholic and the mother Jewish), sent him to an Episcopal church (an affiliation he nominally maintained throughout his life) as part of their effort to Americanize their children; see Ronald Bayor, *Fiorello La Guardia: Ethnicity and Reform* (Wheeling, Ill.: Harlan Davidson, 1993), 9. Leonard Covello's conversion to Protestantism resulted from his association with Anna Ruddy, a Canadian Methodist who founded a settlement house, the Home Garden (the present-day La Guardia Memorial House), in Italian Harlem; see *The Heart Is the Teacher* (New York: McGraw-Hill, 1958), 31–35. Giovannitti's attraction to the social gospel led him to convert to Protestantism and enroll in a seminary. Similar to Norman Thomas, of the same period, his initial commitment to the ministry represented the first step on a trajectory that led to a lifelong commitment to radicalism; see Mangione and Morreale, *La Storia*, 284.

59. Yans-McLoughlin, *Family and Community*, 116.

60. Michael Denning, *The Cultural Front: The Laboring of American Culture in the Twentieth Century* (New York: Verso, 1997), 36.

61. William Shedd, *Italian Population in New York* (New York: Casa Italiana Educational Bureau, 1934). The concentrations of first- and second-generation Italian Americans ranged from 75 to 90 percent in Italian Harlem (the largest), the Lower East Side's Little Italy, and the Belmont section of the Bronx. Another 13 areas (nine of which were in Brooklyn) had concentrations of 50 to 75 percent. Leonard Covello, "The Italians of New York," p. 10 (unpublished manuscript, ca. 1946, in Gerald Meyer's possession).

62. Irving Sollins, "A Socio-Statistical Analysis of Boys' Club Membership" (Ph.D. diss., New York University, 1936), 43. See also Donna R. Gabaccia, *From Sicily to Elizabeth Street* (Albany: State University of New York Press, 1984).

63. On another occasion, he described the Little Italies as "an agglomeration of numerous disjointed groupings." "Casa Italiana Educational Bureau: Its Purposes and Programs" (New York: Casa Italiana Educational Bureau, ca. 1934), 3.

64. Jerry Krase has noted that "Throughout history, Italian American communities have been highly valued by those who live within them, but have been negatively viewed by those outside them." "America's Little Italies: Past, Present, and Future," *Italian Journal* 4, no. 5 (1990): 25.

65. Leonard Covello, a major figure among cultural pluralists, understood the cultural implications of imparting the language of origin to subsequent generations and its importance in elevating the prestige of the community. He developed an educational philosophy, which he termed community-centered education, that honored the cultures and contributions of all ethnic groups. See Gerald Meyer, "Leonard Covello: A Pioneer in Bilingual Education," *The Bilingnal Review* (January–August 1985): 55–61. On Americanization as a deradicalizing process, see John McClymer, "The Federal Government and the Americanization Movement, 1915–1924," *Prologue* 10, no. 1 (1978): 23–41.

66. Vecoli, "The Making and Un-Making of an Italian Working Class," chap. 1 of this book.

67. Rudolph J. Vecoli, "Primo Maggio in the United States: An Invention of the Italian Anarchists," in *Sappi che oggi è la tua festa*, ed. Andrea Panaccione (Venice: Marsilio, 1986), 55–83; Vecoli, "Primo Maggio: May Day Observances among Italian Immigrant Workers, 1890–1920," *Labor's Heritage* 7 (spring 1996): 28–41; Robert D'Attilio, "Primo Maggio: Haymarket as Seen by Italian Anarchists in America," in *Haymarket Scrapbook*, ed. Dave Roediger and Franklin Rosemont (Chicago: Kerr, 1986), 229–31; Topp, "The Italian-American Left," 125–26; Avrich, *Sacco and Vanzetti*, 53–55.

68. Antonio Stella, *Some Aspects of Italian Immigration to the United States* (New York and London: G. P. Putnam's Sons, 1924), 55. Although illiteracy in southern Italy was as high as 80 percent during the era of major migration, the illiteracy rate among immigrants from southern Italy to the United States was lower—the Dillingham Commission, for example, gave a figure of 53.9 percent. E. Sori, in *L'emigrazione italiana dall'Unità alla seconda guerra mondiale* (Bologna, Italy: Il Mulino, 1938), p. 38, estimated illiteracy at 52 percent for those over 10 years of age during the period 1900 to 1914; Tomasi, in *Piety and Power*, pp. 23–24, noted that in 1907–8 fewer than 9 percent of the northerners and almost 60 percent of the southerners were illiterate.

69. Quoted in Pernicone, "Italian Immigrant Radicalism," 82.

70. MSS inscription by Ruotolo, dated July 18, 1935, in *Leonardo, Annual Magazine of the Leonardo Da Vinci Art School* (New York: Leonardo Da Vinci Publishing House, 1925), in possession of Philip V. Cannistraro.

71. See Frances Winwar, *Ruotolo, Man and Artist* (New York: Liveright, 1949), and Josef Vincent Lombardo, *Attilio Piccirilli, Life of an American Sculptor* (New York: Pitman, 1944). On the Da Vinci Art School, see Lucio Ruotolo, "Onorio Ruotolo and the Leonardo da Vinci Art School," *Italian American Review* (winter 2000): 1–20.

72. Fred L. Gardaphè, *Italian Signs, American Streets: The Evolution of Italian American Narrative* (Durham: Duke University Press, 1996), 66; see also Gardaphè, "Follow the Red Brick Road: Recovering Radical Traditions of Italian/American Writers," chapter 13 of this book. On Giovannitti as a poet, see Wallace Sillanpoa, "The Poetry and the Politics of Arturo Giovannitti," in Krase, *Melting Pot and Beyond*, 175–89; Joseph Tusiani, "La poesia inglese di Arturo Giovannitti," *La Parola del Popolo* 147 (November–December 1978): 94–98; Lucilla LaBella Mays, "Arturo Giovannitti: Writings from Lawrence," in *Italian Ethnics: Their Languages, Literature, and Lives*, ed. Domenic Candeloro, Proceedings of the 21st Annual Conference of the American Italian Historical Association

(Staten Island, N.Y.: The American Italian Historical Association, 1990), 79–89; Julia Lisella, "Behind the Mask: Signs of Radicalism in the Work of Rosa Zagnoni Marinoni," chapter 14 of this book; Roberto Ventresca, "A Torch in the Night: Virgilia D'Andrea and Italian Anarchism in America" (paper presented at the conference "The Lost World of Italian American Radicalism," New York, N.Y., 14–15 May 1997).

73. Passing references to New York's radical theater are to be found in Emelise Aleandri, "A History of Italian-American Theatre: 1900 to 1905" (Ph.D. diss., City University of New York, 1983), but the work does not contain a sustained discussion of the subject under that rubric, possibly because it ignored the radical press and was based largely on mainstream newspapers.

74. See also Salerno, *Red November, Black November.*

75. George E. Pozzetta, "Italians and the Tampa General Strike of 1910," in Pozzetta, *Pane e Lavoro*, 29–46.

76. Gary R. Mormino and George E. Pozzetta, "The Reader Lights the Candle: Cuban and Florida Cigar Workers' Oral Tradition," *Labor's Heritage* 5 (spring 1993): 4–26.

77. Gary R. Mormino, "The Radical World of Ybor City, Florida" chapter 12 of this book. See also Mormino and George E. Pozzetta, *The Immigrant World of Ybor City* (Urbana: University of Illinois Press, 1987), and a new edition, published by University Presses of Florida (Gainesville), 1989.

78. Curtis MacDougall, *Gideon's Army* (New York: Marzani & Munsell, 1965), 3:858.

79. Nunzio Pernicone, "Carlo Tresca's *Il Martello*," *Italian American Review* (spring/summer 2001): 7–55.

80. Paola A. Sensi-Isolani, "Italian Radicals and Union Activists in San Francisco, 1900–1920," chapter 8 of this book; Mangione and Morreale, *La Storia*, 280–81.

81. Meyer, *Vito Marcantonio*, 52, 244, n. 29.

82. On the stonecutters of Barre, Vermont, see Patrizia Audenino, *Un mestiere per partire* (Milan: Franco Angeli, 1990); Barre Museum, Aldrich Public Library, *Carlo Abate: "A Life in Stone"* (Barre Museum, n.d.); Mari Tomasi, "The Italian Story in Vermont," *Vermont History* 28 (January 1960): 73–87.

83. Avrich, *Sacco and Vanzetti*, 49–52, 135.

84. Pernicone, "Italian Immigrant Radicalism," 82; Jennifer M. Guglielmo, "*Donne Ribelli*: Recovering the History of Italian Women's Radicalism in the United States," chapter 4 of this book.

85. Jean Vincenza Scarpaci, "Angela Bambace and the International Ladies' Garment Workers' Union: The Search for an Elusive Activist," in Pozzetta, *Pane e Lavoro*, 99–118; Amfitheatrof, *Children of Columbus*, 120. On Italian immigrant women and radicalism, see especially, Donna R. Gabaccia, "Italian Immigrant Women in Comparative Perspective," *Altreitalie* 9 (1993): 163–75; Donna R. Gabaccia and Franca Iacovetta, "Women, Work, and Protest in the Italian Diaspora: An International Research Agenda," *Labour/Le Travail* 42 (fall 1998): 161–81; Betty Boyd Caroli, Robert F. Harney, and Lydio F. Tomasi, eds., *The Italian Immigrant Woman in North America* (Toronto: The Multicultural History Society of Ontario, 1978); Gary R. Mormino and George E. Pozzetta, "Immigrant Women in Tampa: The Italian Experience, 1890–1930," *Florida Historical Quarterly* 61 (January 1983): 296–312; Rose Laub Coser, Laura S. Anker, and Andrew J. Perrin, *Women of Courage: Jewish and Italian Immigrant Women in New York* (Westport, Conn.: Greenwood Press, 1999); Colomba Marie Furio, "Immigrant Women and Industry: A Case Study. Italian Immigrant Women and the Garment Industry, 1880–1950" (Ph.D. diss., New York University, 1979).

86. Lipset and Marks, It Didn't Happen Here, 143. See also Samuel L. Baily, "Italians and Organized Labor in the United States and Argentina, 1880–1910," in Silvano M. Tomasi and Madeline H. Engel, eds., The Italian Experience in the United States (New York: Center for Migration Studies, 1970), 111.

87. Topp, "The Italian-American Left," 131.

88. The literature on the Lawrence strike is substantial. See especially, Foner, History of the Labor Movement, 4:306–350; Dubofsky, We Shall Be All, 227–62; Donald B. Cole, Immigrant City: Lawrence, Massachusetts, 1845–1921 (Chapel Hill: University of North Carolina Press, 1963); David J. Goldberg, A Tale of Three Cities: Labor Organization and Protest in Paterson, Passaic, and Lawrence, 1916–1921 (New Brunswick, N.J.: Rutgers University Press, 1989); Michael Topp, "The Transnationalism of the Italian American Left: The Lawrence Strike of 1912 and the Italian Chamber of Labor in New York City," Journal of American Ethnic History 17 (fall 1997); Milton Meltzer, Bread and Roses: The Struggle of American Labor, 1865–1915 (New York: Random House, 1973); Gerald Rosenblum, Immigrant Workers: Their Impact on American Labor Radicalism (New York: Basic Books, 1973); and Henry Bedford, " 'Not Enough Pay': Lawrence, 1912," in The Private Side of American Society, ed. Thomas Frazier (New York: Harcourt Brace Jovanovich, 1979), 163–80.

89. Philip F. Notarianni, "Italian Involvement in the 1903–04 Coal Miners' Strike in Southern Colorado and Utah," in Pozzetta, Pane e Lavoro, 47–65; Nunzio Pernicone, "Arturo Giovannitti's 'Son of the Abyss' and the Westmoreland Strike of 1910–1911," Italian Americana 17 (summer 1999): 178–92.

90. On the Paterson strike of 1913, see James D. Osborne, "Italian Immigrants and the Working Class in Paterson: The Strike of 1913 in Ethnic Perspective," in New Jersey's Ethnic Heritage, ed. Paul A. Stellhorne (Trenton: New Jersey Historical Commission, 1978), 11–34; Steve Golin, The Fragile Bridge: Paterson Silk Strike, 1913 (Philadelphia: Temple University Press, 1988); and Anne Huber Tripp, The IWW and the Paterson Silk Strike of 1913 (Urbana and Chicago: University of Illinois Press, 1987).

91. Calvin Winslow, "Italian Workers on the Waterfront: The New York Harbor Strikes of 1907 and 1919," chapter 3 of this book.

92. Rudolph J. Vecoli, "Anthony Capraro and the Lawrence Strike of 1919," in Pozzetta, Pane e Lavoro, 3–27. Italians also took part in the Great Steel Strike of 1919; see John Andreozzi, "Italians in a Mill Town: Lackawanna, New York," in Juliani and Cannistraro, Italian Americans: The Search for a Usable Past, 73.

93. Avrich, Sacco and Vanzetti, 54; Pernicone, "Luigi Galleani and Italian Anarchist Terrorism."

94. Augusta Molinari, "L'Internazionale a New York e gli internazionalisti italiani," in Italia e America dal settecento all'età dell'imperialismo, ed. G. Spini and Anna Mar (Venice: Marsilio, 1976), 279–95; in the same volume see also Arnaldo Testi, "L'immagine degli Stati Uniti nella stampa socialista italiana (1886–1914), pp. 313–47.

95. Fenton, Immigrants and Unions, 162; Topp, "The Italian-American Left," 135–36. See also Elisabetta Vezzosi, Il socialismo indifferente: Immigrati italiani e il partito socialista negli Stati Uniti (Rome: Edizioni Lavoro, 1991); Gabriella Facondo, Socialismo italiano esule negli Stati Uniti (1930–1942) (Foggia, Italy: Bastogi, 1993). Il Proletario appeared briefly in 1903–4 as a daily, but its readers could not sustain the attendant expenses.

96. Jerre Mangione wrote a novel loosely based on Carlo Tresca, Night Search (New York: Crown, 1965).

97. Pernicone, "Carlo Tresca's Il Martello." See also Amfitheatrof, Children of Columbus, 292–305.

98. Avrich, *Sacco and Vanzetti*, 175.

99. Ellen Schrecker, "Immigration and Internal Security: Political Deportations during the McCarthy Era," *Science & Society* (winter 1996–1997): 394.

100. Avrich, *Sacco and Vanzetti*, 128.

101. On Italian Americans in World War I, see Fiorello B. Ventresco, "Loyalty and Dissent: Italian Reservists in America during World War I," *Italian Americana* 4 (1978): 93–122; Emilio Franzina, *Gli italiani al nuovo mondo: L'emigrazione italiana in America 1492–1942* (Milan: Arnaldo Mondadori, 1995), 180. On Italy and America during World War I, see Daniela Rossini, *Il mito americano nell'Italia della Grande Guerra* (Bari, Italy, and Rome: Laterza, 2000); John J. Tinghino, *Edmondo Rossoni: From Revolutionary Syndicalism to Fascism* (New York: Peter Lang, 1991); Stefano Luconi, "From Left to Right: The Not So Strange Career of Filippo Bocchini and Other Italian American Radicals," *Italian American Review* 6 (autumn 1997–winter 1998): 59–79; Marcella Bencivenni, "A Magazine of Art and Struggle: The Experience of *Il Fuoco*, 1914–1915," *Italian American Review* (spring/summer 2001); Aldo Tarabella, "Perchè si combatte," *Il Fuoco*, 1 January 1915, 6. On De Biasi, *Il Carroccio*, and the origins of Italian American Fascism, see Philip V. Cannistraro, *Blackshirts in Little Italy: Italian Americans and Fascism, 1921–1929* (West Lafayette, Ind.: Bordighera, 1999).

102. On Italian American Fascism, see Cannistraro, *Blackshirts in Little Italy*, and the bibliography cited therein.

103. Covello, "The Italians of New York City," 7. Massimo Salvadori, *Resistenza ed azione* (Bari, Italy: Laterza, 1951), 163; Gaetano Salvemini, *Italian Fascist Activities in the United States*, ed. Philip V. Cannistraro (New York: Center for Migration Studies, 1977), 4; Luigi Sturzo, "L'Italo-Americano," *Nazioni Unite*, 1 September 1945; Michael J. Parenti, *Ethnic and Political Attitudes: A Depth Study of Italian Americans* (1962; reprint, New York: Arno Press, 1975), 33–34, 61–62 (page citations are to the reprint edition).

104. On the comparison with Italian communities outside the United States, see Gabaccia, "Lost and Found: Italian American Radicalism in Global Perspective" (conclusion of this book); Vecoli, "The Making and Un-Making of the Italian American Working Class," chapter 1 of this book; John P. Diggins, *Mussolini and Fascism: The View from America* (Princeton: Princeton University Press, 1972), 78–80.

105. See, for example, the early article "Fascisti in America to Fight Radicalism," *New York Times*, 21 March 1923.

106. John P. Diggins, "The Italo-American Anti-Fascist Opposition," *Journal of American History* (December 1967): 579–98. For an inside look at the world of Italian anti-Fascism in New York, see Vanni B. Montana, *Amorostico: Testimonianze euro-americane* (Livorno, Italy: Bastogi, 1975).

107. Cannistraro, *Blackshirts in Little Italy*, 37–39, 68–69; Pellegrino Nazzaro, "Il manifesto dell'alleanza antifascista del Nord America," *Affari Sociali Internazionali* 2 (June 1974): 182.

108. The ILGWU's membership was 51 percent Italian American. Hence, the "segregation" of many of its Italian American members into the two Italian locals may have prevented a shift from the ILGWU's almost exclusively Jewish leadership toward a greater representation of Italian Americans. See Robert Laurentz, "Social and Ethnic Conflict in the New York City Garment Industry, 1933–1960" (Ph.D. diss., State University of New York, Binghamton, 1980), 233. No full-length scholarly monograph on Antonini and Local 89 has been published. See John S. Crawford, "Luigi Antonini: His Influences on Italian-American Relations" (master's thesis, University of Wisconsin, 1950); Benjamin

Stolberg, *Tailor's Progress: The Story of A Famous Union and the Men Who Made It* (Garden City, N.Y.: Doubleday Doran, 1944).

109. Gerald Meyer, "The American Labor Party and New York City's Italian American Communities: 1936–1950," in *Industry, Technology, Labor and the Italian American Communities* (Staten Island, N.Y.: American Italian Historical Association, 1997), 40–41.

110. Charles Zappia, "From Working Class Radicalism to Cold War Anti-Communism: The Case of the Italian Locals of the International Ladies' Garment Workers' Union," chapter 5 of this book; Philip V. Cannistraro, "Luigi Antonini and the Italian Anti-Fascist Movement in the United States," *Journal of American Ethnic History* 5 (fall 1985): 21–40. See also James E. Miller, *The United States and Italy, 1940–1950* (Chapel Hill: University of North Carolina Press, 1986), and Vincent J. Tirelli, *The Italian-American Labor Council: Origins, Conflicts, and Contributions* (New York: The Italian-American Labor Council, 1991).

111. Unlike their counterparts in the ILGWU, however, these anti-Fascists were frequently willing to cooperate with the Communists, and during the struggle for power in the ALP, the ACWA coalesced with the Marcantonio-led left wing against the Dubinsky-Antonini wing. These political differences corresponded to the internal politics of their respective unions: the ILGWU's David Dubinsky had fought and won a battle against the Communists for control of the union; the ACWA's leader, Sidney Hillman, while keeping a firm control of the union, worked together with the Communists against racketeers and business unionism. Steven Fraser, *Labor Will Rule: Sidney Hillman and the Rise of American Labor* (New York: The Free Press, 1991).

112. When in 1936 the army, with the support of the Catholic Church and most of the wealthy, fomented an armed uprising, the Socialists and the Communists, with its middle-class allies, mobilized to defend the republic. The anarchists and dissident Communists of the POUM organized peasants and workers in seizures of land and factories as a prelude to full-fledged socialist revolution. These actions alienated those supporters of the republic—such as anticlerical republicans and the linguistic minorities (especially the Basques and the Catalans), who were not necessarily radical. Ultimately, the Communists utilized their own terror under the leadership of Vidali against their political enemies on the Left, crushing the POUM and the anarchist Confederaciòn Nacional de Trabajo (CNT) union, dismantling the industrial and rural collectives that the anarchists and dissident Communists had established, and executing POUM leaders and anarchists. Although not a Trotskyite organization, and despite Trotsky's criticism of it, POUM became identified with his followers.

113. The personalistic, nonorganizational character of *Il Martello* is illustrated by the fact that it only survived (even then in diminished form) for three years after Tresca's death. See Pernicone, "Carlo Tresca's *Il Martello*."

114. Vecoli, "The Making and Un-Making of an Italian American Working Class."

115. A recent study has argued that Vanni Montana, one of the most prominent Italian Americans in these circles, was a Fascist agent. See Fraser Ottanelli, "Fascist Informant and Italian American Labor Leader: The Paradox of Vanni Buscemi Montana," *Italian American Review* 7 (spring/summer 1999): 104–16.

116. There is an increasing tendency to interpret the Left New Deal as a type of social democracy. See especially, Joshua Freeman, *Working Class New York: Life and Labor since World War II* (New York: The New Press, 2000); John Culver and John Hyde, *American Dreamer: A Life of Henry Wallace* (New York: W. W. Norton, 2000); and Denning, *Cultural Front*, passim.

117. Works Progress Administration, *The Italians of New York* (New York: Random House, 1938), 99; "Valenti, Girolamo," in *Il movimento operaio italiano: Dizionario Biografico*, ed. Franco Andreucci and Tommaso Detti (Rome: Editori Riuniti, 1978), 5:171–74.

118. On Communist membership statistics, see Pernicone, "Italian Immigrant Radicalism," 81.

119. Gerald Meyer, "Italian Americans and the American Communist Party," chapter 9 of this book; Roger Keeran, "The Italian Section of the International Workers Order, 1930–50," *Italian American Review* 7 (spring/summer 1999): 63–82.

120. Meyer, Ibid. On Italian American writers in the Communist orbit, see Gardaphè, "Follow the Red Brick Road," chapter 13 of this book. On Cacchione, see Simon Gerson, *Pete: The Story of Peter V. Cacchione, New York's First Communist Councilman* (New York: International Publishers, 1976).

121. Max Salvadori, "Antifascisti italiani negli Stati Uniti," in *Atti del I Congresso internazionali di Storia Americana: Italia e Stati Uniti dall'Indipendenza ad oggi* (Genoa: Bastagi, 1978), 269–80.

122. On Vidali, see Gallagher, *All the Right Enemies*, 137–39; Gallagher, "Revolutionary Requirements, Etc.," *Grand Street*, winter 1985, 226–34; Mario Passi, *Vittorio Vidali* (Pordenone, Italy: Studio Tesi, 1991); on Vacirca, see "Vacirca, Vincenzo," in Andreucci and Detti, *Il movimento operaio italiano*, 5:160–63.

123. Charles L. Killinger, "Salvemini at Harvard: A Case Study in the Intellectual Migration," in Juliani and Cannistraro, *Italian Americans*, 198–215. See also Aldo Garosci, *Storia dei fuorusciti* (Bari, Italy: Laterza, 1953); Salvadori, *Resistenza ed azione*; Charles F. Delzell, "The Italian Anti-Fascist Emigration, 1922–1943," *Journal of Central European Affairs* 12 (April 1952): 20–55.

124. Salvemini, *Italian Fascist Activities in the United States*, 135–64. See also William B. Smith, "The Attitudes of Catholic Americans toward Italian Fascism between the Two World Wars" (Ph.D. diss., Catholic University of America, 1969), and Diggins, *Mussolini and Fascism*, 182–203.

125. On the Mazzini Society, see Maddalena Tirabassi, "La Mazzini Society (1940–1946): Un'associazione degli antifascisti italiani negli Stati Uniti," in *Italia e America dalla Grande Guerra a oggi*, ed. G. Spini, G. G. Migone, and M. Teodori (Venice: Marsilio, 1976), 141–58; Charles L. Killinger, "The *Nazioni Unite* and the Mazzini Society," *Italian American Review* (spring/summer 2001): 151–95. The agenda for a postwar Italy is described in Gaetano Salvemini and George La Piana, *What to Do with Italy* (New York, 1943).

126. Miller, *The United States and Italy*, passim.

127. William Beyer, "Italian-American Generations during World War II," in *The Home-Front War: World War II and American Society* (Westport, Conn.: Greenwood Press, 1995), 64–65.

128. Franca Iacovetta, Roberto Perin, and Angelo Principe, eds., *Enemies Within: Italian and Other Internees in Canada and Abroad* (Toronto: University of Toronto Press, 2000); Stephen Fox, *The Unknown Internment* (Boston: Twayne, 1990).

129. Alba, *Italian Americans*, 79. See also Gary R. Mormino and George E. Pozzetta, "Italian Americans and the 1940s," in Cannistraro, *Italians of New York*, 139–53.

130. Meyer, "Italian Americans and the American Communist Party," chapter 9 of this book. Toward the end of the McCarthy period, novelist Carl Marzani introduced Americans to the ideas of Marxist thinker Antonio Gramsci; see *The Open Marxism of Antonio*

Gramsci, trans. and annotated by Carl Marzani (New York: Cameron, 1957); see also Marzani's *The Survivor* (New York: Cameron, 1958).

131. Ronald L. Filippelli, *American Labor and Postwar Italy, 1943–1953* (Stanford, Calif.: Stanford University Press, 1989).

132. Centola, "American Catholic Church and Anti-Communism," 434–35; Guido Orlando as told to Sam Merwin, *Confessions of a Scoundrel* (Philadelphia and Toronto: John C. Winston, 1954), 178–79; Salvatore J. La Gumina, "Mayor Vincent Impellittieri, Anti-Communist Crusader," in *Italian Americans and Their Public and Private Life,* ed. Frank Cavaioli, Angela Danzi, and Salvatore La Gumina, Proceedings of the 24th Annual Conference of the American Italian Historical Association (Staten Island, N.Y.: American Italian Historical Association, 1993), 172–79.

133. On La Guardia's postwar career, see Herbert Kaufman, "Fiorello La Guardia, Political Maverick: A Review Essay," *Political Science Quarterly* (spring 1990): 113–22; Melvin Holli, *The American Mayor: The Best and the Worst Big-City Leaders* (University Park: Pennsylvania State University Press, 1999); and Bella Rodman, *Fiorello La Guardia* (New York: Hill and Wang, 1962).

134. Tom Kuntz and Phil Kuntz, eds., *The Sinatra Files: The Secret FBI Dossier* (New York: Three River Press, 2000); Gerald Meyer, "Frank Sinatra: The Leftism of an American Icon," *Science & Society* (winter 2002): 311–35.

135. Joseph A. Scimecca and Francis X. Femminella, "Italian-Americans and Radical Politics," in *Power and Class: The Italian-American Experience Today,* ed. Francis X. Femminella, Proceedings of the Fourth Annual Conference of the American Italian Historical Association (Staten Island, N.Y.: American Italian Historical Association, 1973), 12.

136. Richard Goldstein, "John Pastore, Prominent Figure in Rhode Island Politics for Three Decades, Dies at 93," *New York Times,* 17 July 2000; Frank Cavaioli, "Pastore, John (1907–2000)," in *The Italian American Experience: An Encyclopedia* (New York: Garland, 2000), 447–48.

137. Stefano Luconi, "Mario Cuomo (b. 1932)," in *The Italian American Experience,* 160–61; Linda Brandi Cateura, *Growing up Italian* (New York: William Morrow, 1987), 13–18.

138. Stefano Luconi, "Rodino, Peter (b. 1909)," in *The Italian American Experience,* 555–56; Andrew Rolle, *The Italian Americans: Troubled Roots* (Norman: University of Oklahoma Press, 1980), 149.

139. Anne Romano, "Ferraro, Geraldine (b.1935)," in *The Italian American Experience,* 221–22; Cateura, *Growing Up Italian,* 257, 263–66. The list of Italian American liberal politicians is, of course, much longer and includes such figures as Alfred Santangelo, Frank Barbaro, and Anthony J. Celebrezze.

140. Phylis Cancilla Martinelli, "Italian-American Experience," in *America's Ethnic Politics,* ed. Joseph Roucek (Westport, Conn.: Greenwood Press, 1982), 221.

141. Richard Jensen, "The Cities Reelect Roosevelt: Ethnicity, Religion, and Class in 1940," *Ethnicity* (June 1981): 192–93.

142. V. O. Key, *Public Opinion and American Democracy* (New York: Knopf, 1967), 271. It is important to note that the Italian American vote was in part class based, so that in 1940, for example, 61 percent of Italian Americans with average incomes voted for Roosevelt, and some 77 percent of poor Italian Americans did so. See Jensen, "Cities Reelect Roosevelt," 192–93. In New York City, however, the rejection of Roosevelt in 1940

within the Italian American community was substantial. This resulted in part from the long delay of Generoso Pope's *Il Progresso Italo-Americano* to endorse Roosevelt, whose anti-Mussolini stance threatened to pit Italian Americans against Italians, and in part from resentment against La Guardia, who was perceived by many as taking the Italian American vote for granted. See Bayor, *Neighbors in Conflict*, 147–88. Also contributing to the defection in the Italian American vote for Roosevelt in New York City in 1940 was the agitation of the Communist Party and those organizations it led and influenced against Roosevelt as a warmonger and an imperialist. This campaign was led by Marcantonio. In the 18th Assembly District (which was almost coterminous with Italian Harlem), Roosevelt's vote fell from 78 percent in 1936 to 55 percent in 1940. See Meyer, *Vito Marcantonio*, 52.

143. Paul Lazarsfeld and James McPhee, *Voting: A Study of Opinion Formation in a Presidential Campaign* (Chicago: University of Chicago Press, 1954), 62–63.

144. Martinelli, "Italian-American Experience," 227.

145. Mansueto, "Blessed Are the Meek," 117.

146. See, however, Fred Milano, "The Italian American Working Class and the Vietnam War," in Pozzetta, *Pane e Lavoro*, 159–74.

147. Gil Fagiani, "Mario Savio: Resurrecting an Italian American Radical," chapter 11 of this book.

148. Jackie Di Salvo, "Father James E. Groppi (1930–1985): The Militant Humility of a Civil Rights Activist," chapter 10 of this book.

149. Gil Fagiani, "A Summary of Italian Americans for a Multicultural U.S.'s (IAMUS) Work, 1992–1994," in authors' possession.

150. Information supplied by Ron Ilardo.

151. Capone, Leto, and Mecca, *Hey Paesan!*, 2. See also Anthony J. Tamburri, ed., *Fuori: Essays by Italian/American Lesbians and Gays* (West Lafayette, Ind.: Bordighera, 1996).

152. Edvige Giunta, "Where They Come From: Italian American Women Writers as Public Intellectuals," chapter 16 of this book.

153. Mary Jo Bona, "Rooted to Family: Italian American Women's Radical Novels," chapter 15 of this book. See also *The Voices We Carry: Recent Italian American Women's Fiction*, ed. Mary Jo Bona (Montreal: Guernica, 1994), and Bona, *Claiming a Tradition: Italian American Women Writers* (Carbondale: Southern Illinois University Press, 1999).

154. Rosario A. Iaconis, "Right vs. Right," *The Italic Way* 30 (2000): 16–17, 26.

155. Lipset and Marks, *It Didn't Happen Here*, 159.

156. Ibid., 125–66.

157. Amitai Etzioni, "The Ghetto: A Re-evaluation," *Social Forces* 37 (March 1959): 260.

158. Meyer, "Italian Americans and the American Communist Party."

159. His writings (which included translations into nine languages) numbered more than 570 titles—*The Native's Return* was selected as a Book-of-the-Month Club selection, and *My America* went through 10 English-language printings. Robert Harney, "E Pluribus Unum: Louis Adamic and the Meaning of Ethnic History," in *If One Were to Write a History: Selected Writings of Robert Harney*, ed. Pierre Ancil and Bruno Ramirez (Toronto: Multicultural History Society), 182.

160. Roger Keeran, "National Groups and the Popular Front: The Case of the International Workers Order," *Journal of American Ethnic History* (spring 1995): 23–51; Barring-

ton Moore, "The Communist Party of the USA: An Analysis of a Social Movement," *American Political Science Review* (February 1945): 388.

161. The new edition of *I Vote My Conscience*, with a new introduction and a complete bibliography of writings on Marcantonio, was published by the John Calandra Italian American Institute, Queens College (City University of New York).

162. The catalog of the exhibit has been published as Cannistraro, *The Italians of New York: Five Centuries of Struggle and Achievement*.

Part I

Labor

Chapter 1

The Making and Un-Making of the Italian American Working Class

Rudolph J. Vecoli

The building still stands on East 14th Street in lower Manhattan. The marble facade, a lintel bearing the inscription "Italian Labor Center," with medallions depicting the worker and his family—one in a posture of terror, the other showing serenity—is still intact. Once this edifice embodied the noble aspirations for peace and justice of a burgeoning Italian working-class movement in America. Today, the ground floor is occupied by a combination beauty parlor and bar, and the upper stories have been divided into apartments. Decrepit, filthy, forgotten, the building symbolizes the failure of those aspirations and, indeed, the loss of the very memory of such a movement. This essay is an attempt to explain why.[1]

Between 1910 and 1920, Italian immigrants coalesced into a working class imbued with a militant class consciousness. Led by talented organizers—socialists, syndicalists, anarchists—they mobilized powerful radical movements that played decisive roles in strikes. They also formed unions, cooperatives, and cultural organizations, and they found their voices in song, theater, oratory, and popular manifestations. These movements were stimulated not only by a spirit of class struggle but also by an emergent ethnic nationalism. Classified as "black" labor, Italians were the object of loathing by American union leaders and workers as well as by the upper classes. Inspired by a revolutionary élan, Italian workers were not only seeking liberation from economic oppression, but also redemption from ethnic injury. For a time, it appeared that their dual identities, as proletarians and as Italians, were congruent sources of solidarity.[2]

From one point of view, World War I, by creating labor shortages and benign government policies, abetted this transformation: a growing number of Italians enrolled in unions and participated vigorously in the numerous struggles of the war and postwar years. Italian garment workers, textile operatives, miners, shoemakers, longshoremen, and others, were conspicuous in the 1919 wave of strikes.

During these years, Italians underwent a dramatic transformation in reputation, from being vilified as servile wagecutters and strikebreakers, to being hailed by "Big Bill" Haywood as the vanguard of the revolutionary proletariat—and damned by American Federation of Labor (AFL) trade unionists as violent and recalcitrant to their control.[3]

The Russian Revolution, which Vittorio Buttis called the "bolshevik volcano," appeared to Italian radicals to augur the uprising of the American working class, which would overthrow the bastion of capitalism, Wall Street.[4] The establishment of the Italian Chamber of Labor in New York City in 1919 embodied the grand ambitions such leaders entertained in the afterglow of the Communist revolution. Modeled after the *camere di lavoro* in Italy, it was to mobilize and lead all the Italian workers of New York in the coming upheaval. Soon, however, postwar depression, decline in organized labor's strength, and internecine strife dashed these high expectations.[5]

During the two decades of the interwar period, the ethnic and working-class solidarity of the Italian Americans (by which I mean both immigrants and American-born children) was eroded and fragmented by external and internal forces. Although the great majority continued in the ranks of wage earners, by the end of this period they no longer comprised a distinctive Italian working class in America. The radical ideologies and ideologues that had formerly guided them gradually lost their power to inspire. Even the Great Depression did not breathe life back into an Italian labor movement. During the 1930s, Italian Americans participated in unions and labor struggles on a larger scale than ever before, but they did so for the most part as members of a multiethnic working class.[6]

This transformation is not to be explained simply by the working class Americanization thesis as advanced by several historians.[7] Rather than being a tale of assimilation, the "deradicalization" of Italian American workers was as much due to transnational influences as it was to domestic developments. The Bolshevik and Fascist revolutions had profound impacts upon the Italian labor movement in America. Ideological and political forces stemming from Italy and the Soviet Union combined with internal dynamics within the "Little Italies" to radically alter the political character of Italian Americans.

Repression by the American state during World War I dealt the first debilitating blow to Italian radicalism. Smashing their presses, shuttering their offices and meeting places, and arresting thousands, federal and state agencies instituted a reign of terror against the *sovversivi*. The imprisonment or deportation of leading activists, such as Giovanni Baldazzi and Luigi Galleani, decapitated the Italian revolutionary movement. The tar-and-feathering and beating of antiwar and labor organizers, such as Nino Capraro, by vigilantes silenced others. Some, like Angelo Faggi, returned to Italy, while others, like Eligio Strobino, dropped out of the movement.[8]

An even deeper wound inflicted on the immigrant Left was the schism resulting from the issue of Italian intervention in the European war. From 1914 on, a controversy raged within the radical ranks: should the war be resisted? or should it be embraced as an opportunity to bring about the social revolution? Deeply divided, former comrades engaged in passionate debate and bloody combat in the halls and streets of Little Italies. Intoxicated by jingoist propaganda, Italian immigrants turned against radical leaders who opposed the war. Erasmo Abbate recalled that workers who a few months before had followed him in a strike beat him up for his opposition to Italy's war policy. On Minnesota's Iron Range, Italians who had participated in the 1916 strike abandoned the Industrial Workers of the World (IWW) because of the antiwar position of the Finns. In this test of loyalties, ethnic nationalism more often than not prevailed over class solidarity among Italian (as well as other) immigrants.[9] Tracing a political trajectory for others to follow, Edmondo Rossoni, erstwhile editor of *Il Proletario*, moved from syndicalism to nationalism to Fascism. Anarchist Domenico Trombetta, later editor of the Fascist and racist *Il Grido della Stirpe*, also traversed this ideological journey. In the United States, as in the homeland, numerous converts to Fascism were drawn from radical ranks.[10]

The political climate created by the war and the Treaty of Versailles prepared the soil for the seeds of Fascism. A hypernationalism engendered by "Wilson's betrayal of Italy" at Versailles manifested itself in the Italian American vote in the 1920 presidential election. Congressman Fiorello La Guardia shrilled: "Any Italo-American who votes the Democratic ticket this year is an Austrian bastard."[11] During the twenties, Italian Americans increasingly embraced ethnic nationalism as a shield against intensified nativist assault. Carrying its message of hatred of Catholics and foreigners, the Ku Klux Klan burned crosses and paraded in towns and cities of the Northeast and the Midwest. Meanwhile, the nativist movement for immigration restriction made clear to Italian Americans that they were viewed as inferior and undesirable. When federal agents raided their neighborhoods and trashed their homes, they understood that the Eighteenth Amendment and the Volsted Act were aimed at their "un-American" lifestyles. Nicola Sacco and Bartolomeo Vanzetti's seven-year agony was a constant reminder that, for many Yankees, they remained "anarchistic bastards." It is not surprising that Italian Americans responded to such bigotry with a heightened ethnic consciousness, which easily evolved into philo-Fascism.[12]

Italian American Fascism was not an exotic transplant, but, as Philip Cannistraro has demonstrated, an indigenous growth. Before Mussolini's coup of October 1922, Agostino De Biasi, editor of the nationalist journal *Il Carroccio*, had founded the first *fascio* in New York City on April 30, 1921. In San Francisco, editor of *L'Italia* and former socialist Ettore Patrizi also embraced Fascism. Meanwhile, newly arrived immigrants formed the Fascistic Federation of Italian War Veterans in the United States. Once in power, Mussolini sent agents to organize *fasci* among *italiani all'estero* (the Fascist regime's term for the far-flung immigrants). Soon, black-shirted Italian Americans were marching in the streets of Little Italies. Only when deadly clashes with anti-Fascists became an embarrassment did Mussolini in 1929 abolish the Fascist League of North America, with its strong-arm tactics, adopting in its stead a policy of cultural propaganda and economic coercion to influence Italian Americans.[13]

Not black-shirted *squadristi,* but a fraternal association, the Order Sons of Italy in America, played a major role in bringing the masses within the Fascist fold. Influenced by socialists such as Augusto Bellanca, the Order previously had taken a pro-labor position, for example, by supporting the strikes of 1919. Mussolini, however, found an eager adherent in Giovanni M. Di Silvestro, supreme venerable of the Order from 1921 to 1935 (also a former socialist). Shortly after the March on Rome, Di Silvestro telegraphed Mussolini (Il Duce) pledging the loyalty of the Sons of Italy to the Fascist regime. Not all members of the Order shared his devotion to Il Duce. The Grand Lodge of New York, under the leadership of Judge Salvatore Cotillo and Congressman Fiorello La Guardia, criticized Di Silvestro's action as compromising Italian Americans and temporarily seceded. Nonetheless, Di Silvestro continued to be an unwavering supporter of Mussolini. With its extensive network of 1,100 local lodges and a membership of over 160,000 (most of whom were workers), the Sons of Italy became a major component of the Fascist infrastructure, which was to dominate Italian American life until 1941.[14]

Other major institutional supports of Fascism that ensured its hegemony over Italian Americans were the Italian-language media and the Italian national parishes. A survey conducted in 1923 revealed that of 136 Italian American newspapers, only eight were critical of Fascism. As the Italian government tightened its control through subsidies and control of advertising, the ethnic press became even more compliant purveyors of Fascist propaganda. Most importantly, Generoso Pope, New York City contractor, political broker, and owner of *Il Progresso Italo-Americano,* which had a circulation of more than 100,000, became the leading propagandist for Fascism in the United States. With the exception of a handful of struggling publications of the Italian Left, the printed word for Italian Americans was controlled by Fascists. As radios became common, the message of Fascism (including shortwave broadcasts of Il Duce's speeches) penetrated into Italian American homes.[15]

Despite the estrangement of the Vatican and the kingdom of Italy following unification, Italian clergy in the United States, beleaguered by anticlericals on the one hand and an Irish American hierarchy on the other, sought to rally their wayward flocks with appeals to *italianità.* With few exceptions, Italian priests welcomed Fascism, particularly following the Lateran Pact of 1929, which resolved outstanding differences between the pope and Il Duce. Viewing Fascism as a bulwark against atheistic Communism, the American hierarchy, in word and deed, bestowed its blessings upon Mussolini and his works. Through sermons, religious celebrations, societies, and parochial schools, Italian national parishes became conduits for Fascist propaganda.[16]

Rather than speak of the Americanization of the Little Italies during the interwar years, it would be more accurate, then, to speak of their Fascistization. In 1940, refugee historian Gaetano Salvemini estimated that 5 percent of some five million Italian Americans were true Fascists, another 35 percent philo-Fascists, and 10 percent anti-Fascists. The other 50 percent he characterized as apolitical, concerned only with their immediate affairs. The *prominenti*, the business and professional elite, were understandably devotees of Il Duce. Fascism also became the major challenge to the radical ideologies that had held sway over immigrant workers.[17]

Based in the radical movements, which had survived the postwar repression—albeit with depleted ranks and resources—the anti-Fascists constituted a sizeable minority (several hundred thousand, according to Salvemini's estimate). The Galleanisti, anti-organizational anarchists, had gone underground, nurturing the legacy of their prophet, disrupting their rivals' meetings, and committing occasional acts of terrorism. The syndicalist Federazione Socialista Italiana—once the most-dynamic force in the Italian American Left—its leaders imprisoned, deported, or employed as trade-union functionaries, was absorbed by a moribund IWW. Meanwhile, the social democratic Federazione Socialista Italiana (FSI) suffered a devastating schism; in the conflicts that tore apart the Socialist Party of America, the majority of FSI members joined the faction, which became the Federazione Italiana of the Communist Workers Party of America.[18]

Still, the core of the anti-Fascist resistance was composed of veterans of these movements (Carlo Tresca, Arturo Giovannitti, Girolamo Valenti, Raimondo Fazio, and Frank Bellanca, among others), reinforced by the first wave of *fuorus-citi*, refugees from Fascism. The latter included radical leaders such as Carmelo Zito, Vanni Montana, Armando Borghi, Vittorio Vidali, and Serafino Romualdi as well as rank-and-file leftist workers fleeing the cudgels and castor oil of the *squadristi*. From such ingredients, a discordant coalition of socialists, syndicalists, anarchists, Communists, and trade unionists formed the Anti-Fascist Alliance of North America (AFANA) in 1923. Breaking up Fascist rallies, AFANA street-fighters kept the Blackshirts from taking over the Little Italies. For some years, the Alliance also waged a war of words against Fascism through *Il Nuovo Mondo*, a daily newspaper edited by Frank Bellanca. Although New York City was the principal battleground between Fascists and anti-Fascists, the struggle also went on in Boston, Chicago, San Francisco, and other cities. Communities with strong radical traditions, such as Tampa, Barre, Rochester (New York), and mining towns, from Pennsylvania to Colorado, constituted pockets of anti-Fascist resistance.[19]

The mainstay of the opposition to Fascist hegemony, however, was the Italian-dominated labor organizations, in particular the clothing workers' unions. With substantial treasuries and a membership of over twenty thousand in 1920, the Italian locals of the International Ladies' Garment Workers' Union (ILGWU) and the Amalgamated Clothing Workers of America (ACWA), under the leadership of Luigi Antonini and Augusto Bellanca, respectively, became bulwarks of anti-Fascism. Many radicals found jobs as union organizers (and anti-Fascist agitators) with these unions. In addition to sponsoring *Giustizia* and *Il Lavoro*, the ILGWU and the ACWA subsidized other anti-Fascist publications. Bellanca and

Antonini also turned out thousands of garment workers for mass anti-Fascist rallies in Union Square and Madison Square Garden.[20]

Rank-and-file union members, however, did not necessarily share the passionate anti-Fascism of their leaders. One union source described the membership as "apathetic." In fact, many were enthusiastic supporters of Mussolini. Their nationalistic feelings were heightened by the Italians' minority status within the garment unions. Italian locals had been established only after a protracted struggle with the dominant Jewish element. Many Italians felt that they still did not have an equal voice and power in union affairs. Jewish leaders complained about "the Italian problem," accusing them of scabbing, resistance to organization, and lack of discipline. Ethnic mistrust, jealousy, and conflict, which extended from the shop floor to the unions' highest levels, increased the receptivity of Italian garment workers to nationalist appeals.[21]

Fascist agents were quick to exploit such sentiments among the rank and file by "boring from within," or establishing dual unions. In 1924, Italian Local 89 of the ILGWU declared that "hundreds of emissaries of the Italian Tyrant have been unleashed in the United States . . . for the avowed purpose of terrorizing the American workers of Italian extraction into seceding and withdrawing from the ranks of the *bona fide* American Labor Movement."[22] Even shop chairmen and local presidents of the ACWA and the ILGWU were members of the Fascist League. Although the extent of Fascist influence among Italian American workers is yet to be determined, scattered evidence suggests that it made even greater inroads among longshoremen, construction workers, barbers, and some factory employees. Fascists also contested for the allegiance of workers in the sphere of leisure. *Dopolavoro* clubs, after the Fascist model, attracted Italian American working class families with films, drama groups, sporting and musical events.[23]

An even greater threat to established trade-union leadership, however, came from the Communists. Initially enthralled by the Russian Revolution, many anarchists, syndicalists, and socialists, including Luigi Antonini, the head of Local 89 of the ILGWU, joined the Workers Party of America, newly formed by the Communists. But as they learned of killings of anarchists and socialists by Bolsheviks, and as they experienced Communist authoritarianism, an increasing number came to view Communism as Fascism's bastard twin. Following the founding of the Trade Union Education League (TUEL) in 1920, through which the Communists intended to carry out the Third International's directive of boring from within, antagonism among labor leaders toward Communists hardened. During the ensuing "civil war" incited by the Communist attempt to take over the garment unions, Antonini of the ILGWU and Bellanca of the ACWA supported the social democratic Jewish leadership. Charles Zappia interprets their stance as due not to their anti-Communism but to their determination to preserve the autonomy of the Italian locals—and, one might add, their positions—from Communist control. Steven Fraser attributes the receptivity of some Italians to the TUEL to their "political rebelliousness and racial animosity" (presumably toward the Jewish leadership, although Jews also spearheaded the Communist revolt). Only a small minority of Italian militants, such as Angela Bambace, organizer for the ILGWU, and Nino Capraro, ACWA organizer and leader of the Sicilian-dominated section of the Workers Party in Rochester, followed the Comintern's shift to the Red International of Labor Unions in 1928, and few Italians joined Communist-led dual unions, such as the Needle Trades Workers Industrial Union. In fact, the Communist Party regarded its greatest weakness among garment workers to be its failure to secure the support of the Italians.[24]

The Communist strategy to gain control of both the Italian anti-Fascist and the labor movements was personified by Vittorio Vidali, a recent exile from Fascism who had been the militant leader of the Communists in Trieste. An agent of the Comintern, Vidali quickly became secretary of the Federazione Italiana of the Works Progress Administration and editor of its daily newspaper, *Il Lavoratore*. By 1926, Vidali dominated AFANA, prompting the secession of democratic socialists, led by Salvatore Ninfo of the ILGWU and Girolamo Valenti of the ACWA, who formed the Anti-Fascist League for the Freedom of Italy. Tresca's continued collaboration with Vidali and the Communists brought down on his head the wrath of the anti-Communists, particularly of the Galleanisti.[25]

Other than within the needle trades unions, Italian radicals played a minor role in organized labor during the twenties. We know little, however, about the Wobblies, anarchists, and socialists who constituted progressive elements among miners, dockworkers, shoemakers, textile workers, and hotel and restaurant workers. They kept their radical faith alive by working within American Federation of Labor (AFL) unions, such as the United Mine Workers of America (UMWA), and at other times following Communist leadership, as in the Passaic textile strike and the National Miners Union.[26]

Italian American labor leadership was most conspicuous in unions which have been characterized as conservative and corrupt. By the 1920s, labor in entire industries, clothing manufacturing, construction, and working on the docks among others, was largely in the grip of criminal elements. Perhaps more than any other factor, labor racketeering contributed to the debasement and marginalization of Italian radicalism. Labor bosses, such as Domenico D'Allessandro, president of the International Hod Carriers, Building, and Common Laborers Union, and Paolo Vaccarelli (Paul Kelly), vice president of the International Longshoremen's Association, made no pretense of being democratic or progressive. Yet, in their defense, they opened up jobs and unions to Italian laborers against hard-fisted Irish opposition. Even Communist and socialist labor leaders hired gangsters to intimidate and assault their opponents. As a consequence, racketeers, such as Arnold Rothstein and Joe Ryan, gained power over legitimate unions. Although labor racketeering was initially in the hands of the Irish and the Jews, by the 1920s, Italian Americans such as Frank Costello, Emil Camarada, and Al Capone were gaining control of many trade unions. Those without the stomach for such rough tactics were excluded from labor leadership. Of Carlo Tresca, it was said that he was too radical, whereas Vincenzo Vacirca was said to be too honest. Those who challenged the labor racketeers sometimes paid with their lives: Giovanni Pippan, exiled leader of miners in Istria, was assassinated in 1933 while organizing the League of Italian Bread Drivers and Bakery Workers of Chicago, and in 1939 Peter Panto, leader of an insurgent movement of Italian dockworkers against the Camarada family, which controlled the Brooklyn docks, "disappeared." In neither case were the killers ever apprehended.[27]

Beleaguered by anti-radical reaction, employers' open-shop drives, declining union membership, and labor racketeering, the Italian Left in the twenties was further weakened by internal ideological schisms and fratricidal vendettas. Its limited energies were drained by the battle against Fascism and the exhaustive campaign to save Sacco and Vanzetti from the electric chair. By 1930, the Italian American labor movement was but a shadow of what it had been a decade earlier.[28]

The collapse of capitalism following the Wall Street crash of 1929 revived the radical vision of a new social order built upon the ruins of the old. Although the Depression slowed assimilation and social mobility, paradoxically it also opened the way for Italian Americans to participate more actively in American life. Together with other eastern and southern Europeans, they helped to make a new deal for themselves through a revitalized labor movement and progressive politics. The vehicle for their involvement, however, was not a militant Italian working class movement as it had been prior to 1920; rather, it was through participation in Congress of Industrial Organizations (CIO) multiethnic unions and the Democratic Party of Franklin Roosevelt.[29]

The ILGWU exemplified the resurgence of labor under the impetus of New Deal policies. The "uprising of the 60,000" of August 1933, a successful four-day strike of dressmakers and cloakmakers in New York City, initiated a period of dramatic growth in numbers and strength. By 1936, total membership in the ILGWU zoomed from 40,000 (in 1932) to 200,000. Italian locals in New York, Boston, Chicago, and other cities experienced rapid growth; Local 89, with 40,000 members, became the ILGWU's largest local. Long resentful of his subordination to Jewish leadership, Luigi Antonini, reveled in his new influence and power. Attacked as an enemy of *la patria* because of his anti-Fascism, he appealed to ethnic nationalism: "Local 89 in this strange land is the most complete manifestation of the collective greatness of our emigrants. It is the most faithful guardian of our civilization. It is Italy."[30]

Although Italian American women now comprised a major portion of the garment unions' activists as well as their rank and file, the industry's labor force was becoming even more diverse. Veterans of earlier struggles, like Angela Bambace, were organizing African American and Puerto Rican needle workers. Despite their numbers and militancy, women's quest for a greater role in union affairs was frustrated by an entrenched male bureaucracy. Into the 1940s and beyond, Jewish and Italian men continued to hold most offices in the ILGWU and maintained control over a predominantly female and increasingly non-European membership. Gender, racial, and ethnic barriers erected by a self-serving leadership prevented even these "progressive" unions from realizing their potential as agencies of democratic change.[31]

By the 1930s, Italian Americans, in large part second generation, had entered en masse the mass-production industries, such as those producing automobiles, steel, electrical goods, and rubber goods. Some, with radical antecedents, were active in the organizing drives of the CIO. We know some of their names—Ernie DeMaio, of the United Electrical, Radio, and Machine Workers; Julia Maietta, of the ACWA; Joe Germano, of the Steel Workers Organizing Committee; Severino Pollo, of the United Automobile Workers; and George Baldanzi of the Textile Workers Union of America—but we do not know much more about them. Italian Americans also were prominent in the Progressive Miners of America revolt against John L. Lewis's dictatorial control of the UMWA. Veterans of earlier struggles, and their children, such as Mario Manzardo, played a significant role in the American labor movement of the 1930s. Although this is a story yet to be told, one may surmise that a legacy of immigrant radicalism contributed to the labor militancy of Italian Americans. However, now they were acting primarily as members of an American proletariat rather than as an "Italian working class" in America.[32]

Although Italian American workers strongly supported leftist union leadership, in politics they did not follow suit. Why did Italian Americans, among the poorest and most maligned ethnic groups, not rally to the Communist Party U.S.A.? In comparison to Finns and Jews, Italian members were few and far between. Despite Communist Party (CP) efforts to recruit them, a report on national groups in the Party of May 1938 counted a total of between 500 and 800 Italians, as compared to 4,000 Jews. Harvey Klehr's analysis of the Party's central committee between 1921 and 1961 revealed that of 212 members (of whom one-third were foreign born) only three were born in Italy.[33]

Even the Communist-led International Workers Order (IWO), a confederation of mutual benefit societies organized along nationality lines, attracted only a modest number of Italian Americans. The Italian section, the Garibaldi-American Fraternal Society, organized in 1931, had grown to 6,800 members by 1938. As in the case of the other 14 IWO ethnic sections, the Italians draped themselves in the democratic traditions of their countries of origin. The Garibaldi-American Fraternal Society donned the mantle of its namesake and invoked "the glorious traditions of the Italian Risorgimento." Although Jews were by far the largest ethnic element, by 1947 even the Ukrainian, Slovak, and Russian sections had larger memberships. Like IWO members in general, its Italian American contingent were not Communist Party members; many had joined for the insurance benefits.[34] When the Society appeared on the attorney general's list of subversive organizations in 1947 (the only Italian association to be so cited), membership declined rapidly. *L'Unità Operaia* and its successor *L'Unità del Popolo,* which were closely tied to the IWO, ceased publication in 1951.

Nor did the Communist Party receive significant electoral support from Italian Americans. From 1932 on, they tended to vote overwhelmingly for Franklin D. Roosevelt (FDR) and usually the straight Democratic Party ticket. In New York City, Generoso Pope, a pro-Fascist member of the Democratic National Committee and a friend of FDR, delivered the Italian vote for Tammany Hall. The exceptions to this pattern were Fiorello La Guardia and Vito Marcantonio, both of whom first ran as Republicans to break Tammany's stranglehold on city politics. La Guardia's ethnicity, rather than his progressive politics, secured him the Italian American vote in his campaigns for Congress and the mayoralty of New York City.[35]

But how does one explain the overwhelming support of Italian Harlem for Vito Marcantonio? As a Congressman from 1936 to 1950 (except for a hiatus from 1937 to 1938), Marcantonio, although not a party member, closely followed the Communist Party line in his speeches and votes. Gerald Meyer's explanation is persuasive; his constituents voted for him not because they agreed with his ideology, but because he was a native son, born and bred in East Harlem, who championed their interests. As Meyer put it, Marcantonio "was organically a part of . . . the largest . . . and most Italian community in the United States. . . . He lived in the same house with his grandmother and mother, marched in church processions, socialized with Mafia chieftains, and wore religious amulets." Although Marcantonio became the leader of the American Labor Party (ALP), formed in New York City in 1936 to enable socialists and Communists to vote for Roosevelt (and La Guardia and Marcantonio), the ALP attracted many Jewish, but fewer Italian, voters.[36]

The kid gloves with which these progressive politicians dealt with Fascism is indicative of its power over their Italian American constituencies. La Guardia (nicknamed the Little Flower), who personally loathed Mussolini and denounced Nazism, never publicly criticized Il Duce or Fascism. In a 1926 speech in Congress, the Little Flower declared, "It is none of our concern what kind of government the Italian people have."[37] After Marcantonio participated in an anti-Fascist rally in 1935, Pope's *Il Progresso Italo-Americano* endorsed his opponent, who went on to win the 1936 election. Thereafter, Marcantonio rarely attacked Mussolini or Fascism.[38] If anything, Fascist sentiment was even more dominant in other cities with large Italian American populations, such as Boston, Chicago, and New Orleans. For example, Angelo Rossi, mayor of San Francisco (1931–1943) was ardently pro-Mussolini.[39]

Most Italian Americans evidently had no difficulty in joining CIO unions and voting for the New Deal, and at the same time supporting Fascist Italy. As William F. Whyte was told in Boston's Little Italy: "Mussolini for Italy! Roosevelt for America!"[40] Il Duce's propaganda machine had done its work well. Although Italy was widely condemned for its aggression against Ethiopia and subjected to economic sanctions by the League of Nations, philo-Fascism among Italian Americans reached a fever pitch in 1935–1936. The depth of this support, even after Il Duce had become an object of criticism and ridicule, suggests that ethnic nationalism had been incorporated into the core identity of many Italian Americans. As Vanni Montana observed, "Italian Americans were drunk with the heavy wine of patriotism." [41]

Pope, Di Silvestro, and other leaders vigorously defended Mussolini's policies and lobbied President Roosevelt and the Congress to maintain a "strict neutrality." Fascists harangued mass rallies, journalists exhorted readers, and priests offered benedictions in support of Fascist Italy's civilizing mission in Africa. The Fascist anthem, *Giovinezza* (Youth), and the war hymn, *Faccetta Nera* (Little Black Face), resounded in public meetings and homes. To great applause, Italian American volunteers (a modest number) sailed to fight for the new Roman empire. On shop floors, factory workers contributed hard-earned dollars, while their wives donated gold wedding rings to the Italian Red Cross. News of the victory of Italian forces was celebrated by demonstrations from Boston's North End to San Francisco's North Beach.[42] In a clash of ethnic nationalisms, African Americans and Italian Americans fought in the streets of American cities.[43]

We need a study of how Fascism affected the attitudes of Italian Americans on matters of race. Initially many immigrants worked, lived, and even intermarried with African Americans. From the 1900s on, Italian radicals had vigorously condemned racial bigotry and lynchings. Yet by 1943, the editor of the Communist *L'Unità del Popolo* reported that Italian American workers had participated in the Detroit race riot, attacking blacks in a "bestial manner."[44] How did Italian Americans acquire a definition of themselves as "white" and of the other as "black"? Although the adoption of white racism by immigrants is commonly described as a concomitant of Americanization, Fascist Italy's war in East Africa, with its theme of civilizing a primitive people, deeply influenced the racial attitudes of Italian Americans.[45]

The anti-Semitic racial laws of the Fascist regime of 1938 had implications for Italian American relations with African Americans as well as with American Jews. Patrizi, in *L'Italia* of San Franciso, justified Mussolini's anti-Semitic policy as "natural," by pointing to the history of racial slavery and segregation in the United States. In New York, *L'Unità del Popolo* sponsored an "Italians Don't Hate Jews" rally; but in 1939 Tresca warned Antonini of the spread of "Fascist anti-Semitic propaganda among the needle trades."[46]

In a 1939 interview in Bridgeport, Connecticut, an Italian-born factory worker and reader of *Il Progresso*, offered the following observations:

Most of the black people are not civilized, and they should not be together with us people . . . Sometimes I pass by black people's house, and then I hear them . . . make all kinds of noise like they be in Africa . . . Selassie didn't care to civilize the people, so Mussolini is doing it now . . . some day, Mussolini will fix them up, and maybe they get to be like people some day, and not like animals. [He continued:]

The trouble with this country is that all the Jewish people they are running it now, and the working people have no chance to make a living. . . . Look all the factories that the Jewish people have. The Jewish people . . . have plenty of money.[47]

Despite efforts of Italian radicals, particularly the Communists, to combat racism and anti-Semitism during the 1930s, Fascist propaganda insinuated racial and ethnic prejudices into the minds of many Italian Americans. The cherished ideal of Italian radicals, the international solidarity of workers celebrated on Primo Maggio, had been shattered, by war, Fascism, and ethnic and racial rivalries.[48]

Notwithstanding the economic crisis of the 1930s, the various tendencies of the Italian American Left were not reinvigorated. Support among Italian Americans for the Communist Party, as indicated above, was minuscule. Meanwhile, the Italian Socialist Federation affiliated with the Socialist Party of America, dwindled to less than one hundred members as a hard core led by Giuseppe Bertelli refused to endorse Roosevelt and the New Deal and clung to a pacifist position. The depleted ranks of syndicalists and socialists struggled from issue to issue to keep alive their publications, *Il Proletario* and *La Parola del Popolo*. Yet, although vastly outnumbered, the anti-Fascists continued to wage battle against Mussolini's minions. The flourishing garment unions provided the foot soldiers and financial wherewithal for publications, rallies, and lobbying campaigns. In his weekly broadcast, "The Voice of Local 89," Antonini evenhandedly lambasted Fascists and Communists. *La Stampa Libera*, directed by Valenti, and Tresca's *Il Martello*, although with limited circulations, exposed the machinations of the Fascists. The anti-Fascists also sought to undermine the favorable view of Mussolini among Americans in general. In 1938, Valenti testified before the House Committee on Un-American Activities regarding Fascist influence among Italian Americans. His disclosures had little immediate effect, since Congressman Dies was more concerned with Communism. Only when the United States and Italy went to war did the authorities become alarmed about the extent of Fascist influence among Italian Americans.[49]

The Spanish Civil War served as a litmus test of the political attitudes of Italian Americans. A 1938 survey of ethnic groups in New York City reported that Italian Americans were highest in pro-Franco sentiment (50 percent) and lowest in pro-Loyalist sentiment (20 percent). Clearly the pro-Fascist press and the Catholic Church, which vigorously backed il Generalissimo, shaped opinion in the Little Italies. Although the anti-Fascists supported the Loyalists with fundraisers and rallies, relatively few Italian Americans joined the Abraham Lincoln Brigade or the Brigata Garibaldi, the latter sponsored by the Popular Front Comitato Italiano Anti-Fascista. Conflict within the Italian American Left was further exacerbated as reports arrived of the executions in Spain of socialists and anarchists by Communists (allegedly under the direction of political commissar Vidali, now bearing the *nom de guerre* General Carlos). Tresca, who had collaborated with the Communists, now became a severe critic of the Soviet Union and its Italian American partisans.[50]

Following the enactment of the racial laws of 1938 and Italy's entry into the war, a third wave of refugees arrived. These *fuorusciti*, however, were unlike the grassroots combatants who had arrived in the twenties. Among them were leading Italian political leaders and intellectuals, such as Giuseppe Lupis, Max Ascoli, Luigi Sturzo, and Carlo Sforza, representing a broad political spectrum. Rather than merging with the existing anti-Fascist movement, in 1939 they created the Mazzini Society. An elite organization, lacking any appreciable grassroots support among the mass of Italian Americans, the Society sought to persuade influential American opinion makers of the threat to American democracy posed by Mussolini's regime. The perceived arrogance of the recently arrived refugees was resented by the veterans of the anti-Fascist movement in America.[51]

That Italian Americans remained strongly pro-Fascist was revealed by their reaction to President Roosevelt's "stab in the back" speech following Italy's invasion of France. In the 1940 election, a majority voted Republican, and in the 1941 mayoral race in New York City, in large numbers they deserted La Guardia for O'Dwyer. However, as the Roosevelt administration inched toward intervention, the *prominenti* became increasingly circumspect in their expressions of Fascist sympathies. With the declaration of war by Italy on the United States on December 11, 1941, they hastened to declare their total loyalty to the president and to the United States. Although some four thousand Italian Americans were arrested or suffered detention because of suspected Fascist sympathies, as of 1942 only 210 were actually interned. Among them were a few rabid Fascists (such as Domenico Trombetta), but the leading apologists for Mussolini, including Generoso Pope, emerged unscathed. In recognition of their loyalty (and the clout of the Italian American vote), on Columbus Day 1942, Attorney General Francis Biddle removed, without distinction, some 600,000 unnaturalized Italians from the category of "enemy aliens." To the chagrin of the anti-Fascists, the prewar pro-Fascist leadership retained its control over Italian American institutions such as *Il Progresso* and the Order Sons of Italy throughout the war years and beyond.[52] Although Italian Americans unreservedly demonstrated their allegiance to the United States, there was no clear repudiation of their infatuation with Fascism. As a consequence, pernicious elements of what Stanislao Pugliese has termed "nostalgic Fascism" remained embedded in the psyche of many Italian Americans.[53]

By the 1940s, an Italian working-class movement that had been forged in the desperate strikes of the early decades of the century had for all practical purposes ceased to exist. Its death toll may have been rung with the murder of Tresca by an "unknown" assassin on January 11, 1943, in New York City. Many of the old radicals, now labor bureaucrats, co-opted first by the New Deal and then by the security state, enlisted in the cold war. Antonini became an enthusiastic agent of the Department of State's policy of preventing Communists from gaining control of the labor movement in Italy. Those who still retained a radical vision were soon caught in the coils of the Taft-Hartley Act and McCarthyism, and were denied union office, blacklisted, and deported. The old faiths, anarchism, syndicalism, and socialism, which had inspired the immigrant generation to heroic resistance, persisted only in the memories of a dwindling coterie of aging radicals.[54]

In considering the demise of Italian American radicalism, a final crucial question remains: why was it largely a one-generation phenomenon? Why were there so very few Red Diaper Babies among the children of Italian American radicals? The forces of Americanization operated powerfully on young people of immigrant backgrounds. Indoctrinated with American patriotism in the public schools, infatuated with glamorous images on the silver screen, seduced into a consumer culture, children of immigrants were encouraged to view their parents' ways (including their politics) as Old World and embarrassing. Also, the recurring Red scares, with threats of public humiliation and deportation, inspired fear within families. Belonging to the radical minority carried a painful stigma; it often meant being ostracized by neighbors, denounced by the priest, taunted by other children. Not surprisingly, later in life children of radicals often professed not to know about their parents' politics—or refused to discuss them.[55]

Yet, the question remains: why did Italian immigrants, as compared to Jews and Finns, fail to transmit radical ideas and commitments to the second generation? The answer may lie in differing family dynamics among these ethnic groups. The nurturing of children by traditional (often religious) mothers and their alienation from radical fathers might help explain the political rupture between generations. Among Finns and Jews, radicalism was more often a family culture in which wives and mothers participated actively, whereas among Italians, politics was regarded as a male sphere from which women and children were excluded.[56]

Although clearly a subject to be further explored, one may cite a literary source as suggestive. Len (short for Lenin) Giovannitti, son of Arturo, the poet and labor leader, wrote a thinly disguised novel in which he described his father's cruelty toward his mother: "I only knew he made my mother unhappy; he made me miserable and I hated him for it. . . . We never spoke about it, but [my mother and I] shared the same unspoken fear of my father's wrath. . . . In later years, she used the memory of my father's tyranny against us to keep me close to her, to make me feel guilty and repay her for all those years of misery. I could never break the bond."[57]

Over the past several decades, a cohort of scholars has diligently and creatively gone about the task of recovering the "lost world of Italian American radicalism" from the neglect—and often outright denial—engendered by an Italian American triumphal historical narrative. We have learned that there is much in this history that is noble and beautiful as well as that which is ugly and tawdry. Regardless, it constitutes a rich and poignant dimension of the Italian American experience. Certainly, the Italian chapter needs to be incorporated into the labor history of America. Moreover, we Italian Americans, in particular, need to know and draw upon this revolutionary and libertarian legacy to free us from an apologetic ethnicity that is too much dominated by a reactionary, chauvinist, and racist ideology.

NOTES

1. The Italian Labor Center (ILC) was built at 231 East 14th Street in 1919 as the headquarters of Cloakmakers Local 48, ILGWU. Unione dei Cloakmakers Italiani, Locale 48, I.L.G.W.U., *Libro Ricordo. XXV Anniversario 1916–1941* (New York, 1941), 93, 149. The cover is illustrated with a drawing of the ILC. The building also housed the Italian Chamber of Labor, established that same year. The carvings are probably the work of

Onorio Ruotolo, poet and sculptor, whose works in that period dealt with the theme of workers and their resistance to exploitation. Records relating to the ILC are in the E. Howard Molisani Papers and the Onorio Ruotolo Papers, Immigration History Research Center (hereinafter cited as IHRC), University of Minnesota, St. Paul.

2. Rudolph J. Vecoli, "The Italian Immigrants in the United States Labor Movement from 1880 to 1929," in *Gli italiani fuori d'Italia. Gli emigrati italiani nei movimenti operai dei paesi d'adozione 1880-1940*, ed. B. Bezza (Milan, 1983), 257-306; Vecoli, "Etnia, internazionalismo e protezionismo operaio: gli immigrati italiani e i movimento operai negli USA, 1880–1950," in *La Riscoperta delle Americhe Lavoratori e Sindacato nell'emigrazione in America Latina, 1870–1970*, ed. Vanni Blengino, Emilio Franzina, and Adolfo Pepe (Milan, 1994), 507–25; David Montgomery, *The Fall of the House of Labor: The Workplace, the State, and American Labor Activism 1865–1925* (Cambridge, Mass., 1987), 100; Edwin Fenton, *Immigrants and Labor, A Case Study: Italians and American Labor* (New York, 1975), 189, 556–58.

Observing that Italians were regarded as "the garbage of the United States" by other workers as well as employers, Edmondo Rossoni, organizer of the syndicalist Federazione Socialista Italiana (FSI) and editor of its organ, *Il Proletario*, concluded that the struggle of nationality had to supersede that of class. Prior to the rise of Fascism, Rossoni proposed the organization of the Italian Confederation of Labor in North America on the basis of "class nationalism." John J. Tinghino, *Edmondo Rossoni: From Revolutionary Syndicalism to Fascism* (New York, 1991), 42–43.

3. David Montgomery, "Nationalism, American Patriotism, and Class Consciousness among Immigrant Workers in the United States in the Epoch of World War I," in *"Struggle a Hard Battle": Essays on Working-Class Immigrants*, ed. Dirk Hoerder (De Kalb, Ill., 1986), 327–51; Montgomery, "The 'New Unionism' and the Transformation of Workers' Consciousness in America, 1909–1922," *Journal of Social History* 7 (summer 1974): 509–29; William Leiserson, *Adjusting Immigrant and Industry* (New York, 1924); Rudolph J. Vecoli, "The War and Italian American Syndicalists" (unpublished paper, 1978); Michael M. Topp, "Immigrant Culture and the Politics of Identity: Italian-American Syndicalists in the U.S., 1911–1927" (Ph.D. diss., Brown University, 1993); Fiorello B. Ventresco, "Loyalty and Dissent: Italian Reservists in America during World War I," *Italian Americana* 4 (1978): 93–122. Ventresco notes that despite the 100 Per Cent Americanism movement, Italian immigrants, as allies, were encouraged by the U.S. government to "exult in their newfound dual patriotism" (p. 3).

The spirit of 1919 is captured in interviews with Italian workers in Lawrence strike files; Anthony Capraro Papers, IHRC, and David J. Saposs Papers, series 4, box 21, Research Files, Americanization Studies, Wisconsin Historical Society, Madison (Wisconsin Historical Society hereinafter cited as WHS).

4. Vittorio Buttis, *Memorie di Vita di Tempeste Sociali* (Chicago, 1940), 122. Buttis was a longtime socialist and a labor organizer among Italian Americans.

5. Fenton, *Immigrants and Labor*, 188–89; Rudolph J. Vecoli, "Anthony Capraro and the Lawrence Strike of 1919," in *Pane e Lavoro: The Italian American Working Class*, ed. George E. Pozzetta (Toronto, 1980), 3-27; Michael M. Topp, "The Transnationalism of the Italian-American Left: The Lawrence Strike of 1912 and the Italian Chamber of Labor of New York City," *Journal of American Ethnic History* 17 (fall 1997): 39–63; Charles A. Zappia, "Unionism and the Italian American Worker: A History of the New York City 'Italian Locals' in the International Ladies' Garment Workers' Union, 1900–1934" (Ph.D. diss., University of California at Berkeley, 1994), 206–10.

6. In his pathbreaking study, Edwin Fenton concluded that the most significant period of the Italian American labor movement had come to an end by 1920; Fenton, *Immigrants and Labor*, 189, 408, 454, 558. Although I agree with this proposition, I disagree with his explanation that Italian radicals simply assimilated into the U.S. conservative labor model and became "practical trade unionists." In their study of the Italian labor movement in Chicago, Eugene Miller and Gianna S. Panofsky concluded that the radical élan was pretty well spent by the mid-1920s. I have profited from consulting their well-researched, but unfortunately still unpublished, work: "Struggling in Chicago: Italian Immigrants with a Socialist Agenda, 1880–1980," 2:76–79.

7. Lizabeth Cohen, *Making a New Deal: Industrial Workers in Chicago, 1919–1939* (Cambridge, Mass., 1990); Thomas Gobel, "Becoming American: Ethnic Workers and the Rise of the CIO," *Labor History* 29 (spring 1988): 173–81; Gary Gerstle, *Working Class Americanism: The Politics of Labor in a Textile City, 1914–1960* (Cambridge, Mass., 1989); James R. Barrett, "Americanization from the Bottom Up: Immigration and the Remaking of the Working Class in the United States 1880–1930," *Journal of American History* 14 (December 1992): 996–1020.

8. William Preston, Jr., *Aliens and Dissenters: Federal Suppression of Radicals, 1903–1933* (Cambridge, Mass., 1963); Paul Avrich, *Sacco and Vanzetti: The Anarchist Background* (Princeton, N.J., 1991); Fiorello B. Ventresco, "Crises and Unity: The Italian Radicals in America in the 1920s," *Ethnic Forum* 15 (1995): 12–15; Rudolph J. Vecoli, " 'Free Country': The American Republic Viewed by the Italian Left, 1880–1920," in *In the Shadow of the Statue of Liberty: Immigrants, Workers, and Citizens in the American Republic, 1880-1920*, ed. Marianne Debouzy (Saint-Denis, France, 1988), 35–56; Vecoli, "Luigi Galleani," in *Encyclopedia of the American Left* [hereinafter cited as *EAL*], ed. Mari Jo Buhle, Paul Buhle, and Dan Georgakas (New York, 1990), 251–53; Nunzio Pernicone, "Luigi Galleani and Italian Anarchist Terrorism in the United States," *Studi Emigrazione* 30 (1993): 469–89; and interviews with Eligio Strobino, 27 September 1977 and 15 September 1978, in author's possession. The near lynching of Capraro during the Lawrence strike is documented in the Capraro Papers, IHRC.

9. Vecoli, "Italian American Syndicalists"; Michael M. Topp, "The Italian-American Left: Transnationalism and the Quest for Unity," in *The Immigrant Left in the United States*, ed. Paul Buhle and Dan Georgakas (Albany, N.Y., 1996), 119–37. Ventresco, "Italian Reservists in America," reported that although Italian immigrants purchased Italian war bonds, relatively few responded to the call to the colors. Erasmo Abbate (alias Hugo Rolland), "Memoir" (in author's possession); Reports, June–August 1917, War Records Commission, Council of National Defense, Minneapolis Division Correspondence and Records 1918–20, 44G6.9B, Minnesota Historical Society, St. Paul (Minnesota Historical Society hereinafter cited as MHS). One of these reports reads as follows: "Amato Guliani . . . stated that the majority of the Italians and Servians who were last year members of the IWW had withdrawn from that organization on account of the pro-German attitude that their Finn fellow workers had taken against the Allies because they absolutely refuse to side in with Russia." *Reports*, 45, 15 August 1917, Virginia, Minn.

10. Tinghino, *Edmondo Rossoni*; Stefano Luconi, "From Left to Right: The Not So Strange Career of Filippo Bocchini and Other Italian American Radicals," *Italian American Review* 6 (autumn 1997/winter 1998): 59–79. On Trombetta, see his file, Casellario Politico Centrale, Archivio Centrale dello Stato, Rome. He was reported as disseminating, in speech and in writing, propaganda favorable to the Fascist regime; Consolato Generale d'Italia di New York a R. Ministero dell'Interno, 10 November 1933.

11. John B. Duff, "The Italians," in *The Immigrants' Influence on Wilson's Peace Policies*, ed. Joseph P. O'Grady (Lexington, Ky., 1967); John Allswang, *A House for All Peoples: Ethnic Politics in Chicago, 1890–1936* (Lexington, Ky., 1971), 40, 116; Arthur Mann, *La Guardia: A Fighter against His Times 1882–1993* (Chicago and London, 1959), 94, 111, 114. The quote is from Mann, p. 114.

12. John P. Diggins, *Mussolini and Fascism: The View from America* (Princeton, N.J., 1972), 78–81; Agostino De Biasi, *La battalgia dell'Italia negli Stati-Uniti* (New York, 1927); Avrich, *Sacco and Vanzetti*, 3–4; John Higham, *Strangers in the Land: Patterns of American Nativism, 1860–1925*, paperback ed. (New Brunswick, N.J., 1992), 264–330; Salvatore J. La Gumina, *WOP: A Documentary History of Anti-Italian Discrimination in the United States* (San Francisco, 1973); Stefano Luconi, "Anti-Italian Prejudice and Discrimination and the Persistence of Ethnic Voting among Philadelphia's Italian Americans, 1928–1953," *Studi Emigrazione* 29 (March 1992): 113–32.

13. Philip V. Cannistraro, *Blackshirts in Little Italy: Italian Americans and Fascism, 1921–1929* (West Lafayette, Ind.: Bordighera, 1999); Gaetano Salvemini, *Italian Fascist Activities in the United States*, ed. Philip V. Cannistraro (New York, 1977), 3–50; Nunzio Pernicone, "Il caso Greco-Carrillo. Un espisodio della lotta fra Fascismo e anti-Fascismo negli Stati Uniti," *Storia Contemporanea* 27 (August 1996): 611–41. On the conflict in California between Fascists and anti-Fascists, see Gabriella Faconda, *Socialismo italiano esule negli USA (1930–1942)*, (Foggia, Italy, 1993).

14. Baldo Acquilano, *L'Ordine Figli d'Italia in America* (New York, 1925); Robert Ferrari, *Days Pleasant and Unpleasant in the Order Sons of Italy* (New York, 1926); Salvemini, *Italian Fascist Activities*, 91–105; Mann, *La Guardia*, 251–52; John Andreozzi, comp., *Guide to the Records of the Order Sons of Italy in America* (St. Paul, Minn., 1989). The archives of the Order are now in the Immigration History Research Center, University of Minnesota. The papers of Giovanni M. Di Silvestro and George J. Spatuzza are particularly revealing regarding the ties between the Order Sons of Italy and the Fascist regime.

There is need for a detailed history of the relationship between the Order Sons of Italy and Fascism, including studies of local lodges. The Guglielmo Marconi Lodge of Hibbing, Minnesota, disapproved of Di Silvestro's message to Mussolini and supported the Sacco and Vanzetti defense. However, during the Italo-Ethiopian War it donated money to the Italian Red Cross, and it celebrated the Italian victory in 1936. Guglielmo Marconi Lodge, Hibbing Papers, OSIA, MSS P 318, box 1 Minutes, MHS.

15. Benedicte Deschamps, "De La Presse 'Coloniale' à la Presse Italo-Américaine, Le Parcours de Six Periodiques Italiens aux Etats-Unis, 1910–1935," 2 vols. (Ph.D. diss., Université Paris VII-Denis Diderot, 1996), 1:83–89; 2:279–98; Deschamps, "L'épreuve/les preuves de la loyauté: La presse italo-américaine face à la citoyenneté (1910–1935), *Revue Française d'Études Américaines* 75 (January 1998): 47–61; Philip V. Cannistraro, "Generoso Pope and the Rise of Italian American Politics, 1925–1936," in *Italian Americans: New Perspectives in Italian Immigration and Ethnicity* (Staten Island, N.Y., 1985), 264–88; Rudolph J. Vecoli, "The Italian Immigrant Press and the Construction of Social Reality, 1850–1920," in *Print Culture in a Diverse America*, ed. James P. Danky and Wayne A. Wiegand (Urbana and Chicago, 1998), 17–33; Salvemini, *Italian Fascist Activities*, passim; Fiorello B. Ventresco, "The Struggle of the Italian Anti-Fascist Movement in America (Spanish Civil War to World War II)," *Ethnic Forum* 6 (1986): 25–26.

16. Rudolph J. Vecoli, "Prelates and Peasants: Italian Immigrants and the Catholic Church," *Journal of Social History* 2 (spring 1969): 217-68; Salvemini, *Italian Fascist Activities*, 145–64; Peter R. D'Agostino, "Missionaries in Babylon: The Adaptation of Italian

Priests to Chicago's Church" (Ph.D. diss., University of Chicago, 1993); D'Agostino, "The Scalabrini Fathers, the Italian Emigrant Church and Ethnic Nationalism in America," *Religion and American Culture: A Journal of Interpretation* 7 (winter 1997): 121–59; D'Agostino, "Italian Ethnicity and Religious Priests in the American Church: The Servites, 1870–1940," *Catholic Historical Review* 80 (October 1994): 714–40. In 1925, Archbishop George Cardinal Mundelein of Chicago declared: "Mussolini was a great big man—the man of the times" (D'Agostino, "Scalabrini Fathers," p. 145).

17. Salvemini, *Italian Fascist Activities*, 244–45. For vivid descriptions of the influence of Fascism among Italian American workers, see the memoirs of three major anti-Fascists: Vanni B. Montana, *Amarostico: Testimonianze euro-americane* (Leghorn, Italy, 1975); Armando Borghi, *Mezzo secolo di anarchia* (Naples, 1954); and Vittorio Vidali, *Orrizonti di liberta* (Milan, 1980). Borghi recalled that when he arrived in the United States in the mid-1920s, the Little Italies had become "hotbeds of Mussoliniana frenzy" (p. 340).

18. Paul Avrich, "The Revenge of Sacco and Vanzetti" (paper presented at the conference "The Lost World of Italian American Radicalism," New York, N.Y., 14–15 May 1997); Ventresco, "Crises and Unity," 12–34; Pernicone, "Luigi Galleani and Italian Anarchist Terrorism," 469–89; Bruno Cartosio, "Gli emigrati italiani e l'Industrial Workers of the World," in Bezza, *Gli italiani fuori d'Italia*, 359–95; Elisabetta Vezzosi, *Il socialismo indifferente: Immigrati italiani e Socialist Party negli Stati Uniti del primo Novecento* (Rome, 1991). The membership of the Italian Socialist Federation (Socialist Party of America) declined from more than one thousand in 1919 to 343 in 1927, whereas the Italian Federation of the Workers Party of America had 400 members in 1922 (Vezzosi, p. 207; Miller and Panofsky, "Struggling in Chicago," 1:8).

19. John P. Diggins, "The Italo-American Anti-Fascist Opposition," *Journal of American History* 54 (December 1967): 579–98; Nunzio Pernicone, "Carlo Tresca: The Life and Death of a Revolutionary," in *Italian Americans: The Search for a Usable Past*, ed. Richard N. Juliani and Philip V. Cannistraro (Staten Island, N.Y., 1989), 216–35; Ventresco, "Crises and Unity," 18–29.

For brief biographies of leaders of the anti-Fascist movement, consult: *Il Movimento Operaio Italiano Dizionario Biografico* (hereinafter *MOIDB*), 5 vols., ed. Franco Andreucci and Tommaso Detti (Rome: Editori Riuniti, 1975–78); *La Parola del Popolo, Cinquantesmio Anniversario, 1908–1958* (Chicago) 9 (December 1958–January 1959). On concentrations of anti-Fascists see: Vecoli, "Italian Immigrants in Labor Movement," and Gary R. Mormino and George E. Pozzetta, *The Immigrant World of Ybor City: Italians and Their Latin Neighbors in Tampa, 1885–1985* (Champaign, Ill., 1987); on Chicago see Miller and Panofsky, "Struggling in Chicago," 1:20.

20. Charles A. Zappia's dissertation, "Unionism and the Italian American Worker," is the best study of the Italians in the needle trades' unions in the postwar period. See also his article "Unionism and the Italian American Worker: The Politics of Anti-Communism in the International Ladies' Garment Workers' Union in New York City, 1920–1925," in *Italian Americans through the Generations*, ed. Rocco Carporale, American Italian Historical Association Annual Meeting (New York, 1986).

21. Fenton, *Immigrants and Labor*, 458, 537; Zappia, "Unionism and the Italian American Worker," 163, 171–72, 182, 293, 343; Robert Laurentz, "Racial/Ethnic Conflict in the New York City Garment Industry, 1933–1980" (Ph.D. diss., State University of New York, Binghamton, 1980); Steve Fraser, *Labor Will Rule: Sidney Hillman and the Rise of American Labor* (New York, 1991), 110, 229 (Fraser uncritically reiterates harshly negative stereotypes of Italians, 107–9, 203–4); Fraser, "Landyslayt and Paesani: Ethnic Con-

flict and Cooperation in the Amalgamated Clothing Workers of America," in Hoerder, *"Struggle a Hard Battle,"* 327–51; Fraser, "Dress Rehearsal for the New Deal: Shop-Floor Insurgents, Political Elites, and Industrial Democracy in the Amalgamated Clothing Workers," in *Working-Class America: Essays on Labor, Community, and American Society,* ed. Michael H. Frisch and Daniel J. Walkowitz (Urbana, Ill., 1983), 212–55.

For a bitter expression of anti-Jewish sentiment, see Orazio Montalbò, *Dicianove Anni di Vita e di Lotta. Appunti e Ricordi 1905–1924* (New York, 1925). Montalbò recounts how Jews repeatedly thwarted his efforts to organize Italian workers in various unions. Frustrated, he abandoned socialism for Fascism.

22. *Report of the General Executive Board of the Seventeenth Convention of the International Ladies' Garment Workers' Union* (Boston, Mass., 5 May 1924), 72. The resolution goes on to assert that it was "the avowed aim of these international marauders to wean the Italian workers away from the very ranks of our own International Ladies' Garment Workers' Union." At the ACWA convention of 1926, a resolution was offered that "the Fascisti . . . seek to extend their brutal union-smashing activities to . . . America where Fascisti bands . . . are . . . attempting to substitute Fascisti organizations for the bona fide labor movement," and further suggested that "any member . . . caught spreading propaganda in favor of Fascism . . . be expelled from our organization." Report of the General Executive Board of the Amalgamated Clothing Workers of America to the Sixth Biennial Convention (Philadelphia-New York, 12–17 May 1924), 321; *Documentary History of the Amalgamated Clothing Workers of America 1926–1928,* report of the General Executive Board and proceedings of the Eighth Biennial Convention of the Amalgamated Clothing Workers of America (Montreal, Canada, 10–15 May 1926).

23. Fraser, *Labor Will Rule,* 229; Montana, *Amarostico,* 157; Salvemini, "Italian Fascist Activities," 66, 107–34; Nunzio Pellegrino, "Manifesto of AFANA," *Labor History* 13 (summer 1972): 418–19; Christopher C. Newton, "Ethnicity and the New Deal: Italian Language Theatre Sponsored by the Federal Theatre Project in Boston, 1935–1939" (Ph.D. diss., Tufts University, 1994), 156–57.

The inroads of Fascist propaganda among workers was commented on in a resolution of the Italian delegates to the Third Convention of the International Workers Order in 1935: "Among the troops of the Fascist avant-garde in America swarm a good number of Italian workers deceived by the demagogic propaganda of Italian Fascism and deluded that their everyday problems of life will be resolved by Fascism." Resolution of Italian Conference for the Movement against War and Fascism, box 10, file 14, International Workers Order Records, Labor-Management Documentation Center, Martin P. Catherwood Library, Cornell University, Ithaca, N.Y.

24. Diggins, "Italo-American Anti-Fascist Opposition," 580–81; Zappia, "Politics of Anti-Communism"; Fraser, *Labor Will Rule,* 203–5; Montana, *Amarostico,* 106; Vidali, *Orrizonti di libertà,* 201–26; Jean A. Scarpaci, "Angela Bambace and the International Ladies' Garment Workers' Union: The Search for an Elusive Activist," in Pozzetta, *Pane e Lavoro,* 99–118; Miller and Panofsky, "Struggling in Chicago," 1:10–20, 2:10–16. The Tuscan neighborhood on Chicago's West Side was reported to be a Communist stronghold.

25. Nunzio Pernicone, "Carlo Tresca and the Sacco-Vanzetti Case," *Journal of American History* 66 (December 1979): 535–47; Ventresco, "Crises and Unity," 21; Montana, *Amarostico,* 113; Vidali, *Orrizonti di liberta;* E. Collotti, "Vittorio Vidali," *MOIDB,* 5:229–32.

26. Vidali, *Orrizonti di libertà;* Vecoli, "Italian Immigrants in Labor Movement"; Montgomery, *Fall of the House of Labor,* 98. See scattered references in *Il Proletario, Il Lavoratore,*

L'Adunata dei Refrattari, Giustizia, and Il Lavoro. The careers of several of these labor radicals can be traced in their papers: Angela Bambace, Anthony Capraro, Antonino Crivello, Pasquale Mario De Ciampis, and Giuseppe Procopio, in the IHRC.

27. Fenton, *Immigrants and Labor*, 116, 221–39; Montgomery, *Fall of the House of Labor*, 99, 294; Fraser, *Labor Will Rule*, 242–44, 253–57; Buttis, *Vita di Tempeste Sociali*, 132–34, 141; Montana, *Amarostico*, 241; John Hutchinson, *The Imperfect Union: A History of Corruption in American Trade Unions* (New York, 1970), 65–73, 90–124, 222–37; Malcolm M. Johnson, *Crime on the Labor Front* (New York, 1950), 35–38, 96–112, 191; Philip Taft, *Corruption and Racketeering in the Labor Movement* (Ithaca, N.Y., 1958); Salvatore LaGumina, *New York at Mid-Century: The Impellitteri Years* (Westport, Conn., 1992), 23. According to LaGumina, Paolo Vaccarelli was regarded as a Robin Hood figure by the Italians because he defied the Irish leadership of the International Longshoremen's Association; William Mello, "Pete Panto: Rank and File Radical on the Brooklyn Waterfront" (paper presented at "The Lost World of Italian American Radicalism Conference"); E. Collotti, "Pippan, Giovanni," *MOIDB*, 4:158–59; Eugene Miller, "Italian Radical Union Organizing in Chicago: The Contributions of Giovanni Pippan, 1924–1933" (unpublished paper, 1995); Pernicone, "Carlo Tresca: Life and Death," 216–35; Rudolph J. Vecoli, "Tresca, Carlo," *MOIDB*, 5:97–100; G. Miccichè, "Vacirca, Vincenzo," *MOIDB*, 5:160–63.

28. Diggins, "Italo-American Anti-Fascist Opposition," 580–81; Fenton, *Immigrants and Labor*, 554; Zappia, "Unionism and the Italian American Worker," 318; Nunzio Pernicone, "Carlo Tresca and the Sacco-Vanzetti Case," *Journal of American History* 66 (December 1979): 535–47; Adrianna Dada, "L'arrivo di Borghi negli Stati Uniti tra alleanza anti-Fascista e purismo ideologico," *Bollettino del Museo del Risorgimento* (Bologna, Italy) 35 (1990): 145–60; Vidali, *Orizzonti di libertà*, 206, 229, 233. Vidali describes the violent clashes among Communists, socialists, and anarchists. Giuseppe Bertelli, a leader of the Italian American democratic socialists for almost a half century, severely criticized those radicals who exhausted their energies in the struggle against Fascism in Italy instead of instilling socialist principles among the workers in the United States; Miller and Panofsky, "Struggling in Chicago," 1:3–4, 40–42, 55.

29. To this extent, I agree with Lizabeth Cohen et al. (see note 6), but rather than viewing this incorporation into American labor and political movements as due to Americanization, I maintain that transnational influences of Fascism and Communism substantially conditioned Italian American participation in the progressive movements of the 1930s.

30. Fraser, "Dress Rehearsal"; Zappia, "Unionism and the Italian American Worker," 326–30; Scarpaci, "Angela Bambace"; Jennifer Guglielmo, " 'The Uprising of 60,000': The Meanings of Labor Solidarity in the ILGWU, 1933–1940" (unpublished paper, 1996). The source of the quote is *Giustizia*, October 1933. In *Amarostico* (155, 161–62), Vanni Montana, Local 89's public relations man, casts a cold eye on Antonini's personality and mode of operation.

31. Jennifer Guglielmo, "Donne Ribelle: Recovering the History of Italian Women's Radicalism in the United States" (paper presented at "The Lost World of Italian American Radicalism" conference), 60–61, n. 103, 112; Laurentz, "Racial/Ethnic Conflict," 121–26, 164–73; Scarpaci, "Angela Bambace."

32. Steve Rosswurm, ed., *The CIO's Left-Led Unions* (New Brunswick, N.J., 1992), for example, mentions only a few Italian Americans. On Italian American labor organizers, see Miller and Panofsky, "Struggling in Chicago," 1:4–44, 2:4–6, 25, 4:23, 36–44; June Namias, *First Generation: In the Words of Twentieth-Century American Immigrants* (1978),

41–47; Alice Lynd and Staughton Lynd, eds., *Rank and File: Personal Histories by Working Class Organizers* (Boston, 1973), 131–48; Rudolph J. Vecoli, "The Italians," in *They Chose Minnesota*, ed. June Holmquist (St. Paul, Minn., 1981), 458. Interviews with Ernie De Maio, 17 October 1976 and 12 September 1978, in author's possession.

Several oral history projects have recorded interviews with Italian American labor activists: Alice M. Hoffman, coordinator, *Oral History Projects*, Department of Labor Studies, Pattee Library Collections, Pennsylvania State University, University Park, Pa., 1985; and Paul Buhle and Jonathan Bloom, eds., *Guide to the Oral History of the American Left*, Tamiment Library, New York University Libraries, New York, 1984.

The role of second-generation Italian Americans in the labor movement particularly calls for attention. In 1919, James Mark, vice president of District 2, United Mine Workers of America, had this to say about the children of the immigrants: "The second generation has been helpful in making unionists out of the Italians. They are the organizers, officers, and leaders" (interview with David J. Saposs, 24 June 1919, Saposs Papers, WHS).

33. Nathan Glazer, *The Social Basis of American Communism* (New York, 1961), 159, 221–22; Harvey Klehr, "Immigrant Leadership in the Communist Party of the United States," *Ethnicity* 6 (1979): 36; Klehr, *The Heyday of American Communism: The Depression Decade* (New York, 1984), 382; Gerald Meyer, "Italian Americans and the American Communist Party" (paper presented at "Lost World of Italian American Radicalism" conference); Meyer, "Italian Americans and the American Communist Party: Notes on a History," The Balch Institute for Ethnic Studies. On the career of "Eric Lanzetti" (Carl Marzani), see Vivian Gornick, *The Romance of American Communism* (New York, 1977), 117–24; see also the entries for Peter V. Cacchione, Bella (Visono) Dodd, and Al Lannon (Albert F. Vetere), in *Biographical Dictionary of the American Left*, ed. Bernard K. Johnpoll and Harvey Klehr (New York, 1986).

As part of the CPUSA's Americanization strategy, activists with "foreign sounding names" were often given "American" names. Thus, when Mario Alpi was placed in the national office of the party, he became the nondescript Fred Brown; Klehr, *Heyday*, 25–26.

34. Thomas J. E. Walker, *Pluralistic Fraternity: The History of the International Workers Order* (New York, 1991), 96–97; Roger Keeran, "National Groups and the Popular Front: The Case of the IWO," *Journal of American Ethnic History* 14 (spring 1995): 26; Keeran, "The IWO and the Origins of the CIO," *Labor History* 30 (summer 1989); Keeran, "The Italian Section of the International Workers Order, 1930–1950" (paper presented at "Lost World of Italian American Radicalism" conference); Klehr, *Heyday*, 384–85; Committee on Un-American Activities, U.S. House of Representatives, *Guide to Subversive Organizations and Publications* (and appendix), rev. ed. (Washington, D.C., 1951). Considerable documentation on the Italian section of the IWO is in the Fred Celli Papers, IHRC, as well as in the IWO Papers, Cornell University.

35. Cannistraro, "Generoso Pope"; Thomas Kessner, *Fiorello H. La Guardia and the Making of Modern New York* (New York, 1989), 35, 418; Arthur Mann, *La Guardia Comes to Power 1933* (Philadelphia and New York: J. B. Lippincott, 1965), 26, 134–37.

Another exception was Peter V. Cacchione, the first Communist Party candidate to be elected to office in a major city, who served on the New York City Council from Brooklyn, 1942–47. Although he received the votes of Italian American garment workers and longshoremen, a greater percentage of his support came from Jewish and black neighborhoods. Simon W. Gerson, *Pete: The Story of Peter V. Cacchione, New York's First Communist Coun-*

cilman (New York, 1976), 110–11. See Peter V. Cacchione, *Italian-Americans and the War* (New York, 1940).

36. Gerald Meyer, *Vito Marcantonio, Radical Politician, 1902–1954* (Albany, N.Y., 1989), 69, 115–16, 122–29, 175–77; Kenneth A. Waltzer, "The American Labor Party: Third Party Politics in New Deal-Cold War New York, 1936–1954" (Ph.D. diss., Harvard University, 1977). The quote is from Gerald Meyer, "Marcantonio, Vito," *EAL*, 447–48. George Charney, a CP organizer in East Harlem, declared that "among Vito Marcantonio's beloved Calabrese, [the Communist Party] had but a handful of members. . . . The other Leftist groups [had] no presence whatsoever" (quoted in Meyer, *Vito Marcantonio*, pp. 115–16).

More study should be devoted to the political activities of Italian Americans outside the Atlantic Seaboard states. On Minnesota's Iron Range, John T. Bernard, born of Italian parents in Corsica, a miner and organizer for the Steel Workers' Organizing Committee, was elected to Congress on the Farmer-Labor Party ticket in 1936; Vecoli, "The Italians," 458. See Gerald Meyer, "The American Labor Party and New York City's Italian American Communities, 1936–1950," in *Industry, Technology, Labor, and the Italian American Communities* (Staten Island, N.Y.: American Italian Historical Association, 1995), 33–49.

37. Kessner, *La Guardia*, 136, 403; Ronald Bayor, *Neighbors in Conflict: The Irish, Germans, Jews, and Italians in New York City, 1929–1941*, 2d ed. (Urbana, Ill., 1988), 77. The quote is from Mann, *La Guardia*, 252.

38. Meyer, *Vito Marcantonio*, 119.

39. Faconda, *Socialismo italiano*, 21–27.

40. Quoted in Newton, "Ethnicity and the New Deal," 130.

41. Stefano Luconi, "The Influence of the Italo-Ethiopian Conflict and the Second World War on Italian-American Voters: The Case of Philadelphia," *Immigrants & Minorities* 16 (November 1997): 3–7; Fiorello B. Ventresco, "Italian-Americans and the Ethiopian Crisis," *Italian Americana* 6 (fall/winter 1980): 4–27; Brice Harris, Jr., *The United States and the Italo-Ethiopian Crisis* (Stanford, Calif., 1964), 122–25; Diggins, *Mussolini and Fascism*, 302–6; Salvemini, *Italian Fascist Activities*, 196–208; the quote is from Montana, *Amarostico*, 118. Montana continues, "The great mass of Italian Americans was delirious with 'imperial glories' [while] the tune 'Facetta Nera' echoed in all hours of the day and night in the houses and streets of the Little Italies."

42. Diggins, *Mussolini and Fascism*, 302–6; Bayor, *Neighbors in Conflict*, 107–8; Salvemini, *Italian Fascist Activities*, 209–42; Montana, *Amarostico*, 159; Miller and Panofsky, "Struggling in Chicago," 1:60; Faconda, *Socialismo italiano*, 93. Auxillary Bishop William D. O'Brien of the Archdiocese of Chicago at a 1936 ceremony during the playing of *Giovinezza* "raised his arm in a Roman salute and held it in the same position for the duration of the hymn" (D'Agostino, "Scalabrini Fathers," p. 145).

43. Nadia Venturini, *Neri e italiani ad Harlem. Gli anni trenta e la guerra d'Etiopia* (Rome, 1990); Diggins, *Mussolini and Fascism*, 306–12; Harris, *Italo-Ethiopian Crisis*, 41. Boston's *Italian News* discusses a parade celebrating the conquest of Ethiopia: "Carrying Effigy of Selassie through No. End"; Newton, "Ethnicity and the New Deal," 134–35.

44. Nadia Venturini, "African American Riots during World War II: Reactions in the Italian American Communist Press" (paper presented at American Italian Historical Association annual conference, Cleveland, Ohio, 1997), 9–12. The Ku Klux Klan in Detroit was organizing Italian American youth into Mantle Clubs.

45. Meyer, *Vito Marcantonio*, 124–25, reported increased racism among Italian Americans because of the Ethiopian War. See also Vecoli, " 'Free Country,' " 35–56; Vecoli,

"The African Connection: Italian Americans and Race" (paper presented at American Italian Historical Association Annual Meeting, Cleveland, Ohio, 1997); Vecoli, "Are Italian Americans Just White Folks?" *Italian Americana* 13 (summer 1995): 149–61.

46. Faconda, *Socialismo italiano*, 94–96; Fraser, *Labor Will Rule*, 229, 498; Meyer, *Vito Marcantonio*, 119. Even pro-Fascists such as Pope rejected Mussolini's racial laws, yet the growth of anti-Semitism was noted in New York City, especially among "Italians who worked in Jewish sweatshops" (Bayor, *Neighbors in Conflict*, pp. 84–86). In 1943, *L'Unità del Popolo* reported that in Detroit "Anti-Semitism is especially rampant among Italian Americans" (Venturini, "African American Riots," p. 10).

47. "I Fix the Railroad Tracks," Italians in Bridgeport, Peoples of Connecticut, Ethnic Heritage WPA Writers Project 1930s, box 23, Historical Manuscripts and Archives, University of Connecticut, Storrs. The Ethnic Heritage Project includes numerous interviews with Italian Americans, some of which have been published in Bruce M. Stave and John F. Sutherland, eds., *From the Old Country: An Oral History of the European Migration to America* (New York, 1994).

48. Rudolph J. Vecoli, "Primo Maggio: May Day Observances among Italian Immigrant Workers, 1890–1920," *Labor's Heritage* 7 (spring 1996): 28-41.

49. Ventresco, "Italian Anti-Fascist Movement," 17–30; Zappia, "Unionism and the Italian American Worker," 330–33; Diggins, *Mussolini and Fascism*, 111–43; Montana, *Amarostico*, 118; Miller and Panofsky, "Struggling in Chicago," 1:4–24, 118; Rudolph J. Vecoli, "Valenti, Girolamo," MOIDB, 5:171–74, and "Tresca, Carlo," 5:97–100; Dorothy Gallagher, *All the Right Enemies: The Life and Murder of Carlo Tresca* (New Brunswick, N.J., 1988). Luigi Antonini, *Dynamic Democracy* (New York, 1944) is a collection of his writings and radio broadcasts. Extensive documentation on the Italian America Left during the 1930s is in the Fred Celli Papers, IHRC.

50. Ventresco, "Italian Anti-Fascist Movement," 18–24, 31; Gallagher, *All the Right Enemies*; Collotti, "Vidali, Vittorio," MOIDB, 5:229–32; Meyer, *Vito Marcantonio*, 115; Montana, *Amarostico*, 130–37, 167; Borghi, *Mezzo secolo*, 356–58; Miller and Panofsky, "Struggling in Chicago," 2:66–75. Based on current research, Fraser Ottanelli estimates that about two hundred fifty Italian Americans fought with the Loyalists. Communication to the author, 9 March 1998.

A survey of the following reveals few references to Italian Americans: Peter Carroll, *The Odyssey of the Abraham Lincoln Bridge: Americans in the Spanish Civil War* (Stanford, Calif., 1994); John Grassi, *The Premature Anti-Fascists: North American Volunteers in the Spanish Civil War, 1936–39: An Oral History* (New York, 1986); Arthur H. Landis, *The Abraham Lincoln Brigade* (New York, 1967); Cecil D. Eby, *Between the Bullet and the Lie: American Volunteers in the Spanish Civil War* (New York, 1969); Robert A. Rosenstone, *Crusade of the Left: The Lincoln Battalion in the Spanish Civil War* (New York, 1969); Allen Guttmann, *The Wound in the Heart: America and the Spanish Civil War* (New York, 1962).

51. Maddalena Tirabassi, "La Mazzini Society (1940–1946): Un'associazione degli anti-Fascisti italiani negli Stati Uniti," in *Italia e America dalla Grande Guerra ad Oggi*, ed. G. G. Migone, G. Spini, M. Teodori (Venice, 1976); Tirabassi, "Enemy Aliens or Loyal Americans? The Mazzini Society and the Italian-American Communities," *RSA: Rivista di Studi Anglo-Americani* 3 (1984–1985) [*Atti del Settimo Convegno Nazionale: Italy and Italians in America*, ed. Alfredo Rizzardi]: 399–425; Diggins, *Mussolini and Fascism*, 399–421; Montana, *Amarostico*, 172. The politics of the anti-Fascist movement during these years can be followed in the Alberto Cuppelli Papers and Max Ascoli Papers, IHRC.

52. Faconda, *Socialismo italiano*, 135; Meyer, *Vito Marcantonio*, 116; Fraser, *Labor Will Rule*, 498; Tirabassi, "La Mazzini Society (1940–1946): Un 'Associazione degli antifascisti italiani negli stati uniti," in *Italia e America dalla Grande Guerra a Oggi*, ed. Giorgio Spini, Giangiacomo Migone, and Massimo Teodori (Venice: Marsilio, 1976), 141–58; Borghi, *Mezzo secolo*, 362; Montana, *Amarostico*, 172; Stephen Fox, *The Unknown Internment: An Oral History of the Relocation of Italian Americans during World War II* (Boston, 1990); Nadia Venturini, "From Roosevelt and Mussolini to Truman and De Gasperi: The Politics of Italian American Leadership, 1930–1950" (M.A. thesis, University of Minnesota, 1984), also published as "Italian American Leadership, 1943–48," *Storia Nord-americana* (1985); Philip V. Cannistraro, "Luigi Antonini and the Italian Anti-Fascist Movement in the United States, 1940–1943," *Journal of American Ethnic History* 21 (fall 1995); John S. Crawford, *Luigi Antonini* (New York, 1950); Luconi, "Influence of the Italo-Ethiopian Conflict," 7–15; Luconi, "The Changing Meaning of Ethnic Identity among Italian Americans in Philadelphia during World War II," *Pennsylvania History* 63 (autumn 1996): 561–78; George E. Pozzetta, "Alien Enemies or Loyal Americans? The Year of Anxieties," chapter 3 of a work on Italian Americans and World War II that Pozzetta was writing at the time of his death.

53. Stanislao G. Pugliese, "The Culture of Nostalgia: Fascism in the Memory of Italian-Americans," H-Net List on Italian-American History and Culture, 30 July 1997, available at h-italn@h-net.msu.edu. In this perceptive essay, Pugliese questions the meaning of Fascism to Italian Americans, in the past and present. He interprets the idealization of the Fascist era as a nostalgic escape from an unsatisfactory present. Pugliese recounts that an Italian band that plays at religious festivals on Long Island, New York, is asked "invariably" to play the Fascist anthems, *"Giovinezza," "Facetta Nera,"* and *"Marcia su Roma."*

54. Gallagher, *All the Right Enemies*; Pernicone, "Carlo Tresca: Life and Death"; Zappia, "Unionism and the Italian American Worker," 334–36; Zappia, "From Working Class Radicalism to Cold War Anti-Communism: The Case of the Italian Locals of the ILGWU" (paper presented at "Lost World of Italian American Radicalism" conference); Ventresco, "Italian Anti-Fascist Movement," 34–37; Montana, *Amarostico*, 172–215.

On victims of McCarthyism, see David Caute, *The Great Fear: The Anti-Communist Purge under Truman and Eisenhower* (New York, 1978). Giacomo Quattrone, who had lived in the United States 40 years and had eight American-born children, was deported, not for having been a member, but for having attended meetings and having donated money to the Communist Party; Caute, p. 241. Documentation on Quattrone and other Italian Americans can be found in the American Committee for the Protection of the Foreign Born Papers, Labadie Collection, University of Michigan Library, Ann Arbor.

55. In conducting oral histories, I have encountered examples of amnesia among children of Italian radicals, and, on occasion, an outright refusal to talk about radical antecedents. Other researchers have reported similar experiences; a colleague who attempted to interview a son about his anarchist father was told, "some things are better left alone" (letter of Sarah J. Sweeney, 8 January 1998, in author's possession). For insightful comments regarding the effects of Americanization on the politics of the second generation, see Buttis, *Vita di Tempeste Sociali*, 1–2; and Borghi, *Mezzo secolo*, 341–42.

56. This interpretation is supported by the sociological and historical literature; for example, A. Ann Squier and Jill S. Quadagno, "The Italian American Family," in *Ethnic Families in America: Patterns and Variations*, ed. Charles H. Mindel, Robert W. Habenstein, and Roosevelt Wright, Jr. (New York, 1988), 109–37; Raymond A. Belliotti, *Seeking Identity: Individualism versus Community in an Ethnic Context* (Lawrence, Kans., 1995), 39–76;

Leonard Covello, *The Social Background of the Italo-American School Child* (Leiden, The Netherlands, 1967); Colleen Leahy Johnson, *Growing Up and Growing Old in Italian-American Families* (New Brunswick, N.J., 1985); Elizabeth Ewen, *Immigrant Women in the Land of Dollars: Life and Culture on the Lower East Side, 1890–1925* (New York, 1985); and Judith Smith, *Family Connections: A History of Italian and Jewish Lives in Providence, Rhode Island, 1900–1940* (Albany, N.Y., 1985). For a revisionist interpretation that stresses Italian American women's political activism, see Guglielmo, "Donne Ribelle."

57. Len Giovannitti, *The Nature of the Beast: A Novel* (New York, 1977), 37–42.

Chapter 2

War among the Italian Anarchists: The Galleanisti's Campaign against Carlo Tresca

Nunzio Pernicone

A cursory history of the Italian American Left might easily promote the impression that immigrant radicals (*sovversivi*) spent more time and energy squabbling amongst themselves than they did fighting the ruling class. Although such a conclusion would be mistaken, internecine conflict undeniably was an integral feature of the *sovversivi*'s subculture. Some issues of contention originated in Italy and Europe; others stemmed from conditions encountered in America that bore directly on the lives of immigrant workers. The inter- and intradenominational altercations of the *sovversivi* were generally limited to words, subsumed under the rubric of *la polemica*. A polemic might take the form of a doctrinal dispute conducted on a serious intellectual level, or of personal attacks replete with allegations, denunciations, and coarse insults. Polemics were aired in lecture halls and in the radical press, more frequently the latter. Broadsides exchanged between antagonists appeared in host newspapers often for weeks and months on end; their echoes sometimes reverberated for years, even decades. A few polemics degenerated into full-fledged feuds, occasionally provoking violent confrontations.[1]

Among the anarchists, who inherited the tradition of the polemic directly from Giuseppe Mazzini and Mikhail Bakunin, the most important internecine struggle waged in the United States was between Carlo Tresca and the Galleanisti. What began before World War I as a polemic between Tresca and Luigi Galleani over strike tactics was broadened and intensified in the 1920s and 1930s by the latter's disciples, who published the newspaper *L'Adunata dei Refrattari*, into a protracted campaign of character assassination. Motivated principally by jealous resentment of Tresca's popularity and influence, the Galleanisti sought to destroy his political reputation so that he could never attain full leadership of the Italian anarchists in the United States. For sheer malevolence and mindless

fanaticism, the Galleanisti's war against Tresca had no equal among the fratricidal conflicts of the *sovversivi*.

The behavior of the anarchists associated with *L'Adunata* cannot be understood apart from the intellectual and spiritual legacy bequeathed to them by their
"master," Luigi Galleani.[2] Galleani (1861–1931) was an anarchist–communist
(*comunista anarchico*) of the Peter Kropotkin school, with its fatalistic belief that
"natural laws" made revolution inevitable and would create "natural harmony"
in postrevolutionary society. Active in the United States from 1901 to 1918,
Galleani published *Cronaca Sovversiva* in Barre, Vermont (1903–1912) and
Lynn, Massachusetts (1912–1918). Unquestionably the best-written Italian
anarchist periodical in the country, it advocated every means of revolutionary
violence—including assassination and bombs—against the state and the bourgeoisie. *Cronaca* even regularly advertised and sold for 25 cents *La Salute è in Voi!*
(Health Is in You!), "an indispensable pamphlet for all comrades who love self-
instruction," that is, a bomb manual.[3]

Like most Italian anarchists who favored terrorism, Galleani was an *anti-orga-
nizzatore*, unalterably opposed to political parties, federations, labor unions, and
all other forms of organization, which he considered to be harbingers of authoritarianism. Galleani's anti-organizationism reflected a *forma mentis* characterized
by fanatical sectarianism and inflexibility in matters of thought and action.[4]
Fidelity to his anarchist beliefs was more important to Galleani than life itself.
During the reaction of 1898–1900, when the Socialist deputy Oddino Morgari
urged the anarchists condemned to confinement on penal islands (*domicilio
coatto*) to nominate Errico Malatesta and other leaders for election to parliament
as protest candidates, Galleani—himself confined on Pantelleria—rejected the
proposal, declaring that "The Faith Remains Unchanged" (Manet Immota
Fides):

> If, in order to leave here, we must submit before a banner that is not ours, if our liberation
> must be the result of a compromise, if we must leave these shoals counting among our days
> here even one of which we must be ashamed, if we must return as apostates, diminished,
> stunted, transfigured, after having burned incense of false adoration before idols which we
> repudiate—better to remain!
>
> Alone, with the truth, against all the world, even in a garret, that is a sweet and con-
> soling solitude.[5]

Galleani remained true to this rigid standard throughout his life. Unfortunately,
Galleani's notion that his "truth" was the only truth made him completely intol-
erant and contemptuous of anyone who dared to disagree. Paul Avrich has
observed that those who challenged Galleani on major issues often "stood condemned as corrupt allies of government and capital, if not as outright traitors and
spies."[6]

Thus, it would be that whomever Galleani condemned also stood condemned
in the eyes of his followers. Clinging tenaciously to the myth that anarchists do
not recognize leaders, and that their "master" was merely a *primus inter pares*,

they would deny that Galleani's dominance over them was nearly total.[7] In reality, starting in 1903, when he assumed the mantel from Giuseppe Ciancabilla, who died prematurely that year, Galleani was the undisputed chieftain of the Italian-American *anti-organizzatori*. Even after his deportation in 1919, Galleani remained the spiritual leader of his flock, revered almost as an omniscient and infallible deity. More than any other Italian anarchist of his era—in the United States, South America, or Europe—Luigi Galleani represented the quintessential "anarchist leader" described by the Swiss sociologist Roberto Michels. "Though the anarchist leaders are as a rule morally superior to the leaders of the organized parties working in the political field," Michels explained, "we find in them some of the qualities and pretensions characteristic of all leadership." The struggle against authority and coercion "has not stifled in them the natural love of power." Galleani, conforming to Michels's anarchist paradigm, exercised leadership over others through the traditional means of the spiritual leader and the orator: "the flaming power of thought, greatness of self-sacrifice, profundity of conviction." He exercised dominion "not over the organization but over minds," the result "not of technical indispensability, but of intellectual ascendancy and moral superiority."[8] Michels might have added that the anarchist leader's ascendance to power and influence could be greatly facilitated if his oratory and prose were more dazzling than comprehensible for many of his followers, as was the case with Galleani.[9]

Ironically, Galleani's dominance over mind and spirit generated precisely the kind of personal hegemony that Italian anarchists—especially the *anti-organizzatori*—had condemned as authoritarian since the late 1870s. Malatesta, Italy's greatest anarchist, admired Galleani's abilities as a propagandist but disagreed profoundly with his Kropotkinist conception of anarchist communism, his rejection of organization, and his demolitionist approach to revolution. Above all, however, Malatesta harbored serious misgivings about Galleani's position as the anointed leader of Italian anarchism in the United States, noting in 1926 that "he [Galleani] had created in America, around *Cronaca Sovversiva*, an environment of consensus and cooperation that, if anything, had the authoritarian defect of depending too much upon the impetus of a single person."[10] Other anarchists were distressed not only by the authoritarian propensities of Galleani's leadership but also by the cult of personality that revolved around him, a tendency assiduously nurtured by the editors of *L'Adunata*, especially Raffaele Schiavina (aliases Max Sartin and Bruno), who held this position from 1928 until the newspaper's demise in 1971. For example, Sam Dolgoff and Valerio Isca, two of anarchism's best-known and most-knowledgeable militants in the United States, both commented disapprovingly (using the same words) that the comrades of *L'Adunata* "worshipped Galleani like a God."[11]

Carlo Tresca (1879–1943), the bête noire of the Galleanisti, was an altogether different sort of person.[12] Whereas Galleani's personality was austere and his demeanor aristocratic, Tresca's nature was ebullient, friendly, and down-to-earth; he exuded an insatiable joie de vivre.[13] Politically, although Galleani and Tresca were both revolutionaries, the two men were leagues apart in matters of doctrine and behavior. Although in the course of his career, he described himself as a revolutionary socialist (1898–1904), a revolutionary syndicalist (1904–1913), and an anarcho-syndicalist (1913–1943), Tresca really eludes standard radical typology. Among the least-sectarian of revolutionaries, Tresca had little regard for doctrinal orthodoxy and behavioral conformity, and thus never qualified as a "movement" socialist, syndicalist, or anarchist, in the conventional sense. Nor did his supporters—the Treschiani—belong to a single ideological persuasion, drawn, as they were, to the man rather than to his philosophy. Furthermore, unlike Galleani and his followers, who inhabited a subculture composed overwhelmingly of Italian anarchists, after 1912 Tresca lived and worked in a politico-social environment that encompassed not only the Italian American Left but the broader mainstream of American radicalism, where a more pragmatic approach was employed.[14]

Arturo Giovannitti, the poet laureate of the Italian American Left, observed as early as 1916 that because of his rebellious spirit and nondoctrinaire approach to ideology and social struggle, "Tresca was always a little outside the favor of all the subversive theologies, always suspect in the community of the faithful, always in disrepute for heresy among the friars who come and go between old shrines and new baptisteries."[15] A true rebel, who always pursued an independent path, Tresca was a free lance of revolution, a man of action more concerned with winning victories for the workers than with the means by which he helped to achieve them.

The Galleanisti, who recognized only one star in the anarchist firmament, were predisposed from the outset to despise and reject Tresca. The master set the tone. In 1910, following Tresca's imprisonment for libeling a priest, Galleani expressed solidarity with him as a victim of clerical persecution, but not before disparaging his political behavior, specifying that "in the realm of ideas, he is our adversary."[16] Tresca's "adversary" status was reconfirmed during the agitation to liberate Giovannitti and Joe Ettor, who were jailed on trumped-up murder charges when they led the 1912 Lawrence strike. For many weeks, the Industrial Workers of the World (IWW) leaders had promoted an industrywide general strike for September 27, to compel the state government to free the accused. A few days before, however, the IWW canceled the general strike because the risk of failure seemed too great and the tempers of the Italian workers too explosive.[17] Tresca, whom the IWW had recruited to lead the agitation (he was in prison during the strike), was obliged to accede, even though he had campaigned for the general strike. Finally, under pressure from the Italian workers, whom the Galleanisti were spurring to revolt, the IWW opted for a one-day protest strike on September 30, which Tresca led in the front ranks. Furious that they had lost their opportunity for a revolutionary gesture, the Galleanisti—principally Umberto Postiglione and Calogero Speziale—heaped scorn upon the IWW and pilloried Tresca in *Cronaca Sovversiva* for having "eviscerated the enthusiasm of the proletariat" and committing other acts of apostasy.[18]

The inevitable question raised by the clash over the Ettor-Giovannitti agitation was whether the Galleanisti's hostility toward Tresca resulted solely from their different approach to revolutionary action or whether it was enhanced by personal jealousy and animosity on Galleani's part. Schiavina, his foremost disciple, maintained that Galleani never took Tresca seriously enough to consider him a rival or to be influenced by personal jealousy.[19] Dolgoff, however, believed that "the pond was too small for such egos as Galleani and Tresca."[20] Certainly, Galleani's resentment must have been stirred when the IWW declined his offer of assistance during the Lawrence strike, a rejection he attributed to the Wobblies' fear of involving him and the Italian anarchists in the struggle.[21] Nor could he have been pleased that the IWW bypassed him a second time by selecting Tresca to lead the Italian workers during the agitation for Ettor and Giovannitti. Thus, whether Galleani took him seriously or not, because of his role in the Ettor-Giovannitti agitation and the Paterson silk workers' strike that lasted from January to August 1913, Tresca attained national recognition as the most important and feared Italian radical in the United States. By contrast, Galleani remained virtually unknown outside of radical circles until his antiwar activities brought him to the attention of federal authorities.

Soon another issued emerged. As far as the Galleanisti were concerned, Tresca, as a revolutionary syndicalist, by definition was an outsider to the anarchist movement. Then, late in 1913, at a regional conference of the syndicalist Italian Socialist Federation, Tresca declared himself "an anarcho-syndicalist like [Armando] Borghi in Italy."[22] Now Galleani was confronted with the prospect of sharing leadership with a dynamic newcomer who had achieved a national reputation as a fearless strike leader and enjoyed a large personal following of militants. He published a newspaper, *L'Avvenire* (New York), whose circulation of 4,000 exceeded *Cronaca's* circulation of 3,200.[23] Dolgoff was probably correct, therefore, in his belief that Galleani considered Tresca a very serious threat to his position as "pope" of the Italian anarchist movement in the United States.[24]

Indeed, their 1915 polemic revealed that Galleani was determined to undermine Tresca's credibility as an anarchist. The lingering controversy over the Lawrence general strike provided grist for Galleani's mill. In March 1915, after Tresca presented a lecture in Philadelphia on the Ettor-Giovannitti agitation, at which he referred to Postiglione and Speziale as "good young anarchists not yet expert in the excitability of the masses in certain moments," Galleani condemned Tresca for not valuing the collaboration of anarchist propagandists.[25] He hastened to point out, moreover, that in April 1915, Tresca had called himself an "anarcho-syndicalist like Borghi" in one issue of *L'Avvenire*, while stating in another that "neither *La Plebe* nor *L'Avvenire* [his newspapers] have ever been anarchist."[26] As Galleani became progressively more patronizing and insulting—not only toward Tresca but obliquely toward his lover, Elizabeth Gurley Flynn—Tresca abandoned his usual deference toward the veteran revolutionary and began referring to him mockingly as the "the Almighty."[27] Galleani, in his final salvo of 1915, declared Tresca excommunicated from the anarchist movement because he had failed to repent his error in siding with the IWW against the anarchists in Lawrence: "we will no longer travel on the same path: no longer can you be an anarchist—even like Borghi, and I will continue to be an anarchist—like no other."[28]

The 1915 polemic, despite its acrimony, did not cause an immediate break between Tresca and the Galleanisti. That same year, he and several Galleanisti served on the defense committee for Frank Abarno and Carmine Carbone, two anarchists tricked into planting a bomb in St. Patrick's Cathedral by a police agent provocateur.[29] The Galleanisti also participated in the agitation on behalf of Tresca and the other strike leaders and miners imprisoned on trumped-up murder charges during the Mesabi Range strike of 1916.[30] Nevertheless, as confirmed by Schiavina, the 1915 polemic was very important for the future of Italian American anarchism, because it convinced Galleani that Tresca was not a "true" anarchist, meaning he would never be fully accepted or trusted by the Galleanisti.[31]

For Tresca, in contrast, the 1915 polemic did not engender enduring negative feelings or hostile attitudes. Whereas Galleani never forgave his critics (for example, Giacinto Menotti Serrati and Aldino Felicani), Tresca rarely harbored personal grudges against fellow radicals with whom he had exchanged verbal blows. And despite Galleani's contemptuous treatment of him, Tresca never ceased to regard the veteran anarchist with anything less than great admiration and respect.[32] Tresca remained willing, moreover, to provide assistance for personal problems, as in September 1917, when he invited "Gigi" to New York for free medical treatment by his brother Ettore, a well-known physician in the Italian community.[33]

Tresca also never hesitated to help Galleani's followers, especially when they ran afoul of American authorities, and they never hesitated to avail themselves of his assistance when needed. For Tresca was the great "fixer" among the Italian radicals, the man with the best connections with lawyers, politicians, and influential Americans. Although he could not prevent Galleani's deportation in June 1919, Tresca—himself targeted for expulsion—organized the Comitato Italiano Pro-Vittime Politiche in 1919, which obtained legal services from the American Civil Liberties Union and other sources for many Italian radicals. It was Tresca, for example, who persuaded the IWW lawyer Fred Moore to represent Sacco and Vanzetti at their trial in 1921. Nonetheless, the Galleanisti who dominated the Sacco-Vanzetti Defense Committee in Boston distrusted Tresca and denied him a direct role in the defense.[34]

In New York, in 1922, Tresca helped the Galleanisti launch *L'Adunata*—successor to *Cronaca*—by reading proofs, offering technical advice, and giving other assistance. Initially, *L'Adunata* and *Il Martello* advertised one another's fund-raising drives and picnics. Costantino Zonchello, *L'Adunata*'s first editor, belonged to the Comitato Generale di Difesa Contro Il Fascismo, a predominantly anarchist group formed by Tresca in February 1923 that constituted the first Italian anti-Fascist organization in the United States. But comradeship and cooperation between Tresca and the Galleanisti did not survive the year.[35]

Tresca, by now, had distinguished himself as the most-important Italian anti-Fascist leader in the United States. A few weeks before the March on Rome in October 1922, Mussolini himself threatened Tresca with retaliation for *Il Martello*'s attacks against Fascism.[36] The threat was made good with the eager assistance of the federal government, which since 1919 had been preparing a case for Tresca's deportation. In May 1923, after the Italian ambassador lodged an official complaint concerning a scurrilous article about the House of Savoy that Tresca had published in *Il Martello*, the Departments of State, Justice, Labor, and the Postal Service conducted an elaborate campaign to entrap this audacious anti-Fascist. Tried in federal court from November 26 to December 8, 1923, Tresca was convicted not for his article attacking the Italian monarchy but for violating the so-called obscenity statute of the U.S. criminal code. The "crime" for which he received a sentence of a year and a day was having published a two-line advertisement in *Il Martello* for a book in Italian on birth control.[37]

Railroading Tresca proved more difficult than the authorities expected. Because the criminal proceedings against him had obviously been undertaken at the behest of the Fascist government, Tresca's friends in the legal and political establishment, the press, and the American Civil Liberties Union were able to mount an effective protest campaign that compelled an embarrassed President Calvin Coolidge to reduce Tresca's sentence by two-thirds and to acknowledge the original source of the complaint. Tresca's victimization had thus been transformed into the first significant victory for Italian anti-Fascism in the United States.[38]

The Galleanisti—their vision perhaps impaired by the glare of the national spotlight focusing on Tresca—did not see matters that way. During the four months between Tresca's arrest on August 14 and his trial on November 26, *L'Adunata* failed to express a single word of solidarity on his behalf. Later, when several anarchist groups demanded an explanation, *L'Adunata* skirted the issue of its pretrial silence, declaring instead that because Tresca at his trial had "denied ever having been an anarchist or a syndicalist, . . . his misfortunes do not concern us."[39] Tresca had indeed lied about his political allegiance. "The Department of Justice," he explained, "was there in full force to extend its hand and grab Tresca by the neck, shouting 'Ah! You declared yourself an anarchist? So then, it's Ellis Island [for you].' "[40] However, that the Galleanisti should have taken umbrage because Tresca failed to martyr himself only demonstrated the double standard of political morality they applied to their rival.

When Schiavina and seven other disciples were interrogated prior to their deportation with Galleani on June 24, 1919, all eight blatantly lied about the nature of their anarchist beliefs, maintaining that they did "not believe in and had not advocated or taught the destruction of government by forcible means, but were simply believers in the doctrine that government is an unnecessary institution, and had been teaching this doctrine simply as a philosophy."[41] Sacco and Vanzetti also denied they were anarchists when arrested. Furthermore, many other Galleanisti "compromised" their ideals when confronted by the need for self-preservation. After the Palmer raids, dozens of Galleanisti went underground or into exile rather than risk deportation. Some never resurfaced, many restricted their activities, and still others became completely inactive. Only the Galleanisti's predisposition to condemn Tresca's every act can explain why the compromises they sanctioned among their own comrades were unpardonable when committed by him. For years after the birth-control trial, they stubbornly ignored the circumstances that accounted for Tresca's courtroom evasion and continued to condemn him for having denied he was an anarchist in federal court.[42] Within just a few months of his conviction, moreover, the Galleanisti would accuse Tresca of yet another act of heresy.

Released from Atlanta Federal Penitentiary in May 1925, Tresca stopped in Washington while en route to New York and decided to visit the White House like any tourist. Inside the Blue Room, Tresca became surrounded by school children awaiting an audience with President Coolidge. When an attendant, mistaking him for their teacher, instructed Tresca to lead the students into a receiving room, Tresca found himself in the presence of the president. Coolidge briefly greeted the students and exited. Tresca left the White House delighted with his deception. He, the most notorious anarchist in the country—albeit shorn of his beard and 20 pounds lighter—had been standing just a few feet from the president, but Secret Service guards had failed to recognize him.[43] Back in New York, Tresca related this incident to a New York World reporter, who embellished the story, claiming that Tresca wanted to thank Coolidge for commuting his sentence but had time only for a quick handshake.[44] In a subsequent interview for the New Leader, Tresca indicated that the bourgeois press had misrepresented his visit to the White House, and for years to come, at countless anarchist meetings, he would explain that he "had neither the occasion to speak nor shake hands with that salami of a president."[45]

By now conditioned to perceive apostasy in Tresca's every act, the Galleanisti chose to believe the reporter's version rather than Tresca's. Osvaldo Maraviglia, the manager of L'Adunata, insisted that Tresca himself had confirmed his handshake with Coolidge.[46] He also denounced Tresca as a renegade for allegedly telling the New York World that "I seek only freedom—not anarchy, therefore I do not have bombs in my pockets."[47] Besides misquoting his remarks, Maraviglia lamented that Tresca had tarnished the image of the anarchists by associating them with bombs—conveniently forgetting the bomb manual Galleani had advertised regularly in Cronaca Sovversiva since 1905 and the many occasions that comrades known to him had utilized bombs against their enemies: for example, the bombing of Attorney General A. Mitchell Palmer's home in Washington on June 2, 1919, and the Wall Street explosion of September 16, 1920. [48]

Maraviglia's attack received a strong endorsement from Galleani himself, whose chagrin at the prospect of Tresca replacing him as leader of the Italian American anarchists had now become palpable. Writing privately to his disciples at L'Adunata, Galleani urged that Tresca be prevented from obtaining the "dictatorship about which the rogue has dreamed since our departure and the end of

'C.S'. It is well that he should be disabused, and that the unmasking continue until the immutable characteristics of his muddled and Jesuitic countenance are revealed."[49] Galleani's call to undermine Tresca ensured that the story of the "handshake" with Coolidge would acquire the authority of dogma. Eventually, after endless repetition, the tale passed permanently into the realm of anarchist legend. Even anarchists favorably disposed to Tresca came to believe it.[50]

L'Adunata's double standard was soon back in evidence after Armando Borghi, Italy's foremost anarcho-syndicalist, arrived from France in November 1926. Fearing his influence, the Italian Consul of Boston denounced Borghi as an anarchist to the State Department in hope of securing his deportation. Subsequently arrested and interrogated by immigration officials, Borghi—as he himself acknowledged—evaded a direct "yes" or "no" answer when asked if he was an anarchist.[51] Yet Borghi's concealing his political identity to avoid deportation, unlike Tresca's in 1923, did not scandalize the Galleanisti. Among Italian anarchists, the former secretary general of the Unione Sindacale Italiana was second only to Malatesta in prestige and influence, so despite his different tactical orientation, *L'Adunata* wanted to secure Borghi's assistance and invited him to join its editorial staff.[52]

Borghi's alignment with *L'Adunata* had not been widely anticipated. On the contrary, many anarchists had expected Tresca and Borghi—both anarcho-syndicalists and men of action—to cooperate and to revitalize the movement. Tresca, too, had entertained this hope and welcomed Borghi's arrival. However, Tresca's ties with the Communists precluded collaboration.[53] Although he opposed Bolshevik dictatorship, Tresca regarded the Communists as revolutionaries and militant anti-Fascists. More immediately, he considered them essential allies and participants in the Anti-Fascist Alliance of North America (AFANA), which he had helped to resurrect in 1925. All this was unacceptable to Borghi. After meeting Lenin and attending the second Comintern Congress in July 1920, Borghi left Russia convinced that Bolshevism was synonymous with tyranny. Thereafter, he opposed any form of cooperation between anarchists and Communists, and while in France he had already censured Tresca for such associations. Disapproval of Tresca's pragmatic approach to the Communists was an entirely appropriate position for an anarchist; but Borghi resumed his attacks upon arrival without ever trying to persuade Tresca amicably (they met only twice) to sever his ties with AFANA.[54] Furthermore, by lending *L'Adunata* the authority of his prestige, Borghi contributed a measure of political legitimacy and intellectual respectability that lent credibility to the Galleanisti's campaign.

By the late 1920s, Tresca's position as the preeminent Italian anti-Fascist in America was recognized by friend and foe alike. *Il Nuovo Mondo*, the daily newspaper published by social democrats and trade unionists, hailed Tresca in 1926 as "the dean of the antifascist movement."[55] *The Nation* elected Tresca to its Honor Roll for 1927 because he had "repeatedly risked his own life in his successful effort to save fellow Italian-Americans from the long arm of Fascist vengeance."[56] Fascist assessments were even more telling. The Italian Consul

General of New York informed Rome in 1925 that "the most dangerous [antifascist newspaper], because of the able manner in which it is edited and the influence it exercises among certain elements of the people, is *Il Martello*, belonging to the noted Carlo Tresca, who has published it for years and who knows the mentality of the subversives."[57] The Italian ambassador reported the following year that "the three renegades whom we have the greatest interest in having expelled from this country are specifically Tresca, [Vincenzo] Vacirca, and [Pietro] Allegra.[58] By 1928, the Fascist Political Police in Rome referred to Tresca as "the *deus ex machina* of anti-Fascism" in the United States.[59]

The Galleanisti had no appreciation whatsoever of Tresca's importance to the anti-Fascist movement. On the contrary, precisely when Tresca reached the height of his influence and prestige, *L'Adunata* descended to new depths of abuse and slander in its campaign against him. The attack was led by Emilio Coda, a former coal miner who had played a central role in the Galleanisti's bombing conspiracy of 1917–1920. After escaping the Palmer Raids, Coda took refuge in Paris, where together with Schiavina he edited the journal *La Difesa di Sacco e Vanzetti* (1923–1924); he returned to the United States in 1924 to serve as secretary of the Sacco-Vanzetti Defense Committee and became editor of *L'Adunata* in 1925. He continued to influence the paper's orientation after the editorship passed to Borghi and Ilario Margarita between late 1926 and the summer of 1928. Disliked even by some Galleanisti for his rudeness, arrogance, and violent temper, Coda harbored a personal hatred of Tresca that bordered on the pathological—hence the perfect man for character assassination.[60]

Coda's technique had been perfected years earlier by Galleani. After Tresca's release from prison, Coda published an article describing several past exchanges with a "comrade" (unnamed but unmistakably Tresca) that had caused him concern. In 1917, the comrade told Coda to warn Galleani that he was in danger because the Justice Department was translating his antiwar articles. In 1920, when Coda questioned him about another Italian anarchist, the comrade revealed that the Justice Department was offering a reward for the man's capture. A year later, after the conviction of Sacco and Vanzetti, the comrade warned Coda that the Defense Committee in Boston might be arrested. On each occasion, Coda allegedly asked the comrade how he had obtained such information; each time, the latter indicated that he had a confidential source in the Justice Department. Expressing gratitude to the comrade for his warnings on behalf of the Galleanisti never seems to have occurred to Coda. Instead, by neglecting to inform *L'Adunata*'s readers that the comrade in question—as he well knew—did indeed have confidential informants in high places, Coda was intentionally seeking to create suspicion that the comrade could have obtained such sensitive information only if he were a spy in the pay of the Justice Department.[61]

Italian anarchists had always had good reason to fear spies. Since the days of the First International, infiltration of anarchist ranks by spies and agents provocateur greatly facilitated government persecution of the movement. Fear of infiltration and persecution constituted much of the basis for the anti-organizationist tendency that emerged in the late 1870s and 1880s, of which Galleani was the classic exemplar.[62] In more-recent memory, the spy Eugenio Ravarini had penetrated the anarchist circles of *Cronaca Sovversiva* and *L'Era Nuova* (Paterson) in 1919–1920, and—until unmasked by Tresca—his revelations enabled the Justice Department to suppress these anarchists, thereby precipitating the chain of events responsible for the Sacco-Vanzetti case.[63] Even Tresca's conviction in 1923 had been facilitated by a spy working on *Il Martello*'s staff.[64]

Inevitably, there were Italian anarchists who gave automatic credence to Coda's allegations because they had appeared in *L'Adunata*, a source they presumed infallible, or because they disliked Tresca and were inclined to believe the worst about him. Others—not necessarily Treschiani—would never believe Tresca guilty of such an offense unless incontrovertible proof was provided. Since none existed, Coda's only choice was to nurture the seeds of suspicion he had sowed by endlessly repeating his insinuations and accusations and obfuscating their lack of foundation. Coda escalated *L'Adunata*'s campaign in February 1928, after Tresca dared "to attribute deficiencies to Galleani whose name he contaminates merely by pronouncing it."[65] Included among the expletives in Coda's latest barrage was the cryptic word *Pagnacca*.[66] Unknown to ordinary Italians, *Pagnacca* to the *sovversivi* was a code word for spy.[67] Galleani had been the first to use the word *Pagnacca* during his bitter polemic with the socialist Giacinto Menotti Serrati in 1902–1903.[68] Galleani also hurled the epithet "spy" at anarchists such as Aldino Felicani and Erasmo Abate (alias Hugo Rolland), who had dared to criticize him for various reasons.[69] By smearing Tresca with the name "Pagnacca," the irascible acolyte Coda was merely aping his master. However, when incredulous anarchists demanded proof of Tresca's guilt, Coda "clarified" his accusation by reiterating it in revised form: "I have never said that Carlo Tresca is an agent provocateur in the service of the Justice Department; I have never said he is an agent of the Fascist government, nor has anyone at *L'Adunata* ever said it. [If] Tresca said this, he lies. I have said and I say that Carlo Tresca has—willfully—committed an act of SPYING, has acted as a SPY."[70] Tresca's "act of SPYING," Coda charged, involved a photograph of an anarchist sought by the "international police," which Tresca obtained from comrades in New London, Connecticut, and gave to a "lawyer-policeman." Coda refused to provide names. To do so, he argued, would enable Tresca to call the editors of *L'Adunata* spies. Nor did Coda explain why he was repeating an accusation he had already made in 1925, concerning an incident that had taken place in 1921.[71]

In reality, Tresca explained, the incident referred to by Coda had involved not one but two photos: one of "Mike Boda" (real name: Mario Buda), a Galleanista terrorist who perpetrated the deadly Wall Street bombing to avenge the murder indictments against Sacco and Vanzetti; the other of Tresca's own associate, Mario Gioia. The "lawyer-policeman" to whom Tresca entrusted the photographs was actually two attorneys: Fred Moore, who defended Sacco and Vanzetti, and Isaac Shorr, a specialist in deportation cases, who was representing

Borghi at the very time Coda branded Tresca a spy. Although Moore and Shorr were Tresca's personal friends, not even the Galleanisti could suspect them of colluding with the authorities.[72]

The climax of Coda's smear campaign occurred on May 13, 1928, when he presided over a "jury of honor" convened in Hartford, Connecticut, to try Tresca for his "crimes." Tradition among the *sovversivi* specified that a jury of honor be composed of comrades acceptable to all parties involved. But the Hartford jury of honor, with the exception of Felice Guadagni, a respected syndicalist who had served on the Sacco-Vanzetti Defense Committee, consisted of six Galleanisti handpicked by Coda. Nor had Tresca been informed about the intended proceedings. Invited to a "meeting" at the home of Girolamo Grasso, a Galleanista in Hartford, Tresca suspected that something nefarious was afoot and did not attend. No matter—he was tried and convicted in absentia. *L'Adunata*, without even specifying Coda's charges, published a declaration from the jury of honor (minus Guadagni, who refused to sign it), stating: "after the serene documentary statement delivered by Coda, the indisputable corroboration by other depositions from comrades worthy of trust, and the evaluation of Tresca's own absence, . . . the accusations are found to be more than verified."[73]

Some of the most-prominent figures in the international anarchist movement were greatly disturbed by *L'Adunata*'s campaign and incredulous of the charges against Tresca. Emma Goldman wrote to a friend: "I feel that the accusations against Carlo Tresca are false and, as you have correctly observed, prompted by personal motives. I have known Carlo Tresca for many years. . . . To claim that he is a spy is absurd."[74] After *L'Adunata* ignored his request for evidence of Tresca's misdeeds, Harry Kelly, the veteran American anarchist, wrote to Alexander Berkman: "I do not feel I can accept the mere statement of people who are frankly antagonistic to Carlo so I cannot withhold friendly intercourse with him and [still] consider him an honest worker in the movement. . . . He makes statements at times that I do not like but that is an entirely different matter from calling him a spy."[75] When Berkman received a letter from Maraviglia, which had condemned Tresca as a "spy" and "worse than a Communist," he responded: "I must say that the whole thing, and all that is involved in it, makes me very sad. Our whole movement is eaten by an ulcer, which corrodes the best elements and almost paralyses all real work. . . . I refer here to charges, counter-charges, incriminations and recriminations which fill our movement with filth, in almost every country."[76]

Across the spectrum of Italian anti-Fascists, everyone outside the anarchist camp considered *L'Adunata*'s allegations absurd and malicious. On May 27, 1928, a few days after Coda's Star Chamber Court had rendered its verdict, some two thousand Italian anti-Fascists met at Cooper Union in New York to welcome the renowned Italian syndicalist Arturo Labriola, who recently had assumed the editorship of *Il Nuovo Mondo*. After Labriola's speech, a passing reference to Tresca made by the chairman Arturo Giovannitti brought the entire audience to its feet, applauding and shouting "Viva Tresca!" and "parli Tresca!"[77] This spontaneous demonstration revealed how much Tresca continued to be admired and respect by most Italian anti-Fascists. The poet Nino Caradonna expressed the general consensus when he wrote that *L'Adunata*'s campaign "had been launched with the firm knowledge that Tresca was not a spy, but with the sole objective of depriving Tresca of some of the fame he enjoys among the subversive element in America."[78]

Although gratified by such support, Tresca was concerned nonetheless about what the anarchists believed. He did not heed Pietro Allegra and other close associates who advised him to treat *L'Adunata*'s accusations as being too ridiculous to dignify with a response.[79] Tresca understood the sectarian mentality of the Italian anarchists, especially the tendency of the most credulous among them to regard *L'Adunata* as the fount of truth and wisdom. In their eyes, failure to deny the charges of spying would be tantamount to an admission of guilt. So, Tresca blasted back at his detractors with each new accusation, demanding they either prove him a spy or desist.[80] But since the Galleanisti's objective was not to prove Tresca a spy but to destroy his standing in the anarchist movement, *L'Adunata*'s campaign continued unabated. Less-partisan readers of *L'Adunata* and *Il Martello*, meanwhile, had become disillusioned by the sordid conflict, but they lacked the influence to intervene.[81]

Besides the Galleanisti, the only observers rooting for *L'Adunata* to bring down Tresca were the Fascists. Mussolini's political police were delighted with the jury of honor verdict, concluding that "anti-Fascism, which is headed in America by Carlo Tresca, has received a terrible blow. Its major exponent has been definitely liquidated."[82] Fascist hopes grew less sanguine when confidential agents reported that the downfall of Tresca and *Il Martello* should not be anticipated soon "because there are too many people who swear upon the innocence of Tresca despite all the warnings [of *L'Adunata*]."[83] Nonetheless, the Fascists were encouraged by the knowledge that *L'Adunata*'s campaign remained "a substantially important question for the subversive movement in the United States of America, and that the definitive liquidation of Carlo Tresca, imposed upon his followers as well, would administer a moral blow to anti-Fascism which depends so much on Tresca."[84] Fascist hopes for continuing dissension among the *sovversivi* brightened in November 1928, when Armando Borghi escalated his attacks against the Italian AFANA. "Since Tresca is the *deus ex machina* of anti-Fascism," the political police concluded, "to bring down the Alliance means the possibility of bringing down Carlo Tresca."[85] Thanks largely to *L'Adunata*'s latest attacks against Tresca and AFANA, the Fascists became newly optimistic that "American anti-Fascism in nearly dead (dying)."[86]

In 1930, hoping to end the cycle of attack and counterattack, Tresca announced a unilateral cessation of hostilities: "for me the personal polemic is finished."[87] But not even a truce, much less peace, could be secured from *L'Adunata* with the newspaper now under the control of Raffaele Schiavina. The former manager of *Cronaca Sovversiva*, and the man most responsible for creating the personality cult of Luigi Galleani, Schiavina had been deported to Italy together with his mentor in June 1919. After fleeing to Paris in 1923, Schiavina edited his own newspaper, *Il Monito,* before reentering the United States illegally, with Coda's help, in 1928. Throughout his tenure as editor of *L'Adunata* (1928–1971) and beyond, Schiavina lived a clandestine existence, almost never attending public functions, his whereabouts known only to a few trusted comrades.[88]

Nearly a half-century later, Schiavina sought to minimize the ferocity of *L'Adunata*'s campaign against Tresca with a disingenuous assertion that the conflict between them had been merely a typical polemic: "we attacked him; he attacked us."[89] In fact, Schiavina was just as sectarian and unforgiving of rivals as Galleani, and he was as determined as his predecessors to undermine Tresca. Thus, in the early 1930s, *L'Adunata* dredged up old accusations refurbished with new insults: "The affair of the photograph has not been forgotten"; "Tresca asked for and received a pardon from Coolidge"; "violent, idiotic, personal diatribes are Pagnacca's only resource."[90] Tresca responded to "Pope Sartin" with bromides of his own, but then in 1938 he enabled *L'Adunata* to invigorate its campaign by committing the most self-destructive blunder of his political career.

Tresca's uneasy collaboration with the Communists had ended in 1929, when he quit the Anti-Fascist Alliance in disgust with its tactics. The Spanish Civil War transformed him into an implacable foe of Soviet dictatorship, and he missed no opportunity thereafter to fight the Stalinists. In September 1937, Tresca infuriated the Stalinists by assisting the John Dewey Commission that investigated and rejected the charges made against Trotsky during the Moscow purge trials. In February 1938, stirred by the disappearance and apparent murder of Juliet Stuart Poyntz, an American Communist Party founder and Comintern operative whom he had known for years, Tresca publicly accused the Stalinists of her abduction and testified before the Federal Grand Jury investigating the case, claiming that Poyntz had been eliminated because she was disillusioned with Stalinism and "knew too much."[91]

Denounced and threatened in the pages of the *Daily Worker* and *L'Unità Operaia,*[92] Tresca was unafraid of the danger the Stalinists might pose, and he challenged them to do their worst. He seemed far more anxious about the attack he knew would be forthcoming from *L'Adunata* because he had testified before the grand jury. In a self-exculpatory article, Tresca insisted that he had never been, consciously or otherwise, a tool of the government or in its service. Recourse to the federal authorities was "not something pleasant," but "life" sometimes requires "compromises" in order to accomplish what "one is obliged to do," he wrote. "I 'used' the Federal Jury," he explained, "as a platform to speak to the public. I 'used' the Federal Jury to denounce to the world the monstrous crimes of the police system organized by Stalin. I fulfilled a duty. My conscience is clear."[93]

Hoping to calm the gathering storm, Tresca also published a sympathetic letter Emma Goldman had written to him concerning the Poyntz affair: "it's a rather disagreeable job to have to apply to a Capitalist court to expose the Stalinist gangsters. All in all I do not envy your job though I think you should go ahead and expose the disappearance of Miss Poyntz."[94] Goldman's letter provoked a stern reprimand from Schiavina and failed to restrain *L'Adunata*'s denunciation of "Pagnacca" for "an act of collaboration with the police, an act of informing and of spying."[95] "Collaborating with the police," Schiavina declared, "is the foulest form of collaboration with the State."[96] Tresca's good intentions were irrelevant: "Whoever, out of hatred for the Communists, resorts to the office of the bourgeois police, puts himself on a level with the most perverse Communists, and . . . does the work of a spy."[97]

Tresca, in response, accused "Pope Sartin" of never fighting the Communists with anything save words. He denigrated his absence from the front lines of struggle, calling him "a mole, traveling underground" who possessed "the courage of a rabbit."[98] *Il Martello* then published a second letter from Goldman, which underscored the danger Tresca had courted by exposing Stalinist crimes. "It was not your appeal to the authorities that I approved of," she wrote, "but your courage in concerning yourself with [certain] matters, knowing that by lifting the veil from the activities of the GPU you run the risk of losing your life."[99] Tresca reiterated his motives for helping the authorities, and explained to Goldman that the conflict between him and *L'Adunata* was a matter of "old rancor." "The *L'Adunata* group," he lamented, "is blinded by hatred, personal hatred. I absolutely cannot explain it."[100]

Despite his self-justification and Goldman's qualified endorsement, even Italian anarchists who rejected *L'Adunata*'s depiction of him as a "spy" were dismayed that Tresca had willingly provided information to the government. His action, in their view, had violated a sacred tenet of the anarchist creed, no matter how well intended. Even among the Treschiani, many never forgave Tresca for this transgression; some severed their ties with him because of it.[101] In retrospect, the Poyntz affair not only hurt Tresca's reputation among the anarchists but hastened the decline of his career. During the last five years of his life, Tresca lost a good deal of the prestige and influence he had enjoyed in the 1920s.

Whether the Galleanisti understood that Tresca's standing had been diminished by his own actions or believed that their campaign had achieved its objective, *L'Adunata* ceased to attack him after the Poyntz affair. Only Tresca's murder on January 11, 1943, prompted a brief article—on the last page—noting with smug understatement that "with regard to Carlo Tresca's ideas, we always found ourselves on opposite poles from him and his methods."[102] Even in the face of the tremendous outpouring of affection, sympathy, and respect for the slain rebel that emanated from the Italian American and American communities upon his death, the Galleanisti remained silent and apart.[103]

What, in the final analysis, did the Galleanisti accomplish by their long campaign against Carlo Tresca? That the harassment and slander to which they subjected him over the years tarnished his image and reduced his influence among Italian American anarchists cannot be doubted. In the process, however, the Galleanisti sullied their own reputation in the eyes of many anarchist comrades, especially outside of Italian circles. Emma Goldman wrote in 1940 that "the *L'Adunata* people . . . are bigots and narrow-minded to the highest degree."[104] Furthermore, by reinforcing the factional tendencies inherent in the movement, *L'Adunata* weakened Italian American anarchism and diminished its contribution to the anti-Fascist resistance. The Fascists recognized as much in 1928: "the conflict between Carlo Tresca and the anarchists [of *L'Adunata*] has brought considerable disorder not only to the anarchist movement but to the antifascist movement in general."[105] Comprehending that fact, however, was beyond the capabilities of the Galleanisti. They were so "blinded by hatred, personal hatred," as Tresca said, that nothing he had contributed during his 40 years of struggle on behalf of the working class would ever be acknowledged, much less appreciated by them. Thus it is not surprising that throughout the 28 years *L'Adunata* continued to publish following his death, Tresca was never again mentioned in its pages, as if treating him as a nonperson would consign his memory to the scrap heap of history. But as the history of Italian American radicalism continues to be explored and Tresca's role defined, there can be no doubt that toward this end the Galleanisti's campaign failed utterly and completely.

NOTES

1. The most notable of these feuds were the polemic between the anarchists Errico Malatesta and Giuseppe Ciancabilla in 1900, and that between the anarchist Luigi Galleani and the socialist Giacinto Menotti Serrati in 1902–1903. At a lecture in Paterson, New Jersey, one of Ciancabilla's supporters shot Malatesta in the leg. The Galleani-Serrati feud resulted in a fight in Barre, Vermont, at which a socialist shot and killed an anarchist.

2. The essentials of Galleani's anarchist philosophy are given in his *La fine dell'anarchismo?* (Newark, N.J., 1925). For biographical material, see Nunzio Pernicone, "Luigi Galleani and Italian Anarchist Terrorism in the United States," *Studi Emigrazione* 30 (September 1993): 469–88; Ugo Fedeli, *Luigi Galleani: Quarant'anni di lotte rivoluzionarie (1891–1931)* (Cesena, Italy, 1956); Pier Carlo Masini, "La giovinezza di Luigi Galleani," *Movimento Operaio* 3 (May–June 1954): 445–58; Mariella Nejrotti, "Le prime esperienze politiche di Luigi Galleani (1881–1891)," in *Anarchici e anarchia nel mondo contemporaneo: Atti del convegno promosso dalla Fondazione Luigi Einaudi (Turin, 5, 6 e 7 dicembre 1969)* (Turin, Italy, 1971), 208–16; Nejrotti, "Luigi Galleani," in *Il movimento operaio italiano: Dizionario biografico, 1853–1943*, 5 vols., ed. Franco Andreucci and Tommaso Detti (Rome, 1976), 2:418–24; Augusta Molinari, "Luigi Galleani: Un anarchico italiano negli Stati Uniti," *Miscellanea Storica Ligure* 11 (1974): 261–86; Robert D'Attilio, "*La Salute è in Voi*: The Anarchist Dimension," in *Sacco-Vanzetti: Developments and Reconsiderations-1979* (Boston, 1982), 81–83; Rudolph J. Vecoli, "Luigi Galleani," in *Encyclopedia of the American Left*, ed. Mari Jo Buhle, Paul Buhle, Dan Georgakas (New York and London, 1990), 251–53.

3. *Cronaca Sovversiva*, 26 December 1908.

4. For an analysis of the rise of anti-organizationist anarchism in Italy, see Nunzio Pernicone, *Italian Anarchism, 1864–1892* (Princeton, N.J., 1993), 168–202, 238–43, 270–72.

5. *I Morti* (Ancona), 2 November 1899. The last sentence originated with the French revolutionary Auguste Blanqui.

6. Paul Avrich, *Sacco and Vanzetti: The Anarchist Background* (Princeton, N.J., 1991), 52.

7. Raffaele Schiavina insisted on this point; Schiavina, interview by author, New York, 10 January 1974. Over a period of more than fifteen years, the author had many conversations with Schiavina about Galleani, Tresca, Malatesta, and other anarchists. At no time would he acknowledge even the slightest flaw in Galleani.

8. Roberto Michels, *Political Parties: A Sociological Study of the Oligarchical Tendencies of Modern Democracy* (New York, 1966), 326.

9. Galleani's vocabulary was beyond the comprehension of many of his working-class followers. Joe Moro, a devoted Galleanista, admitted: "Galleani . . . was a little deep for a man like me without an education." Alberico Pirani, a highly literate admirer, said: "A lot of people didn't understand Galleani, but they loved him anyway" (Paul Avrich, *Anarchist Voices: An Oral History of Anarchism in America* [Princeton, N.J., 1995], 113, 142).

10. Errico Malatesta, " 'La fine dell'anarchismo?' di Luigi Galleani," *Pensiero e Volontà* (Rome), 1 June 1926, in Malatesta, *Scritti*, 3 vols., ed. Luigi Fabbri (Geneva and Brussels, 1936), 3:234.

11. Sam Dolgoff, interview by author, New York, 8 December 1973; Valerio Isca, interviews by author, New York, 29 October 1973 and 5 June 1975.

12. For Tresca, see Nunzio Pernicone, "Carlo Tresca: Life and Death of a Revolutionary," in *Italian Americans: The Search for a Usable Past*, ed. Richard N. Juliani and Philip V. Cannistraro (New York, 1989), 216–35; Pernicone, "Carlo Tresca and the Sacco-Vanzetti Case," *Journal of American History* 60 (December 1979): 535–47; *Omaggio alla memoria imperitura di Carlo Tresca* (New York, 1943); Dorothy Gallagher, *All The Right Enemies: The Life and Murder of Carlo Tresca* (New Brunswick, N.J., 1988).

13. Concetta Silvestri, a Galleanista, said of him: "Galleani was a very severe man: whatever he says goes" (Avrich, *Anarchist Voices*, p. 107). For descriptions of Tresca's personality, see *Omaggio alla memoria imperitura*.

14. For the best descriptions of Tresca by comrades who knew him intimately, see Arturo Caroti, *Per Carlo Tresca* (Milan, 1916), 28–29, and Arturo Giovannitti, "Ecco Carlo Tresca," *L'Avvenire* (New York), 25 August 1916, reprinted in *Controcorrente*, n.s., 16 (January–February 1960): 3–6.

15. Giovannitti, "Ecco Carlo Tresca."

16. *Cronaca Sovversiva*, 26 November 1910.

17. *Il Proletario*, 5 October 1912; Elizabeth Gurley Flynn, *The Rebel Girl* (New York, 1955), 148.

18. *Cronaca*, 19 October 1912. For Tresca's version, see *Il Proletario*, 19, 26 October 1912.

19. Schiavina, interview.

20. Dolgoff, interview.

21. *Cronaca*, 3 March, 2 October 1915.

22. *Il Martello*, 8 June 1929.

23. *Il Comune* (Philadelphia), June 1912; D'Attilio, *"La Salute è in Voi,"* 81.

24. Dolgoff, interview.

25. *Cronaca*, 3 March 1915.

26. *Cronaca*, 2 October 1915. The April 3 and 10 issues of *L'Avvenire* have not survived, so Tresca's exact words cannot be verified. Probably as a precautionary measure, Tresca, in interviews with the American press, had said: "I am not an anarchist but a syndicalist" (*New York World*, 3 April 1915).

27. *Cronaca*, 2, 30 October, 4 December 1915. Galleani signed his articles attacking Tresca with the pseudonyms Gigi and l'Altissimo. His criticism of Flynn pertained to her

tactics and behavior during the Paterson strike of 1913. Again, Tresca's responses are known only as quoted in *Cronaca*.

28. *Cronaca*, 4 December 1915.
29. Avrich, *Sacco and Vanzetti*, 189.
30. Avrich, *Sacco and Vanzetti*, 189; *Cronaca*, 15, 22, 29 July, 1 August 1916.
31. Schiavina, interview; Schiavina, letter to the author, 15 January 1974.
32. Beatrice Tresca Rapport, interview by author, 12–14 November 1973.
33. Carlo Tresca to Raffaele Schiavina, New York, 25 September 1917. Letter quoted in Bureau of Investigation's summary report of 7 May 1920. See United States Department of Justice, Federal Bureau of Investigation, Tresca file (hereinafter cited as FBI, Tresca file). See also *Il Martello*, 20 July 1919.
34. Pernicone, "Carlo Tresca and the Sacco-Vanzetti Case," 535–47.
35. *Il Martello*, 9 June 1923; Isca, interview, 29 October 1973.
36. *Il Popolo d'Italia* (Rome), 4 October 1922.
37. Dozens of government documents pertaining to the frame-up are found in FBI, Tresca file. See also American Civil Liberties Union, *Foreign Dictators of American Rights: The Tresca and Karolyi Cases* (New York, 1925), 3–8; Pernicone, "Carlo Tresca: Life and Death," 221–23; Gallagher, *All the Right Enemies*, 98–109.
38. See *New Republic*, 16 January 1924, 188; *Baltimore Sun*, 29 January 1925; *New York World*, 17 February 1925.
39. *L'Adunata dei Refrattari* (New York), 5 January 1924.
40. *Il Martello*, 22 December 1923.
41. "The Boston Case," Bureau of Immigration, 1919, INS 54235/36C, as quoted in Avrich, *Sacco and Vanzetti*, 135.
42. Typically, when Tresca was conducting lecture tours devoted to serious issues, the Galleanisti in the audience would change the subject during the question period and demand that he explain why he had denied being an anarchist at his trial. See the unsigned spy report of June 30, 1929, on Tresca's lecture in Cleveland, in Archivio Centrale dello Stato, Ministero dell'Interno, Affari Generali Reservati, 1927–1933, Anno 1929, sez. 1, busta 188 (hereinafter abbreviated as ACS, Min. Int., AGR).
43. Tresca related part of this story in *Il Martello*, 23 May 1925. He gave a more detailed account, taken down almost verbatim by a spy, at a meeting in Cleveland in 1929. See unsigned spy report in ACS, Min. Int., Direzione Generale della Publica Sicurezza (DGPS), AGR, 1927–33, sez.1, anno 1929, busta 188.
44. *New York World*, 11 May 1925.
45. See Cleveland spy report of 30 June 1929, in ACS, Min. Int., DGPS, AGR, 1927–1933, a. 1929, b. 188; Esther Lowell, "Carlo Tresca Home from Jail," *New Leader* (New York), 16 May 1925.
46. *L'Adunata*, 30 May 1925.
47. Ibid.
48. Ibid. Tresca was quoted in the *New York World* (11 May 1925) as saying: "I don't carry bombs—despite the stories of the Mussolini Government. I seek only freedom—not anarchy."
49. Galleani's letter of May 30, 1925, was not published until 13 years later, during another phase of the anti-Tresca campaign. See *L'Adunata*, 20 May 1938.
50. Dolgoff, interview; Joseph Ienuso, letter to the author, Gilroy, Calif., 3 August 1977.
51. See Armando Borghi, *Mezzo secolo di anarchia, 1898–1945* (Naples, 1954), 344–46.

52. After World War II, the Galleanisti would ostracize Borghi because they disapproved of his personal life. See Sam Dolgoff, *Fragments: A Memoir* (Cambridge, England, 1986), 33. Not surprisingly, Borghi's memoirs say little about his association with *L'Adunata* other than to mention that he was a "voluntary collaborator" (Borghi, *Mezzo secolo*, p. 353).

53. *Il Martello*, 4 December 1926; Isca, interviews, 29 October 1973 and 5 June 1975.

54. *Il Nuovo Mondo* (New York), 18 January 1926; Armando Borghi, *Gli anarchici e le alleanze* (New York, n.d.), 15–18, 25–45; *L'Adunata*, 10, 24 March 1928, 6 October 1929.

55. *Il Nuovo Mondo*, 5 September 1926.

56. *The Nation*, 4 January 1928, 4.

57. Consul General of New York to Minister of the Interior, Rome, 10 October 1925, in ACS, Min. Int., DGPS, AGR, a. 1925, b. 130.

58. Italian Ambassador in Washington to Minister of the Interior, Rome, 3 July 1926, in ACS, Min. Int., DGPS, AGR, a. 1926, b. 102. Allegra was an anarcho-syndicalist and Tresca's closest associate on *Il Martello*'s editorial staff; Vacirca, a former socialist deputy, was a member of *Il Nuovo Mondo*'s editorial staff.

59. Report of 6 November 1928, in ACS, Min. Int., Divisione Polizia Politica (hereinafter DPP), Stati Uniti—Anarchici dal 1928 al 1935, b. 13, f. 5.

60. Avrich, *Sacco and Vanzetti*, 61–63, 102–3, 110, 158, 168–69, 215–16; Avrich, *Anarchist Voices*, 118, 131; Isca, interview, 5 June 1975. Additional biographical material is found in the ACS, Min. Int., DGPS, Casellario Politico Centrale (CPC), Emilio Coda, b. 1390. Schiavina (interview) claimed that Coda had an affair with Elizabeth Gurley Flynn after Tresca left her. He assumed that Flynn must have told Coda many "dark secrets" about Tresca, although Coda only "hinted" at what they were, and Schiavina could not remember any specifics. There is no corroborating evidence that Flynn had an affair with Coda, although she undoubtedly knew him through her work for the Sacco-Vanzetti Defense Committee.

61. *L'Adunata*, 4 July 1925.

62. Pernicone, *Italian Anarchism*, 176–78, 185–91, 271–72, et passim.

63. Avrich, *Sacco and Vanzetti*, 178–80.

64. *Il Martello*, 22 December 1923, 23 May 1925.

65. *L'Adunata*, 25 February 1928.

66. Ibid.

67. After Gaetano Bresci assassinated King Umberto I, the anarchists of Paterson exposed a mill worker named Pagnacca, who served as a spy for the Italian Consulate of New York.

68. Luigi Galleani, *Metodi della lotta socialista*, [ed. Raffaele Schiavina] (New York, 1972); Ugo Fedeli, *Luigi Galleani: Quarant'anni di lotte rivoluzionarie, 1891–1931* (Cesena, Italy, 1956), 119–31.

69. Isca, interview, 5 June 1975.

70. *L'Adunata*, 31 March 1928.

71. Ibid. Coda had related the photo incident in *L'Adunata* of July 4, 1925, but his accusation failed to arouse suspicion at the time.

72. *Il Martello*, 29 September 1928.

73. *L'Adunata*, 19 May 1928. The Galleanisti who signed the declaration were Girolamo Grasso (Hartford, Conn.), Giovanni Scussel (Needham, Mass.), Tony Mascioli (Old Forge, Pa.), Domenico Rosati (New York), Frank Guida (New York), and Ilario Bettolo (Chicago).

74. Letter quoted in *Il Martello*, 11 August 1928.

75. Kelly to Berkman, London, 12 November 1928, Alexander Berkman Archive, International Institute for Social History, Amsterdam. Quotation provided by Paul Avrich.

76. Osvaldo Maraviglia to Alexander Berkman, Newark, N.J., 6 July 1928, and Berkman to Maraviglia, New York, 19 November 1928, Berkman Archive, International Institute for Social History, Amsterdam. Information provided by Paul Avrich.

77. *Il Martello*, 2 June 1928.

78. *Il Martello*, 30 June 1928.

79. *Il Martello*, 3, 17, 31 March 1928.

80. *Il Martello*, 23 May 1925; 23, 30 October 1926; 11, 18 February, 3, 17, 31 March, 14 April, 26 May, 2, 9,16, 23, 30 June, and 7 July 1928.

81. Giuseppe Popolizio, letter to the author, Rivesville, W. Va., 8 January 1977.

82. Divisione Polizia Politica, note of 28 June 1928, in ACS, Min. Int., DGPS, CPC, Carlo Tresca, b. 5208.

83. Direttore, Capo Divisione Polizia Politica to Divisione Affari Generali Riservati, 22 October 1928, ibid.

84. Ibid.

85. Untitled report, 6 November 1928, in ACS, Min. Int., Divisione Polizia Politica [DPP], "Stati Uniti-Anarchici dal 1928 al 1935," b. 13, f. 5.

86. Ibid.

87. *Il Martello*, February 8, 1930.

88. For biographical information, see Cenno biografico, Prefettura di Ferrara, in ACS, Min. Int., DGPS, CPC, Raffaele Schiavina, b. 4690; Avrich, *Sacco and Vanzetti*, 63, 82, 122–25, 135, 146–47, 158, 209, 213–14, 217; Paul Berman, "The Torch and the Axe: The Unknown Aftermath of the Sacco-Vanzetti Affair," *The Village Voice*, 17 May 1988.

89. Schiavina, interview.

90. *L'Adunata*, 14 June, 5 July 1930, 2 September 1933.

91. *New York Times*, 8, 9, 22 February, 1938; *Il Martello*, 21 February 1938.

92. See Tresca Memorial Committee, *Who Killed Carlo Tresca?* (New York, 1945), 10–13; Pietro Allegra, *Il suicidio morale di Carlo Tresca* (n.p. [New York], n.d. [1938]).

93. *Il Martello*, 11 April 1938.

94. Italian translation, ibid. For the original, see Gallagher, *All the Right Enemies*, 173–74.

95. *L'Adunata*, 7 May 1938.

96. Ibid.

97. *L'Adunata*, 22 October 1928.

98. *Il Martello*, 9 May 1938.

99. *Il Martello*, 11 July 1938.

100. Ibid.

101. Isca, interview, 5 June 1975; Dolgoff, interview. The author's father, Salvatore Pernicone, who directed an amateur theatrical group (*filodrammatica*) that performed plays for *Il Martello*, broke with Tresca over the Poyntz affair.

102. *L'Adunata*, 16 January 1943. The independent anarchist Erasmo Abate (alias Hugo Rolland), who had angered both Galleani and Borghi, believed that the *L'Adunata* group had murdered Tresca, a theory unworthy of serious consideration; interview by author, 18 June 1975.

103. In addition to the daily American and the Italian-American anti-Fascist press, see *Omaggio alla memoria imperitura.*

104. Emma Goldman to Eleanor Fitzgerald, Toronto, 12 January 1940, in Emma Goldman Papers, Letters 1938–40, Tamiment Institute Library, New York University.

105. Note, Capo Divisione Polizia Politica, 30 September 1929, in ACS, *Min., Int.*, DPP, Stati Uniti—Anarchici dal 1928 al 1935, b. 13, f. 5.

Chapter 3

Italian Workers on the Waterfront: The New York Harbor Strikes of 1907 and 1919

Calvin Winslow

> This is Red Hook, not Sicily. This is the slum that faces the bay on the seaward side of Brooklyn Bridge. This is the gullet of New York swallowing the tonnage of the world.
>
> Arthur Miller, *A View from the Bridge*

In May, 1907, Italian longshoremen in Brooklyn, New York, sparked a strike that ultimately involved thirty thousand workers in an industrywide general strike, a revolt that lasted six weeks. In 1919, they rebelled again. Italian longshoremen in Brooklyn rejected a wage settlement negotiated by the U.S. Shipping Board and their union, the International Longshoremen's Association (ILA). In defiance of the shippers, the government, and their own union, Italian strikers shut down the Brooklyn waterfront and marched over the bridges to Manhattan, where they were joined by other longshoremen, chiefly Irish, in what quickly became another general strike idling 150,000 workers—the largest waterfront strike in U.S. history.

This essay explores these rebellions and the radicalism of the Italian longshoremen who led them. It also considers these Italian strikers in relation to the other ethnic and racial groups in the waterfront workforce, in particular the African American and Irish longshoremen. In addition, it places these longshoremen within the context of the working-class radicalism that developed in the United States in these years. Finally, it documents the contributions of these workers to the development of Italian American radicalism in this crucial decade.

These were the years of great strikes, characterized by mass involvement and direct action. These strikes were often led by immigrants and were multinational in composition. Workers challenged managerial authority, even when their demands were "pure and simple," that is, related strictly to wages and working conditions. Such challenges could quickly become "all or nothing" movements; they frequently spilled out of workplaces and into working-class neighborhoods. They reflected the growth of class consciousness among American workers and the widespread development of a radical spirit. As a result, ethnic isolation was often broken down and new solidarities were established.[1]

The traditional unions, foremost the craft unions of the American Federation of Labor (AFL), were often swept up in these movements. "One Big Union" increasingly was a popular demand, and the movement for industrial unions sometimes seemed irresistible. The conservative AFL leaders—who prided themselves in collaborating with the employers and the state, who insisted on the sanctity of contracts, on jurisdictional division by craft, and on the authority of the trade union leaders—were frequently rejected.[2]

Longshoremen were powerful workers. They could shut down harbors and tie up the world's commerce.[3] They were not always victorious, however, and they rarely fought in circumstances they chose. Sometimes even their own unions were beyond their control. This was the case in the ILA, the AFL union that came to dominate waterfront unionism on the East and Gulf Coasts.

In the 1920s, gangsterism was established on the New York waterfront. Powerful images shape our impressions of this development. The 1951 film *On the Waterfront* recalled "president for life" Joe Ryan, the West Side Irish gangster who dominated the ILA.[4] Similarly, lurid tales from the Brooklyn side revealed a union that was the property of the Anastasia brothers and "Murder, Inc."[5] Gangsterism, however, was not inevitable. The history of these strikes shows that there were alternatives to crime and corruption, as well as to Jim Crow and the right-wing unionists of the ILA. Crime and corruption were not something inherent in the nature of the work, nor were they determined by the structure of the industry; certainly their source was not the workers themselves. This becomes clear when we view the history of these strikes "from the bottom up."

In the 1907 strike, workers of all occupations, from all parts of the harbor, blacks as well as whites, all the ethnic groups, united in a general strike for 10 cents an hour more in pay—and an industrial union.[6] In 1919, Italian longshoremen in Brooklyn rejected a wage settlement negotiated by the ILA and the U.S. Shipping Board, which was still empowered with wartime authority. The longshoremen called the settlement the "Woolworth award," a raise of 5 cents an hour on regular work, 10 cents on overtime (5 and 10!). This strike idled 650 ships in the port, including 50 passenger liners.[7] It produced a remarkable display of working-class solidarity and internationalism. These strikes each produced movements for industrial unionism, movements that were multinational and implicitly democratic. In the end, the strikes were defeated. This, however, does not diminish their significance, nor does it invalidate the demands and aspirations of the longshoremen.

* * *

The New York Harbor included some seven thousand miles of waterfront along both sides of the Hudson River, the East River, and along the Brooklyn waterfront to Bay Ridge. By the turn of the twentieth century, it was the world's largest and busiest port—a vast complex of piers, warehouses, and railroad terminals. Abutting these work sites was a series of working-class neighborhoods.[8]

The new ocean liners arriving at the piers of the Cunard, North German Lloyd, and White Star Lines were symbols of modernity. These ships represented the highest levels of technology. They were the results of the fierce competition between the giant steamship companies, including J. P. Morgan's new shipping trust, the International Merchant Marine, founded in 1902.[9] The docks, however, were old-fashioned and mechanization was rare. The shippers lobbied to have piers extended farther and farther into the rivers to accommodate ever larger ships. The *Titanic* was bound for the White Star Line's Chelsea piers. But on the docks, the work was primitive. It was heavy, grueling and dangerous. The hours were long; men sometimes worked 20 hours in a stretch or more. Other jobs would last only a few hours. Longshoremen were required to stay on a job until it was done. Then, however, they might wait days, or weeks, for the next job. Consequently, the longshoremen feared unemployment; it created continuous insecurity, and, whatever the rate of pay, reduced their standard of living.[10]

The shippers considered the longshoremen unskilled common laborers, and thus hired them as casual workers, one job at a time. They contended that shipping timetables demanded rapid turnarounds, but that the seasons, the seas, and the tides made arrivals and departures unpredictable. Still, "the ship must sail on time!"[11] The leaders of the ILA supported this position.[12]

The shippers hired the longshoremen in early morning "shape-ups," that is, in gatherings of longshoremen at the heads of the piers. Italian longshoreman Rosario Ferrintino said of a Brooklyn shape-up in the 1920s, "It was bad, very bad." Thousands of men would gather in Columbia Street in Red Hook, often overflowing up Carroll, President, and Union Streets. The police were always on hand to keep order. "They harassed the men," recalled Ferrintino. "They beat them with sticks."

The foremen arrived at five and six in the morning, looking for specialists and favored gangs. When the locations of work were discovered, or announced, the longshoremen would stampede to those piers for another shape-up. "The foreman might announce he needs 100 men," said Ferrintino. "Down at the pier there are 1000."[13]

Charles Barnes, the foremost investigator of the industry, estimated that in 1915 for every job in New York Harbor there were three longshoremen.[14] This did not count transient laborers and men from other trades. In such circumstances, longshoremen would fight for their survival.

Ethnic rivalry intensified competition for work on the waterfront. The working class neighborhoods that crowded waterfront piers and warehouses reflected not just the occupations of the workers but also the racial and ethnic segregation of American society. German longshoremen and their families lived in the tenements along the Hoboken docks on the New Jersey side of the Hudson River. Chelsea in Manhattan was the Irish stronghold. The South Brooklyn district of Red Hook was Italian. There were large numbers of Polish longshoremen in Greenpoint.[15]

Still, racial and ethnic boundaries were not altogether rigid. There were Irish longshoremen everywhere. Scandinavian longshoremen were scattered among the Italian streets of Red Hook. Italians were increasingly found in Hoboken and Jersey City. African Americans fought for jobs and homes throughout the harbor. In Chelsea, at the turn of the century, settled immigrants, some second- and third-generation Americans, were joined by newcomers from Ireland. The New Immigrants of the late nineteenth century, then, were not all from southern and eastern Europe.[16] Interestingly, the new Irish were sometimes radical nationalists from the counties of western Ireland. Dockside neighborhoods were almost always in transition. They were far from stable and only rarely homogeneous. Segregation was the rule on the New York waterfront, and the workers were divided. Segregation inevitably produced conflict. "There was a time," black longshoremen told investigator Franklin Frazier, "when a Negro could not walk down Atlantic Avenue," the street leading to the Red Hook waterfront.[17] The difficulties such divisions presented for trade unions are obvious.

The Irish constituted the longshoremen of longest standing. They established their presence before the Civil War. The antiblack racism of the Irish was legendary. They began driving blacks from the waterfront in the 1840s and 1850s. Then, in the New York City draft riots of 1863, they took advantage of the turmoil to introduce "whites-only" rule on the waterfront. Committees of the Longshoremen's Association patrolled the piers in the daylight hours, insisting that "the colored people must and shall be driven to other parts of industry, and that work on the docks . . . shall be attended to solely and absolutely by members of the 'Longshoremen's Association' and such white laborers as they see fit to permit on these premises." After sundown, these "committees" were replaced by parties of men and boys, including longshoremen, which were responsible for a number of the rioters' most-grisly killings.[18]

When Italian immigrants entered the waterfront workforce, they were also categorized as "colored." Barnes expressed the prevailing prejudice when he classified Italian longshoremen as "inferior workers" who, because of their "low standard of living" and their "inability to manage strikes" were also responsible for "the deterioration of the occupation."[19] When a *Brooklyn Eagle* writer reported in May 1907 that three gangs of "white men" had been hired to replace strikers on Brooklyn's East Central piers, he meant that Irish were replacing Italians.[20] "Race" relations on the waterfront were complex and always shifting. Some hiring foremen apparently preferred African Americans to Italians, alleging the former were stronger workers. But this was not the norm. At first, apparently, Italians worked willingly with African Americans; by 1920, black longshoremen informed Frazier that Italians, "the first to admit the Negroes," were "assimilating the prejudices of the white men, in order apparently to insure their own standing."[21]

The employers responded to strikes with strikebreakers, and they consciously fueled ethnic rivalries. Consider just the first days of the 1907 strike. Brooklyn shippers, for example, hired Italian strikebreakers on the Ward and Mallory Line piers to replace striking African American longshoremen.[22] On the Barber Line piers, African Americans were hired to replace Italian longshoremen.[23] The *Eagle* reported a contingent of Russian Jews, led by a rabbi, replacing Italians on the Atlantic docks. It also called attention to "scores of scrub women [predominantly Irish] gathered up in the city . . . performing the work usually done by the striking stewards." French sailors were discovered working on Manhattan piers; Belgian ships carried their own longshoremen.[24]

The results could be lethal. The first casualty of the 1907 strike was Joseph Bovano, a housepainter. He was killed as he and his son attempted to make their way home from work in Chelsea on the White Star Line pier. They were attacked by a crowd of Irish as they boarded a streetcar on 23rd Street and 11th Avenue.[25]

There were, however, factors that united longshoremen. These included the poverty of the waterfront neighborhoods, the chronic unemployment and the fear this produced. The horrendous working conditions; the grinding, dangerous work; the experience of casual labor; and the shape-up also determined the outlook of longshoremen. In addition, the gangs shaped the longshoremen's identity. Longshoremen worked in gangs, often groups of a dozen or more, where relationships were intimate and intense. Cooperation was an absolute necessity—life depended on it. All this produced a common identity and created a collective consciousness.

Moreover, although racial and ethnic segregation was a fact, observers simultaneously noted the "cosmopolitan character" of the waterfront worker. According to Barnes, "the work of the ordinary longshoreman [took] him to so many parts of the port" that there was a "continual interchange of individuals and nationalities in almost every locality."[26] Class consciousness on the waterfront developed rapidly in these circumstances, though it was almost always partial and inconsistent. Nevertheless, there were times when the longshoremen's identity transcended craft, and locality, as well as race and ethnicity. The slogan of the 1907 strike was: "We are all longshoremen!"[27]

* * *

Italians from the Lower East Side worked throughout the harbor, but the majority of Italian longshoremen came to live near where they worked, in Red Hook, adjacent to the Erie and Atlantic basins, and southward along the Brooklyn waterfront to the Bush Terminal piers and Bay Ridge.

Italian immigrants, wrote an early historian, lived in "wretched tenements" along the waterfront, "not because they like to, but because they are too poor to go elsewhere."[28] One small house on President Street in Red Hook, for example, was home to 25 longshoremen in 1910.[29] These neighborhoods, according to Frederick Hersey, a manager at the Bush Terminals, constituted a "reserve." He said, "The greater part of the Italian labor comes from a district of its own, and it is very easy to draw from that district."[30]

Italians initially "invaded" the waterfront workforce as strikebreakers.[31] They found work in 1887 in the course of "the Big Strike," the revolt of Irish longshoremen, led by the Knights of Labor.[32] One ironic result of the Knights of Labor defeat was that a number of shippers deliberately adopted a policy of hiring only Italians, or only African Americans, as a way of eliminating the Irish, whom they viewed as the fomenters of trade unionism on the waterfront. In the 1890s, there were new invasions, and by 1910, Italians were virtually equal in number with the Irish, constituting more than a third of the waterfront workforce.[33]

When Italians worked on the piers as individuals, they were treated in a way analogous to blacks—they worked at the least-skilled tasks and were consigned to menial work. According to Barnes, they were rarely assigned to work on the ships' decks. The tendency, however, was for Italians to work on all-Italian piers, such as those of the Kerr Line. By 1915, the majority of Italian longshoremen worked on all-Italian piers or in occupations dominated by Italians. Coaling, for example, was virtually all Italian. The all-Italian piers and occupations were frequently the least desirable—such as coaling and work in the coastal and seasonal trades.[34]

The status, then, of the Italian-American longshoreman was contradictory. On all-Italian piers, Italian longshoremen worked in all capacities on the docks and the ships, often under the supervision of Italian foremen. This was segregation, of course, but the Italians used such segregated piers to develop bases of workplace activism. They formed their own local unions and acquired trade union experience. By 1906, there was an Italian local union in Brooklyn.[35] It was affiliated with the Irish-led Longshoremen's Union Protective Association (LUPA). All this would have been impossible for Italian longshoremen had they worked in isolation from one another, a minority scattered throughout the harbor.

The Italian immigrant longshoremen, then, made the best of their situation. They fused their experience in the United States with the traditions of their homeland, and they became, when their numbers allowed it, the backbone of the movement for industrial unionism in New York Harbor.[36]

* * *

On May Day 1907, the New York World announced a record number of immigrants arriving in the port: "yesterday . . . more than 15,000 [migrants] . . . got their first view of the city." The paper predicted 150,000 more would arrive within the month.[37] At the same time, the New York Times reported 15,000 migrants were waiting on ships in order to disembark in the harbor. It estimated that the largest single group among them was from Sicily and the south of Italy.[38]

New York City's papers also reported on May Day activities around the world, that is, on workers' demonstrations and protests, including in the United States. They did not mention, however, the demonstrations of Italian longshoremen in Brooklyn. These May Day marchers, carrying red flags and the flags of various countries, were demanding higher wages, and their numbers grew as longshoremen quit work and joined the demonstrations.[39]

There was widespread dissatisfaction with wages in the spring of 1907, and this led to conflict in all parts of the harbor.[40] Unemployment was low and work was plentiful. Consequently, there were strikes and "all sorts of rumors of strikes," reported the *Eagle*. Emboldened longshoremen attempted to push their wages up, one job at a time, one dock at a time. Black longshoremen on the Ward and Mallory Lines were already on strike on May Day, despite attempts to replace them with white strikebreakers.[41]

This pattern of strikes changed as a result of the May Day marches. In the first of these, a crowd of Italian longshoremen marched through Brooklyn's Atlantic docks carrying red flags, "only to be driven from the Union Stores [warehouses] by armed superintendents."[42]

Then they crossed the Brooklyn Bridge. In Manhattan, hundreds of striking Italian longshoremen from Brooklyn were reported in Battery Park. Again, they carried red flags, Italian flags, Irish, German, and American flags, and "dividing their forces and cheering vociferously, one section attempted to march up West Street to clear out the longshoremen on the North River (Hudson) in a sympathetic strike."[43] Another group went up the East River front. More marchers were reported on May 2; hundreds of Italians marched along the Clinton Street wharves in Brooklyn, demanding that all work be stopped.[44]

This was more than simply a strike. It was also a demonstration of immigrant laborers, as well as a May Day appeal for working-class solidarity. "There is a general impression along the waterfront," reported the *Eagle*, "that there will be serious trouble before this strike is settled."[45] Furthermore, the report continued, "a peculiar feature" had emerged. "The Irishmen are joining issue with the Italians."[46]

This happened again, on a larger scale, in 1919. Impatient with contract negotiations then proceeding in Washington, D.C., Italian longshoremen in Brooklyn struck on October 5. They returned to work; however, their dissatisfaction with the results of the negotiations between the ILA and the U.S. Shipping Board caused them to strike again. This time they crossed the bridges, took their picket lines to the Chelsea piers, where they again drew out the Irish and together proceeded to shut down the harbor.[47]

The longshoremen's strikes of 1907 and 1919 in New York Harbor were not ordinary strikes. These conflicts were intense and radical; they involved significant participation by rank-and-file longshoremen, as well as their family members, including women and children, and their neighbors.

Violence was common. When John Riley, an ILA district leader, waded into a crowd of strikers on the first day of the 1919 strike, ordering them back to work, he was beaten and left unconscious in a mud puddle.[48] The strikers were confronted everywhere with strikebreakers protected by the police and, in 1919, the threat of the U.S. Army. In 1907, in the Williamsburg section of Brooklyn, longshoremen attempted with pickets to close down the waterfront. According to the press, this escalated into "savage rioting" when on May 7, some two thousand sugar workers at the Sugar Trust's American Sugar Refining Company walked out in a wildcat strike. The company brought in Italian strikebreakers. The two strikes merged in the streets, and by the end of the day, the *World* reported "fifty wounded" in a "pitched battle" as longshoremen and refinery workers "rioted from daylight until dark." "The strikers," the report continued, "were armed with monkey-wrenches, iron bars and big sticks and lay in wait in doorways for the hundreds of strikebreakers. . . . *Ten thousand sympathizers with the strikers looked on.*"[49]

On May 11, 1907, in Manhattan, audacious strikers seized a ship and attacked the strikebreakers working on it. The strikers "rushed the gates" of the 34th Street pier "when the foremen opened them to bring in freight in the morning" and stormed the big liner *Campagnia*. The police and supervisors were reported to have fired their weapons, but they were unable to stop the strikers who, for a short time, took control of the ship. Several strikers entered the hold of the ship where they were alleged to have destroyed property and set the ship on fire.[50]

Sometimes there were peaceful conclusions. On May 18, 1907, three hundred strikebreakers quit work on the White Star Line piers and "marched to Greenwich Hall, the union's headquarters." Jeremiah Condon, a LUPA delegate, met them. "It was decided that they should parade to the headquarters of the White Star Line on Broadway. . . . All the strikebreakers being Italian, an Italian flag was obtained and the march began."[51]

Such conflicts often involved clashes between the ethnic groups. But there was also conflict within the various communities, including the Italian communities. Again in Brooklyn, in 1907, Sanci Leli, a striker, was killed in a cellar on Columbia Street, "hacked to death," according to the press, by strikebreakers. Leli was reported to have "wanted to continue the strike." He said, "It was time for all workmen to recognize unionism and American methods." But Markel Basilio, according to police, said he was against the strike: "he was a strikebreaker . . . he was going to make a great deal of money . . . he would become a great padrone."[52] Basilio was charged with the murder. A similar conflict took place on East 109th Street in Manhattan, when Vito Franolo, a union longshoreman, attempted to kill Philip Coggiano but hit a bystander, a young boy, instead. Franolo accused Coggiano, identified in reports as a *padrone*, of supplying strikebreakers for the steamship companies and sought revenge in the fight that followed.[53]

Il Proletario, an Italian American socialist newspaper, exposed Italian labor contractors who organized strikebreakers, as well as the Italian bankers who financed them and the Italian newspapers that carried their advertisements.[54] *Il Proletario* also supported the Irish longshoremen of LUPA, who eventually took formal leadership of the strike. So did the Brooklyn Italians.[55] On May 10, 1907, the police estimated seven thousand Italian longshoremen in Prospect Hall in South Brooklyn, overflowing into the streets. "For three hours," reported the *Eagle*, "they were harangued by Italian orators . . . not a word of English was spoken." The strike leaders' speeches were greeted with "the wildest kind of cheering and howling, waving of banners and tossing of hats in the air." These Italian strikers joined LUPA en masse—requesting and receiving, the following day, 10,300 union badges.[56]

James Connolly, the Irish revolutionary, came to New York in 1907 to work for the Industrial Workers of the World (IWW). He was impressed with the radicalism of these workers and was optimistic about recruiting New York longshoremen to the IWW's Marine Transport Workers Union (MTWU). Even when the strike was defeated, he predicted that ten thousand of these workers, including significant numbers of Italians, would join the "One Big Union."[57]

The 1919 strike was equally radical. By that year, the ILA, an AFL union that originated in the Great Lakes, represented New York longshoremen. The union was largely imposed upon them, top down, as a result of the wartime collaboration of the ILA, the shippers and the government. The ILA opposed strikes.[58]

T. V. O'Connor, the international president of the ILA, immediately ordered the 1919 strikers back to work. "This is not a strike," he insisted. Instead, it was the work of "the Italian element, aided by German sympathizers," men from "166 Sackett Street in Brooklyn," the Red Hook headquarters of the IWW.[59] The press discovered a "bolshevik conspiracy," led by foreigners, chiefly Italians, and members of the IWW.[60] Samuel Gompers, president of the AFL, wired the strikers, warning that the strike violated "the fundamental principle of the American Federation of Labor. The agreement to abide by the award [of the U.S. Shipping Board] was a sacred contract."[61]

Nonetheless, in 1919, the IWW—victimized by state repression, including the Palmer Raids, and also by local courts and police, as well as vigilantes—was in no position to lead such a colossal strike. In fact, the strike was not led by the IWW, nor was it a Bolshevik conspiracy. It was, however, a rank-and-file rebellion, and very radical indeed.

In a series of mass meetings, thousands of longshoremen turned out to support the strike, voice their demands and denounce the union leaders. At one such meeting, John Hylan, the Tammany mayor of New York, appeared, urging the longshoremen to return to work. With him, he brought Paolo "Paul Kelly" Vaccarelli, the first Italian American to rise to the rank of vice president in the ILA. Vaccarelli, according to the *Eagle*, "his fingers sparkling with diamonds," was, "a picturesque survival of the old East Side gangsters."[62] The *New York Call* reported "four times he tried to swing the Italians to his side." He spoke to them "in Italian . . . he translated the Mayor's statements." But the strikers "overwhelmingly disapproved his recommendations . . . to go back to work [which] repeatedly brought the same old 'No!' "[63]

James Connolly's hopes to recruit large numbers of radical longshoremen to the IWW did not materialize. Still, the IWW established a modest presence. In the absence of official support for the strike, the IWW served as a center for the Brooklyn strikers.

The *Brooklyn Eagle*, investigating the anti-Red hysteria of the press and the authorities, sent a reporter for a firsthand account of the IWW: "He had no difficulty locating its headquarters. . . . It does not attempt to hide itself. It is in a congested Italian neighborhood. In a window above an Italian fruit and vegetable store is a large colored sign reading 'Industrial Workers of the World.' "[64]

The reporter entered the building, climbed the stairs, and found a small room. His description must have been meant to reassure worried readers. The room was "not altogether clean, but clean enough." The men there, two or three dozen, "talked volubly, but without disorder, in Italian. These men, although they wore black and dark-colored suits and usually no collars, gave an altogether clean impression."[65]

On other days, during the strike, Italian longshoremen gathered in large numbers beneath this office. They sought information, debate, and direction. The *Eagle* reported there were times when "*thousands* of Italian longshoremen" would surround the Sackett Street IWW hall, apparently in spontaneous, informal strike rallies. The IWW claimed it recruited twelve hundred Italian longshoremen in the course of the strike, not, if true, an insignificant number.[66]

* * *

Against the odds, the longshoremen were able to unite in 1907 and 1919; their strikes showed the power this unity gave them. It is important to stress, however, that this unity involved more than the simple substitution of class consciousness for racial, ethnic, and sectional consciousness. There was, in fact, a remarkable increase in the level of class consciousness of the longshoremen. This consciousness, though, developed not just in the conflict between the longshoremen and the shippers. Class consciousness also developed within the various ethnic communities. The ethnic mobilizations—the Italian May Day marchers, for example—were an expression of this.

These strikers confronted, after all, not just employers and the police. They lived in divided communities, which included hostile labor contractors, the *padrone*, strikebreakers from every group, ethnic trade unionists, clergy, and politicians, nearly all of whom opposed the strikes.

The mobilizations of 1907 and 1919 began within the separate groups of longshoremen and proceeded through them. They produced harborwide, rank-and-file rebellions. In these strikes, independent (that is, separate, racially and ethnically distinct) mobilizations and organization, far from impeding working class solidarity, were indispensable components in the movement for industrial unionism. Consequently, considering longshoremen in these strikes, racial and ethnic and class consciousness were intertwined; they cannot be counterposed.

The longshoremen's strikes of 1907 and 1919 were led by immigrants, blacks and whites, and rank-and-file workers. These workers were far from "tractable." Red Hook—the Italian Quarter—was the center of waterfront radicalism. The Italian longshoremen were the dynamic group in the strikes. They had the courage, ability, and audacity to transform the local agitations of March 1907 and October 1919. They were capable of identifying with other groups of longshoremen, and, in spite of staggering barriers to common action, they succeeded in drawing them into the general strikes.

The Italians brought, with their May Day red flags, imagination, commitment, and rebelliousness to the labor movement in New York Harbor.

*****

The strikes of 1907 and 1919 were defeated—the longshoremen, fighting in the very shadows of Wall Street, were outlasted and overpowered. The consequences of these defeats were long lasting. Other workers would achieve industrial unions, although almost a generation later, in the upheavals of the 1930s. The New York longshoremen never would. There was not another major strike in the harbor for 20 years.[67]

In these years, crime and corruption prevailed on the New York waterfront. Beginning in the 1920s, Irish and Italian gangs cooperated in carving up the waterfront. The shippers and the American Federation of Labor allowed this; they too opposed industrial unions. Joe Ryan personally presided over both the New York State and the New York City labor federations in these years.[68]

The longshoremen, however, continued to challenge this system. The results were mixed. Before World War II, brave longshoremen organized a "Rank-and-File Committee." But the best-known member, Pete Panto, an Italian American from Brooklyn, was murdered, his body dumped in a lime pit in New Jersey.[69] The opposition of African American members of ILA Local 968 to Jim Crow on the waterfront constituted an early chapter of the Civil Rights movement.

There were wildcat strikes following the end of World War II. Mary Heaton Vorse, the veteran labor journalist, covered these. She reported the prevalence of favoritism and casual work—"no matter how long he's worked on the docks, every man is hired fresh every day"—as well as deprivation and the threat of unemployment. She revealed the collaboration of the union leadership and the shippers. She exposed Joseph Ryan, "the President for Life of the International Longshoremen's Association" and his belief that "the system" was "best suited for the port of New York." She called these strikes a "revolt" and gave voice, again, to the thousands of "anonymous longshoremen . . . still living for the day of liberation from this system."[70]

NOTES

I would like to thank Gil Fagiani for his help in translating from *Il Proletario.*

1. See Charles Barnes, *The Longshoremen* (New York: Survey Associates, 1915); Edwin Fenton, *Immigrants and Unions, A Case Study: Italians and American Labor, 1870–1920* (New York: Arno Press, 1975); and David Montgomery, *The Fall of the House of Labor* (New York: Cambridge University Press, 1987).

2. David Montgomery, "The New Unionism and the Transformation of Workers' Consciousness in America," in *Workers' Control in America* (New York: Cambridge University Press), 91–112.

3. See E. J. Hobsbawm, "National Unions on the Waterside," in *Labouring Men* (New York: Anchor Books, 1967), 242.

4. Eli Kazan, director, *On the Waterfront*, 1951.

5. Colin Davis, "All I Got's a Hook," in *Waterfront Workers: New Perspectives on Race and Class*, ed. Calvin Winslow (Urbana: Illinois University Press, 1998), 138.

6. See Calvin Winslow, "Men of the Lumber Camps Come to Town: New York Longshoremen in the Strike of 1907," in Winslow, *Waterfront Workers*, 123–87.

7. See Calvin Winslow, "On the Waterfront: Black, Italian, and Irish Longshoremen in the New York Harbor Strike of 1919," in *Protest and Survival: Essays for E. P. Thompson*, ed. John Rule and Robert Malcolmson (New York: New Press, 1993), 355–93.

8. See Barnes, *Longshoremen*.

9. See Ron Chernow, *The House of Morgan* (New York: Atlantic Monthly Press, 1990), 145.

10. Barnes, *Longshoremen*, 75.

11. See Ernest Poole, "The Ship Must Sail on Time," *Everybody's Magazine*, August 1908, 176–86.

12. Committee on Industrial Relations, 3, (Washington, D.C., 1916), 2064. (Hereinafter *CIR*).

13. City University of New York Oral History Project, Tamiment Library, New York University.

14. Barnes, *Longshoremen*, 72.

15. Ibid., 3.

16. David Brundage, "The 1920 New York Dockers' Boycott: Class, Gender, Race, and Irish American Nationalism" (unpublished paper, in author's possession).

17. Franklin Frazier, "The Negro Longshoremen" (unpublished manuscript, 1921, Russell Sage Foundation, New York), 4.

18. Iver Bernstein, *The New York City Draft Riots* (New York: Oxford University Press, 1990), 27–28.

19. Barnes, *Longshoremen*, 7–12.

20. *Brooklyn Eagle*, 2 May 1907.

21. Frazier, "Negro Longshoremen," 27.

22. *Brooklyn Eagle*, 2 May 1907.

23. *Brooklyn Eagle*, 3 May 1907.

24. *Brooklyn Eagle*, 9 May 1907; *New York Times*, 12, 28 May 1907; *New York Evening Journal*, 13 May 1907.

25. *New York Times*, 5 May 1907.

26. Barnes, *Longshoremen*, 10, 27.

27. *Brooklyn Eagle*, 10 May 1907.

28. Antonio Mangano, *Sons of Italy* (New York: Missionary Education Movement, 1917), 24.

29. Barnes, *Longshoremen*, 7–12.

30. *CIR*, 3, 2095.

31. Franklin Frazier used this expression; Frazier, "Negro Longshoremen," 4.

32. See New York State, *Fifth Annual Report of the Bureau of the Statistics of Labor* (Albany, N.Y., 1887).

33. Barnes, *Longshoremen*, 5.

34. U.S. Census, 1910, NARA, Microfilm Publications, T624, reel 956; Barnes, *Longshoremen*, 115.

35. Barnes, *Longshoremen*, 115.

36. See Donna R. Gabaccia, *Militants and Migrants: Rural Sicilians Become American Workers* (New Brunswick, N.J., Rutgers University Press, 1988), and Rudolph J. Vecoli, "Italian American Workers, 1880–1920: Padrone Slaves or Primitive Rebels?" in *Italian*

Americans: New Perspectives in Italian Immigration and Ethnicity, ed. S. M. Tomasi (New York: Center for Migration Studies, 1977), 25–49.

37. *New York World*, 1 May 1907.
38. *New York Times*, 3 May 1907.
39. *Brooklyn Eagle*, 1 May 1907; Fenton, *Immigrants and Unions*, 253.
40. *Brooklyn Eagle*, 1 May 1907.
41. Ibid., 2 May 1907.
42. Ibid.
43. Ibid.
44. Ibid.
45. Ibid., 4 May 1907.
46. Ibid.; *New York Times*, 11 May 1907.
47. *New York Call*, 8 October 1919.
48. *New York Times*, 10 October 1919.
49. *New York World*, 8 May 1907 (emphasis added).
50. *New York Times*, 11 May 1907.
51. Ibid., 14 May 1907.
52. *New York Evening Journal*, 13 May 1907.
53. *New York World*, 9 May 1907.
54. *Il Proletario*, 26 May 1907.
55. Ibid., 2 June 1907.
56. *Brooklyn Eagle*, 10 May 1907; *New York Evening Journal*, 16 May 1907.
57. *Industrial Union Bulletin*, 1 February 1908.
58. See John R. Commons, "The Longshoremen of the Great Lakes," *Labor and Administration* (New York, 1913): 267–68. See also Maud Russell, *Men Along the Shore: The I.L.A. and Its History* (New York: Brussel and Brussel, 1966).
59. *New York Times*, 10 October 1919.
60. *New York Call*, 24 October 1919.
61. AFL Records, *The Samuel Gompers Era*, "Longshoremen," reel 39, *New York Call*, 22 October 1919.
62. *Brooklyn Eagle*, 16 October 1919.
63. *New York Call*, 22 October 1919.
64. *Brooklyn Eagle*, 12 October 1919.
65. Ibid.
66. Ibid (emphasis added); *Rebel Worker*, November 1919; *New Solidarity*, 15 November 1919. It is worth noting that these longshoremen fought without the assistance of Joseph Ettor (born in Brooklyn), Carlo Tresca, and Arturo Giovannitti, the best-known Italian American radicals of the period, who were no longer members of the IWW.
67. Mary Heaton Vorse, "The Pirate's Nest of New York," in *Rebel Pen* (New York: Monthly Review Press, 1985), 219–33.
68. Gary Fink, ed., *Biographical Dictionary of American Labor* (Westport, Conn.: Greenwood Press, 1984), 444.
69. Davis, "All I Got's a Hook," 139.
70. Vorse, "Pirate's Nest," 233.

Chapter 4

Donne Ribelli: Recovering the History of Italian Women's Radicalism in the United States

Jennifer Guglielmo

In 1905, Maria Barbieri issued this call to action: "To my women comrades, these thoughts are dedicated to you, from another woman worker: It is the thought and palpitation of my soul in which I feel all the social injustices, that for centuries we have been humble and obedient slaves; I am a rebel who rises up against all these inequities, and I also invite you to the struggle." Beginning with the title "Ribelliamoci!" (Let's Rebel!), Maria addressed her *compagne* in an anarchist *circolo* that included as many as ninety Italian women and men, most of whom were textile workers from Como and Biella in northern Italy who worked in Paterson, New Jersey's, silk factories. She also reached other Italian women throughout the United States who read (or had someone else read to them) her essays in one of the more popular Italian American radical newspapers, *La Questione Sociale*.[1] Her words reveal a world of Italian American women's radicalism that we have yet to document in its complexity, nuance, and creativity.

To date, very little has been published on Italian American women's community organizing, much less their participation in radical movements. Fortunately, Colomba Furio, Vincenza Scarpaci, Donna Gabaccia, Franca Iacovetta, Nancy Hewitt, Ardis Cameron, Elizabeth Ewen, Caroline Merithew, and others, have documented some stories of Italian women's radical activities in the United States.[2] Within most histories, however, Italian American women often appear as peripheral actors and occasional supporters to the men who are positioned at the center of these movements. Because of this, scholars continually assert that Italian American women rarely participated in community politics, much less revolutionary movements. What has emerged in most historical literature is an image of Italian American women as apolitical, unable to mobilize community resources when necessary, and without a history or culture of resistance.[3] However, in order to understand the history of Italian American radicalism, we must make meaning of women's political actions rather than dismiss them as rare or peripheral manifestations; we must examine these so-called margins of struggle.

Stereotype has taken hold of scholarship on Italian American women in large part because it is validated within certain historical documents. Entire runs of Italian radical newspapers were filled with the words of male leaders, with only occasional essays by women. Carlo Tresca, Errico Malatesta, Luigi Galleani, Pietro Gori, Saverio Merlino, Gigi Damiani, Augusto Bellanca, Luigi Antonini, Arturo Giovannitti, and other men, occupied central stage in many forms of Italian American radical performance. Italian immigrant men more often held formal positions of leadership in neighborhood and labor organizations, and many presented themselves as the ones best suited to teaching radicalism to women. Additionally, other European immigrant working-class women regularly asserted that Italian immigrant women were absent from radical movements and that they were "unorganizable," especially when compared to their own styles of activism.[4] Alongside this narrative, however, exists Maria Barbieri, her *compagne*, and many others like her, women who, in their time, were far from invisible or hidden.

Although a great deal of public discourse on the Left perpetuated stereotypical images of Italian women, there existed another world, where Italian American women formulated strategies of resistance and survival that called into question systems of power and authority within their families, communities, and larger society. For example, in reflecting on her career as a radical labor organizer, Elizabeth Gurley Flynn proclaimed, "there were practically no women in the Italian movement—anarchist or socialist. Whatever homes I went into with Carlo [Tresca] the women were always in the background, cooking in the kitchen, and seldom even sitting down to eat with the men."[5] Ironically, in the same cities and movements where Flynn organized workers, anarchist Italian immigrant women workers in places like Paterson, New York City, and Spring Valley, Illinois, were meeting regularly to study the writing of proletarian Italian feminist theoreticians, writing and publishing testimonies on the particular struggles of women, leading discussion groups within their communities, and finding innovative ways to organize their coworkers and neighbors, alongside and separately from men. They did so within a larger community that included family, *paesani, compagni*, and other immigrant radicals from around the world. Clearly, we must peek into the kitchen and listen to what these women were saying and planning as they nourished these movements with "una buona salsa di pomodoro."

This essay relates several stories of Italian American women's radicalism to demonstrate the variety with which women acted to bring about a society without coercive authority or unequal distribution of community resources. This essay is not meant to be comprehensive, but to survey some areas of Italian American women's radical activity over the first decades of the twentieth century. In the absence of an adequate body of writing on this history, any analysis is necessarily tentative and provisional. My broader purpose, then, is to suggest how we might more successfully read, interpret, and understand Italian women's radicalism in the United States. The recovery of these stories is an essential first step toward understanding the history of Italian American radicalism in its multivocality, comprising many different experiences and debates, both within and outside organized social movements.[6] These stories teach us strategy, they disrupt stereotypes, and they force us to examine and interrogate the way power operates within and between communities to erase women's histories of protest and resistance. They also reveal the variety of ways Italian American women confronted power in their daily lives, enabling us to more concretely assess the consequences of their choices today. Within this essay I have chosen to trace the experiences of different individuals and follow them into the many communities they formed and joined over time. This strategy of recovery enables us to glimpse into the private lives of activist women and explore the many ways they participated in radical social movements. Their stories complicate the way we think of Italian American radicalism. They also encourage us to consider the ways revolutionary ideologies, movements, and acts not only led exceptional people to devote their lives to activism, but also influenced and shaped the lives of thousands.

The history of Italian American women's radicalism begins in Italy, where at the end of the nineteenth century female traditions of grassroots protest and radical activism were foundational to local resistance movements against the oppressive authority of the state, wealthy landowners, and the Church. The widespread poverty, recurring economic depressions, labor upheavals, and government repression, which shaped the lives of most Italians in this period, caused Italians, throughout the peninsula, to form organizations, such as the *fasci dei lavoratori* (unions of workers), and struggled for a reconstruction of society in which industry and government were brought under the control of workers. The Italian government condemned these actions. They shut down newspapers, arrested socialist and anarchist leaders, and brutally suppressed popular movements. Workers' demonstrations often culminated in clashes with the military in which hundreds of people were killed. When Mussolini came to power in 1922, repression intensified as he sought to eradicate all proletarian opposition. The Italian labor movement extended internationally, as Italians traversed the globe and brought traditions of militancy, protest, and rebellion with them.[7]

Many historians have richly documented the ways women formed a critical component of popular movements in Italy throughout the nineteenth and twentieth centuries. Their studies show how women's collaborative activities offered them an autonomous space where they could, under certain circumstances, collectively assess systems of power, and organize in opposition to them. Thousands of women participated in organizing drives and strikes in textile, mining, and agricultural industries, and they helped to build organizations such as the Unione Sindacale Italiana, the Partito Socialista Italiano, and Camere del Lavoro.[8] Activism also occurred around women's traditional responsibilities, where neighborhood and kin networks were converted into powerful weapons of resistance and protest. As Donna Gabaccia has argued, "In Italy, the mob would long remain an important protest form among groups most visibly excluded, especially peasants and women."[9] For example, in 1898, hundreds of women, men, and children demonstrated in Ancona for lower bread prices and an end to the tax on flour with the cries "Viva la anarchia!" and "Viva la rivoluzione sociale!" In addition, Sicilian women took to streets in the 1890s with the cry "Viva il socialismo e abbasso il militarismo!" and responded to tax officials' advice that they should take jobs as servants if they could not pay their taxes by destroying municipal offices. They demanded: "There should no longer be either rich or poor. All should have bread for themselves and for their children. We should all be equal."[10]

To date, we know very little of the ways Italian women brought this history of protest and revolutionary activism into their lives in the United States. Fortunately, Salvatore Salerno, George Carey, and Patrizia Sione unearthed the story of Maria Roda, who organized workers in Italy and France before she crossed the Atlantic in 1892, at 15 years of age, and settled with her father and sister in Paterson, New Jersey. In France, Maria was briefly incarcerated after Sante Caserio, a *compagno* in her anarchist circle assassinated Sadi Carnot, the president of France. Prior to that, the Rodas had been forced to leave Como, their native town in Lombardy, after Maria was convicted of organizing a strike in the silk factory where she worked as a weaver, a trade she and her sister had learned from their father, Cesare. Consequently, the Rodas came to Paterson to find work in the city's silk mills, alongside other *paesani*. Like other Italian immigrant women, she and her sister arrived in the United States having developed some skills for the industrial marketplace and with the day-to-day experiences of resistance and struggle in Italy. Maria migrated, she told one of her mentors, Emma Goldman, because she "felt that she had work to do among her countrymen in the United States." The daughter of an anarchist and a self-proclaimed socialist–anarchist herself, as a teenager Maria responded to the poverty and repression she witnessed around her by becoming active within anarchist circles in Como. Before leaving Italy, she had studied revolutionary practice with Ada Negri, known widely among Italian radicals as the "ardent poetess of revolt." And in this way, Maria's reputation preceded her.[11]

Upon her arrival in Paterson, Maria (and her father) joined a radical circle known as Gruppo Diritto all'Esistenza, which included Maria Barbieri and other Italian anarchist immigrants, similarly committed to connecting their struggles in the silk factories to those of other workers throughout the world. At only 16 years of age Maria began speaking before large assemblies of workers, where she immediately impressed seasoned radicals and rank-and-file workers with her ability to rouse audiences. Her activities brought her into daily contact with many of the leading immigrant revolutionaries. Soon after she arrived in the United States, she fell in love with the prominent Spanish anarchist, Pedro Esteve, an internationally renowned labor organizer, close friend of Malatesta, and the editor of several anarchist newspapers, including *La Questione Sociale*. While raising eight children and laboring in Paterson's silk mills, Maria and Pedro became part of the community of intellectual working-class leaders that extended beyond

Paterson and across the United States. A charismatic and powerful speaker, Maria regularly traveled with Pedro to assist and support the collective struggles of Mexican, Cuban, Spanish, Puerto Rican, African American, Eastern European Jewish, Italian, and other textile, cigar, mine, and dock workers in the United States. While they were based in Paterson, at different times they also set up a home in Brooklyn and Tampa in order to connect the revolutionary activities in these different communities.[12]

Maria Roda's commitment to the anarchist and socialist movements led her to devote the majority of her time to organizing other women workers, because, as she stated, "Chi conosce le miserie più della donna?" In order to accomplish this, she helped to found a *gruppo anarchico femminile*, the Gruppo Emancipazione della Donna, in Paterson in 1897, with the purpose of creating a place for women to discuss and produce revolutionary theory and strategy and to build coalitions with other workers. "And it is right," Maria stated, when announcing in *La Questione Sociale* that women were meeting on their own, "because we feel and suffer; we too want to immerse ourselves in the struggle against this society, because we too feel, from birth, the need to be free, to be equal."[13] Over the next decade, the Paterson-based Gruppo Emancipazione della Donna, worked closely with a similar circle of Italian anarchist women workers in New York City and collaborated with other workers throughout the country and internationally. By the early 1900s, Italian women's anarchist groups in Paterson and New York City were in regular correspondence with other *gruppi femminili di propaganda* (women's propaganda groups), as they called them, and their supporters in industrial centers such as Philadelphia and Boston and in the mining communities of Pennsylvania, Illinois, and Vermont.[14] Across the country, Italian women came together to examine their particular struggles and bring *l'emancipazione della donna* to the center of working-class revolutionary debates and practice. Together, they voiced their need to collectively struggle, "For the emancipation of women, together with those struggles that must occur in order to attain the rights that all of oppressed humanity demand, a woman must struggle with great zeal to emancipate herself from the tyranny and prejudice of men, and from those who foolishly consider women inferior and often treat her like a slave."[15] Women active in the *gruppi* used community-wide meetings and the radical press to publicize and share their activities, ideas, and objectives, and to develop activist networks among women workers from different regions in Italy who resided throughout the United States.

The women who participated within these radical communities—such as Maria Barbieri, Maria Roda, Ida Merini Catastini, Maria Raffuzzi, Ninfa Baronia, Angela Marietti, Ernestina Cravello, Maria Croce, Alba Genisio, Rosa De Alberti, Rosa Castelli, and Maria Livi—came from the ranks of the Italian revolutionary émigrés who undertook the formidable task of politicizing and organizing the masses of Italian women workers in America. They wrote and published testimonies on the particular struggles of women, led discussion groups and hosted lectures in their communities, circulated the writing of Italian feminist theoreticians such as Anna Maria Mozzoni,[16] and spoke out at rallies—whatever it took to bring together their coworkers and neighbors.

They also participated within larger working-class radical communities that included men. Within their families, in community discussions at local meeting halls, festivals, dances, and picnics, in jointly hosted seminars and in workplace actions, they collaborated with men in the movement. Indeed, it was the Italian anarchist women in Paterson who formed one of the first locals of the Industrial Workers of the World (IWW), which sought to organize all workers—American-born and foreigners—regardless of race, ethnicity, gender, or skill. Such an alliance laid important groundwork for workers' collective action in the years that followed.[17] These women also met and organized separately to ensure that their own concerns were addressed within the larger international working-class movement. In addition to fostering an environment that was conducive to orga-nizing their *compagne*, the women found it necessary to assert their commitment to *il movimento operaio*. Repeatedly, they confronted men in the movement who asserted, "that the woman, for all her efforts, can never elevate herself from sub-servience." Rather, they argued, "We agitate, we organize to prove to the world that accuses us, that we too are capable of something."[18]

Within their writing we find the intricacies of Italian immigrant women's debates and the emergence of their own distinctive proletarian feminism. Many of these women advocated the "organizational" current of anarchist thought, believing that solving material problems required working-class mobilization and collective action in the context of the industrial union movement. The newspa-pers more commonly associated with anti-organizationalist anarchists, such as *Cronaca Sovversiva*, did not publish women's essays on their role within the radi-cal movement with as much frequency as the organizationalist papers, such as *La Questione Sociale* and *L'Era Nuova*.[19] Revolution was not something they waited for; it was the daily act of bringing about a society without domination or inequality. As Maria Barbieri stated, "A struggle continues each and every day, to pull out the deep roots that a false education has cultivated and nourished in my heart."[20] Within their essays, these women gave voice to the exploitation they endured as a source of cheap labor within the expanding capitalist world system. They denounced imperialism, nationalism, the Church, racism, and nativism, as well as contributed to theoretical debates concerning syndicalism, parlimentari-anism, and free love.[21] However, unlike the men in the movement, they regularly exposed and opposed cultural traditions that condoned the abuse of authority and power within families and communities. Some of the women wrote using pseudonyms, presumably to enjoy greater creative and political license under the cover of anonymity and also to evade deportation and the loss of employment. One of the more-prolific women authors wrote under the alias "Titì." In 1906 she began a series of essays with the title *"Alle Donne, Emancipiamoci!"* (To The Women: Let's Emancipate Ourselves!) in which she called on her radical com-munity to apply revolutionary theories to their intimate relationships: "I have reached the height of my individuality and I submit only to *myself*. But I say and write this because no one has told me to put this to the test yet. . . . In fact, we should take a glance not only at the bourgeois society but at ourselves, workers who are part of the anarchist family."[22] On occasion, the women found the public support of men who, like Camillo Di Sciullo, reminded his brothers: "We anarchists have predicated our work on the emancipation of women. . . . Don't you know that the first campaign to do is that of the family? Build a little anarchist world within your family and you will be able to see how it strengthens, how it becomes easier to launch other campaigns!"[23] Within the public culture of the press, women brought forth their critiques and forced their radical communities to confront the ways power operated internally. It was through their activism that *l'emancipazione della donna* became a part of the Italian anarchist debates.

Italian women's writing opposed belief systems that socialized them to be "umili e sottomesse." They asked, "Who are these people, these absolute masters of ourselves, our happiness, and our life? We are these people, because we approve of everything that enslaves us." One strategy they proposed was to raise their daughters to think and act on their own behalf: "The axiom of domination in fact begins at birth, when a girl learns her place in life. . . . She is infused with ideas that are different from those that we want to teach, ideas that will lead her to be an illiterate and poor seamstress as an adult. . . . If our girls could rebel against our authority, they would do so willingly, and it will be much better for her and for all of humanity."[24] They asserted that as women they occupied "a great position and huge influence in the individual and collective life of humanity," which could be used to educate "a new generation of conscious workers stripped of prejudice, and for us to have protection and comfort in the struggle for human emancipation." On several occasions, women publicly chastised men in the community whom they believed were *anti-femministi*. They argued, "It is necessary, indeed urgent that men concern themselves, above all else, with the emancipation of women."[25] Italian women active within the anarchist and socialist movements argued consistently that revolutionary work within the family, community, and larger society required feminist organizing. The feminism they advocated was not, "The manner of certain bourgeois feminists who claim the equality or supremacy of our sex, and would be satisfied with the realization of these dreams." Rather, feminism meant that working-class and poor women's struggles, concerns, and strategies informed revolutionary praxis.[26]

By following women activists through their many communities, we are able to explore how Italian American radical culture was established through dialogue and collaboration between women and men, and rooted in the material reality of everyday life. As their stories suggest, many women active in anarchist and socialist movements came from radical families. Maria Roda, Ersilia Grandi Cavedagni, Caterina Caminita, Ella Andolini, Ernestina Cravello, Maria Livi, and many others grew up within families and found partners who were similarly committed to the movement. Many learned strategies of resistance and oppositional politics within their households before they entered the workplace and grassroots movements. As their writing suggests, women brought this early knowledge to bear when they entered community politics. Families were a central location where political ideologies were formed and reproduced for men and women, and these relationships hold a key to understanding the history of Italian American radical culture and praxis.[27]

Revolutionary organizing was not confined to the exceptional efforts of several hundred anarchist women. In these same years thousands of Italian women walked off jobs and took to the streets alongside men and other working-class women in labor uprisings and industrywide strikes across the United States. In Paterson, Newark, Lowell, Passaic, Little Falls, New York City, Boston, Hopedale, Rochester, Lawrence, Lynn, Chicago, Tampa, Cleveland, and Providence, Italian women organized strikes with other immigrant working-class women that drew on communal protest traditions and women's neighborhood networks, as well as on the revolutionary ideals of socialism and anarchism.[28] Although Italian women workers rarely held leadership positions in unions or formal strike committees during this period, their ability to organize their coworkers and neighbors proved crucial in winning labor struggles, especially in the textile, clothing, and tobacco industries, where they often outnumbered men in the rank and file. Large-scale collective actions radicalized many women. Initially drawn into a strike by dangerous working conditions, low wages, and long hours, thousands of women came to see their struggles as connected to that of other workers throughout the world. In the process, critiques of capitalist development became infused with their own day-to-day experiences of household and community struggle. Indeed, in the years before the First World War, the masses of Italian immigrant women (and men) came together most often within the revolutionary industrial union movement, which was inspired by anarchist, socialist, and syndicalist ideologies. Fortunately this history has found its chroniclers. Historians often focus on spectacular dramas such as strikes because they catch our attention. They also reveal how less-visible acts of survival and opposition have a cumulative effect on power relations and on the development of mass-based movements. Examining activism in large-scale industrial upheavals alongside everyday acts of resistance and smaller collective mobilizations enables us to consider the large numbers of Italian women who participated in revolutionary working-class movements.

Stories of Italian women's activism on the frontlines of U.S. labor struggles are numerous and filled with rich evidence of their audacity, courage, and inventiveness in confronting abusive and demeaning conditions in their lives. However, scholars writing on working women's labor struggles in New York City in this period often assume Italian women were absent from such movements. These conclusions are drawn from evidence that Italian women, the majority of whom labored in the city's garment trades, were reluctant to join strikes that were organized by the Jewish women who led the rank and file in garment shops and unions at the beginning of the twentieth century. During the first major garment strike in the city, the famous Uprising of 20,000 in 1909, Jewish women workers aligned themselves with middle-class progressives and feminist activists in the Women's Trade Union League (WTUL), after the male-dominated International

Ladies' Garment Workers' Union (ILGWU) was reluctant to support their decision to strike. Italian women garment workers on the other hand, had not developed faith in either the ILGWU or the WTUL, since neither proved committed
to their particular struggles. Indeed, leaders from these organizations routinely
expressed the belief that Italian women were "hopeless" because they were
"absolutely under the dominance of men of their family, and heavily shackled by
old customs and traditions."[29] Because of this, Italian women garment workers in
New York City formed different alliances to confront the abuse of their labor.

The city's anarchist, socialist, and syndicalist circles, provided one of the primary ways Italian women addressed labor grievances and formulated oppositional
strategies during this period.[30] Gabaccia discovered that in the early twentieth
century, Brooklyn's Italian "shoe and garment workers struck without much initial help from the reform-minded Socialists." Rather, many Italian women and
men built coalitions with "Spanish-speaking and Jewish groups in the neighborhood" through *circoli* such as Club Avanti, a group founded by Sicilian anarchists
and freethinkers in Brooklyn, which "supported education, sponsored lectures on
peace, religion, and sexual and family questions, on women's emancipation,
nationalism, imperialism, major immigrant strikes, the Mexican Revolution, the
problems of political prisoners in Italy, and, more generally, current events."[31]
Vincenza Scarpaci's research revealed how shirtwaist factory operatives Angela
and Maria Bambace were drawn into labor activism in 1916 by attending meetings sponsored by Italian socialists and anarchists in their neighborhood in
Harlem. It was also at these gatherings that they met labor organizers within the
IWW and learned direct action (syndicalist) strategies. Tina Cacici, a garment
worker who would become a renowned leader of a radical faction in the
Lawrence strike of 1919, first became known for her rousing speeches on
women's emancipation at a local socialist club in Brooklyn.[32] Furthermore,
Gabaccia argues, "only with the organization of the IWW [in 1905] did workplace agitation increase in Brooklyn."[33] Italian women garment workers were
drawn to the IWW because of its anarcho-syndicalist ideology and support for
their labor struggles. For example, following the 1909 uprising it was the IWW
that demanded that the ILGWU make all of its decisions in mass meetings rather
than in committees where Italians were absent or underrepresented. Unlike the
ILGWU and the WTUL, the IWW also drew support and membership from
many local Italian working-class radical circles throughout the city.[34] The masses
of Italian garment workers were not yet willing to join the ILGWU in the 1909
uprising. However, the successes workers had been able to achieve in the earlier
uprising inspired them to become visible and active participants in the cloakmakers' strike of 1910. A total of 2,800 Italian workers joined the union in the
first three days of the strike, and three weeks later approximately 20 Italian workers, including large numbers of Italian finishers, who identified with the cloakmakers, joined the strike.[35]

In the years following the 1910 strike, Italian women in New York City were
able to carve out a space within the ILGWU and the Amalgamated Clothing

Workers of America (ACWA), where they mentored and mobilized the thousands of Italian women who entered these unions over the next several decades. However, since many of the prominent early leaders in the ILGWU and the ACWA were men, historians have assumed that they were responsible for the successful organization of Italian women in the unions.[36] In view of this, the role Italian women played in building solidarity within their own ranks has not been considered central to understanding the history of working-class radicalism in this period. It was in New York City's garment locals, that Italian workers found a powerful organization to negotiate on their behalf from the 1920s through the 1960s. These movements drew the energies of many prominent Italian male radicals, but it was Italian women who composed the majority of workers in the garment industry and unions.

Rather than solely focus on the men who were initially hired to organize Italian women garment workers, or those who assumed leadership positions in the unions and formal strike committees, we need more studies that consider the role Italian women played in organizing themselves. From the outset, Angela and Maria Bambace, Susanna Angretina, Rosalina Ferrara, Rose De Cara, Giordana Lombardi, Anna Coocha, Sadie La Rosa, Laura Di Guglielmo, Lina Manetta, Angelina Limanti, Maria Prestianni, Anna Squillante, Millie Tirreno, Anna Fama, Anna Cassio, Clara Zara, Rose Grasso, Rosalie Conforti, and countless other women formed the first organizing teams that successfully brought thousands of their *compagne* into the ILGWU. They labored as operatives, drapers, finishers, hemstitchers, and examiners in the industry and became radicalized by the desperate and deteriorating labor conditions in the factories. Often they would find work in dress shops that were nonunion, meet other workers, listen to their grievances, and recruit them into the union. They did so at great risk, as many of them experienced arrests and beatings at the hands of employers and police. They tested modes of organizing workers through workplace committees, house visits, leaflets and educational programs, community-wide publicity, cultural activities, community coalitions, demonstrations, strikes, picket lines, soup kitchens, and family involvement.[37] Their tactics paid off when unprecedented numbers of Italian women joined the garment worker uprisings in 1910, 1913, and 1919. It was also due to their efforts that women joined the ILGWU once Italian members had their own autonomous locals in 1916 and 1919.[38] Colomba Furio's research demonstrated that by 1919, "an overwhelming majority of Italian women and girls joined the ranks of those who went out on strike that year." During the strike, "Italian women distinguished themselves on picket lines, at strikers' meetings, and on organizational committees." As one older Italian immigrant woman recounted, she joined the union's struggles that year because "me sick of the boss, me sick of work, me sick of go hungry most time." She then showed the interviewer her deformed finger, the bone worn down into the shape of a hook, and the space where her front teeth had once been, the result of decades of quickly twisting cotton and biting buttonholes to save time and keep her job in a garment factory. She concluded, "me sick, me tired, me can stand no longer, that's why me all strike."[39] The first administration of the Italian Dress-makers' Local 89 (chartered in 1919) included many of the women who had been most active in the strike that year, which had finally brought garment work-ers the 40-hour week. By the 1920s, New York City's garment unions became one of the primary centers of Italian American radical activity, and a principle bat-tleground for struggles over fascism, nationalism, and communism.[40] Yet, few scholars have examined Italian women's participation within these debates.

After the 1919 strike, Italian women workers utilized the garment unions as community organizations. They conducted meetings and distributed literature in Italian, hired and trained their own organizers, employed community-based orga-nizing strategies, and connected union activities to other movements in their neighborhoods.[41] For example, on August 9, 1927, days before Italian anarchists Sacco and Vanzetti were executed, over 2,000 women and men left their jobs throughout New York City in protest and marched from the Italian neighbor-hood in the Lower East Side to City Hall, and then gathered at Union Square for a rally that included over 25,000 women and men, most of whom represented the garment unions. Factories across the country were brought to a standstill as Ital-ians joined with other workers and used their unions to oppose American nativism and repression against the Left.[42]

As Italian American garment workers became increasingly sympathetic to Mussolini's vision of a "New Italy," anarchists, syndicalists, communists, social-ists, and other radicals led oppositional movements in their homes, neighbor-hoods, workplaces, and unions. Evidence of Italian women's participation in the anti-Fascist movement exists in photographs of rallies, often sponsored by the garment unions, which included large numbers of Italian women supporters and speakers. It is also revealed in newspaper accounts of women's actions in the Ital-ian-language press. During the summer of 1923, for example, several Italian women in New Haven, Connecticut, sneaked into a local Fascist celebration and took to the floor during speeches shouting "Viva l'Italia! Abbasso Mussolini!" Simultaneously, they attacked reputed Fascists, causing fights to break out and the meeting to end.[43]

The histories of specific individuals also provide evidence of the ways Italian immigrant women led anti-Fascist activities. Margherita di Maggio not only ran the organizational department of the Italian dressmakers' local of the ILGWU in the 1920s, she was also well known in her Sicilian family for challenging those who "felt drawn by Mussolini's promise of grandeur to the Italian people." Di Maggio's niece recalled, "she and my grandfather were always arguing. . . . She wanted to buy him a round-trip ticket to go back to Italy and see how things were." When the arguments "got worse" Margherita bought him a one-way ticket and "within two months he wrote back here begging her to send him the return ticket."[44] Ginevra Spagnoletti joined an anti-Fascist group in her Greenwich Village neighborhood after becoming active in the ACWA, and before long she began to host anti-Fascist gatherings in her home. Her children (including the famous painter Ralph Fasanella) recalled such meetings as a critical part of their own education, but Ginevra's husband grew resentful of her political and intellectual life, and such tensions escalated until she left him with her six children.[45] Hundreds of other women, including Angela Bambace, Lucia Romualdi, Lillie Raitano, and Josephine Mirenda, also entered the anti-Fascist movement through labor activism in the ACWA and the ILGWU.[46]

The Needle Trades Workers Industrial Union, a Communist Party dual-union, became another avenue for Italian women's activism after factional disputes within the ILGWU led the general executive board to the expel Communists and women activists struggling for more-democratic representation within the union in the 1920s. Charles Zappia has argued that Italian union leaders aligned themselves with the ILGWU leadership during this "civil war" in order to safeguard their autonomy in the newly formed Italian-language locals. Yet, there was some opposition in the ranks. Women such as Angela Bambace and Albina Delfino opposed these actions and became active in Communist Party meetings and strikes, where they formed alliances with anarchist and Communist insurgents in the union.[47] As the Italian American rank and file became increasingly anti-Communist and supportive of Mussolini, Italian radicals were forced to contend with new political divisions in the socialist movement they sought to build in the garment unions.

Although labor unions provided one setting for activism on the Left, Italian women also mobilized support for the anti-Fascist movement within local anarchist circles. Through the radical press, Italian anarchist women called on their *compagne* to oppose Fascism as they would any systemic and pervasive form of domination. Many women sent letters and essays for publication in New York City's popular anarchist newspaper *L'Adunata dei Refrattari*. One woman from Philadelphia addressed herself to other women and called upon them to oppose the coercive motherhood that Fascists were calling for: "If you are able to see the contradictions of fascism, the illiterate masses will be able to pass for those with great knowledge. . . . Uplift yourselves, throw oppression and iniquity into the face of this vile society which imposes them upon you. . . . Become women . . . you must be free, not prostitutes, the comrades of men in life and in the struggle."[48] In addition, anarchist women continued to voice their opposition to the men in the movement who did not recognize the importance of women to workers' struggles. "Men should know," wrote another woman, "that humanity cannot elevate itself if women are not elevated and that the emancipation of the proletariat cannot move forward without the emancipation of women."[49]

Radical movements also benefited from the activism of anarchist *fuorusciti*, refugees of the Fascist regime. Throughout the 1920s, Italian workers filled meeting halls to capacity to hear Virgilia D'Andrea, an anarchist labor organizer and schoolteacher from Sulmona (Abruzzi) who fled Fascist police in 1928 and settled in Brooklyn with her *compagno* and lover, Armando Borghi. A noted organizer and renowned *compagna poetessa*, Virgilia was invited to speak at workers' assemblies throughout the United States. From city to city, as far west as California, she spoke before thousands of Italian workers and urged them to oppose

nationalism and imperialism, "based as it is on colonial conquest and the subju-
gation of peoples of color." Rather, she argued, all should see themselves as a "citizen of the world, a child of father Sun and mother Earth." Virgilia also told of
the metalworkers who took over their factories in northern Italy and of her own
imprisonment during the strike. She spoke out against the escalating campaign
of violence and physical intimidation against workers in Italy and the United
States and protested the execution of Sacco and Vanzetti, her comrades in the
movement.[50]

When we consider that, according to Gaetano Salvemini, anti-Fascists comprised only 10 percent of the Italian American population of 4,600,000 in 1930,
the efforts of Italian socialist and anarchist women to build an oppositional
movement might seem particularly negligible. Yet, interestingly, the garment
workers had more success repelling Fascist agents from recruiting supporters in
their unions than did longshoremen, barbers, and workers in other trades.[51] Even
though the numbers of anarchist women were even less than those of anti-Fascists, their circles, and other radical workers' clubs, would continue to provide a
setting where Italian Americans actively confronted the racism and sexism
within their own ranks into the 1930s.

Political divisions within the Italian American left widened during the
Depression, yet Italian women garment workers were able to organize one of the
most-effective labor mobilizations of the period. In August of 1933, sixty thousand dressmakers in New York, New Jersey, and Connecticut walked off their
jobs and took to the streets. Joined by Puerto Rican, West Indian, African American, and Jewish women dressmakers, Italian women filled strike halls to capacity, stormed nonunion shops calling workers to join them, marched through the
streets of their neighborhoods, and formed picket lines outside shops demanding
decent wages and working conditions and an end to sweatshops once and for all.
The Italian women dressmakers who participated in orchestrating the strike,
such as Angela Bambace, Tina Catania, Antonetta Lazzaro, Tina Gaeta,
Margherita Di Maggio, Lillie Raitano, Josephine Mirenda, Grace De Luisa, Lucia
Romualdi, Albina Delfino, Maria Primavera, Lena Ferrari, Maria Dattilio, and
hundreds of others, followed in a long tradition of Italian women's labor militancy and activism. Yet, they also ushered in a new era, one that Italian garment
workers would come to call *l'alba radiosa* (the radiant dawn).[52]

The five-day strike was the crucial event by which Italian garment workers,
both immigrant and American-born, assumed an overwhelming numerical
majority within the ILGWU. For the first time, they not only held a measure of
power in the industry and union, but before the state, which appeared to support
their organizational appeals for economic justice. In March of the following year,
Margherita Di Maggio, Minnie Badami, Dorothy Drago, Yolanda Liguori,
Angelina Farruggia, and other prominent organizers of the Italian Dressmakers'
Local 89, traveled to Washington, D.C., to present President Franklin D. Roosevelt with a bronze plaque and pledge the support of Italian garment workers to
the National Industrial Recovery Act. Although Italian women were still not

proportionately represented in the hierarchy of the union, they made up close to 80 percent of the Italian Dressmakers' Local 89, which became the largest local in the nation, with forty thousand members, and the majority of workers in other large locals. As the largest segment of the rank and file, Italian women continued to run their locals' organizational drives and struggle with Italian and Jewish men for a voice in union affairs.[53]

Following the uprising, the ILGWU locals became important centers of Italian American life in New York City. As the third largest union in the American Federation of Labor, Italian radical leaders and labor organizers, once isolated from the federal government, now embraced the belief that "a strong state and strong unions could remedy the failures of capitalism so glaring in the Great Depression."[54] Recently, scholars have suggested that reliance on the state and politically powerful unions spelled the downfall of Italian American radicalism, as many former revolutionaries moved from desiring the overthrow of state capitalism to accommodation.[55] The Italian American radical community was seriously diminished in its influence with its increased reliance on reformist socialist unions and support for Fascism among Italian American workers. By the 1930s, Italian American workers in socialist unions no longer sought to dismantle private property, the government, and other systems of oppressive authority, but to utilize the apparatus of the state, community institutions, and labor unions, to assert identities as Americans. New Deal reforms were critical in cementing this transition, since these programs channeled workforce protections and benefits to white industrial workers. This gave groups like Italians (and other southern and eastern European immigrants and their descendants), who may not have identified as white, a powerful reason to assert such an identity. In the decades following the Second World War, whiteness guaranteed access to federally subsidized loans, which they used to abandon the inner city for segregated suburbs and maintain positions of authority in the newly empowered trade unions. Yet, as Tom Guglielmo's recent work points out, although Italians began to see themselves and their interests as white in this period, they were in many of the most-critical ways "white on arrival" in the United States: they could become citizens, own property, vote, represent themselves in a court of law, and marry whomever they chose—rights that were routinely denied to Chinese, Japanese, Mexicans, Puerto Ricans, African Americans, Native Americans, and other people of color.[56] By the late 1940s, Italian American women and men garment workers in New York City began to insist on their whiteness, entitling them to privileged political rights, better-paying jobs, and leadership of the union. They often did so by practicing and institutionalizing policies of racialized exclusion in the union and industry, which enabled them to gain control over higher-paying jobs and deny democratic representation to African American, Puerto Rican, and West Indian women and men in the union.[57]

In their public statements, however, Italian American labor organizers often sought to avoid the issue of race as much as possible and instead drew attention to the "culture of unity" offered by a multi-ethnic socialist union.[58] In a speech commemorating the anniversary of the strike four years later, Antonino Crivello, veteran labor organizer and manager of ILGWU Local 144 in Newark, recounted the event before hundreds of Italian American women dressmakers who had participated in the uprising: "Jews, Germans, Hungarians, Italians, Colored and members of every nationality working and suffering together in the shops and who had been divided by all sorts of prejudices and by the evil arts of the bosses at last realized that only through workers' unity and solidarity they could conquer their rights and they stood up together and fought and won one of the most splendid victories of the labor movement."[59] Italian garment workers also celebrated the writings of Arturo Labriola, whose essay "Le Razze di Colore e il Socialismo" was published in full text for Italian workers in commemoration of the ideologies they felt informed the founding of the Italian Dressmakers' Local 89. Labriola indicted "those with white skin" for the atrocities of racism, slavery, and colonialism. White people, or "those with European stock" only counted for a fraction of the world's population, he argued, while "at least 1,500 million of the world's population are *not* from European races: black, yellow, olive, mixed, and so forth. Together, *this is humanity.*"[60] This rhetoric of shared oppression and worker solidarity enabled Italians to link their cause with that of other workers, while at the same time it obscured the ways they had built upon labor successes to secure preferential positioning within the union and industry at the expense of other workers. Considering the vigilance with which Italian women and men defended their whiteness and the "racial purity" of their neighborhoods from the 1940s onward—in places where the garment unions were both weak and strong—we have to examine how race fractured this "culture of unity" that many Italian American radicals sought to project in the 1930s. Several women, such as Albina Delfino, who left the ILGWU and charged the socialist leaders of the Italian Dressmakers' Local 89 with "working together with the boss" by advancing the interests of Italians to the detriment of other workers, drew attention to these deep tensions that existed within Italian American radical culture in this period.[61]

Italian American women also remained active outside of their unions and participated within a number of different neighborhood coalitions and radical political circles to confront the Depression, the spread of Fascism and imperialism, and the persistent racism and discrimination in the United States. The Communist Party, which was often on the frontlines of grassroots popular movements in this period, provided new ways for Italian immigrant women and their American-born daughters to build radical culture and become active in local movements. After leaving the Italian Dressmakers' Local 89, Albina Delfino became a labor organizer for the Communist Party in the 1930s. She traveled between Lawrence, Providence, Boston, Paterson, and New York City, to assist Italian workers on the verge of striking or already on strike, and to combat racial antagonism within these working-class communities. Often, she held open-air meetings six days a week with Frances Ribaldo, another Italian woman organizer in the party, where they encountered antagonistic Italian men who proclaimed that they had nothing to learn from women. During the Spanish Civil War, both women worked to bring Italian women in New York City into the movement for Republican Spain. Before long, she recalled, "those women were organizing affairs, going from house to house collecting clothes for the children."[62] Additionally, it was often through the Communist Party and other radical circles, such as the Italian Workers' Club in Harlem, that Italians joined neighborhood movements to protest the Italian invasion of Ethiopia in December 1934 and to confront the Italians who responded to the war by hanging effigies of Emperor Haile Selassie. Indeed, the Communist Party played a pivotal role in uniting many Harlem organizations in support of Ethiopia. One parade, held in 1935, began in two separate contingents, one led by Italian Americans and the other by African Americans, that merged into a unified line of march at 129th Street and Seventh Avenue to conclude with a mass outdoor rally of more than 25,000 participants.[63]

In the Italian American Communist press, young journalists such as Aurora De Gregorio publicly expressed shame that similar experiences of oppression could lead Italians to see their struggles as against, rather than with, people of color around the world. In an open letter to John Williams (a young African American man who was convicted of rape without evidence by an all-white jury), De Gregorio called on Italian American radicals to condemn the Italian Judge Brancato, who said "I would give him twenty years if I could. Remember, she is a white woman." "He forgets," wrote De Gregorio, "that at one time in America, our Italian-American boys were looked upon as knife-wielding, suspicious villains, and often framed on similar outrageous charges, received little better treatment at the hands of the law. He forgets that even today, our Youth are faced with discrimination and our parents are being classified as 'second-class citizens'. . . . [The same people] who deny your people the right to vote, who would doom your Youth to the poverty and lynch mobs of the South, are the same fellows who brand us Italian-Americans as 'Fifth Columnists,' 'Trojan Horses,' and 'Gangsters,' and are fingerprinting our parents. . . . [Judge Brancato] does not speak for the Italian people."[64] Italian American women also used the Party to organize along lines of gender. In the late 1930s, several hundred Italian American women organized within the Progressive Women's Council, which emerged out of the United Council of Working-Class Women and included both Communist-affiliated organizations and non-Communist women's groups. The council, which served as an umbrella organization to the network of working-class women's councils throughout the city's immigrant neighborhoods, linked woman's consumer and tenant advocacy with workplace issues. These groups provided Italian American women with a space to connect their struggles with those of their neighbors. In 1936, Elsie Canepa, an activist in the council, led several hundred Italian women in a May Day parade and other radical demonstrations in the city, where she claimed their right to participate in shaping the revolutionary movement.[65]

Italian women in the Bronx, Brooklyn, the Lower East Side, and throughout New Jersey also joined the Italian section of the Communist Party's International Workers Order (IWO), which was founded in 1931 to help build coalitions around international movements against Fascism, racism, and imperialism. Throughout the 1930s and 1940s, Italian women in New York City organized their own *logge femminili,* and also participated within women's auxiliaries in lodges run primarily by the men in their community. Italian women active in the IWO organized drama groups, strike kitchens, and wartime knitting groups; they also participated in the postwar campaign to provide aid to Italian children. They issued a monthly publication titled *La Donna Italiana,* which focused on their particular struggles within the movement. Although most of women's organizing occurred on the local level, some women occupied positions of national leadership. Domenica Pontremoli, Eleanor Johnjulio, and Elvira and Jennie Mingroni were elected delegates to the first National Convention of the Italian Section, and Anne Fiorentino, in large part because of her success as a community organizer, served as the president of the Italian National Committee of the Italian Section. The Italian National Committee also included such other women organizers as Wanda Perraccini, Drusilla Devese, and Josephine Bilancio. By the late 1940s, Mary Provenzano held one of the more-prominent offices as the chair of the New York Grand Council of the Italian Section. Activism at the national level enabled Italian women in the New York metropolitan area to build coalitions with other working-class women in the IWO and with Italian women's lodges in Chicago, Philadelphia, Detroit, Pittsburgh, Cleveland, and other cities.[66] Vito Magli, the national secretary of the Order, recalled that in the Italian-language newspapers *L'Unità Operaia,* and, later, *L'Unità del Popolo,* which were closely associated with the lodges "we emphasized our Italian background . . . the paper reflected more the politics of Italy rather than the politics of the United States . . . Most of the leadership of *L'Unità* went back to Italy." Yet, he recalled that many members in the lodges focused their activism on domestic issues. "We had situations where we had to intervene," Magli stated, "and explain to the brothers and sisters about racism in the Italian American community. . . . We had to combat racism, a problem in the progressive movement."[67]

Although neighborhood coalition movements and radical circles drew much-smaller memberships than the garment unions, on occasion they provided a place for Italian American women and men to confront the increased poverty and inter-ethnic tensions within their neighborhoods and to question a growing white consciousness among their *paesani.* From the archival records of community leaders such as Vito Marcantonio and Leonard Covello, we know that several hundred Italian American women in East Harlem came together in the 1940s and pledged their commitment to "fight against discrimination because of race, color, and creed," and "establish amicable relations" between Italians and their neighbors. They represented a variety of groups, including local Parent-Teacher Associations, the Italian Social Workers Association, the Italian Teachers Association, the IWO, the American Labor Party (ALP), the Harlem Center Civic Association, the Italian Unemployed Association, the La Guardia Political

Club, the Italian Mothers' Club, the Lower and East Harlem Youth Congress, the Harlem Legislative Council, and a variety of benevolent and mutual-aid societies. Italian American anarchist women formed another component of this network, meeting regularly throughout the depression in a *gruppo femminile anarchico* called Nosotras, which they formed with Puerto Rican, Cuban, and other Latin American women workers in the metropolitan area.[68]

Coalitions among women also took other forms. Throughout the late 1930s, for example, hundreds of Italian American women, men, and children, under the aegis of the East Harlem Housing Committee, jammed the streets of their New York City neighborhood, shouting "We refuse to die like rats in dirty old tenement flats! Make East Harlem a model town, tear the old law tenements down!" At the center of this movement for better housing was a group of women, both immigrant and American-born—Mary Bassano, Adoneta Cuoco, Anna Russo, Cammilla Pagano, Rose Di Geronimo, Mary Cammorota, Angelina Perrone, and dozens of other women from the community; most of whom were married with children. Within the first few months of organizing hundreds of supporters, the women moved beyond the initial goal of constructing low-cost publicly funded housing projects along the East River and began to connect their activities to other movements in the city. The movement started from anger at greedy landlords and unresponsive state and city officials, but it generated a coherent and sustained attack upon an entire system of economic and political exploitation and led many women in the housing movement to link their grievances to their Puerto Rican, African American, Jewish, and West Indian neighbors. When public housing was finally built in East Harlem in the 1940s, however, the units increasingly went to more than twelve thousand low-income African American and Puerto Rican families, whose migration to the city was fueled, in part, by the promise of jobs in wartime industries. Most Italians were unable to gain access to the apartments because of their relatively higher incomes. Ironically, the majority of East Harlem's Italians turned to blaming their Puerto Rican and African American neighbors for the loss of "their" community rather the urban renewal programs that decimated poor, urban communities under the guise of "slum clearance" while subsidizing the development of racially segregated suburbs.[69]

By the 1940s, those Italians who remained active in U.S. radical movements confronted the loss of a mass base of support by drawing on the strategies of the earlier generation of anarchist Italian immigrant women: They focused on confronting issues of power within the Italian American community in order to expose the ways a praxis of domination in any form eroded their ability to successfully bring about revolution. But the ability of revolutionary socialist, anarchist, and syndicalist ideas to mobilize large numbers of Italian Americans within a multi-ethnic and egalitarian popular movement would not be recaptured after the Second World War. Indeed, by then, distancing oneself from radicalism was a primary way Italians could position themselves as less foreign and more American. The appeal of both American and Italian nationalism, and the widespread political repression against anarchists, Communists, and revolutionary socialists in the United States, caused a fracturing of the radical political culture and a fragmenting of memory. Consequently, the history of Italian American women's activism within revolutionary movements has remained for the most part in archives and oral histories.

This essay offers only a glimpse into the worlds of Italian women's radicalism in the United States. These stories are just some of the thousands that wait to be told. Italian American women crafted large-scale acts of resistance, they wrote and spoke out publicly about the conditions of their lives, they exposed the ways power operated within their communities, they organized neighbors and coworkers, and they debated revolutionary ideology and practice. Such activities were possible because of the everyday acts Italian women devised to confront oppressive conditions in their families and communities. The day-to-day struggle to make ends meet led women to devise practical actions and collective strategies, that when necessary were transformed into weapons of resistance. When we consider women's presence within Italian American radical movements, we are attending to the ways culture is created through dialogue and debate—not only among prominent leaders, but among the thousands of women and men whose lives became influenced by revolutionary ideas and actions.

NOTES

This essay benefited immeasurably from the assistance, support, and guidance of the following: Donna Gabaccia, David Roediger, Salvatore Salerno, Franca Iacovetta, Philip Cannistraro, Kym Ragusa, Edvige Giunta, Rosette Capotorto, Joseph Sciorra, Giorgio Bertellini, Danilo Romeo, Lucio Ruotolo, Nan Enstad, Marjorie Bryer, Gaye T. M. Okoh, Rachel Maxine Koch, and the entire Guglielmo family. I am especially grateful to Gerald Meyer for his editorial expertise.

1. Maria Barbieri, "Ribelliamoci!" *La Questione Sociale* (herein after referred to as *LQS*), 18 November 1905. The original text reads: «Vi giungano gradite, a voi tutte o compagne, queste poche righe che un'altra proletaria come voi vi dedica. E' il pensiero, è il palpito della mia anima che sente tutte le ingiustizie sociali per cui noi da secoli siamo le schiave umili e sottomesse; è una ribelle che insorge contro tutte queste iniquità, e invita anche voi alla lotta.»

2. To date, the only book-length study of Italian American women's radicalism remains unpublished: Colomba Marie Furio, "Immigrant Women and Industry: A Case Study. The Italian Immigrant Women and the Garment Industry, 1880–1950," (Ph.D. diss., New York University, 1979). Other materials that document this history are the following: Furio, "The Cultural Background of the Italian Immigrant Woman and Its Impact on her Unionization in the New York City Garment Industry, 1880–1918," in *Pane e Lavoro: The Italian American Working Class*, ed. George E. Pozzetta (Staten Island, N.Y.: American Italian Historical Association, 1980): 81–98; Jean Vincenza Scarpaci, "Angela Bambace and the International Ladies' Garment Workers' Union: The Search for an Elusive Activist," in *Pane e Lavoro*, 99–118; Donna R. Gabaccia, *Militants and Migrants: Rural Sicilians Become American Workers* (New Brunswick, N.J.: Rutgers University Press, 1988); Gabaccia, *From the Other Side: Women, Gender, and Immigrant Life in the U.S., 1820–1900* (Bloomington: Indiana University Press, 1994); Elizabeth Ewen, *Immigrant Women in the*

Land of Dollars: Life and Culture on the Lower East Side, 1890–1925 (New York: Monthly
Review Press, 1985); essays by Caroline Merithew, Franca Iacovetta, and Robert Ven-
tresca, in *Women, Gender, and Transnational Lives: Italian Workers of the World*, ed. Donna
R. Gabaccia and Franca Iacovetta (Toronto: University of Toronto Press, 2003); Ardis
Cameron, *Radicals of the Worst Sort: Laboring Women in Lawrence, Massachusetts,
1860–1912* (Urbana: University of Illinois Press, 1993); Nancy A. Hewitt, *Southern Dis-
comfort: Women's Activism in Tampa, Florida, 1880s–1920s* (Urbana: University of Illinois
Press, 2001); Ruth Laub Coser et al., *Women of Courage: Jewish and Italian Immigrant
Women in New York* (Westport, Conn.: Greenwood Press, 1999); Gary R. Mormino and
George E. Pozzetta, "Immigrant Women in Tampa: The Italian Experience, 1890–1930,"
Florida Historical Quarterly 61 (January 1983): 296–312; Charles Zappia, "Unionism and
the Italian American Worker: A History of the New York City 'Italian Local' in the
International Ladies' Garment Workers' Union, 1900–1933" (Ph.D. diss., University of
California, Berkeley, 1994); Maria Parrino, "Breaking the Silence: Autobiographies of
Italian Immigrant Women," *Storia Nordamericana* 5, no. 2 (1988); Brigid O'Farrell and
Joyce L. Kornbluh, *Rocking the Boat: Union Women's Voices, 1915–1975* (New Brunswick,
N.J.: Rutgers University Press, 1996), 34–57; Paul Avrich, *Anarchist Voices* (Princeton,
N.J.: Princeton University Press, 1995); and Paul Avrich, *Sacco and Vanzetti: The Anar-
chist Background* (Princeton, N.J.: Princeton University Press, 1991).

3. For a fuller discussion of why Italian American women's histories have been marginalized, see Donna R. Gabaccia, "Italian American Women: A Review Essay," *Italian Americana* (fall/winter 1993): 38–61; Gabaccia, "Immigrant Women, Nowhere at Home?"
Journal of American Ethnic History 10, no. 4 (1991): 61–87; Gabaccia, "Italian Immigrant
Women in Comparative Perspective," *Altreitalie* 9 (1993): 163–75; and J. Vincenza
Scarpaci, "La Contadina: The Plaything of the Middle Class Woman Historian," *Journal
of Ethnic Studies*, vol. 9 (summer 1981).

4. For an insightful discussion of the ways Jewish women have stressed their own mili-
tance and class consciousness in contradistinction to the values and behavior of Italian
American women, see Susan A. Glenn, *Daughters of the Shtetl: Life and Labor in the Immigrant Generation* (Ithaca, N.Y.: Cornell University Press, 1990), 191–94.

5. Elizabeth Gurley Flynn, *Rebel Girl, An Autobiography: My First Life (1906–1926)*
(New York: International Publishers, 1955), 333.

6. I am following the lead of Elsa Barkley Brown, whose work has demonstrated how
social movements should be conceived as "multivocal" processes, wherein different positions are revealed as interconnected. See her "Polyrhythms and Improvisation: Lessons for
Women's History," *History Workshop Journal*, vol. 31 (spring 1991).

7. Rudolph J. Vecoli, "Italian Immigrants in the United States Labor Movement from
1880 to 1929," in *Gli italiani fuori d'Italia, gli emigrati italiani nei movimenti operai dei paesi
d'adozione 1880–1940*, ed. Bruno Bezza (Milan: Franco Angeli, 1983); Gabaccia, *Militants
and Migrants*; Mario De Ciampis, "Storia del Movimento Socialista Rivoluzionario Italiano," *La Parola del Popolo* 9 (Dec. 1958–Jan. 1959): 136–63; George E. Pozzetta and
Bruno Ramirez, *The Italian Diaspora across the Globe* (Ontario: Multicultural History Society of Ontario, 1992); Gianfausto Rosoli, ed., *Un secolo di emigrazione italiana, 1866–1976*
(Rome: Centro Studi Emigrazione, 1978); Nunzio Pernicone, *Italian Anarchism,
1864–1892* (Princeton, N.J.: Princeton University Press, 1993).

8. Jole Calapso, *Donne Ribelli: Un secolo di lotte femminili in Sicilia* (Palermo, Italy: S. F.
Flaccovio, 1980); Calapso, *Una donna intransigente: Vita di Maria Giudice* (Palermo, Italy:
Sellerio Editore, 1996); Franca Pieroni Bortolotti, *Alle origini del movimento femminile in*

Italia, 1848–1892 (Turin, Italy: Einaudi, 1975); Bortolotti, *Socialismo e questione femminile in Italia* (Milan: G. Mazzotta, 1974); Bortolotti, *Sul movimento politico delle donne, Scritti inediti*, ed. Annarita Buttafuoco (Rome: Cooperativa Utopia, 1987); Teresa Noce, *Gioventù senza sole* (Rome: Editori Riuniti, 1978); Camilla Ravera, *Breve storia del movimento femminile in Italia* (Rome: Editori Riuniti, 1978); Jane Slaughter, *Women and the Italian Resistance, 1943–1945* (Denver: Arden Press, 1997); Victoria de Grazia, *How Fascism Ruled Women, Italy, 1922–1945* (Berkeley: University of California Press, 1992); Lucia Chiavola Birnbaum, *Liberazione della donna/feminism in Italy* (Middletown, Conn.: Wesleyan University Press, 1986); Claire La Vigna, "Women in the Canadian and Italian Trade Union Movements at the Turn of the Century: a Comparison," in *The Italian Immigrant Woman in North America*, ed. Betty Boyd Caroli, Robert F. Harney, and Lydio F. Tomasi (Toronto: The Multicultural History Society of Ontario, 1978); Elda Gentili Zappi, *"If Eight Hours Seem Too Few": Mobilization of Women Workers in the Italian Rice Fields* (Albany: State University of New York Press, 1991); Gabaccia, *Militants and Migrants*.

9. Donna R. Gabaccia, "Migration and Militancy among Italy's Laborers," in *Roots of the Transplanted*, ed. Dirk Hoerder et al. (New York: Columbia University Press, 1994), 247.

10. Calapso, *Donne Ribelli*, 175; Chiavola Birnbaum, *Liberazione*, 13, 23, 25; also quoted in E. J. Hobsbawm, *Primitive Rebels: Studies in Archaic Forms of Social Movement in the 19th and 20th Centuries* (New York: Praeger, 1959), 183.

11. Salvatore Salerno, "No God, No Master: Italian Anarchists and the Industrial Workers of the World," chapter 7 of this book; Patrizia Sione, "Industrial Work, Militancy, and Migrations of Northern Italian Workers in Europe and in Paterson, New Jersey, 1880–1913" (Ph.D. diss., State University of New York, Binghamton, 1992), 1, 199–200; George Carey, *"La Questione Sociale*, an Anarchist Newspaper in Paterson, New Jersey (1895–1908)," in *Italian Americans: New Perspectives in Italian Immigration and Ethnicity*, ed. Lydio Tomasi (New York: Center for Migration Studies, 1985); Emma Goldman, *Living My Life* (Garden City, N.Y.: Garden City Publishing, 1931), 150–1.

12. Salerno, "No God, No Master"; Salerno, *Red November, Black November: Culture and Community in the Industrial Workers of the World* (Albany: State University of New York Press, 1989), 49–50, 58, 89; Sione, "Industrial Work, Militancy, and Migrations," 1, 199–200; Carey, *"La Questione Sociale,* " 292; Carey, "The Vessel, the Deed, and the Idea: Anarchists in Paterson, 1895–1908," *Antipode* 10, no. 11 (1979): 51; Avrich, *Anarchist Portraits* (Princeton, N.J.: Princeton University Press, 1988), 173; Avrich, *Sacco and Vanzetti*, 55; Avrich, *Anarchist Voices*, 143, 391–93; Gianna S. Panofsky, "A View of Two Major Centers of Italian Anarchism in the United States: Spring Valley and Chicago, Illinois," in *Italian Ethnics: Their Languages, Literature, and Lives*, ed. Dominic Candeloro, Fred L. Gardaphè, and Paolo A. Giordano (Staten Island, N.Y.: American Italian Historical Association, 1990), 279; Joan Casanovas, "Pere Esteve (1865–1925): Un Anarquista Catala a Cavall de Dos Mons i de Dues Generacions," Papers of George E. Pozzetta, Immigration History Research Center (IHRC), University of Minnesota, St. Paul; Bernardo Vega, *Memoirs of Bernardo Vega: A Contribution to the History of the Puerto Rican Community in New York*, ed. Cesar Andreu Iglesias (New York: Monthly Review Press, 1984); Angelo Massari, *The Wonderful World of Angelo Massari*, trans. Arthur D. Massolo (New York: Exposition Press, 1965), 107; Gary R. Mormino and George E. Pozzetta, *The Immigrant World of Ybor City: Italians and Their Latin Neighbors in Tampa, 1885–1985* (Urbana and Chicago: University of Illinois Press, 1987); George E. Pozzetta, "Italians and the

Tampa General Strike of 1910," in *Pane e Lavoro*, 31; Pozzetta, "An Immigrant Library: The Tampa Italian Club Collection," *Ex Libris* 1 (spring 1978): 12.

13. «Ed è appunto perchè sentiamo e soffriamo che noi pure vogliamo immischiarci nella lotta contro questa società, perchè anche noi ci sentiamo nate per esser libere, per esser uguali» (Maria Roda, "Alle operaie," *LQS*, 15 Sept. 1897).

14. See Luigia Reville, "Ai Rivoluzionarii, in nome del gruppo 'L'azione femminile' di Parigi," *LQS*, 5 May 1900; "Cronaca di Spring Valley, Il Gruppo Femminile" and Il Gruppo I Nuovi Viventi, Il Gruppo Femminile Luisa Michel, "La questione della donna," *L'Aurora*, 22 Dec. 1900; "I gruppi femminili di propaganda," *LQS*, 23 Nov. 1901; "Le nostre compagne" *LQS*, 6 Nov. 1901, 23 Nov. 1901, 14 Dec. 1901, 4 Jan. 1902, 11 Jan. 1902, 5 April 1902; Il Gruppo Anarchico Femminile, Paterson, "Il Gruppo Anarchico femminile," *LQS*, 12 July 1902; Gruppo Emancipazione della Donna, Paterson, "Comunicati," *LQS*, 26 July 1902; Gruppo Emancipazione della Donna, Paterson, "Pubblicazione di Propaganda," *LQS*, 10 May 1902; "Gruppo Emancipazione della Donna," Paterson, *LQS*, 16 Aug. 1902. See also Carey, "*La Questione Sociale*," 292; Panofsky, "A View of Two Major Centers," 275–76; Caroline Merithew, "Anarchist Motherhood: Toward the Making of a Revolutionary Proletariat in Illinois Coal Towns," in Gabaccia and Iacovetta, *Women, Gender, and Transnational Lives*.

15. «Per l'emancipazione della donna, la quale oltre alla lotta che deve fare per la conquista dei diritti che tutta l'umanità oppressa rivendica, deve lottare con non minore ardore per emanciparsi dalla tirannia e dai pregiudizii degli uomini, i quali scioccamente considerano la donna come un essere inferiore, quando non la trattino addirittura come una schiava.» "Cronaca di Spring Valley, Il Gruppo Femminile," *L'Aurora*, 22 Dec. 1900.

16. Pamphlet, Gruppo Emancipazione della Donna, A. M. Mozzoni, *Alle fanciulle che studiano* (Paterson, N.J.: Tipografia del *Despertar*, 1902); Gruppo Femminile, Emancipazione della Donna, Paterson, "Alle figlie del popolo di Anna Maria Mozzoni," *LQS* (26 April 1902). During the Risorgimento, Mozzoni brought "l'emancipazione della donna" to the forefront of Italian socialist debates through her activism within the Socialist Party and La Lega Promotrice degli Interessi Femminili, an independent association that she helped to found at Milan in 1881 "to stimulate women's consciousness of their rights." Chiavola Birnbaum, *Liberazione*, 19–21; Zappia, "If Eight Hours Seem Too Few," 71–76. See also Anna Maria Mozzoni, *Liberazione della donna*, ed. Franca Pieroni Bortolotti (Milan: G. Mazzotta, 1975); Mozzoni, *Un passo avanti nella cultural femminile, tesi e progetto* (Milan: G. Mazzotta, 1975); Mozzoni, "Alle Figlie del Popolo," *LQS*, 15 July 1895.

17. For examples of the anarchist feminist writing by Italian immigrant women workers, many of whom participated within the *gruppi*, see Virginia Buongiorno, "Alle compagne lavoratrici" *LQS*, 15 Oct. 1895; Ersilia Grandi, "A un'operaia," *LQS*, 12 Oct. 1898; "La Donna e la famiglia," *LQS*, 17 March 1900; "Emancipazione della Donna I," *LQS*, 7 July 1900; "Emancipazione della Donna II," *LQS*, 14 July 1900; "Emancipazione della Donna III," *LQS*, 21 July 1900; Ernestina Cravello, "Lettera Aperta al Bolletino della Sera," *LQS*, 1 Sept. 1900; Una Sartina, "Ma tu sei una donna!" *LQS*, 24 Aug. 1901; Alba, "Alle mie compagne," *LQS*, 21 Aug. 1901; Alba, "Eguali diritti," *LQS*, 15 Oct. 1901; Maria Barbieri, "Alle Madri," *LQS*, 7 Sept. 1901; Titì, "Alle Mie Sorelle Proletarie," part 1, *LQS*, 9 June 1906; Titì, "Alle Mie Sorelle Proletarie," part 2, *LQS*, 16 June 1906; Titì, "Alle Mie Sorelle Proletarie," part 3, *LQS*, 23 June 1906; Titì, "Alle Donne, Emancipiamoci!" *LQS*, 7 July 1906; Caterina Sebastiani, "L'Ultima Parola," *LQS*, 8 Dec. 1906; Augusta De Angelis, "Redenta," *LQS*, 22 Dec. 1906; Ida Merini Catastini, "La Donna nella Famiglia," *LQS*, 16 Nov. 1907; Alba Genisio, "Alle Donne Proletarie," *LQS*, 7

March 1908; Candida M. D'Arcangelo, "Alle Donne Proletarie" *LQS*, 11 Jan. 1908; and Anna De Gigli, "L'Amore, La proprietà e i delitti," *L'Era Nuova*, 31 May 1913. For material on local activism in the IWW, see Salerno, "No God, No Master"; David J. Goldberg, *A Tale of Three Cities: Labor Organization and Protest in Paterson, Passaic, and Lawrence, 1916–1921* (New Brunswick, N.J.: Rutgers University Press, 1989); Anne Huber Tripp, *The IWW and the Paterson Silk Strike of 1913* (Urbana and Chicago: University of Illinois Press, 1987); Philip S. Swanton, ed., *Silk City: Studies on the Paterson Silk Industry, 1860–1940* (Newark: New Jersey Historical Society, 1985); and Steve Golin, *The Fragile Bridge: Paterson Silk Strike, 1913* (Philadelphia: Temple University Press, 1988).

18. «Che la donna, per quanto si sforzi, non potrà mai elevarsi dallo stato d'abbiezone in cui si trova» (Alba, "Eguali diritti," *LQS*, 5 Oct. 1901). «Noi ci agitiamo, ci organizziamo per provare al mondo che ci accusa, che anche noi siam capaci a qualche cosa» (Roda, "Alle operaie"). For other essays by women who defended their commitment to the movement, see Alba, "Eguali diritti," *LQS* (Oct. 15, 1901); Caterina Sebastiani, "L'Ultima Parola," *LQS*, 8 Dec. 1906; "I gruppi femminili di propaganda," *LQS*, 23 Nov. 1901; and Una Sartina, "Ma tu sei una donna!" *LQS*, 24 Aug. 1901.

19. Salerno, "No God, No Master"; Sione, "Industrial Work, Militancy, and Migrations"; Carey, "*La Questione Sociale.*" See also "Perchè siamo Organizzatori," *LQS*, 30 March 1897. There was some crossover, as a few women published their essays in many different papers. For example, Ersilia Cavedagni (who was also Ersilia Grandi and the partner to Giuseppe Ciancabilla) published essays in *La Questione Sociale* and *Cronaca Sovversiva*, such as "Unione libera," *Cronaca Sovversiva*, 23 Dec. 1905, and "Comunicati," *Cronaca Sovversiva*, 20 Jan. 1906.

20. «[U]na lotta continua di tutti i giorni per poter svellere le profonde radici che una falsa educazione aveva coltivate e cresciute nel mio cuore» (Maria Barbieri, "Ricordi? Al Compagno lontano," *LQS*, 4 Nov. 1905).

21. Since the essays are too numerous to list, the following is a sampling: Teresa Ballerini, "Ai Diatribi," *LQS*, 15 Oct. 1896; Ersilia Cavedagni (Ciancabilla e Grandi), "La caccia agli Anarchici Italiani," *LQS*, 15 April 1898; Una Donna, "Scab!" *LQS*, 12 Nov. 1904; Anna Rio, "Paura della Libertà!" *LQS*, 3 June 1905; Aurora, "Gli anarchicissimi," *LQS*, 2 June 1906; Caterina Caminita, "Dopo la Grazia," *LQS*, 16 June 1906; Cristina Melone, "Lettera Aperta: Ai Preti della Chiesa di San Michele di Paterson," *LQS*, 20 April 1907; Susanna Zannotti, "L'altra campana," *LQS*, 7 Sept. 1907; Susanna Zanotti, "Una Parola Ancora," *LQS*, 12 Oct. 1907); Michelina de Luca, "Lettera di Propaganda," *LQS*, 15 Feb. 1908; Angiolina Algeri, "Le delizie del secolo XX," *L'Era Nuova*, 22 April 1911; and Anna De Gigli, "La potenza del danaro," *L'Era Nuova*, 5 July 1913.

22. «Io ho raggiunto l'altezza della mia individualità e non mi piego che al mio proprio io. Ma questo lo dico e lo scrivo perchè ancora non mi è stato detto di mettere alla prova tutto ciò. . . . Infatti, diamo uno sguardo alla società borghese e un altro a noi, proletarie che facciamo parte della famiglia anarchica» (Titì, "Alle Donne, Emancipiamoci!" *LQS*, 7 July 1906). Titì's writing appeared regularly in *La Questione Sociale* between 1906 and 1907.

23. «Noi anarchici si è predicato ai quattro venti l'emancipazione della donna. . . . Non sapete che la prima propaganda da farsi è quella della famiglia? Fate un piccolo mondo anarchico nella famiglia vostra e poi vedrete come sarete temprati, come vi riuscirà più facile il propagare gli altri!» (Camillo Di Sciullo, "La Donna," *LQS*, 26 Oct. 1907). For other examples of support from men in the movement, see A. Ferritti, "La Donna, Come era, come è, e come sarà" *LQS*, 29 Feb. 1896; "Considerazioni sulla donna,"

LQS, 15 Aug. 1897; "Gli Anarchici e la Donna," *LQS*, 4 April 1897; "N.di R." printed after Roda, "Alle operaie"; Albert Guabello, "Alle Donne," *LQS*, 18 Feb. 1899; Evening, "La Donna dell'Avvenire" *LQS*, 18 Feb.1899; Giuseppe Corna, "Il Martirio della donna," *LQS*, 17 June 1899. See response to Luigia Reville, "Ai Rivoluzionarii," *LQS*, 5 May 1900; Il Gruppo I Nuovi Viventi, Il Gruppo Femminile Luisa Michel, "La questione della donna," *L'Aurora*, 22 Dec. 1900; A. Visalli, "Alla Donna," part 1, *LQS*, 19 Jan. 1901; A. Visalli, "Alla Donna," part 2, *LQS*, 26 Jan. 1901; "I gruppi femminili di propaganda," *LQS*, 23 Nov. 1901; and Il Mefistofelico, "Intorno all'Emancipazione della Donna," *LQS*, 2 Nov. 1907.

24. Maria Barbieri, "Ribelliamoci!" 18 Nov. 1905. The following quotation, «Chi è questa gente padrona assoluta della nostra persona, della nostra felicità, della nostra vita? Questa gente siamo noi, perche noi approviamo tutto ciò che ci fa schiave. . . . Dominati, infatti, da questo assioma, appena nasce una bambina le si assegna il suo posto nella vita. . . . ha infuso a quella bambina attitudini diverse di quelle che noi vogliamo imporle, di modo che ella, adulta, sarà una pessima cucitrice e una analfabeta. . . . Se la bambina potesse ribellarsi alla nostra autorità, essa lo farebbe ben volentieri, e sarebbe molto meglio per lei e per l'umanità tutta,» is from Titì, "Alle Mie Sorelle Proletarie," *LQS*, 6 June, 16 June 1906.

25. «[U]n gran posto e una grande influenza nella vita individuale e collettiva dell'umanità» which could be used to educate «una nuova generazione di lavoratori coscienti e spogli di pregiuidizii, e per aver noi stessi un appoggio e un conforto nella lotta per l'emancipazione umana. . . . sia necessario, anzi urgente, preoccuparsi, prima di tutto, dell'emancipazione della donna» (Il Gruppo I Nuovi Viventi, Il Gruppo Femminile Luisa Michel, "La questione della donna," *L'Aurora*, 22 Dec. 1900).

26. «delle femministe a modo di certe borghesi che reclamano l'eguaglianza o la supremazia del nostro sesso, e che sarebbero soddisfatte dalla realizzazione di quei sogni» (Luigia Reville, "Ai Rivoluzionarii, in nome del gruppo 'L'azione femminile' di Parigi," *LQS*, 5 May 1900). See also "Il Femminismo," part 1, *LQS*, 16 March 1901; "Il Femminismo," part 2, *LQS*, 23 March 1901.

27. Several U.S. labor historians have demonstrated the importance of family to working-class resistance and struggle. See, for example, Elsa Barkley Brown, "Mothers of Mind," *Sage*, vol. 6 (summer 1989); Robin D. G. Kelley, " 'We Are Not What We Seem': Rethinking Black Working Class Opposition in the Jim Crow South," *Journal of American History* 80 (June 1993): 75–112; Alice Kessler-Harris, "Treating the Male as 'Other': Redefining the Parameters of Labor History," *Labor History* 34 (spring/summer 1993): 190–204.

28. From a vast literature, see Cameron, *Radicals of the Worst Sort*; Hewitt, *Southern Discomfort*; Judith E. Smith, *Family Connections: A History of Italian and Jewish Immigrant Lives in Providence, Rhode Island, 1900–1940* (Albany: State University of New York Press, 1985); Meredith Tax, *The Rising of the Women: Feminist Solidarity and Class Conflict, 1880–1917* (New York: Monthly Review Press, 1981); Joan M. Jenson and Sue Davidson, eds., *A Needle, A Bobbin, A Strike: Women Needleworkers in America* (Philadelphia: Temple University Press, 1984); Golin, *Fragile Bridge*; Mormino and Pozzetta, *Immigrant World of Ybor City*.

29. Quotes from WTUL leaders are reprinted in Glenn, *Daughters of the Shtetl*, 190–93. For ILGWU attitudes toward Italian women in this period, see Furio, "Immigrant Women and Industry," 99–104; Scarpaci, "Angela Bambace," 102; Edwin Fenton, *Immigrants and Unions: A Case Study, Italians and American Labor, 1870–1920* (New York: Arno Press, 1975), 483–85.

30. Interview with Capraro by Blodgett, 11 Sept. 1969, tapes 4, 6 and 7, Capraro Papers, IHRC; Gabaccia, *Militants and Migrants*, 139–41; Fenton, *Immigrants and Unions*, chap. 9; Ewen, *Immigrant Women*, 259; Scarpaci, "Angela Bambace"; Vecoli, "Italian Immigrants in Labor Movement," 274–75; Glenn, *Daughters of the Shtetl*, 198; Steve Fraser, "Landslayt and Paesani: Ethnic Conflict and Cooperation in the Amalgamated Clothing Workers of America," in *"Struggle a Hard Battle": Essays on Working-Class Immigrants*, ed. Dirk Hoerder (De Kalb, Ill., 1986); De Ciampis, "Note sul movimento socialista."

31. Gabaccia, *Militants and Migrants*, 139–41.

32. Scarpaci, "Angela Bambace," 101. See also "Notes to interview questions dictated by Angela Bambace to Marian," 18–20 Feb. 1975. My thanks to Philip Camponeschi, Angela's son, for sharing this and other documents concerning Angela with me. They are now included in the Bambace Papers at the IHRC. For more on the Bambace sisters and Tina Cacici, see interview with Capraro by Blodgett, 11 Sept. 1969, tapes 5 and 7, Capraro Papers, IHRC; *Il Proletario*, 17 Feb. 1911; Rudolph J. Vecoli, "Anthony Capraro and the Lawrence Strike of 1919," in Pozzetta, *Pane e Lavoro*, 14–15.

33. Gabaccia, *Militants and Migrants*, 140.

34. See also Furio, "Immigrant Women and Industry," 156–57, 242–46; Annelise Orleck, *Common Sense and a Little Fire: Women and Working-Class Politics in the United States, 1900–1965* (Chapel Hill: University of North Carolina Press, 1995), 76; Salerno, *Red November, Black November*, 48–9, 58, 89; Gabaccia, *Militants and Migrants*, 117, 140–2; Fenton, *Immigrants and Unions*, 308–10, 479–91; Bruno Cartosio, "Gli emigrati italiani e l'Industrial Workers of the World," in Bezza, *Gli italiani*; Zappia, "Unionism and the Italian American Worker"; De Ciampis, "Storia del Movimento Socialista," 154; Vecoli, "Italian Immigrants in the Labor Movement"; Vecoli, "Italian American Workers, 1880–1920: Padrone Slaves or Primitive Rebels?" in *Perspectives in Italian Immigration and Ethnicity*, ed. Silvio Tomasi (New York: Center for Migration Studies, 1977), 28–29. See also "Comunicazioni" in *L'Adunata dei Refrattari* and regular articles in *Il Proletario* throughout the 1910s and 1920s for more information on IWW organizing among Italian workers in New York City.

35. "Cloak Makers Vote to Strike," *New York Call*, 5 July 1910; "Lo Sciopero dei Sarti," *L'Araldo*, 21 July 1910. See also Furio, "Immigrant Women and Industry."

36. Furio, "Immigrant Women and Industry," 156, 162.

37. Angela Bambace, "Notes to interview questions dictated by Angela Bambace to Marion," 18–20 Feb. 1975, Bambace Papers, IHRC; *L'Operaia*, 13 Sept. 1913, 4 April 1914, 13 Aug. 1914, 3 Sept. 1914, 17 Oct. 1914, 24 Oct. 1914, 31 Oct. 1914, 2 Jan. 1915, 27 Feb. 1915, 24 April 1915; Furio, "Immigrant Women and Industry."

38. The Italian Cloak, Suit, and Skirt Makers' Union Local 48 received its first charter in 1916, and the Italian Dressmakers' Local 89 was chartered in 1919; Local 48-ILGWU, *"48" Libro Ricordo del XXV Anniversario della Unione dei Cloakmakers Italiani* (New York: International Newspaper Printing, 1941), 25–30; Furio, "Immigrant Women and Indus-try"; Zappia, "Unionism and the Italian American Worker: The Politics of Anti-Commu-nism in the International Ladies' Garment Workers' Union," in *Italian Americans through the Generations*, ed. Rocco Caporale (Staten Island, N.Y.: American Italian Historical Association, 1986).

39. This quote, taken from Theresa Malkiel, "Striking for the Right to Live," *The Com-ing Nation* 1 (25 Jan. 1913), is reprinted in Furio, "Immigrant Women and Industry," 188.

40. Zappia, "Unionism and the Italian American Worker"; Philip V. Cannistraro, "Luigi Antonini and the Italian Anti-Fascist Movement in the United States,

1940–1943," *Journal of American Ethnic History*, vol. 21 (fall 1995); Cannistraro, *Black-shirts in Little Italy: Italian Americans and Fascism, 1921–1929* (West Lafayette, Ind.: Bordighera, 1999); John P. Diggins, "The Italo-American Anti-Fascist Opposition," *Journal of American History* 54 (December 1967): 582; Diggins, *Mussolini and Fascism, The View from America* (Princeton, N.J.: Princeton University Press, 1972), 111–43; Gaetano Salvemini, *Italian Fascist Activities in the United States*, ed. Philip V. Cannistraro (New York, 1977); Fiorello B. Ventresco, "Crises and Unity: The Italian Radicals in America in the 1920s," *Ethnic Forum* 15, nos. 1–2 (1995).

41. "Una tessitrice," *L'Adunata dei Refrattari*, 12 May 1923; Romualdi, "Storia della Locale 89," in *Local LXXXIX: XV Anniversary* (org: ILGWU, 1934). See also Furio, "Immigrant Women and Industry"; Scarpaci, "Angela Bambace"; Carmen Lucia, "First a Troublemaker, Then a Troubleshooter," in O'Farrell and Kornbluh, *Rocking the Boat*, 34–57.

42. "Primavera Nostra," *L'Adunata dei Refrattari*, 24 Aug. 1927; *Germinal*, 15 Aug. 1927. See also Avrich, *Sacco and Vanzetti*.

43. Corrispondenze, West Haven, Conn., *L'Adunata dei Refrattari*, 9 June 1923.

44. Colomba Furio interview with Diane Romanik, ILGWU officer and niece of organizer Margaret di Maggio, New York City, 1 April 1977, reprinted in Furio, "Immigrant Women and Industry," 417–26.

45. Paul D'Ambrosio, *Ralph Fasanella's America* (Cooperstown: New York State Historical Association, 2001), 26–27.

46. Scarpaci, "Angela Bambace," 104–7; Furio, "Immigrant Women and Industry"; Romualdi, "Storia della Locale 89"; Philip Camponeschi, "Speech prepared for Oscar," 15 Nov. 1908, Bambace Papers, IHRC.

47. Zappia, "Unionism and the Italian American Worker"; Scarpaci, "Angela Bambace"; Furio, "Immigrant Women and Industry"; interview with Albina Delfino by Ruth R. Prago, 9 Jan. 1981, Oral History of the American Left, Wagner Archives, Tamiment Collection, New York University.

48. «s'è permesso di vedere il fascismo per le contrade d'Italia, e gli analfabeti passare per archi di scienza . . . Alzatevi, sbattete in faccia a questa vile società tutte le nefandezze e le angherie che v'impone. . . . Divenite donne. . . . Siate libere, ma non prostitute, siate le compagne dell'uomo nella vita e nella lotta» (Delie, "Alle Donne, L'Italia Grande Espone i Suoi Grandi Uomini a Moralizzare!" *L'Adunata dei Refrattari*, 15 Jan. 1923).

49. «[L'uomo] dovrebbe sapere che l'umanità non può elevarsi se non si eleva la donna e che l'emancipazione proletaria non può camminare che a pari passo coll'emancipazione femminile» (Una Donna, "Parole al Vento al Mio Sesso," *L'Adunata dei Refrattari*, 30 Aug. 1922). See also "L'emancipazione della donna," *L'Adunata dei Refrattari*, 15 Jan. 1927.

50. I am thankful to Robert Ventresca and Franca Iacovetta for sharing their important research on D'Andrea with me. See their essay, "Foreign, Female, and Dangerous: Virgilia D'Andrea, Politics of Protest, Poetry of Exile," in Gabaccia and Iacovetta, *Women, Gender, and Transnational Lives*. See also poster from Il Circolo di Cultura Operaia announcing Virgilia D'Andrea's lecture at La Casa del Popolo in Somerville, Mass., 22 Feb. 1929, Fabrizi Papers, IHRC; *L'Adunata dei Refrattari*, 26 March 1932, 3 Sept. 1932, 24 Sept. 1932. The quotations are from her lecture, "I Delitti della Patria Borghese, I Diritti della Patria Umana," Somerset Hall, Somerville, Mass., 3 Dec. 1931, and other cities throughout the United States, reprinted in D'Andrea, *Richiamo All'Anarchia: Protesta e proposta anarchica in otto conferenze* (Imda: Cooperative Editrica Paolo Galeati, 1965), 142, 147.

51. Diggins, "Italo-American Anti-Fascist Opposition," 582; Diggins, *Mussolini and Fascism*; Salvemini, *Italian Fascist Activities*; Vecoli, "Making and Unmaking of the Italian American Working Class," 22.

52. *New York Times*, 16, 17 Aug. 1933; Fannia M. Cohn, "The Uprising of the Sixty Thousand, The General Strike of the Dressmakers' Union," *Justice*, 1 Sept. 1933; *Daily Worker*, 17, 18, 19 Aug. 1933; *Il Progresso*, 16–20 Aug. 1933; see materials on 1933 strike in Papers of Charles Zimmerman, box 28, file 5, and in Papers of David Dubinsky, box 69, file 2, ILGWU Archives, Kheel Center for Labor Management Documentation and Archives, Cornell University; Serafino Romualdi, "Storia della Locale 89," in *Local 89 Fifteenth Anniversary Commemoration Pamphlet* (New York, Local 89: ILGWU, 1934); ILGWU, *Report of the General Executive Board to the 23rd Convention of the ILGWU* (Atlantic City, N.J., 3 May 1937), 48.

53. Romualdi, "Storia della Locale 89"; Local 48-ILGWU, *Libro Ricordo*; "Il Sindacato dell'Abbigliamento Femminile-ILGWU," *La Parola del Popolo*, 50th Anniversary Publication, 1908–1958, 195; Local 89, ILGWU, *We, the Italian Dressmakers Speak* (New York, 1944); *Giustizia*, October 1933, April 1934; *Local 89 Fifteenth Anniversary Commemoration Pamphlet* (1934); "Administration of Local 89, 1944–46" in ILGWU, *Jubilee, 1919–1944* (1944); "New York: Our City-Our Union, 24th Convention of the ILGWU, Fortieth Anniversary" (1940), box 1, Crivello Papers, IHRC. See also interviews with Tina Catania, Grace de Luisa, and Tina Gaeta in Furio, "Immigrant Women and Industry," 427–35, 436–45, 446–57; Scarpaci, "Angela Bambace"; Nancy L. Green, *Ready-to-Wear, Ready-to-Work: A Century of Industry and Immigrants in Paris and New York* (Durham, N.C.: Duke University Press, 1997).

54. Lizabeth Cohen, *Making a New Deal: Industrial Workers in Chicago, 1919–1939* (New York: Cambridge University Press, 1990), 253.

55. These were the sentiments expressed by many participants at the conference that inspired this anthology, "The Lost World of Italian American Radicalism: Labor, Politics, and Culture," Calandra Institute, City University of New York, New York City, 14-15 May 1997. See also Gabaccia, *Militants and Migrants*, 145–48.

56. Thomas A. Guglielmo, *White on Arrival: Italians, Race, Color, and Power in Chicago, 1890–1945* (New York: Oxford University Press, forthcoming). For more on this process, see George Lipsitz, *The Possessive Investment in Whiteness: How White People Profit from Identity Politics* (Philadelphia: Temple University Press, 1998); Robert Orsi, "The Religious Boundaries of an 'Inbetween' People: Street *Feste* and the Problem of the Dark-Skinned Other in Italian Harlem, 1920–1990," in *Gods of the City: Religion and the Urban Landscape*, ed. Robert Orsi (Indianapolis: Indiana University Press, 1999); Jennifer Guglielmo and Salvatore Salerno, eds., *Are Italians White? How Race Is Made in America* (New York: Routledge, 2003).

57. See the following documents in the Zimmerman Papers, ILGWU Archives, LMDC: statement, signed by the Spanish Section of the Dressmakers' Local 22 of the ILGWU, box 8, file 4; Letters to *La Prensa*, 23 Dec. 1933, 2 Jan. 1934, box 33, file 11; Memorandum on Puerto Rican Workers, box 53, file 6; "Spanish Dressmakers" leaflet, box 33, file 11; "To Union Square May 1st!" poster, box 4, file 6. See also Altagracia Ortiz, "Puerto Rican Workers in the Garment Industry of New York City, 1920–1960," in *Labor Divided: Race and Ethnicity in the United States Labor Struggles, 1835–1960*, ed. Robert Asher and Charles Stephenson (New York: State University of New York Press, 1990); Ortiz, " 'En la aguja y el pedal eché la hiel': Puerto Rican Women in the Garment Industry of New York City, 1920–1980," in *Puerto Rican Women and Work, Bridges in Transnational Labor*, ed. Altagracia Ortiz (Philadelphia: Temple University Press, 1996); Robert Laurentz, "Racial/Ethnic Conflict in the New York Garment Industry" (Ph.D. diss., State University of New York, Binghamton, 1980); Herbert Hill, "Labor Unions and the Negro," *Commentary* (December 1959); Hill, "Racism within Organized Labor," *Journal of*

Negro Education 2 (1961); Hill, "Racial Inequality in Employment: The Patterns of Discrimination," *Annals of the American Academy of Political and Social Science* (January 1965); Hill, "The ILGWU: Fact or Fiction," *New Politics*, winter 1963.

58. This discourse was not confined to Italian American workers. For more on this, see Cohen, "A Symposium on *Making a New Deal*," *Labor History* (1992).

59. Speech given by Antonino Crivello, organizer and district manager for the Italian Dressmakers' Local 89 at fourth anniversary of the 1933 strike, ILGWU Local 144, Newark, New Jersey (1937), box 1, file 1, Crivello Papers, IHRC.

60. «[Q]uelli che hanno la pelle bianca . . . son di stripe europea . . . almeno 1,500 milioni di esseri umani NON sono di razza derivata dalle sorgenti europee: neri, gialli, olivastri, mescolati, e così via. *Sono essere umani*, esseri, cioè, che, insieme» (Arturo Labriola, "Le Razze di Colore e il Socialismo," in *ILGWU, Local 89 Anniversary, Commemoration Booklet* [1934], 87–89).

61. Delfino, interview by Prago.

62. Delfino, interview by Prago.

63. *New York Times*, 6 May 1936; Fiorello Ventresco, "Italian-Americans and the Ethiopian Crisis" *Italian Americana* 6 (fall/winter 1980); Nadia Venturini, *Neri e Italiani ad Harlem, Gli anni Trenta e la guerra d'Etiopia* (Rome: Edizioni Lavoro, 1990); Mark Naison, *Communists in Harlem during the Depression* (New York: Grove Press, 1983), 138–40, 157, 195–96.

64. Aurora De Gregorio, "Open Letter to a Young Negro," *L'Unità del Popolo*, 13 July 1940.

65. Elsie Canepa, "Tribuna delle Donne," *L'Unita Operaia*, 2 May 1936, 2. See also Orleck, *Common Sense*, 240, 248, 255, 268–69.

66. Roger Keeran, "National Groups and the Popular Front: The Case of the International Workers Order," *American Ethnic History* (spring 1995). See also the following from the Papers of the IWO, LMDC: Natalina Arcangeli to Constantino Lippa, 16 Aug. 1950, box 10, file 14; Lippa to Sorella Geraci, 18 April 1950, box 10, file 14; Lippa to Salvatore Geraci, 22 Aug. 1950, box 10, file 14; Gallapaga to Lippa, 21 Aug. 1950, box 10, file 11; Rapporto della Conferenza dei Delegati Italiani alla Terza Convezione Biennale, 7–9 May 1935, box 10, file 14; Conferenza dei Delegati Sezione Italiana alla Quarta Convenzione Nazionale, 28–29 April 1938, box 10, file 14; Riunione del Comitato Nazionale della Sezione Italiana, 7 Dec. 1938, box 10, file 8; Riunione del Comitato Nazionale della Sezione Italiana, 9 Sept. 1940, box 10, file 8; Meeting of the Italian American National Committee, Italian American City Committee of New York City and Lodge Functionaries, 26 June 1941, box 10, file 8; Minutes of the Italian National Committee, 7 Aug. 1943, box 10, file 8.

67. Vito Magli, interview by Paul Buhle, Oral History of the Left, Tamiment Library, New York University.

68. Esta Pingaro to Vito Marcantonio, 5 Oct. 1941, box 67, file 6, Papers of Vito Marcantonio, New York Public Library; John W. Sutter to Vito Marcantonio, 24 Oct. 1938, box 3, file 3, Marcantonio Papers. "Comunicazioni: New York, N.Y.," *L'Adunata dei Refrattari*, 16, 30 April 1932.

69. See the following documents from the Leonard Covello Papers at the Balch Institute for Ethnic Studies, Philadelphia: pamphlet, *Harlem Parade for Better Housing* (1938), Housing File, box 43; Leonard Covello, "Building Democratic Ideals through a School-Community Program," *Library Journal*, 1 Feb. 1940, 108; Minutes of the First Meeting of

the East Harlem Housing Committee of the Harlem Legislative Conference, 15 Jan. 1938, East Harlem Housing Committee Meetings, box 43; "The East Harlem Housing Committee of the East Harlem Legislative Conference Presents a Campaign, 1938," box 43; Petition, East Harlem Tenants, 1939; "Who Wants Better Housing?" 22 March 1938; "Notes from Minutes, 1937–1940," Community Centered School, box 43; Leonard Covello Speech, ca. 1939, Community Centered School, box 43; "The East Harlem Housing Committee of the East Harlem Legislative Conference Presents a Campaign, 1938," box 43.

Chapter 5

From Working-Class Radicalism to Cold War Anti-Communism: The Case of the Italian Locals of the International Ladies' Garment Workers' Union

Charles A. Zappia

Scholars attempting to reconstruct the rich history of Italian American left-wing radicalism prior to World War II have struggled with the question of why the Italian immigrant radical sensibility rarely survived more than one generation of American life. This essay will explore this conundrum by identifying the most-significant factors that transformed the politics of the union leaders among New York City's Italian American ladies' garment workers from a generally socialist perspective before World War I to an uncritical endorsement of mainstream anti-Communism by the end of World War II. The story begins in southern Italy.

By the 1890s, a process of proletarianization was transforming agricultural production in the Italian *mezzogiorno;* human relations were increasingly based on the production of goods. Although still relying on the traditions of "familism" for support and comfort, peasants began to build mutual-aid societies, labor unions, and *fascii* to conserve whatever benefits and stability traditional life had granted, as well as to advance political solutions for peasant problems that often were rooted in nineteenth-century social relations. Many of these organizations adopted socialist, anarchist, or syndicalist analyses to explain the worsening situation.[1] Some of those whose worldview was affected by both proletarianization and radicalization joined the growing numbers who left Italy between 1880 and 1920. The deteriorating Italian agricultural economy pushed peasants from their home provinces, and the availability of wage labor in the United States lured them.

LE SARTINE ITALIANE

Although few Italians had settled in New York City before the 1880s, hundreds of thousands of Italian immigrants found work and hope in that American city, which was their most-frequent port of entry during that decade. New York provided a wide range of low-paid, unskilled manufacturing and service jobs to a people hungry for a way to subsist in the present while building a base for improvement in the future. The city's rapidly expanding clothing industry was one that offered many Italian laborers their first American jobs. Italian women had worked in the needle trades since the late 1880s as home finishers, and by the mid-1890s, Italian men found work as machine operators and pressers, both in "inside shops" and for subcontractors.[2] By 1909, 55 percent of the workers in the shirtwaist and dress trades were Jewish, and 35 percent were Italian. Many observers agreed that the employers opened their arms to the Italians because they perceived them not only as cheaper labor, but also as much less susceptible than their Jewish coworkers to the virus of unionism.[3]

In contradiction to their employers' perceptions, Italian needleworkers soon turned to unionization as the most effective way of ameliorating the exploitative conditions of their trades. In fact, before 1910, southern Italians who worked in the garment industry were unionized in a percentage exceeding the overall ratio of garment trades labor-force organization. The perception of Italians as resistant to unionization throughout the first decade of the twentieth century occurs because they have been compared to the far more organized, more numerous, and more permanently situated Jewish garment workers. Many Italian workers of this period, who considered themselves to be temporary American workers, focused on sustaining employment under any conditions as a way to save while planning for futures in Italy. Jewish workers, many of whom were refugees from the anti-Semitic violence of the collapsing Russian czarist empire, were in the United States to stay. Thus, they focused on building organizations that could win lasting improvements in the American industrial context.[4]

The generally favorable outcome of the storied Uprising of 20,000, the 1909 New York City dressmakers' strike, convinced many Italian workers, particularly those who were acquiring some commitment to remain in this country, that unionizing was critical to their future prospects of economic and social well-being. Consequently, ever more Italian workers embraced unionization. Some were attracted to the Industrial Workers of the World, or to even smaller sectarian groups; however, most joined the International Ladies' Garment Workers' Union (ILGWU), an American Federation of Labor (AFL) affiliate, founded primarily by Jewish socialists in 1901.[5]

Between 1916 and 1919, Italian-born garment workers in New York City won charters for two ILGWU locals, Local 48 (cloakmakers) and Local 89 (dressmakers). Primarily for organizational reasons, these locals were constituted on the basis of ethnicity rather than craft. The founders of these Italian unions were both cultural traditionalists and union militants. These locals were Italian in more than name, their members read *Giustizia*, the Italian-language version of *Justice*, the ILGWU's newspaper, the meetings were conducted in Italian, and the minutes of thee meetings were written in Italian into the early 1950s. From the 1930s on, brief summaries of Local 89's Executive Board meetings were provided. In short, these institutions not only expressed, but also preserved, the language and culture of the Italian American workers. The cultural values of those Italian Americans who built labor organizations in the sweatshops of New York City's garment districts between 1900 and 1919 stressed the significance of family: the primary nature of familial relationships (even when these were established apart from biological or formal links); the importance of honor and loyalty to one's family, friends, and community; and the efficacy of voluntary association intended to sustain the stability of the family circle. These values, transported from the *mezzogiorno*, strengthened Italian workers in their struggles to organize. More significant, however, in molding the drive toward unionization among the Italian workers were the conditions Italian immigrants faced in their everyday work lives, as well as the discrimination and exploitation they faced in all other areas of their lives in the United States. The motivations of the Italian workers to unionize, then, were based mainly on class interests, as they were first perceived in Italy and then sharpened in the United States. Most of the engaged Italian unionists of this period conceived of the purposes of union activity in broad sociopolitical terms. Belief in class struggle was strong, as was an unarticulated conviction that alienated labor characterized the conditions under which most garment workers toiled. To better their lives in *all* areas, Italian garment workers organized unions and engaged in union and community politics. In the process of doing so, they "negotiated" their ethnicity by forming their own locals to secure a foothold in the ILGWU.[6]

In winning the establishment of their own locals, the Italian garment workers gained more than just an institutional position of influence within the ILGWU: they also enjoyed a relatively secure base from which to involve themselves in a much broader range of activities. The Italians of Locals 48 and 89 contributed to a host of humanitarian causes and built bridges to immigrant workers in other industries, in the New York area and nationally. They led the anti-Fascist crusade within the Sons of Italy, protested state and federal government policies and actions during the period of the first "Red Scare," supported workers' education, and attempted to elevate the status of Italian Americans generally. Within the locals, particularly Local 89, Italian labor activists sought to build and protect their own leadership structure, expand new organizational efforts, improve the social lives of all members by opening a union-sponsored vacation facility, and champion certain reforms within the ILGWU and throughout the garment industry. Most significant to the focus of this study, they also kept the socialist faith.

RESPONSES TO THE RED SCARE

Italian American garment workers took strong positions of opposition to the growing anti-radical hysteria that erupted during 1919 both in mainstream electoral politics and in the AFL. There are many examples of the Italian position. In January 1920, they denounced the actions of the New York Assembly when it voted to suspend five duly-elected socialists, after the Speaker of the House accused them of belonging to a party which had "declare[d] its adherence and solidarity with the revolutionary forces of *Soviet* Russia and did pledge itself and its members to the furtherance of the international Socialist revolution."[7] Local 89's Executive Council sent a resolution to the assembly, the governor, the mayor of New York City, each city alderman, and all the metropolitan newspapers, branding the expulsions a "czarist" action.[8] Local 48's Executive Council proclaimed the general politics of the United States to be "reactionary" and tending to suppress every attempt by workers to share in the liberties of the republic by decrying the workers' aspirations as manifestations of "Bolshevism."[9] Partly to support the reelection bids of the socialists, and more generally to protect radical ideals from right-wing attacks, Local 89, in 1920, endorsed the efforts of New York City Italian socialists to establish *Avanti,* a daily workers' journal. In fact, delegates from Local 89 presented a motion to the Chicago International Convention proposing an ILGWU donation of $5,000 to fund this project, arguing that it would serve the cause of organizing the Italian workers, much as the *Forward* had done for the Jewish workers.[10] The delegates also bought shares in *Avanti,* invested in a radical propaganda group (Labor Film, Inc.), and donated money to the socialist *New York Call.*[11] The dressmakers continued to regard May Day as the principal day of celebration for all workers. Luigi Antonini, the general secretary of the Dressmakers' Local, urged the local's members to abstain from work on that day, and to attend one of the rallies organized to commemorate the occasion.[12]

Luigi Antonini was born in the southern Italian town of Vallata Irspina on September 11, 1883. His family was respectably middle class, but his father, a teacher, extolled the virtues of radical republicans like Giuseppe Garibaldi and Giuseppe Mazzini. After completing high school, he was drafted into the Italian army, where his family's predisposition to radical republicanism was transformed into ardent socialism. In 1908, at 25 years of age, he left Italy for the United States, already committed to the revolution of the proletariat. Between 1908 and 1919, Antonini worked as a cutter, presser, and machine operator in several New York City garment factories, while educating and organizing his fellow immigrant workers. An ILGWU local official since 1914, Antonini was one of the primary founders of Local 89 and had served as its general gecretary since its chartering.[13]

Italian immigrant workers in general and Italian radicals in particular had much to fear at the dawn of the nation's first Red Scare. American nativism and the near hysterical fear of Bolshevism threatened the "new" immigrants. The expression of unpopular opinion by these immigrants could, and sometimes did, have mortal consequences. In the spring of 1920, police "Red Squads," in New York and elsewhere, rounded up a number of Italian radicals, primarily purported anarchists. One of those arrested, Andrea Salsedo, died on May 4 while in police custody, as a result of a fall from the 14th floor of a building on Park Row in New York City.[14] It remains unclear whether Salsedo was murdered or whether he committed suicide; regardless, his death provoked outrage among New York City's Italian dressmakers. Antonini, in one of his most emotional addresses, implied that Salsedo had killed himself after he had been tortured by the police into admitting to crimes he did not commit and, more distressing, revealing the names of certain comrades. Antonini promised that one day the workers would avenge Salsedo's death and would win the power to protect "the rights of the oppressed that now are violated with the connivance of the law."[15]

Like most workers' organizations in the immediate post–World War I period, Locals 48 and 89 condemned the U.S. intervention in the Russian Civil War and supported the recognition of the Soviets as the legitimate successor of the former czarist empire.[16] Local 89's Executive Council donated medical supplies to the Bolsheviks, joined and supported monetarily the pro-Bolshevik American Labor Alliance for Trade with Soviet Russia, and authored resolutions of protest against the U.S. blockade of the revolutionary state.[17] Antonini held fast to his position of support for the Soviets throughout his period of elected service (1920–1926) as a delegate to the international convention of the AFL. In fact, Antonini publicly opposed Samuel Gompers' anti-Soviet policies at the 1920 Montreal Congress of the AFL, and in 1921 he voted against Gompers' reelection to the presidency at Denver.[18] The majority of ILGWU delegates to the Denver Congress supported Gompers, with or without enthusiasm, and even advised Antonini to stifle his anti-Gompers sentiments.[19] After the convention, ILGWU spokesperson Saul Yanovsky criticized Antonini's Denver actions in the pages of *Justice*, the union's official newspaper; however, Local 89's Executive Council endorsed Antonini's position with high praise. This episode demonstrated both Antonini's independence within the ILGWU leadership cadre and the fact that he held the confidence of his Local 89 comrades.[20]

THE SACCO-VANZETTI DEFENSE

The Italian garment workers devoted much of their attention during the 1920s to the defense of Nicola Sacco and Bartolomeo Vanzetti.[21] Members of the Italian locals of the ILGWU remained committed to the conviction that Sacco and Vanzetti had been selected for political martyrdom. Antonio Crivello, an official of Local 89, wrote a poem, published in a pamphlet circulated throughout the ranks of the Italian ladies' garment workers, in which he referred to Sacco and Vanzetti as the "designated victims of a capitalist conspiracy."[22] On August 28, 1920, Antonini was among the featured speakers at the first New York City demonstration in support of Sacco and Vanzetti.[23] In addition, he consistently encouraged assistance for his two countrymen within the various sections of Local 89.[24] During Sacco and Vanzetti's seven-year incarceration, the Italian garment workers participated in rallies, collected legal-defense funds, and pushed their union into the front ranks of Sacco and Vanzetti's supporters. Local 89's Executive Council, at a May 1926 meeting, unanimously voted to send a letter to the Commonwealth of Massachusetts protesting the recent confirmation of the death sentence.[25] The Executive Council took the same action in April 1927, after the Massachusetts Supreme Court denied Sacco and Vanzetti's last appeal.[26]

In July of 1927, Local 89 endorsed a general strike in support of "the two inno-cents."[27] As Sacco and Vanzetti awaited execution in July 1927, Antonini joined Congressman Fiorello La Guardia and representatives from the Italian Chamber of Labor and other organizations in a desperate attempt to win a grant of clemency from the governor of Massachusetts. Antonini was in Boston on August 23, 1927, as the Commonwealth's executioner ended the lives of Nicola Sacco and Bartolomeo Vanzetti.[28]

ANTI-FASCISM, THE COMMUNITY, AND THE LABOR MOVEMENT

While Sacco and Vanzetti sat on death row, Italian American leftists faced another formidable danger. Fascism evidenced wide support. Benito Mussolini's government received relatively favorable press in the United States. Within the Italian American community, many *prominenti* began to support the Fascists, and pro-Fascism even began to gain some respect among immigrant workers. In response to the menace of Fascism, the leaders of Locals 48 and 89 took strong steps. In 1923, the Italian Chamber of Labor, with garment worker support, inau-gurated the citywide Anti-Fascist Alliance. Antonini urged the Central Trades and Labor Council to condemn Italian Fascism, and Local 89's delegates to the 1924 Boston convention of the ILGWU presented a motion committing the union to the anti-Fascist movement.[29] That movement seemed more urgent when the news reached the United States of Italian socialist Giacomo Mat-teotti's murder by the Fascists. At a Carnegie Hall protest rally, on the evening of June 26, 1924, Antonini was among those who condemned the Italian Fascists and who urged strengthening American efforts to defeat them.[30] Antonini, who worked particularly hard to unite the entire labor movement in opposition to Fascism, succeeded in drawing the AFL's William Green into publicly condemn-ing Italian Fascism. In September 1926, while addressing a New York meeting of the Anti-Fascist Alliance,[31] the usually reserved Green pledged that the AFL would "stand with you and work with you until we have succeeded in driving fas-cism from the face of the earth."[32] The Italian locals also were successful in obtaining from the ILGWU a pledge of financial support for a new anti-Fascist Italian-language daily, *Il Nuovo Mondo,* edited by Frank Bellanca, an official of the Amalgamated Clothing Workers of America (ACWA).[33]

BOLSHEVISM: THE AMBIVALENT RELATIONSHIP

The politics of the Italian locals generally reflected the preferences of their leaders. This was most obvious in the case of Antonini's Local 89. Antonini, who had considered himself a left-wing socialist during his early years in New York, joined the Workers' (Communist) Party shortly after the Bolshevik revolution, and once ran for congress as a Communist. His local continued to contribute money to the Italian Socialist Federation as well.[34] During the early 1920s, Local

89 was isolated from mainstream electoral politics; in fact, many among the dressmakers were convinced that electoral politics were irrelevant because a workers' revolution would soon redraw the political map. Local 89 published a pamphlet, *Libertas*, which was filled with testimonials to radical unionism and contained photographs of both "Carlo" Marx and "Nicola" Lenin, who was referred to as "the grandest and most beautiful figure in contemporary history."[35] However, in July 1923, Antonini resigned from the Workers' Party. He later explained his reasons in two long articles published in *Justice*, wherein he avowed his continued admiration of the Bolshevik Revolution and his opposition to the drastic measures the ILGWU had taken against union members who also belonged to the Communist Party's Trade Union Education League (TUEL).[36] Nevertheless, he wrote, he was unwilling to accept Party dictates which limited freedom of expression and divided the labor movement.[37] After his resignation from the Workers' Party, Antonini began to move more toward the mainstream, at least as it flowed through the labor movement. His local, not surprisingly, followed in his wake. This rightward movement greatly accelerated, however, when the Communists challenged the integrity of Local 89 more directly.

THE ITALIANS AND THE UNION'S "CIVIL WAR"

The devotion of many garment trades workers to socialism was primarily a response to the exploitation and discrimination industrial workers suffered in the United States; but it was also a product of historical and cultural factors experienced by American immigrant workers in the lands of their birth. By the start of the First World War, Jewish immigrants from eastern Europe and the Russian Empire had helped to make the ILGWU one of the most socialist unions in the AFL. The shock waves of the Bolshevik Revolution further radicalized some garment trades socialists and spurred the growth of a left wing within the socialist ranks of the ILGWU. This left wing, particularly strong among the Jewish dressmakers, soon merged with the new Communist Party and set its sights on winning control of the ILGWU. The struggle for power between the insurgent Communists and the union's social democratic leadership resulted in a bitter "civil war" that persisted throughout most of the 1920s and devastated the ILGWU.

American Communist activists, trying to implement Lenin's policy of "boring from within," found their greatest success among the Fur Workers, where they were able to displace the AFL leadership, and among the ladies' garment workers, where they temporarily dominated the largest locals of the ILGWU.[38] In 1924, the Communists won elections in New York City ILGWU Locals 2, 9, and 22, which consisted of the largest number of workers in the cloak and dress trades that were most crucial to the union's organizing goals. When the anti-Communist president of the ILGWU, Morris Sigman, isolated the Communists by manipulating his control over the "out-of-town" locals, full-scale sectarian war exploded.[39] The internal turmoil that characterized politics in the ILGWU during the remainder of the 1920s caught the leaders and members of the new Italian locals in a difficult position. Like their Jewish comrades, many of the Italian activists were socialists who had moved leftward after 1917. This was in part because the socialism espoused by the leaders of the International was both too "Jewish" and too conservative to suit the Italian leftists. Jewish socialism was always unique, in the sense that it served as a vehicle for a secular Jewish culture tied to the preservation of the Yiddish language. Italian socialism was a response to the same kinds of economic pressures and developments experienced in the Russian Pale, but it was not for the Italians a means of cultural maintenance. More significantly, the evolutionary socialism endorsed by many prominent Jewish leaders within the ILGWU left workers with little more than the conviction that they were on the side of history. Those who were less comfortable demanded immediate change, and the success of the Bolsheviki in Russia seemed to hold the promise of proletarian revolution that would better the lives of workers sooner rather than later. Consequently, some Italian activists, like Antonini, had earlier joined and supported the Workers' Party of America. However, when the Communists within the ILGWU tried to capture its central administration, Antonini; the Cloakmakers' general secretary, Salvatore Ninfo; and most other Italian union activists supported the moderate International administration. They did *not* do so because they had, at that point, embraced a comprehensively anti-Communist point of view. The Italian response was based on an assessment of power politics within the ILGWU. The Communists, in 1925, advanced a program for union amalgamation that would have destroyed the hard-won autonomy of the Italian locals. The Italian support for the moderate administration of Morris Sigman represented a move to protect the growing power of Locals 48 and 89 from *any* challenge, regardless of the ideology of the challengers. Moreover, the Italians still supported, even at the critical convention of 1925, other Communist proposals that were not aimed directly at capturing union power. Yet, once the fight was joined, it became so bitter, personal, and, at times, violent, that, increasingly, Communism itself became the enemy.

In an effort to further polarize the membership and defeat the Sigman administration, in the summer of 1926 the Communists launched a poorly led, underfunded massive cloakmakers' strike, which lasted for 28 weeks. In the end, the workers won nothing, the International tottered on the edge of bankruptcy, and the Communists lost much of their influence. The ILGWU limped through the rest of the 1920s, largely because of the wounds inflicted in the "civil war," the blame for which most Italians placed on the Communists.[40]

DEPRESSION AND RESURGENCE

Once the national economy collapsed in late 1929, poor conditions in the garment trades severely strained the garment workers' meager resources and presented political problems for the Italian locals' leadership, particularly among the dressmakers.

Within the ranks of Local 89, unemployment, shorter working seasons, and worsening conditions on the job fueled another spate of opposition to Antonini's policies and administration. A group of male pressers, some of whom had long differed with Antonini on a host of issues, provided a core of dissent within the local. Still, even though he could point to no great achievements since 1930, Antonini remained popular with the largely female general membership. In the local elections of April 1932, Antonini retained his seat as general secretary by capturing 91 percent of the vote.[41]

The ILGWU did not begin its historic resurgence until after the inauguration of Franklin Delano Roosevelt and the passage of the National Industrial Recovery Act in 1933. The New Deal's National Recovery Administration (NRA) reversed the situation of only a few years earlier by accepting cloak and dress codes favorable to the workers. The union's ranks were also tremendously augmented by a very successful dressmakers' strike in August 1933.

The Italian dressmakers shared significantly in the fruits of the 1933 strike and later NRA victories. Antonini and other Local 89 activists had played important coordinating roles during the short dress-trade workers' strike. By the end of 1933, the success of that strike brought a rush of Italian dress trade workers into Local 89, which increased its membership to approximately forty thousand, 70 percent of whom were women.[42] Italian women and men worked in virtually every dress factory in New York City, and constituted large majorities in many important shops.[43] According to the charter of Local 89, *all* unionized Italian dressmakers in the city fell under the jurisdiction of the single Italian dress local; and now there were so many of them! The officers of Local 89, who as recently as a year earlier had worried about how to pay their bills with so small a dues base, now were faced with the happy prospect of deciding how to manage a local with such a massive membership.[44]

Antonini continued to use *Giustizia* as a vehicle for educating the membership in the issues confronted by the union. He soon realized, however, that the local's greatly expanded membership now required other methods of communication as well. Consequently, in 1934 Antonini began the "Voice of Local 89," a weekly radio program that was broadcast into the late 1940s. In this Italian-language version of FDR's fireside chats, the general secretary praised the Italian American workers and exhorted them to remain dedicated unionists. He also blasted the Fascists and the Communists, warmly supported the New Deal, and began to articulate a new version of Italian Americanism that would be molded more finely during the Second World War.[45]

The great growth of Local 89 also gave Luigi Antonini a far-stronger voice in the uppermost echelons of the ILGWU. At the International's 1934 convention in Chicago, after Julius Hochman, a prominent union official, nominated Antonini for the office of first vice president of the International, he was elected unanimously.[46] Antonini's preeminence among the Italian activists and the new significance of the Italian dressmakers was now formalized by his presence on the ILGWU's General Executive Board. When the Italian dressmakers gathered in

New York several months later to celebrate their organizational successes, the 15th anniversary of Local 89, and the vice presidential election of Antonini, they filled the largest arena in the city, Madison Square Garden. In a decade and a half, Local 89 had grown from a fledgling organization of only several thousand, to the largest local union in the ILGWU and one of the largest union locals in the United States.[47]

FROM DEPRESSION TO COLD WAR

The sizeable Italian presence in the ILGWU was duplicated within the ranks of the Amalgamated Clothing Workers of America (ACWA), another generally industrial union firmly within the Roosevelt coalition. The national political importance of union leaders like David Dubinsky, elected president of the ILGWU in 1932, and particularly Sidney Hillman, who had led the ACWA since 1914 and would later, in 1944, found the CIO's political action committee (PAC), perhaps has been overstated. Nonetheless, the garment unions were important building blocks in the New Deal structure, and the Italians were major players in the politics of the garment unions. Local 89 continued to maintain its close ties to Fiorello La Guardia, but Antonini initially supported and then resisted the rise of La Guardia's protégé, Vito Marcantonio, the radical congressman from East Harlem. In fact, Antonini tried to block Marcantonio's labor support in the congressional election of 1936 and was dissuaded from doing so only after La Guardia, who had been lobbied privately by the ACWA's Augusto Bellanca, interceded on Marcantonio's behalf. Further signifying his move toward the right, Antonini increasingly warred with Bellanca—a La Guardia, Marcantonio, and FDR supporter—claiming that he was too close to the garment trades' Communists. Simultaneously, Antonini mended fences with his old political foe Generoso Pope, the publisher of Il Progresso Italo-Americano, despite the fact that he remained clearly pro-Fascist until December 11, 1941.[48]

The anti-Fascist crusade carried by Antonini and other Italian garment unionists since the early 1920s continued to gather strength in the 1930s. Clashes between Fascist and anti-Fascist Italian Americans increased in frequency and severity after 1925. Mussolini's supporters attacked anti-Fascist groups and offices, while coming under attack themselves at Columbus Day festivities, Garibaldi Day ceremonies, and even at the funeral of Rudolph Valentino. At least a dozen people died in New York City's streets battling for the soul of its Italian community. Following the 1933 killing of a young Italian American anti-Fascist, who had been heckling the pro-Mussolini speakers at a Khaki Shirts of America rally in Queens, there seems to have been a change in the political complexion of Italian American anti-Fascism. Before Hitler's rise in Germany, Fascism did not appear to threaten American interests or world peace; consequently, the ideological battle among the Italian Americans of New York City seemed to many outsiders to be an insignificant squabble of left- and right-wing extremists. However, after 1933, when the characteristics and ambitions of

Nazism became more apparent, anti-Fascism became more compelling to mainstream American political opinion molders. Very quickly, Italian American anti-Fascism became less radical and more integrative. In fact, as the Roosevelt administration turned its attention to the threat of Fascism in Europe, and as Communists forged popular fronts against Fascism between 1935 and 1939, anti-Fascism increasingly became a vehicle for the Americanization of many Italian American garment workers.[49]

The coming of the Second World War brought new problems and possibilities to the Italian locals. In opposing the use of the Enemy Alien Act against Italian Americans who were not citizens of the United States, Local 89's leaders reminded the Justice Department of the garment unionists' long history of anti-Fascist involvements. Anti-Fascism now became a cornerstone of emerging Italian American patriotism, since one now could be anti-Fascist and pro-American without being pro-Communist and anti-Italian.[50] Moreover, the argument that the best interests of the Italian people and the wartime policies of the United States were identical seems to have emerged at this time. Antonini was instrumental in forming the Italian-American Labor Council, in December 1941, partly to construct an interpretation of "Italian-Americanism" that was far more conservative than that which had earlier prevailed among the garment workers.[51]

The increasing conservatism among the leadership of the Italian garment unionists grew even more apparent when, during the war, Antonini became involved in the "Columbus Citizens Committee," an organization that included several former Fascist sympathizers and reputed mob figures. In 1944, Antonini traveled to Allied-occupied Italy under State Department auspices, where he promoted the creation of "free" (that is, non-Communist) labor unions once the war ended. In fact, by the end of World War II, Local 89 became much more supportive, in a wholly uncritical sense, of overall U.S. foreign policy, and, in the process, even more explicitly anti-Communist.[52]

The new political turn was implemented quickly to combat challenges to Antonini's local leadership. In 1943, when dissident pressers within Local 89 tried to bolt and obtain a separate charter under the leadership of one of Antonini's old nemeses, Giuseppe Provvidenti, the movement was mercilessly Red-baited by Antonini and others. Certainly, this fit the pattern established in internal power struggles in other unions during and after this period. It seems that Antonini and his supporters also used intimidation and, on occasion, force to deal with internal critics identified as Communists. At a meeting attended by approximately one thousand pressers, Provvidenti, after criticizing Antonini severely, was attacked by several men, one of whom hit him over the head with a chair, sending him to the hospital. As was the case in other unions, whenever tactics of direct repression were used by Local 89's leaders to maintain their control, those tactics were legitimized as defenses against Communists seeking to destroy democracy in the American labor movement.[53]

The postwar changes in the structure of the garment industry, the influx of African Americans and Spanish-speaking newcomers into the trades, and the changes within the Italian community—out-migration, increasing exogamy, decline in the use of the Italian language, occupational mobility out of the garment trades, greater assimilation—reshaped the political sensibility of the leaders and members of Locals 48 and 89. The commitment to socialism and class-conscious unionism became ever more diluted, in part because labor organization made more effective by this commitment had brought so many of the first-generation Italian American garment workers out of the sweatshops and helped even more of their children find their ways to the suburbs. For the most part, the Italian locals' leaders helped to direct the general anti-Communist hysteria of the postwar period. Local 89, with State Department encouragement and assistance, worked to influence a conservative turn in the development of trade unionism in Italy and encouraged Italian American garment workers to write their families and friends in Italy beseeching them to vote against the Communist Party in the important postwar elections, particularly in 1948. By 1950, Antonini was the president and Local 48's Edward Molisani the vice president of the Italian American Labor Council, which by then fully endorsed the Truman-Acheson version of the cold war.

The Italian dress- and cloakmakers of New York City doubtlessly responded, as individuals, in a variety of ways to the changes that swept through their lives between the "Great War" and the cold war. Nevertheless, in terms of organized political action, they invariably mirrored the lead of the most politically prominent of their union chiefs, Luigi Antonini. Between 1919 and 1950, Antonini's political journey had taken him from membership in the Workers' Party and advocacy of working-class revolution to junior membership in the cold war policy elite and advocacy of placing the fight against Communism above virtually all other union concerns.[54] The post–World War I Red Scare, the nativism and conservatism of the 1920s, the pragmatic anti-Communism molded in the crucible of the ILGWU's "civil war," and the gradual "Americanization" of anti-Fascism obscured the original progressive, and often socialist, dreams of the immigrant activists. Idealism yielded to acceptance of the status quo, and the preservation of the Italian locals became an end in itself. The most effective strategy for their protection was to present those unions now as major defenders of Italian American workers, not primarily from the exploitation of their bosses but rather from the alleged threats of Communism, both external and internal.[55]

EPILOGUE: "È FINITA"

Although the complex mix of Italian American anarchism, socialism, and non-sectarian left-wing radicalism was but a memory in the ILGWU by the 1950s, the leaders of Locals 48 and 89 were able to preserve the *italianità* of their organizations for another generation. Nonetheless, between 1950 and the mid-1980s, Italian American membership in the ILGWU declined sharply, from over 100,000 to about 16,000, many of whom were retirees.[56] The demographic base for a labor organization whose paper was printed in Italian, whose radio broadcasts were communicated in Italian, and whose meetings and their records were in Italian no longer existed. Under the twin pressures of changing labor-force demographics and increasing local administrative costs, the preservation of distinctly Italian locals became a burden ILGWU administrators would bear no longer.

Local 48, the older of the two Italian locals, was the first to lose its autonomy. Between late 1977 and early 1978,[57] Local 48 merged with its younger, but larger, sister, Local 89, and became part of the newly created Coat, Dress, and Rainwear Joint Board. The new bargaining entity consisted also of the merged Locals 1 and 35 and David Dubinsky's old Cutters' Local 10. E. Howard Molisani, the manager of Local 48, general manager of the old Cloak Joint Board, and the first vice president of the International, retired from all three positions. He was appointed as the first general manager of the Coat, Dress, and Rainwear Joint Board. The Italian cloakmakers were integrated into the merged Local 89-48.[58]

As late as October 1983, Local 89-48 operated a very active Retirees Club, which was comprised wholly of people of Italian birth or ancestry.[59] Nevertheless, membership continued to decline as budgets tightened. At a September 1984 retreat of the International's General Executive Board, President Sol Chaikin, citing "severe operating losses," recommended that the New York Coat, Dress, and Rainwear Joint Board be replaced by a "super local," Local 89-22-1. Of the member locals of the Joint Board, only Local 10 retained its historic identity and original charter. Locals 89-48, 22, and 1-35 would merge, and, in the process, the identities of Locals 48 and 35 would disappear forever. Chaikin noted that executive board members of the locals would all continue to serve, but only until the end of their current terms. Realizing that his recommendation was both historic and wrenching for those who made that history, Chaikin lamented that "the necessity of providing for our future forces us to deal harshly with our past." The General Executive Board accepted Chaikin's proposals.[60]

The leaders of the affected locals really had little choice other than to accept the ILGWU General Executive Board's decision. In September, the Executive Board of Local 89-48 passed a resolution accepting "restructuring." Predictably, Frank Longo, Local 89-48 manager and International vice president, announced that he would retire immediately "as part of a general consolidation of staff." On October 3, at what was described as an "emotion-filled" meeting, the Coat, Dress, and Rainwear Joint Board accepted the restructuring as well.[61]

On November 14, 1984, Samuel Byer, who had started his ILGWU career as a staff auditor and who had no strong ties to any particular local, was appointed as the manager of the new "super local" 89-22-1. Its staff of business agents was reduced by 30 percent, and only one important local official, Anthony Claudino, came from the ranks of the old Local 89. Later, in February 1987, Claudino would be appointed as one of two assistant managers of Local 89-22-1, purportedly to ease Byer's administrative burdens, but perhaps also to placate Italian American "old-timers" who complained of being forgotten by their union.[62]

With no Italian locals and ever fewer Italian members, it was inevitable that the venerable voice of the Italian ladies' garment workers would fade into silence as well. In December 1986, editor Lino Manocchio announced that *Giustizia*, the Italian-language newspaper of the ILGWU, published continuously since January 25, 1919, was printing its last issue. The International's official news organ announced the event in an article poignantly headlined "*Giustizia* è finita."[63] The nearly seventy-year history of the Italian locals in the ILGWU had ended.[64]

NOTES

1. Charles A. Zappia, "Unionism and the Italian American Worker: A History of the New York City 'Italian Locals' in the International Ladies' Garment Workers' Union, 1900–1934" (Ph. D. diss., University of California, Berkeley, 1994), 28–84.

2. "Inside shops" were those owned by the largest manufacturers, who both employed labor to make the garments and sold finished garments to consumers. Often, the entire production process took place in these shops, which were owned by the largest and most influential manufacturers. Smaller manufacturers often parceled out parts of the manufacturing process, at set prices, to subcontractors, who operated "outside shops." These subcontractors were in essence middlemen between clothing company owners and garment workers. They usually employed workers to rough up and cut garments, which then would be delivered to the manufacturer for finishing and distribution. Louis Levine, *The Women's Garment Workers* (New York: B. W. Huebsch, 1924), 14.

3. Benjamin Stolberg, *Tailor's Progress* (Garden City, N.Y.: Doubleday, Doran, 1944), 59; Pearl Goodman and Elsa Ueland, "The Shirtwaist Trade," *Journal of Political Economy* (December 1910): 817; Levine, *Garment Workers*, 145; Edwin Fenton, *Immigrants and Unions, A Case Study: Italians and American Labor, 1870–1920* (New York: Arno Press, 1975).

4. *Report of the United States Immigration Commission*, by William Dillingham, Chairman (Washington, D.C.: U.S. Government Printing Office, 1911), 2:313, 11:660.

5. Serafino Romualdi, "Storia della Locale 89," in *Local 89 Fifteenth Anniversary Commemoration* (pamphlet, 1934), 36, Immigration History Research Center (hereinafter IHRC), University of Minnesota, St. Paul.

6. Romualdi, "Locale 89," 36.

7. "Albany's Ousted Socialists," *Literary Digest*, 24 January 1920, 19–20.

8. Locale 89, *Processo Verbale*, Consiglio Esecutivo, 10 January 1920, 1–2; *Processo Verbale*, Sezione Centrale, 17 January 1920, 2; 24 April 1920, 2; 2 October 1920, 2. All minutes of Local 89's executive board and section meetings, and all minutes of Local 48's executive board meetings were examined either in the ILGWU Collection, now at the Martin P. Catherwood Library of the New York State School of Industrial and Labor Relations (hereinafter ILR), Cornell University, Ithaca, N.Y., or on microfilm at the Center for Migration Studies (hereinafter CSM), New York, N.Y.

9. Locale 48, *Processo Verbale*, Consiglio Esecutivo, 20 January 1920, 1.

10. Convention of the ILGWU, *Proceedings* (1920), 41, 110; Locale 89, *Processo Verbale*, Sezione Centrale, 29 May 1920.

11. Locale 89, *Processo Verbale*, Consiglio Esecutivo, 3 May, 30 July, 8 August 1920.

12. Locale 89, *Processo Verbale*, Sezione Centrale, 24 April 1920.

13. John S. Crawford, *Luigi Antonini* (New York: Educational Department of the Italian Dressmakers' Union, 1959), 12–21; Stolberg, *Tailor's Progress*, 238–41; *Who's Who in*

Labor (New York: Dryden Press, 1946), 8; Arturo Giovannitti, "Luigi Antonini: The Man and the Leader," in *Local 89 Fifteenth Anniversary*, 21–23, IHRC.

14. Louis Joughin and Edmund M. Morgan, *The Legacy of Sacco and Vanzetti* (Chicago: Quadrangle Books, 1964), 71.

15. Locale 89, *Processo Verbale*, Sezione Centrale, 9 July 1920.

16. Locale 89, *Processo Verbale*, Sezione Centrale, 18 December 1920.

17. Locale 89, *Processo Verbale*, Consiglio Esecutivo, 2 July, 3 November, 4 December 1920.

18. Romualdi, "Locale 89," 44; Locale 89, *Processo Verbale*, Consiglio Esecutivo, 1 July 1921.

19. Romualdi, "Locale 89," 44.

20. Locale 89, *Processo Verbale*, Consiglio Esecutivo, 1 September 1921.

21. For the most-recent treatments of the Sacco-Vanzetti case, see Francis Russell, *Sacco and Vanzetti: The Case Resolved* (New York: Harper and Row, 1986) and William Young and David E. Kaiser, *Postmortem: New Evidence in the Case of Sacco and Vanzetti* (Amherst: University of Massachusetts Press, 1985).

22. Antonio Crivello, "A Sacco e Vanzetti," in *A Libertas: Ricordo della Italian Dress and Waistmakers Union, Local 89, ILGWU* (8 April 1922), unpaginated, ILR.

23. Romualdi, "Locale 89," 45.

24. Locale 89, *Processo Verbale*, Sezione Centrale, 14 January, 22 April 1922.

25. Locale 89, *Processo Verbale*, Consiglio Esecutivo, 25 May 1926.

26. *Sommario delle deliberazioni del Consiglio Esecutivo, emesse nel periodo 29 marzo—24 maggio, 1927*, 11 April 1927, Antonini Papers, IHRC.

27. Romualdi, "Locale 89," 44.

28. *New York Times*, 23 August 1927, 1–2.

29. Convention of the ILGWU, *Proceedings* (1924), 19.

30. *New York Times*, 27 June 1924, 21.

31. Romualdi, "Locale 89," 50.

32. John P. Diggins, *Mussolini and Fascism: The View from America* (Princeton, N.J.: Princeton University Press, 1972), 173.

33. ILGWU, Local 89, *Jubilee, 1919–1944* (New York, 1944), 12, ILR.

34. Locale 89, *Processo Verbale*, Consiglio Esecutivo, 10 October 1920.

35. *A Libertas*, 8 April 1922 (New York: ILGWU), unpaginated.

36. Luigi Antonini, "Why I Left the Workers' Party: Part One," *Justice*, 7 November 1924, 5.

37. Luigi Antonini, "Why I Left the Workers' Party: Part Two," *Justice*, 14 November 1925, 4.

38. For the theory behind the Comintern's policy of "boring from within," see: V. I. Lenin, *Left-Wing Communism: An Infantile Disorder* (New York: International Publishers, 1934), which was first published as a pamphlet in 1921. Also, see Fraser Ottanelli, *The Communist Party in the United States: From the Depression to World War II* (New Brunswick, N.J.: Rutgers University Press, 1991), 9–13. Ottanelli demonstrates that the boring-from-within strategy also emerged in the United States prior to the change in the Comintern's policy in 1921, as did even the Trade Union Education League. For a brief description of the situation among the Furriers, see Irving Bernstein, *The Lean Years: A History of the American Worker, 1920–1933* (Baltimore: Penguin Books, 1960), 139.

39. David Dubinsky, *A Life with Labor* (New York: Simon and Schuster, 1977), 61–64; *Justice*, 19 June 1925, 1.

40. Stolberg, *Tailor's Progress*, 136–37; Romualdi, "Locale 89," 52.

41. Local 89, "Excerpts of the Executive Board Minutes—Italian Dressmakers' Union, 1919–1936," 5, Antonini Papers, ILGWU Collection, ILR.

42. Locale 48, *Libro Ricordo*, 121.

43. Romualdi, "Locale 89," 59.

44. Ibid., 60.

45. Luigi Antonini, *Dynamic Democracy* [an anthology of Antonini's radio addresses] (New York: Eloquent Press, 1944).

46. Convention of the ILGWU, *Proceedings* (1934), 426–28.

47. Julius Hochman, "Hail Local 89," in *Local 89 Fifteenth Anniversary*, 19–20, IHRC.

48. See letters between Luigi Antonini and Frank Bellanca, Augusto Bellanca, and Vito Marcantonio, 1935–1959. See also letters from Antonini to various dignitaries urging Columbus Day celebration participation, 1939–1942; undated attacks on the Antonini-Pope relationship by the Antonio Gramsci Club, Communist Party-U.S.A., Garment Section, New York City (probably 1942 or 1943); Antonini Papers, ILGWU Collection, ILR; August Bellanca to Fiorello La Guardia, 18 September 1936, Bellanca Papers, ACWA Collection, box 146, ILR. For more information on the remarkable career of Marcantonio, see Gerald Meyer, *Vito Marcantonio: Radical Politician, 1902–1954* (Albany: State University of New York Press, 1989). For Hillman's establishment of the CIO's PAC and of its impact on labor politics, see Steven Fraser, *Labor Will Rule: Sidney Hillman and the Rise of American Labor* (Ithaca, N.Y.: Cornell University Press, 1991), 495–538.

49. Diggins, *Mussolini and Fascism*, 125–34; Gaetano Salvemini, *Italian Fascist Activities in the United States* (New York: Center for Migration Studies, 1977), 77–88; *New York Times*, 5 July 1932, 1; "Fascist Propaganda in the United States," anonymous undated manuscript, Girolamo Valenti Papers, Tamiment Library, New York University.

50. On Columbus Day, 1942, Attorney General Francis Biddle announced that Italian nationals in the United States would be exempted from enemy alien classification; Antonini, *Dynamic Democracy*, 455–57.

51. Luigi Antonini, "Luigi Antonini Protests to Phillip Murray," *Sunday Review*, December 1943, 1.

52. Programs and letters regarding 1940 Columbus Day celebration, Luigi Antonini Papers, box 11, folder 9, ILGWU Collection, ILR; undated pamphlet (c. 1944), Antonio Gramsci Club, Communist Party, USA, Garment Section, New York City, Antonini Papers, box 11, folder 8, ILGWU Collection, ILR. See also evidence of Antonini's early attempts to pressure Marcantonio to reject any common action with Communists or any criticism of emerging U.S. foreign policy. See Antonini to Marcantonio, 11 June 1935; Marcantonio to Antonini, 14 August 1935, Antonini Papers, box 24, folder 1, ILGWU Collection, ILR. For reference to Antonini's 1944 Italian mission, see Italian American Labor Council, "Highlights of a Quarter of a Century," *Silver Jubilee* (New York, 1966), unpaginated, IHRC.

53. "Antonini Opponent Slugged at Meeting," undated and unidentified newspaper clipping, most likely from a Communist publication from about 1943; Cupelli Papers, box 1, folder "L. Antonini," IHRC.

54. Italian American Labor Council, "Highlights," unpaginated, IHRC.

55. In one sense, Antonini's late-1940s rhetoric anticipated that of the leaders of the national American labor movement, George Meany and Walter Reuther, who, at the moment of the AFL-CIO merger, jointly declared that they had "been able to bring about

unity of the labor movement at a time when the unity of all American people is most urgently needed in the face of the Communist threat to world peace and civilization." Quoted in Foster Rhea Dulles and Melvyn Dubofsky, *Labor in America: A History,* 5th ed., (Arlington Heights, Ill.: Harlan Davidson, 1993), 361.

56. *Justice,* January 1987, 16.

57. The official depository of ILGWU records, formerly held in the Union's own archives in New York City, is the Martin P. Catherwood Library, New York State School of Industrial and Labor Relations, Cornell University. The archives have no holdings for Locals 48 and 89, or of their successors, beyond 1977, and I have been unable to locate those records elsewhere. Consequently, I have reconstructed much of what follows from articles in *Justice* and from telephone discussions with Robert Pignatelli, who started with Local 89 in the 1950s and is currently a business agent for Local 89-22-1; Bob Lazar, former ILGWU archivist and now also a business agent with Local 89-22-1; and Patrizia Sione, archivist at the Catherwood Library.

58. *Justice,* July–August 1987, 4; telephone interview with Robert Pignatelli, 23 August 1999.

59. *Justice,* November 1983, 7.

60. *Justice,* October 1984, 3.

61. Ibid., 5.

62. *Justice,* December 1984, 6; February 1987, 7; telephone interviews, Bob Lazar and Robert Pignatelli, 8 June 1999.

63. *Justice,* January 1987, 16.

64. On June 29, 1995, the ILGWU merged with the Amalgamated Clothing and Textile Workers' Union, itself the product of an earlier merger between the Amalgamated Clothing Workers and the Textile Workers.

Part II

Politics

Chapter 6

Sacco and Vanzetti's Revenge

Paul Avrich

"The good shoemaker and the poor fishpeddler." This is one of the most often quoted descriptions of Sacco and Vanzetti. It was made by Vanzetti himself shortly before he and Sacco were executed. The description, as far as it goes, is not an inaccurate one. Yet, it obscures the true character of the two men. For they were not merely "philosophical" anarchists or Tolstoyan pacifists, as some of their friends described them. Both, on the contrary, were social militants, advocates of relentless warfare against government and capitalism. Far from being the innocent dreamers so often depicted by their supporters, they belonged to a branch of the anarchist movement that preached insurrectionary violence and armed retaliation, including the use of dynamite. Such activities, they believed, were replies to the monstrous violence of the state. The greatest bomb throwers and murderers were not the isolated rebels driven to desperation but the military resources of every government—the army, militia, police, firing squad, hangman.

Such was the position of Sacco and Vanzetti, as it was of their mentor Luigi Galleani, who showered praise on every rebellious deed and glorified the perpetrators as heroes and martyrs, sacrificing themselves for the oppressed. "Both Nick and I are anarchists," Vanzetti himself declared, "the radical of the radical, the black cats, the terrors of many, of all the bigots, exploiters, charlatans, fakes, and oppressors." Their code of honor taught that revolutionaries should retaliate against the repressive use of force, that submission to the government was cowardly and unworthy of a true anarchist. To be a rebel, they insisted, was to refuse to cringe before the authorities.

Starting in 1917, they began to put these ideas into practice. It was in April of that year that the United States entered Word War I, to which Galleani and his followers were uncompromisingly opposed. This brought down upon them the full panoply of government repression. Throughout the country their clubhouses were raided, men and women beaten, equipment smashed, libraries and files seized and destroyed. Their lectures and recitals were disrupted. and their news-papers and journals suppressed, among them Galleani's *Cronaca Sovversiva* (the Subversive Chronicle), in which he denounced conscription and the war.

The Galleanists viewed these developments with mounting indignation. Men of energy and determination, they could not stand idly by while their comrades were being imprisoned, their presses silenced, their meetings disrupted and dis-persed. An overwhelming desire to retaliate, to strike back at the state that was stifling and crushing their movement, took possession of them. So it was that between 1917 and 1919, the height of the Red Scare, a group of anarchists came into being whose function was to carry out bombings. Sacco and Vanzetti were among them. They refused to turn the other cheek. Uncompromising militants, they rejected docile submission to the state. They were determined, on the con-trary, to answer force with force, not only as a matter of self-defense but of prin-ciple and honor.

The climax was reached in 1919, following a rash of anarchist deportations. Among those evicted from the country was Galleani himself. This proved the last straw. The Galleanists issued a leaflet threatening retaliation. "You have shown no pity to us," it declared. "We will do likewise. And deport us! *We will dynamite you!*" An enemies' list was drawn up, to whom package bombs were sent in the mail. This occurred on the First of May, the premier working class and anarchist holiday. The list consisted of 30 names, including Attorney General A. Mitchell Palmer, Postmaster General Albert S. Burleson, Secretary of Labor William B. Wilson, Supreme Court Justice Oliver Wendell Holmes, Commis-sioner General of Immigration Anthony Caminetti, and U.S. District Judge Kenesaw Mountain Landis, as well as John D. Rockefeller, and J. P. Morgan, among others. Each of the intended victims had antagonized the Galleanists in some unforgivable way: arrested their comrades, closed down their newspapers, deported them to Italy, and the like. Additional bombs were delivered by hand to the doors of intended recipients. None of them was hurt, although the house-maid of one had her hands blown off and an elderly security guard was killed.

To men of the bombers' stamp, the use of violence was not a crime; it was a jus-tifiable response to persecution. They considered themselves at war with the forces of government, and if they resorted to bombs it was as the government used bombs, for the purpose of war. Violence, in any event, was one of the few weapons at their disposal, a necessary means of self-defense. How else were they to retaliate against their tormentors? As Vanzetti expressed it: "I would give my blood to prevent the shedding of blood, but neither the abyss nor the earth nor the heavens have a law which condemns self-defense. Death for death," he declared. "We fight for the triumph of a cause—not to be crushed by the keep-ers—we will never win without vanquishing them. They are mercenary, we ide-alist; should a free man or a rebel allow them to do what they please to him?"

Sacco and Vanzetti continued to feel this way after their arrest, charged with robbing a shoe factory in South Braintree, Massachusetts, and killing the paymaster and his guard. Aware that their chances of acquittal were not great, they began to prepare measures of retaliation. These measures took two forms. The first was to attempt to escape from prison and thus deprive the authorities of their prey. The second, should this fail and the worst come, was to exact retribution against those responsible for their death, above all the judge in the case, Webster Thayer.

The authorities were cognizant of such possibilities. They had long suspected that Galleanists were responsible for the 1919 bombings, not to mention the Wall Street explosion of 1920, in which 33 people were killed. So they were not going to take any chances. At the 1921 trial in Dedham, Massachusetts, every precaution was taken. The courthouse was an armed camp. To prevent escape or a dynamite attack, a metal plate was placed over the window of the holding cell adjacent to the courtroom. The cage in the courtroom in which the defendants sat was kept under heavy guard. Every spectator was searched for concealed weapons and bombs. For the first time in their career, newspapermen were frisked for guns. A troop of state police on horseback paraded about the town, while other troopers on motorcycles swept up and down the main street. Each day, Sacco and Vanzetti, manacled, were taken from the jail to the courthouse surrounded by heavy guard, who took them back to the jail at night.

Throughout the length of the trial, rumors abounded of plans for a forcible rescue of the defendants. And such plans, in actual fact, were being considered. Sacco and Vanzetti and their comrades were aware that in 1861 the Russian anarchist Mikhail Bakunin had made a dramatic escape from Siberia, and that in 1876, Peter Kropotkin had escaped from a prison hospital in St. Petersburg. Closer to home, moreover, in 1900, Alexander Berkman, the anarchist who shot Henry Clay Frick during the Homestead Strike of 1892, had made a nearly successful attempt to tunnel his way out of a Pennsylvania prison with the help of Italian anarchist miners. In his cell at Dedham, it might be noted, Vanzetti was reading Berkman's *Prison Memoirs of an Anarchist*, with its detailed account of the attempt.

The 1921 escape, however, was never actually attempted, due in all probability to the heavy presence of police. But in 1923 rescue plans were again afoot. That year, a meeting of Galleanists was held in Springfield, Massachusetts, to discuss the possibility. The idea was to free the men when they would be at the Dedham courthouse, where motions for a new trial were to be argued before Judge Thayer. The key figure at the Springfield meeting was Cesare Stami, an ultramilitant and participant in illegal activities. He published an underground paper called *La Rivolta degli Angeli* (*The Revolt of the Angels*, the title of a book by Anatole France). The subtitle of Stami's paper was *Giornale degli Anormali—A Journal of the Abnormal*. Apart from publishing this paper, Stami and his gang of expropriators carried out holdups in Pennsylvania, Ohio, and West Virginia, as well as of a bank in Detroit. He now demanded $5,000 to liberate Sacco and Vanzetti (information given to the author by an anarchist who attended the meeting). But the Springfield group did not have the cash, and the deal fell through. Stami, the following year, held up a train in Pennsylvania that was carrying a shipment of gold. But one of his henchmen turned out to be a stool pigeon and tipped off the police. The train was surrounded by policemen, and Stami was killed in a shoot-out, along with several of his men.

Later that year, in October 1924, Judge Thayer denied the appeals for a new trial, and in May 1926, his ruling was affirmed by the Massachusetts Supreme Judicial Court. Thus the time had come again to consider an escape. In January 1927, Vanzetti hinted at this in a letter to Alice Stone Blackwell. "I may get out within this year," he wrote, "no matter if alive or dead. And I hope with all my force that it will come true. By it, I do not mean suicide."

But events were moving against the two men. On April 9, in the Dedham court, Judge Thayer imposed the death sentence. On July 1 both men were removed from the Dedham jail to the Charlestown state prison in Boston. On August 4, Governor Alvan Fuller refused the men clemency. The time had come to act. There could be no further delay.

A plan was hastily concocted. The idea was to get anarchist miners from Pennsylvania to come and blow up the prison in order to effect the escape. In the meantime, Aldino Felicani, treasurer of the Sacco-Vanzetti Defense Committee, attempted through an ex-con named Jack Grey, a safecracker who had spent 20 years in prison, to bribe an electrician at Charlestown so that the execution would not take place at the appointed time. The electrician agreed, and the bribe was passed. He was figuring things out two days before the execution, but after monkeying with the electrical system it broke down. All the lights in the prison went out, "and all hell broke loose," said Gardner Jackson of the Defense Committee. So the plan did not materialize. This same fellow, Grey, according to Jackson, had tried in the final weeks to connive with some of the guards to assist in the men's escape, but to no avail.

Vanzetti, it might be noted, had drawn a design of the interior of the prison. It outlined an escape route, indicating the positions of the guards. Once, when Roger Baldwin, head of the American Civil Liberties Union, and Elizabeth Glendower Evans, a member of the New England Civil Liberties Committee who had become interested in the men during the trial, were visiting Vanzetti in his cell, he told them about the planned escape. Mrs. Evans, according to Baldwin, scolded Vanzetti about the folly of the idea, and he desisted. That he actually desisted, however, seems to me doubtful. More likely, the plan had to be abandoned only when the electrician caused the lights prematurely to fail.

Both Vanzetti and Sacco, of course, knew that escape plans might prove defective. Thus, forever in their minds was the alternative—retribution. Already in 1924, when Judge Thayer was about to reject their motions for a new trial, Vanzetti wrote a letter to Alice Blackwell. "I will ask for revenge," he said. "I will tell that I will die gladly by the hands of the hanger, after having known to have been vindicated. I mean 'eye for an eye, ear for an ear,' and even more, since to win it is necessary that a hundred enemies fall to each of us."

In October of that year, as previously stated, Thayer denied the defendants' motions. After announcing his decision, he rewarded himself by attending the

Dartmouth-McGill football game in Hanover, New Hampshire (Thayer was a Dartmouth alumnus). While there, he ran into James Richardson, Dartmouth's professor of law. "Did you see what I did with those anarchistic bastards the other day?" he said. " I guess that will hold them for a while." Vanzetti exploded with rage when he learned of this remark. "Death for death," he wrote. "I think that the times require to bring with us some enemies, some blackguards—I should say the more that is possible." In the meantime William Thompson, attorney for Sacco and Vanzetti, appealed Thayer's decision to the Supreme Judicial Court of Massachusetts. On May 12, 1926, however, the court rejected the appeal and upheld the guilty verdict against the defendants.

A few weeks later there appeared an article in *Protesta Umana*, the Italian-language organ of the Defense Committee. The front-page headline proclaimed: "As the Day of Execution Approaches, the Prisoners Warn: *LA SALUTE È IN VOI!*" *La Salute è in Voi*—which means Salvation is up to You—was the title of Galleani's bomb manual. The article that followed, signed by Sacco and Vanzetti, carried an appeal for retaliation. "Remember," it concluded, *"LA SALUTE È IN VOI!"* What this meant, as their comrades understood, was a resumption of bomb attacks against the authorities, such as those they had carried out in 1919. Until their death on August 23, 1927, the prisoners returned repeatedly to this theme. "If we have to die for a crime of which we are innocent," declared Vanzetti, "we ask for revenge, revenge in our names and in the names of our living and dead. I will make a list of honor of the perjurers who murdered us. I will try to see Thayer dead. I will put fire in the human breaths."

Sacco was equally vehement. In the spring of 1927, when his comrade Armando Borghi visited him in jail, his eyes glittered with hate as he echoed the protests of Emile Henri and Michele Angiolillo, of Paolino Pallas and Gaetano Bresci, Bresci being the assassin of King Umberto. "We are proud for death," Sacco wrote after Governor Fuller refused clemency, "and fall as the anarchists can fall. It is up to you now, brothers, comrades!"

Their comrades did not disappoint them. On June 1, 1926, a bomb exploded at the home of Samuel Johnson in West Bridgewater, Massachusetts. Whoever planted it apparently mistook Johnson's house for that of his brother Simon, whose call to the police had led to the arrest of Sacco and Vanzetti. On May 10, 1927, a package bomb addressed to Governor Fuller was intercepted in the Boston post office. No one was injured and there was no arrest. Three months later, on August 6, bombs exploded in the New York subway, in a Philadelphia church, and at the home of the mayor of Baltimore. On August 15, an explosion occurred in the East Milton, Massachusetts, home of Lewis McHardy, a juror in the Dedham trial. A bomb placed on the porch of his two-story house exploded at 3:30 in the morning. More than half of the house was demolished. McHardy, his wife, and three children were thrown from their beds but escaped serious injury. Apparently, McHardy was chosen as a target because he had opposed the governor's appointment of an advisory committee to review the case. The day after the bombing, McHardy hung a huge American flag above his front door—or at least what was left of it.

On August 22, 1927, William Thompson met with Vanzetti in the death house just a few hours before the executions. He told Vanzetti that he hoped he would advise his friends against reprisal. Vanzetti, however, refused. He replied that "as he read history, every great cause for the benefit of humanity had had to fight for its existence against entrenched power and wrong." He reminded Thompson of the cruelty of seven years of imprisonment, with alternating hopes and fears, that he and Sacco had been made to suffer. He reminded Thompson of the remarks attributed to Judge Thayer by Professor Richardson and others and asked him what state of mind he thought such remarks indicated. He asked him how any candid man could believe that a judge capable of referring to men accused before him as "anarchistic bastards" could be impartial, and whether he thought that such cruelty as had been practiced upon him and Sacco ought to go unpunished. Thompson was at a loss to reply.

The bombings did not cease with the execution of the two men. At the funeral parlor in Boston a floral piece proclaimed *Aspettando l'ora di vendetta*—Awaiting the hour of vengeance. Vengeance came on the night of May 17, 1928, when a bomb exploded at the Richmond Hill, Queens, home of Robert G. Elliott, the executioner of Sacco and Vanzetti. No one was hurt, but the house was badly damaged. Elliott was the country's most active and famous executioner. Twelve years later, in 1939, he executed the Lindbergh baby's kidnapper, Bruno Hauptmann. At the time of Sacco and Vanzetti's execution, he was 56 years old and had been executing prisoners for 30 years.

In conclusion, let me mention something that occurred during my research on the case a number of years ago. It involves Judge Thayer, one of the principal figures in the drama. I needed more information about him and wrote to the address where he had lived in 1927, which I had found in a Boston newspaper. I addressed my letter to "Occupant, 180 Institute Road, Worcester, Massachusetts," hoping that some relative might live there, or someone who knew something about the case. As it happened, I had no luck. My letter came back stamped "No Such Address." Not "Addressee Unknown," mind you, but "No Such Address." What could this mean? The bomb had demolished the house. A new house was later built on the site, a corner lot, but with its entrance on the street around the corner. The address had become 2 Beachmont Street, and the residents there knew nothing.

It was on September 27, 1932, that the bomb wrecked Thayer's home. The judge escaped serious injury. Shaken by the experience, however, he moved to his club in Boston. There he remained until his death seven months later. There were no further explosions, and none of the bombers were caught. My old friend Valerio Isca offered further information about Thayer. Valerio, the last of the Italian anarchists in New York, died in 1997 at the age of 95. He had struggled throughout the 1920s to save Sacco and Vanzetti, unfortunately, to no avail. But the two men, he told me, received a posthumous measure of revenge. For Thayer, he said, died on the toilet seat, "and his soul went down the drain."

BIBLIOGRAPHY

Avrich, Paul. *Anarchist Voices: An Oral History of Anarchism in America.* Princeton, N.J.: Princeton University Press, 1995.

———. *Sacco and Vanzetti: The Anarchist Background.* Princeton, N.J.: Princeton University Press, 1991.

Baldwin, Roger N. Interview in Oral History Project, Columbia University, 1954.

Galleani, Luigi. *Faccia a faccia col nemico: Cronache giudiziarie dell'anarchismo militante.* East Boston: Edizione del Gruppo Autonomo, 1914.

———. *La Salute è in voi!* N.p., [1905].

Jackson, Gardner. Interview in Oral History Project, Columbia University, 1955.

Pernicone, Nunzio. "Carlo Tresca and the Sacco-Vanzetti Case," *Journal of American History* 66 (December 1979): 535–47.

Russell, Francis. *Tragedy in Dedham: The Story of the Sacco-Vanzetti Case.* New York: McGraw-Hill, 1962.

Sacco, Nicola, and Bartolomeo Vanzetti. *The Letters of Sacco and Vanzetti.* Edited by Marion Denman, Felix Frankfurter, and Gardner Jackson. New York: Viking, 1928.

Sacco-Vanzetti: Developments and Re-considerations. Boston: Boston Public Library, 1982.

The Sacco-Vanzetti Case: Transcript of the Record of the Trial of Nicola Sacco and Bartolomeo Vanzetti in the Courts of Massachusetts and Subsequent Proceedings, 1920–27. 6 vols. New York: Henry Holt, 1928–1929.

Un trentennio di attivita anarchica (1914–1945). Edited by Raffaele Schiavina. Cesena, Italy: Antistato, 1953.

Chapter 7

No God, No Master: Italian Anarchists and the Industrial Workers of the World

Salvatore Salerno

I remember how carefully she held the worn photograph face down in her lap as she talked about her late father's role in the strike. She had found it in an envelope of deteriorating clippings her father had kept tucked between books piled in the corners of their small apartment. After we talked for a while, she showed it to me. It was a picture of a group of impassioned rebels holding a banner that read "No God, No Master." "Who were they?" I asked. "Friends of my father," she answered. "They were once part of a large *circolo*, I don't remember what happened to them all. A few of them were deported, others went to jail, the rest just disappeared—sometime around World War I. They were Italian anarchists, you know, members of the Industrial Workers of the World (IWW)." "Were they anarcho-syndicalists," I asked? "Syndicalists? Well not exactly, I don't really remember what they called themselves, but I remember that they debated these things endlessly."[1]

Syndicalism began attracting worldwide attention following the founding of the French anarcho-syndicalist union, Confédération Générale du Travail (CGT) in the late 1890s. The militancy of French workers found echoes in the activities of workers across the Atlantic. This essay looks at one such group, a group of Italian anarchists in Paterson, New Jersey, a small city with a large radical and labor history. Il Gruppo Diritto all'Esistenza (Right to Exist Group) began agitating for unions based on a model of revolutionary unionism similar to the program advanced by the CGT. Its newspaper, *La Questione Sociale (LQS)*, would become the leading voice of organizationalist anarchists and anarcho-feminists. Max Nettlau, chronicler of fin de siècle anarchism, considered *LQS* to be among the 17 authoritative organs of anarchist thought in the 1900s. He compared *LQS* with *L'Anarchie* of Paris and *Freedom* of London.[2] Pedro Esteve, a Spanish anarchist, was the paper's most consistent editor and among the group's central figures. In addition to his work on *LQS*, he published pamphlets on syndicalism. Esteve also edited *El Despertar*, a Spanish-language anarchist paper popular among cigar workers from Brooklyn to Tampa.[3] He, along with other members of ll Gruppo Diritto all'Esistenza, was continuously involved with disseminating propaganda and organizing tours, particularly among Western miners, and also engaged in union-forming activities among cigar, dock, and textile workers.[4] The group's position on the subject of syndicalism is best illustrated in an article written by Esteve's longtime friend Errico Malatesta, the leading organizationalist anarchist of his time. Esteve translated it into Italian from the French version that appeared in the 1907 issue of *Tempe Nouveaux*. Malatesta's article discussed the dilemma that syndicalism posed for anarchists:

Anarchists must abstain from identifying with the syndicalist movement; they should not take as an end that which is but one of the means for action and propaganda. They must remain in the syndicate in order to give the impulse to march forward and attempt to make of the syndicates, as much as it is possible, instruments of struggle toward social revolution. They must work to develop in syndicates all that can augment their educational influence, their readiness to battle, the propaganda of ideas, strikes, proletariat spirit, the disapproval and hatred of authority and of politicians, the practice of solidarity toward individuals and groups in struggle with the owners.[5]

Malatesta's position on syndicalism is very close to that later adopted by the IWW. This can especially be seen in the writing of Wobblies like Vincent St. John, as well as footloose workers who occasionally contributed articles to the *Industrial Worker* or *Solidarity*.[6]

The anarchists of ll Gruppo Diritto all'Esistenza embraced syndicalist tactics and were part of the movement culture, but they did not identify with syndicalism as an ideology, platform, or structure for a new political party. Instead, they considered themselves anarcho-socialists.[7] *LQS* had running discussions about both the philosophical and the practical meaning of the merger they posed between anarchism and socialism. Vito D'Amico, in a long article, wrote that the question of what anarcho-socialism represented posed a problem. A good number of *compagni*, in fact, did not understand what anarcho-socialism meant; some argued that such a hybrid doctrine was absurd and doomed to failure, whereas others saw the importance of the position. We want the abolition of private property, D'Amico wrote, but "we also want the freedom to govern ourselves individually. Thus we want to abolish government, in other words we want anarchy in addition to socialism."[8] Add to the group's political philosophy the tactics of the general strike, direct action, and sabotage, and there were all the ingredients of revolutionary syndicalism.

In the early 1920s, while active in the factory council movement in Turin, Antonio Gramsci commented on the enigma that revolutionary syndicalism continued to pose for the Italian Left. "Syndicalism," he wrote, "has achieved one result and one only—it has multiplied the number of political parties representing the working class. This multiplicity of political parties is precisely the major obstacle (if not the only obstacle) that stands in the way of proletarian unity and the one big union which is nevertheless an element of the syndicalist program."[9] Gramsci illustrates an important way in which syndicalism stood in the way of its own development or realization. His comments indicate that Wobbly industrial unionist influences ("the one big union") were present in pre- and postwar Italy and important to the Italian Left's discourse. There is also in Gramsci's observations a different diffusion and vision of syndicalism, one that did not lead to, or end in, Fascism.[10]

This essay examines the role of Italian anarchists in the industrial union movement in the United States in the first quarter century of their contact with America. It discusses their role in the development of the IWW and contrasts their efforts with those of Italian socialists, who also made overtures to syndicalism. The example of the Paterson group is used to demonstrate the importance of the foreign-language local to the American industrial union movement and to discuss the absence of this influence in labor historiography.

Of all the tendencies within the Italian American Left, those Italians identifying themselves as anarcho-syndicalist, anarcho-socialist, or industrial unionist remain the least known or understood.[11] There are few studies to draw upon to reconstruct the activities of Italian immigrant workers who defined themselves in these ways.[12] We know little about their milieu, networks of their *circoli* (affinity groups), family, and community life. From the few newspaper sources that have survived, we find anarchist groups active within the industrial union movement, organizing on the shop floor, and building community through social and cultural organizations.

In Paterson, for example, Il Gruppo Diritto all'Esistenza sponsored public talks, plays, and dances in several local taverns. Italian anarchist weavers gathered in local taverns to read their newspapers in Italian, but also in Spanish and French. In the backrooms of taverns, meetings of a broad range of anarchist societies were held that enlivened the Paterson community. There were drama groups such as La Cosmopolita and Circolo Sociale e Filodrammatico, a band called La Simpatica, and a chorus known as Figli del Lavoro that met regularly. In the late 1890s, women in Il Gruppo Diritto all'Esistenza founded Gruppo Emancipazione della Donna to spread the ideas of women's emancipation among textile workers.[13] Eventually the Paterson group formed the Università Popolare, which organized public lectures, social gatherings, and study groups. They eventually introduced a series titled *Libreria Sociologica,* which expanded the group's publications. *The Libreria Sociologica* made available inexpensive Italian-language editions of works by anarchist thinkers, playwrights, poets, and activists. Among the selections of the *Libreria Sociologica,* one could find the writings of Pietro Gori, Elisée Reclus, Peter Kropotkin, Errico Malatesta, Ada Negri, Leda Rafanelli, Saverio Merlino, Michael Bakunin, and Johann Most. The milieu of the Italian American anarchist community in this period revealed an extensive web of associations that mixed cultures, languages, and ideologies.[14]

The anarchist silk workers who made up Il Gruppo Diritto all'Esistenza used syndicalist tactics in their union long before the IWW's 1905 founding convention. Paterson anarchists had spent months in the western part of the United States working on union-forming activities with both the Western Federation of Miners and the United Mine Workers.[15] They were part of the movement that contributed to the founding of the IWW and were connected to struggles for national liberation.[16] The Paterson anarchists were in communication with Ricardo Flores Magón and other Mexican anarchists who helped to establish the Partido Liberal Mexicano (PLM), an anarchist organization responsible for initiating the Mexican Revolution. Among the subscribers to *LQS* was Tierra y Libertad, a club similar to other community organizations set up by Mexican anarchists throughout the Southwest. In 1911, Ludovico Caminita,[17] a former editor of *LQS*, began writing an Italian-language column for the Spanish newspaper *Regeneración*, as well as contributing graphics to the newspaper.[18] In *Rebellion in the Borderlands*, James Sandos writes that Ricardo Flores Magón found his deepest support for the PLM and the plight of the people of Mexico from Italian and Spanish anarchists. Although the details of the associations between these groups remain obscure, these influences are evident in the movement's expressive culture. This can be seen in a poster printed as part of the newspaper in 1910. The top part of the poster displays the *Regeneración* masthead, but over the sun are portraits of five anarchists: Peter Kropotkin at the center; to his right Errico Malatesta and the French anarchist Charles Malato; to Kropotkin's left are the Spanish anarchists Fernando Tarrida del Mármol and Anselmo Lorenzo, a Catalan anarchist and mentor to the young Esteve. These portraits are set against an open book on which are written two titles: Malato's *Philosophy of Anarchism* and Malatesta's *Conversation between Two Workers*. Below them are the portraits of the Flores Magón brothers, Librado Rivera, Angelmo Figueroa, and Antonio de P. Araujo.[19]

Like the *Industrial Worker*, the successor of *LQS*, *L'Era Nuova* carried extensive front-page coverage of the Mexican Revolution. The IWW also had early contact with Mexican anarchists through the Spanish anarchist Florencio Bazora, a close associate of Ricardo Flores Magón. Bazora initiated a relationship between the PLM and the IWW that would weather the defeats of the Liberal armies in northern Mexico and the imprisonment of Flores Magón.[20] Bazora made important contributions to the PLM's campaign, by helping the Magónistas to publish and distribute *Regeneración*, in building coalitions, and in organizing propaganda tours.

The story of the revolutionary syndicalist movement is like a hidden text within both socialist and anarchist history.[21] The bulk of scholarly attention directed at the Italian American anarchist community has focused on the anti-organizationalists and anarchist individualist tendencies. Historical studies of anti-organizationalists have consistently downplayed the contributions of industrial unionism to the labor movement. As a result, it is generally thought that Italians played only a small role in the immigrant wing of the American labor movement, especially in comparison to their Russian Jewish comrades.[22]

There has also been a tendency among historians interested in socialism to collapse the various forms of syndicalism within the industrial union movement. The literature on the Italian Left in the United States relies on the scope and activities of the Italian Socialist Federation (ISF) and its paper *Il Proletario* to evaluate the Italian contribution to the industrial union movement. There are few studies that look at other aspects of the Italian Left's relationship to the IWW and nothing that looks comparatively at the various groups that comprised the Italian Left and the relationship of these groups to syndicalism.[23]

The ISF did not send delegates or observers to the IWW's founding convention, nor did it immediately affiliate with the IWW.[24] The years leading up to the IWW's founding were difficult ones for the ISF. Mario De Ciampis, in his history of the Federation, writes that following the IWW's convention, the ISF entered a "moral and material crisis" of severe proportions. The crisis began in 1906 when Carlo Tresca, a prominent IWW organizer and anarchist, left his position as editor of *Il Proletario* to found his own paper.[25]

Tresca left the ISF not only to play a more prominent role in the industrial union movement but also because of his commitment to direct action on a community, as well as an industrial, level. He recognized the urgency of channeling the energies of the growing masses of southern Italian immigrants and left the ISF to propagate the idea of organizing the *camere di lavoro* (chambers of labor), which were based on a model used by the French anarcho-syndicalists, *bourses de travail* of the CGT. In both France and Italy, the major tasks of these chambers were to represent workers at a regional level, to control the labor market, and to organize sympathy strikes and boycotts during industrial disturbances. These organizations helped local working-class communities develop a sense of solidarity between the skilled and unskilled workers and also worked to build alliances between rural and urban populations. The chambers were therefore not limited to economic or strictly political functions, but rather they served equally as community centers through which festivals and picnics were organized, as spaces for drama and poetry, and as places for neighborhood meetings. The *camere del lavoro* anticipated the emergence of the mixed local (an organizational structure that included skilled and unskilled, employed and unemployed workers with community residents), which were important to the IWW's overall organizational structure.[26]

Not long after Tresca's departure, Giuseppe Bertelli, his replacement as editor of *Il Protelario* also left the ISF to found his own newspaper—*Socialiste senza Aggettivi* (Socialism Without Adjectives).[27] We can see the seriousness of the crisis in a letter written by a Federation member and published in *Il Proletario* in 1906:

In a city in America (New York) that has 650,000 Italians those who are socialist party members are a couple of hundred. . . . If we take into account that at least two-thirds of these comrades were already socialists when they came to America, then tell me comrades, tell me, to what has amounted our work? The naked truth is this: we are not doing our duty, for immigrants shun our sections and because we have isolated ourselves from everyone, despising and offending those who do not think like us, closing ourselves in our halls and having discussions on theories and on comrades—when do we actually fight— while outside priests and *prominenti* infiltrate themselves all over the place and turn immigration to their advantage.[28]

Elisabetta Vezzosi, in her discussion of the ISF's history, writes that doctrinal arguments and tactical disagreements separated the ISF from others on the Italian left. Although the Federation borrowed from both the IWW and the Socialist Party (SP), the ISF did not clearly define itself as either a labor union or a political party. Vezzosi concluded that the failure of the ISF to break the barriers of its isolation meant that the ethnic structure that formed the stable reference points in Italian American immigrant communities became the privileged channels for Americanization rather than centers that nurtured a radical culture.[29] Bruno Ramirez, who also examined the history of ISF, adds that the Federation's affiliation with the IWW represented less an expression of maturity in the Federation's strategic judgment than political opportunism. The affiliation did not create organizational inroads for Italian immigrant workers. nor did it stop factional disputes.[30]

The problems encountered by the ISF following the IWW's founding convention were not unique. They were similar to problems experienced in other socialist organizations as they reacted to syndicalism. We can only understand Italian participation in the IWW if we extend our analysis beyond the ISF. The anarchist socialist position is interesting because although its adherents affiliated with the IWW and adopted syndicalist tactics, they remained critical of syndicalism. They became part of the movement culture of revolutionary syndicalism while maintaining a distinctive tendency. They made the literature of syndicalism available through their *Libreria Sociologica,* hosted public debates, and held internal discussions of the tactics emerging out of the revolutionary syndicalist movement. They also sponsored study groups through their Università Popolare and generally made use of the aesthetic of revolutionary syndicalism in their selection of graphics, poetry, songs, and plays, which emphasized a workers' culture of struggle.

Organizationalist anarchists greeted the IWW founding convention with enthusiasm. The Italian anarchist group, Germinal, from Spring Valley, Illinois, sent observers to Chicago; their report was published as a series in *LQS*.[31] These examples suggest how extensive the web of association was among Italian anarchists in the pre–World War I period. Complex connections existed between the Paterson anarchists and labor struggles throughout the United States, as well as with other anarchist groups representing a range of tendencies. Prior to *LQS*'s suppression in 1908 by federal authorities, its readership extended beyond national borders, and contributors increasingly addressed theoretical and practical issues of concern to world anarchism.

Following the IWW's founding convention, Il Gruppo Diritto all'Esistenza immediately invited IWW organizers to speak in a hall in Paterson. William E.

Trautmann, a German immigrant who was soon to become the general secretary of the IWW, along with several other Wobblies, spoke to a small but enthusiastic group. Following this meeting, Il Gruppo Diritto all'Esistenza affiliated with the IWW and began a series of strikes against silk manufacturers in Paterson. Although critical of the IWW for not completely purging itself of parliamentarianism, they nevertheless felt a certain commonality and became one of the IWW's first charter members. Their comrades in the *Mother Earth* group (*Mother Earth* was an anarchist journal edited by Emma Goldman) were also in solidarity with the IWW, calling its formation a partial anarchist victory.[32] Along with the appearance of the IWW logo, articles condemning parliamentarianism became more frequent in the columns of *LQS*.

The IWW's form of industrial unionism differed from the syndicalism of the ISF, the left wing of the SP, or the Socialist Labor Party. This would become increasingly apparent as the IWW adopted the syndicalist tactics of sabotage and direct action.[33] To understand this form of syndicalism, we must also look at the contributions of migrant workers, unaffiliated to party or union, which were essential elements of the industrial union's movement culture. The complexity of the IWW's amalgam of syndicalism and anarchism can most clearly be seen in its expressive culture.

The powerful but anonymous role of Italian laborers became part of the lore and culture of the industrial union movement in a story that was widely circulated in the first decade of the twentieth century. Sometime around 1906, in Harvey, Illinois, contractors of railway construction workers announced a 50-cents-per-day reduction in wages. In response, the Italian workers cut their shovels one-half inch in protest and shouted, "Short pay, short shovels!" The actions of these construction workers forced the contractors to restore the former wages.[34]

This story was used in one of the IWW's earliest pamphlets to address the tactics of industrial unionism. In "Industrial Unionism: New Methods and New Forms," William E. Trautmann, a major architect of the IWW's form of industrial unionism, used the short-shovel story to demonstrate principles fundamental to industrial unionism, qualities not typically associated with anarchists or Italian workers. Trautmann recommended that workers follow the example of the Italian construction workers in situations where it was difficult to overcome police, injunction judges, or jailers. The short-shovel tactic of these workers prefigured the strategy of "striking on the job," popularized by the Wobblies in the 1910s.[35]

The example of the Italian construction workers also shows a tension between spontaneous activity that is not part of the organized expression of a particular movement and the desire to make such activity conform to a particular theory of what constitutes concerted action. This tension between spontaneity and organized expression was central to the debates among anarchists, socialists, and syndicalists within the industrial union movement and defined a considerable part of the movement's programmatic literature and expressive culture.[36]

More than anything else, the revolutionary industrial union movement was a culture of struggle. Its activities challenge the prevailing view of the boundaries between foreign-language groups and the Left, as well as the strategies employed by immigrant workers in building a community of struggle. The lives and activism of Ludovico Caminita, Pedro Esteve, and women like Maria Roda and Titì, who established an early feminist group connected to *LQS*, all contradict assumptions that have silenced many of the movement's key players. Caminita and Esteve were at home in several different communities; they were integral members of Paterson's Italian anarchist community, they both represented worker–intellectuals, who bridged communities through their linguistic acumen and organizing skills. Important to the "Latin" anarchists, Esteve also forged important connections to Russian Jewish anarchists. He also interacted with native-born anarchists such as Lucy Parsons, a woman of color and a working-class anarchist who was the widow of Albert Parsons, one of the Haymarket martyrs. Initially, Esteve formed close ties to the Italian anarchist community, first through his friendship with Malatesta. Later, his ties to the community were strengthened through his work in Il Gruppo Diritto all'Esistenza and his marriage to Maria Roda. Esteve often represented Il Gruppo Diritto all'Esistenza in public meetings sponsored by other anarchist groups. At those venues, Esteve typically spoke in Italian or served as a translator in meetings with anarchists from mixed ethnic groups.

Maria Roda was another central figure of Il Gruppo Diritto all'Esistenza. Unfortunately, little is known about her life and activism. Born in the town of Como in the Lombardy region of Italy in 1887, Maria was the daughter of Cesare Balzarini Roda and Monti Luigia. She learned silk weaving from her father, who was a militant anarchist, and found work as a teenager in the local mills. The family eventually moved to Milan, a city that offered better wages and employment opportunities. It was there that Maria first came to the attention of authorities. Although only in her teens, she was fined and imprisoned for a period of three months for singing subversive songs in the streets during a strike. Women in Paterson also found themselves arrested, jailed, and fined for similar crimes. In Paterson, a group of young women strikers had developed the strategy of blowing on fancy fish horns, all painted the same color, as a means of creating a spectacle that drew attention to, ridiculed, and shamed scabs.[37]

Roda emigrated from France after serving another term of imprisonment. She, along with other members of her group, were imprisoned following the assassination of President Sadi Carnot of France by one of the group's members, Sante Caserio. Upon her release, she immigrated to the United States, began to organize textile workers in New Jersey, and became part of the Paterson group. Emma Goldman heard her speak at a meeting set up to welcome Goldman home following her release from Blackwell's Island. Roda addressed the Italian comrades present in the hall to welcome Emma home after her term of imprisonment. After hearing Roda's speech, Goldman described her as "a veritable ray of sunlight" and praised her oratory skills. In addition to her membership in Il Gruppo Diritto all'Esistenza, she also had a hand in establishing Gruppo Emancipazione della Donna.[38]

The Gruppo Emancipazione della Donna was organized by Gruppo Anarchico Femminile and acted as a kind of umbrella organization for the various feminist *circoli* within the wider anarchist community. How many women participated in the organization is not known. Some of its members, like Titì, wrote under pseudonyms. Although a prolific contributor to *LQS*, next to nothing is known about her life and activism. Only a few pamphlets from her series have survived. Fortunately, *LQS* published the news stories, essays, editorials, and poetry of these women. In the writing of the group's feminists, we see the beginnings of a discourse that examined the origins of women's oppression as based in private property and the Church. Their position differed from that of individualists and anarcho-communists. The anarcho-socialist feminists who were part of Il Gruppo Diritto all'Esistenza examined the specific ways women were oppressed, not only by capitalism, but also by patriarchy. These feminists opened new lines of analysis within Il Gruppo Diritto all'Esistenza as well as the larger community of anarchists. As Jennifer Guglielmo has discovered, "within their writings, we find the intricacies of Italian immigrant women's ideologies and debates and the emergence of their own distinctive proletarian feminism."[39] Women who contributed to *LQS* continually underscored the importance of economic independence and viewed both masculinity and femininity as social constructions. They questioned how women used power in the community to set standards and redefine what was appropriate, and they theorized about the ways in which the Church and the family socialized girls into docile workers and obedient wives.[40] We also see in the stories they chose to write the beginnings of an anti-imperialist critique. Titì, for example, wrote an editorial that exposed and condemned the genocidal practices of the Belgian government in the Congo.[41]

Il Gruppo Diritto all'Esistenza played an active role in the birth of the industrial union movement. Well in advance of the IWW's inaugural convention, the group leaned toward a workers' union organizational model based on anarchist and socialist principles and syndicalist tactics. Paterson anarchists spent months in the western United States working on union-forming activities with the Western Federation of Miners, one of the IWW's most important forerunners, and ran a weekly column in *LQS* that reported on the struggles of both hard- and soft-coal miners in the region. They were also among the first of the foreign-language groups to affiliate with the IWW. The Paterson weavers became an official local of the IWW in March 1906, and *LQS* was one of the first papers to carry the IWW's logo. In 1906, the IWW conducted 24 strikes in Paterson; of these, two resulted in victories for the workers.[42]

IWW historiography has portrayed the Wobblies as a specifically "native" radical organization, or in the words of Dan Georgakas, "the finest expression of an indigenous radical tradition."[43] In this view, the IWW was born out of the struggles of hard-rock miners, "men who were by and large Americans and the most Americanized immigrants."[44] David Brundage, for example, has argued that all the talismans of syndicalism were present in a trajectory of unions and organizations that came to be exemplified in the American Labor Union, which frontier theorists see as the IWW's most proximate precursor.[45] Although it was central to the IWW's formation and development, these historians fail to analyze the role that anarchists played in the struggles between syndicalism and socialism.

In general, IWW historiography continues to reflect an unwillingness to look at the contributions of anarchism to the building of industrial unionism. For example, Verity Burgmann used the IWW manifesto to conclude that the new movement "clearly reflected a Marxist world vision, which IWW theorists such as Trautmann and Hagerty had derived from books."[46] Trautmann, as we have seen, was helping Italian anarchist silk workers conduct strikes in the early months of 1906. Hagerty, an anarcho-syndicalist and early architect of industrial unionism, had worked tirelessly in the defense of the Haymarket martyrs. At the IWW's founding convention, he acknowledged the contributions of Spanish anarchists to the birth of industrial unionism, invoking the wider movement's debt to European anarcho-syndicalists. Hagerty, as well as the other anarchists who played instrumental roles in the development of the industrial union movement in the United States, saw the IWW as the rebirth of the "Chicago idea," the model of unionism advanced by the Haymarket anarchists.[47]

The industrial union movement was not the result of a particular cultural sphere, nor was it a movement limited to native-born, national, or regional characteristics. It did not develop autonomously within a closed system or specific geographical boundaries. It was a worldwide movement carried by workers who spoke many different languages. Nurtured in intricate patterns of cross-fertilization, syndicalism traveled between states, countries, and continents. Its hybrid nature was matched only by its fluid characteristics, because its chief form of diffusion was the geographical mobility of workers brought about by worldwide patterns of industrialization.

The frontier activist thesis, which has dominated the IWW labor historiography, has also had its effects on the ways immigrant and migrant workers are viewed within labor history. This approach divests the immigrant worker of any cultural substance and transforms radicalism into a direct and spontaneous response to exploitation. In *Militants and Migrants*, Donna R. Gabaccia has critiqued this perspective by arguing that it divorced the ideas and experiences immigrant and migrant workers derived from their participation in Europe's class wars.[48] The Paterson anarchists were the very lifeblood of the IWW's organizational culture, a culture that was rooted in migrant and immigrant groups and the kinds of informal strategies and ideologies they carried with them.

Il Gruppo Diritto all'Esistenza remained active in the IWW throughout the new organization's bitter factional disputes, which were centered around the use of direct action and other syndicalist principles and strategies versus parliamentarianism of the Socialist Party and the Socialist Labor Party.[49] During this period, the bulk of the membership abandoned the IWW as it embraced syndicalist tactics. By 1908, the IWW's membership was limited to a handful of foreign-language locals in the East and a few hundred migratory workers in the West.[50] During these lean years, the bulk of IWW activity took place in the eastern textile industries, where the majority of workers were Italian. When *LQS* was suppressed by federal authorities on March 21, 1908, the group changed the name of its paper to *L'Era Nuova* and continued publishing it until it was again suppressed in 1917. In 1920, when the Federal Bureau of Investigation, assisted by the American Legion, raided the community and arrested 29 members of Il Gruppo Diritto all'Esistenza, now called L'Era Nuova, they thought they had finally subdued America's leading "terrorist" group.[51]

The experience of groups like Il Gruppo Diritto all'Esistenza, Germinal, and Tierra y Libertad raise larger questions about the role of Spanish, Italian, Mexican, Cuban, Puerto Rican, and other Latin American anarchists in the industrial union movement. Their absence from the narrative of Italian American experience shows how incomplete our knowledge and understanding of the Left is, in spite of its importance to the historical experience of Italians in the North America. The absence of this knowledge from the narrative of immigration history is also symptomatic of larger historiographical problems. Although the new social and cultural history has challenged the notion of a master narrative of immigrant experience, that critique has failed to address the fact that the history of the immigrant experience has been largely based on English-language sources.

The history of Il Gruppo Diritto all'Esistenza challenges the dominant way that Italian immigrant radicalism has been portrayed as either marginal to the labor movement or antithetical to the purpose of unionism. The Paterson anarchists also demonstrate the IWW's transnational roots and provide a window into the multi-ethnic organizing strategies that emerged out of mixed local and foreign-language groups. The experience of Il Gruppo Diritto all'Esistenza reveals the tensions between community-based and work-based organizing. Much of the writing of Italian immigrant anarcho-socialist women was about family and community as sites of radical practice.[52] The strategies of their activism involved whole communities, not just wage earners. They established links between their feminism and the politics of the anarcho-socialists who formed Il Gruppo Diretto all'Esistenza. Moreover, the example of the Paterson anarchists revises the labor historians' understanding of the origins of multi-ethnic labor organizing. This is usually associated with the Congress of Industrial Organizations (CIO) in the 1930s and the English-speaking second generation of industrial workers. In fact, it was the first generation, Italians among them, who pioneered what they saw as international practice.

NOTES

I would first like to thank Franco Ramella and Ferdinando Fasce who, each in their own ways, suggested the topic and encouraged me to pursue the links between the Paterson anarchists and the IWW. Thanks are also due to Monica Barbieri, Philip Cannistraro, Renu Capelli, Donna Gabaccia, Jennifer Guglielmo, Fabio Losurdo, Denise Mayotte, Peter Rachleff, James A. Sandos, Rudy Vecoli, and Elisabetta Vezzosi for their help, support, and suggestions.

1. This story is based on oral history interviews I conducted while doing the research for my book *Red November, Black November, Culture and Community in the Industrial Workers of the World* (New York: State University of New York Press, 1989). Although many of the people whom I interviewed remembered an incident in Lawrence, Massachusetts, in which an anarchist group carried a banner that read "No God, No Master," no one could identify the group or knew who made the banner. The phrase is from an IWW placard carried through the streets of Lawrence during the 1912 strike; it read: "XX Century civilization . . . For the progress of the human race we have jails, gallows and guillotines, . . . and the electric chairs for the people who pay to keep the soldiers to kill them when they revolt against Wood [President of American Woolen Company, indicted for placing dynamite among strikers in Lawrence] and other czars of capitalism."

Arise!!! Slaves of the World!!!
No God! No Master!
One for all and all for one!

Quoted in Paul F. Brissenden, *The IWW: A Study of American Syndicalism* (New York: Russell & Russell, 1957), 294. A photograph of this placard appears in M. B. Schnapper, *American Labor: A Bicentennial History* (Washington, D.C.: Public Affairs Press, 1975), 382. In interviews, people typically described the placard as having a disruptive influence and credited anarchists in the IWW for creating it. In her book *The Rebel Girl: An Autobiography, My First Life 1906–1926* (New York: International Publishers, 1955), Elizabeth Gurley Flynn identifies the banner as the work of an anarchist group from Boston or possibly that of an agent provocateur (p. 150). The banner appeared in Lawrence during a parade on behalf of Ettor and Giovannitti, IWW leaders who were arrested and charged in the murder of a young girl shot during one of the demonstrations. The banner, Flynn wrote, "gave the Lawrence police a pretext to break up the parade." A few days later, she claimed, it caused a riot in Quincy. "That banner was worth a million dollars to the employers and may have been a deliberate act of provocation," she concluded.

2. George Carey, "*La Questione Sociale*, An Anarchist Newspaper in Paterson, N.J. (1895–1908)," in *Italian Americans: New Perspectives in Italian Immigration and Ethnicity*, ed. Lydio F. Tomasi (New York: Center for Migration Studies, 1985), 289.

3. Little is known about Pedro Esteve (1866–1925). Considered the leading Spanish anarchist in the United States, Esteve's relationship to anarchism began in Barcelona, where he participated in the Catalan anarchist movement and worked with Barcelona's principal anarchist newspaper, *El Productor*. Early in the 1890s, Esteve left Barcelona for the United States. In the United States, he moved between New York, where he organized seamen, and Tampa, Florida, where he organized cigar makers. He frequently shared the platform with Emma Goldman and acted as her interpreter. In addition to intermittently editing *La Questione Sociale* (*LQS*) between 1899 and 1906, Esteve also edited *El Despertar* (Paterson, 1892–ca. 1895, 1900), *El Esclavo* (Tampa, 1894–ca. 1898), and *Cultura Obrera* (New York, 1911–1912, 1921–1925). In Ybor City, Florida, he ran *La Poliglota*, a small anarchist press. He married the Italian anarchist Maria Roda. Correspondence, Candice Falk, Emma Goldman Papers, University of California, Berkeley, 16 April 1997. See also Paul Avrich, *Anarchist Voices: An Oral History of Anarchism in America* (Princeton, N.J.: Princeton University Press, 1995), 143, 391, 393; Gary R. Mormino and George E. Pozzetta, *The Immigrant World of Ybor City: Italians and Their Latin Neighbors in Tampa, 1885–1985* (Chicago: University of Illinois Press), 150; Emma Goldman, *Living My Life* (Garden City, N.Y.: Garden City Publishing, 1934), 150; Carey, "*La Questione Sociale*."

4. George Carey, "The Vessel, the Deed, and the Idea: Anarchists in Paterson 1895–1908," *Antipode* 10, no. 11 (1979): 56.

5. Errico Malatesta, "Anarchismo e Sindacalismo," *LQS*, 18 January 1907, 1.

6. Vincent St. John, *The IWW: Its History, Structure, and Methods*, 3d ed. (Cleveland, Ohio: IWW Pub. Bureau, 1913), 17; "Are Our Tactics Revolutionary?" *Industrial Worker*, 16 May 1912. See also Salerno, *Red November, Black November*, 120–40.

7. In 1904, for example, Daniel DeLeon supported the revolutionary proletarian faction of the Italian syndicalist movement led by Antonio Labriola, who was lauded by socialist intellectuals as one of the two most important leaders of Italian syndicalism. DeLeon supported Labriola's early position in spite of his attack on parliamentary socialism as a "degeneration of the Socialist spirit." Later, however, DeLeon would emphasize the fact that Labriola combined syndicalism with party activity: "Labriola belongs with the 'syndicalist' wing . . . of the Socialist PARTY of Italy," he declared. "Labriola's position . . . is [as] exactly that of the SLP as two positions in two different countries can be." For a more detailed discussion of the complexities of the early revolutionary syndicalist movement, see Salerno, *Red November, Black November*. In addition, for examples of the kind of writing one might find on the subjects of philosophy, tactics, and methods of the Paterson group, see Maria Roda, "Alle operaie"; Titì, "Alle Mie Sorelle Proletarie," part 1, *LQS*, 9 June 1906; Titì, "Alle Mie Sorelle Proletarie," part 2, *LQ,S*, 16 June 1906; *LQS*, 15 September 1897; Duvico [Ludovico] Caminita, "Perchè siamo Socialisti-Anarchici," *LQS*, 29 December 1906, 1. *LQS* also made available an extensive literature on these subjects through its Libreria Sociologica, which included such pamphlets as [F. Niquet], *Gli anarchici, chi sono, cosa vogliamo* (Paterson: Libreria Sociologica, 1904); Nicolo Converti, *Che cos'è il Socialismo?* (Paterson: Libreria Sociologica, 1906); Fernand Pelloutier, *Sindacalismo e Rivoluzione Sociale* (Paterson: Libreria Sociologica, 1906); and Errico Malatesta, *La politica parlamentare nel movimento socialista* (Paterson: Libreria Sociologica, 1906).

8. *LQS*, 29 December 1906, 1.

9. Quintin Hoare, ed., *Antonio Gramsci, Selections from His Political Writings 1910–1920* (New York: International Publishers, 1977), 176.

10. Fred Thompson, "They Didn't Suppress the Wobblies," *Radical America* 1 (September–October 1967): 1–5.

11. Rudolph J. Vecoli, "The War and American Syndicalists" (unpublished essay, 1978); Bruno Ramirez, "Immigration, Ethnicity, and Political Militancy: Patterns of Radicalism in the Italian-American Left, 1880–1930," in *From "Melting Pot" to Multiculturalism: The Evolution of Ethnic Relations in the United States and Canada*, ed. Valeria Gennaro Lerda (Italy: Bulzoni Editore, 1990).

12. Carey, "Vessel, Deed, Idea"; Augusta Molinari, "L'attività degli anarchici italiani negli Stati Uniti nel primo ventennio del XX secolo" (Tesi di Laurea, University of Genoa, 1971–72); Edwin Fenton, "Immigrants and Unions, a Case Study: Italians and American Labor, 1870–1920" (Ph.D. diss., Harvard University, September, 1957); Rudolph J. Vecoli, "The Italian Immigrant Experience in the United States Labor Movement from 1880 to 1929," in *Gli italani fuori d'Italia: Gli emigrati nei movimenti operai dei paesi d'adozione 1880–1940*, ed. Bruno Bezza, (Milan: Franco Angeli Editore, 1983); Gianna S. Panofsky, "A View of Two Major Centers of Anarchism in the United States: Spring Valley and Chicago, Illinois," in *Italian Ethnics: Their Languages, Literature, and Life: Proceedings of the 20th Annual Conference of the American Italian Historical Association*, ed. Dominic Candeloro et al. (Staten Island, N.Y.: American Italian Historical Association, 1990), 271–96; Donna R. Gabaccia, *Militants and Migrants: Rural Sicilians Become*

American Workers (New Brunswick, N.J.: Rutgers University Press, 1988). For studies that provide a multigenerational perspective on Italian women immigrant and migrant radicalism, see Jennifer Guglielmo, "Donne Ribelli: Recovering the History of Italian Women's Radicalism in the United States" (chapter 4 of this book) and "Lavoratrici Coscienti: Italian Women Garment Workers and the Politics of Labor Organizing in New York City, 1880–1940," in *Women, Gender and Transnational Life: Italian Workers of the World*, ed. Donna R. Gabaccia and Franca Iacovetta (Toronto: University of Toronto Press, 2002).

13. Patrizia Sione, "Industrial Work, Militancy, and Migration of Northern Italian Workers in Europe and in Paterson, New Jersey, 1880–1913" (Ph.D. diss., State University of New York, Binghamton, 1992), 167–70. For more information about the *gruppi femminile*, see Guglielmo, "Donne Ribelli."

14. Carey, "Vessel, Deed, Idea," 248; Ettore Zoccoli, *I gruppi anarchici degli Stati Uniti e l'opera di Max Stirner* (Modena, Italy: Libreria Editrice G. T. Vincenzi e Nipoti, 1901), 21–28; Angelo Massari, *The Wonderful World of Angelo Massari*, trans. Arthur D. Massolo (New York: Exposition Press, 1965), 107. See also Mormino and Pozzetta, *Immigrant World of Ybor City*, 143–75.

15. Carey, "Vessel, Deed, Idea," 56.

16. This community probably also included Cuban, Puerto Rican, and other Latin American workers. Diego Abad de Santillán, *Ricardo Flores Magón, el Apostól de la Revolución Social Mexicana* (Mexico City: Grupo Cultural Ricardo Flores Magón, 1925); James D. Cockcroft, *Intellectual Precursors of the Mexican Revolution, 1900–1913* (Austin: University of Texas Press, 1968); Ellen Howell Myers, "The Mexican Liberal Party, 1903–1910" (Ph.D. diss., University of Virginia, 1970), 34–35; Florencio Barrera Fuentes, *Historia de la revolución Mexicana: La etapa precursora* (Mexico City: Biblioteca del Instituto de Estudios Historicos de la Revolución Mexicana, 1955); John M. Hart, *Anarchism and the Mexican Working Class 1860–1931* (Austin: University of Texas Press, 1978), 89–90.

17. Ludovico Caminita, an Italian printer and draftsman, converted from socialism to anarchism after a debate with Esteve. Caminita followed Esteve to Paterson and worked with him on *LQS*. Caminita became editor of *LQS* in November 1905; he was discharged from his responsibilities as editor by the Gruppo Diritto all'Esistenza in 1908 after writing a series of articles that resulted in the removal of the paper's postal privileges under obscenity statutes. *LQS* was succeeded in 1908 by *L'Era Nuova* until its suppression in 1917. It was edited by Frank Widmer and Caminita, who in 1919 briefly edited an illegal anarchist newspaper, *La Jacquerie*. In *Anarchist Voices* (p. 502), Avrich writes that when threatened with deportation, Caminita supplied information to J. Edgar Hoover about the 1919 bomb conspiracy. Other accounts in Avrich's oral histories contradict this conclusion; see *Anarchist Voices*, 159; Carey, "Vessel, Deed, Idea;" and *"La Questione Sociale."*

18. James A. Sandos, interview by author, 2 December 1997. See also *Regeneración*, 11 November 1911, 3, for an announcement of Caminita's tour. *Regeneración* contains examples of Caminita's graphics from the period 1912 to 1916. Sandos includes a poster designed by Caminita in his book, *Rebellion in the Borderlands: Anarchism and the Plan of San Diego, 1904–1923* (Norman: University of Oklahoma Press, 1992), 53.

19. Sandos, *Rebellion*, 3–62; Max Nettlau, *A Short History of Anarchism* (London: Freedom Press, 1996); David Poole, ed., *Land and Liberty: Anarchist Influences in the Mexican Revolution* (Over the Water, U.K.: Cienfuegos Press, 1977).

20. Piero Ferrua, interview by author, Portland, Oregon, 26 August 1984; Dirk W. Raat, *Revoltosos: Mexico's Rebels in the United States, 1903–1923* (College Station: Texas A&M University Press, 1981), 44–45.

21. James C. Scott, *Domination and the Arts of Resistance: Hidden Transcripts* (New Haven, Conn.: Yale University Press), 1990.

22. Paul Avrich, *Anarchist Portraits* (Princeton, N.J.: Princeton University Press, 1988), 171–72; Nunzio Pernicone, "Luigi Galleani and Italian Anarchist Terrorism in the United States," *Studi Emigrazione* 11 (1993): 478; Paul Buhle, "Anarchism and American Labor," *International Labor and Working Class History* 23 (spring 1983); and Buhle, "Italian American Radicals: Labor in Rhode Island, 1905–1930," *Radical History Review* 17 (spring 1978).

23. For the best discussions of the role of Italian immigrants in the IWW, see Bruno Cartosio, "Gli emigrati Italiani e L'Industrial Workers of the World," in Bezza, *Gli italiani*; Elisabetta Vezzosi, "La federazione socialista italiana del nord America, 1911–1921" (Tesi di Laurea, University of Florence, 1979–80); and Molinari, "L'attività degli anarchici." For an insightful analysis of politics around *Il Proletario* and the relationship of the ISF to the IWW, see Vezzosi, "Class, Ethnicity, and Acculturation in *Il Proletario*: The World War One Years," in *The Press of Labor Migrants in Europe and North America, 1880–1930*, ed. Christina Harzig and Dirk Hoerder (Bremen, Germany: Labor Newspaper Preservation Project, 1985). For an analysis of the ISF's form of syndicalism, see Michael Topp, "Immigrant Culture and the Politics of Identity: Italian-American Syndicalists in the U.S., 1911–1940" (Ph.D diss., Brown University, 1993) and "Transnationalism and Masculinity in the Italian American Syndicalist Movement: The World War I Interventionist Debate" (paper presented at conference "For Us There Are No Frontiers: Global Approaches to the Study of Italian Migration and the Making of Multi-Ethnic Societies, 1800 to the Present Conference," Tampa, Fla., 3–5 April 1996).

24. Cartosio, "Gli emigrati Italiani," 363–65. See also, Vezzosi, "Class, Ethnicity, and Acculturation" and Ramirez, "Immigration, Ethnicity."

25. Mario De Ciampis, "Lavoratori Industriali del Mondo: Storia del Movimento Socialista Rivoluzionario Italiano," *Parola del Papolo* 36 (1958): 136–63.

26. Carl Levy, "Italian Anarchism 1870–1926," in *For Anarchism: History, Theory, and Practice*, ed. David Goodway (New York: Routledge, 1989).

27. De Ciampis, "Lavoratori Industriali del Mondo."

28. Ramirez, "Immigration, Ethnicity," 129.

29. Vezzosi, "Class, Ethnicity, and Acculturation."

30. Ramirez, "Immigration, Ethnicity." For the history of the Italian Socialist Federation, see Elisabetta Vezzosi, *Il socialismo indifferente: Immigrati italiani e Socialist Party negli Stati Uniti del primo novecento* (Rome: Lavoro, 1991) and "La federazione socialista."

31. A. Andrà and Joe Corna, "A convenzione Finita," *LQS*, 15 July 1905, 1. See also, "Industrial Workers of the World," *LQS*, 9 September 1905, 2; "I. W. of the W. La convenzione di Chicago," *LQS*, 13 October 1905, 2; and "La Convenzione di Chicago dell'IWW: Nostri Comenti," *LQS*, 27 October 1905, 1.

32. Parliamentarian forms of socialism were based on the idea that radical social change could be accomplished through existing forms of government based on electoral politics. See Goldman, "The Situation in America," *Mother Earth* 2 (October 1907): 323–24; "Observations and Comments," *Mother Earth* 2 (October 1907): 2; Jean Spielman, "Are the IWW Still Revolutionary?" *Mother Earth* (December 1907): 457, 459–60.

33. Tatsuro Nomura, "Partisan Politics in and around the IWW: The Earliest Phase," *Journal of the Faculty of Foreign Studies* 10 (1977): 86–139; Salerno, *Red November, Black November*, 77–79, 84–86; and Salerno, ed., *Direct Action and Sabotage: Three Classic IWW Pamphlets of the 1910s* (Chicago: Charles H. Kerr Publishing, 1997). See also De Ciampis, "Lavoratori Industriali del Mondo"; Ira Kipnis, *The American Socialist Movement: 1897–1912* (New York: Columbia University Press, 1952); and Vezzosi, "La federazione socialista."

34. William E. Trautmann, *Industrial Unionism: New Method and New Forms* (Chicago: Charles H. Kerr, 1909), 24–25. The story has manifold origins, dating to about 1875, when the story was about Chinese workers on the Central Pacific Railroad. See Archie Green, "Short Shovels," in *Wobblies, Pile Buts, and Other Heroes: Laborlore Exploration* (Chicago: University of Illinois Press, 1993), 327–41. The story takes on a new beginning when Italian workers move beyond the dominant stereotypes and nativist hatred that had labeled them criminals and scabs unworthy of membership in American unions.

35. Salerno, *Direct Action and Sabotage*.

36. Green, *Wobblies*; Salerno, *Red November, Black November*, 119–41.

37. Grace Hutchins, *Labor and Silk* (New York: International Publishers, 1929), 135.

38. Franco Ramella, interview by author, Turin, Italy, 16 March 1999; Patrizia Sione, "Industrial Work, Militancy, and Migration, 1–2, 199–200; Goldman, *Living My Life*, 150; Richard D. Sonn, *Anarchism and Cultural Politics in Fin de Siècle France* (Lincoln: University of Nebraska Press, 1989). Candice Falk, correspondance, Emma Goldman Papers Project, Berkeley, California, April 1997. See also Jennifer Guglielmo, "Lavoratrici Coscienti: Italian Women Garment Workers and the Politics of Labor Organizing in New York City, 1890–1940," in Gabaccia and Iacovetta, *Fighting Back*, and Guglielmo, "Donne Ribelli."

39. Guglielmo, "Donne Ribelli."

40. Maria Barbieri, "Ribelliamoci!" *LQS*, 18 November 1905; Titì, "Alle Mie Sorelle Proletarie," pts. 1 and 2; "Alle Mie Sorelle Proletarie," pt. 3, *LQS*, 23 June 1906; Titì, "Alle Donne: Emancipiamoci!" *LQS*, 7 July 1906; Titì, "Alle Donne, La Proprietà Privata," *LQS*, 14 July 1906; Titì, "Alle Donne: Governo," *LQS*, 21 July 1906; Titì, "Alle Donne: Autorità," *LQS*, 18 August 1906; Titì, "Alle Donne: Il Matrimonio," *LQS*, 25 August 1906; Ida Merini Catastini, "La Donna nella Famiglia," *LQS*, 16 November 1907; Alba Genisio, "Alle Donne Proletarie," *LQS*, 7 March 1908; George Carey, "Vessel, Deed, Idea," 100. I would like to thank Jennifer Guglielmo for sharing her important work on Italian American radical women and for her help in exploring the writings and role of the Paterson feminists. Our work will ultimately form a book that will introduce both scholars and activists to the writings of the men and women of Il Gruppo Diritto all'Esistenza.

41. Il Congo, *LQS*, 26 January 1907; see also Salvatore Salerno, "I Delitti della Razza Bianca (Crimes of the White Race): Racial Discourse among Italian Anarchists 1895–1920," *Italian American Review*, forthcoming.

42. Carey, *The Vessel, the Deed, and the Idea: The Paterson Anarchists, 1895–1908*, n.d., unpublished manuscript, 269–86.

43. Steward Bird, Dan Georgakas, and Deborah Shaffer, *Solidarity Forever: An Oral History of the IWW* (Chicago: Lake View Press, 1985), 2.

44. Melvyn Dubofsky, "The Origins of Western Working-Class Radicalism, 1890–1905," *Labor History* 7 (1966): 153.

45. David Brundage, *The Making of Western Labor Radicalism: Denver's Organized Workers, 1878–1905* (Chicago: University of Illinois Press, 1994), 25–81.

46. Verity Burgmann, *The Industrial Workers of the World in Australia* (New York: Cambridge University Press, 1995), 43–44.

47. Salvatore Salerno, "The Impact of Haymarket on the Founding of the IWW: The Anarchism of Thomas J. Hagerty," *Haymarket Scrapebook*, ed. David Roediger and Franklyn Rosemont (Chicago: Charles H. Kerr Publishing, 1996), 189–91.

48. Gabaccia, *Militants and Migrants*, 122–48; Catherine Collomp and Marianne Debouzy, "European Migrants and the U.S. Labor Movement 1880–1920," in *Roots of the Transplanted*, ed. Dirk Hoerder et. al (New York: Columbia University Press, 1994), 2:361–65.

49. Nomura, "Partisan Politics;" Salerno, *Red November*, 69–90.

50. Paul E. Brissenden, *The IWW: A Study in American Syndicalism* (New York: Russell and Russell, 1919), 213–14; Carey, *The Vessel, the Deed, and the Idea*, 287–318; Melvyn Dubofsky, *We Shall Be All: A History of the IWW* (Chicago: Quadrangle Books, 1969), 141.

51. Salerno, "I Delitti della Razza Bianca."

52. See for example, Barbieri, "Ribelliamoci!"; Titì, "Alle Mie Sorelle Proletarie," pts. 1, 2, and 3; Titì, "Alle Donne: Emancipiamoci!"; Titì, "Alle Donne, La Proprietà Privata"; Titì, "Alle Donne: Governo"; Titì, "Alle Donne Autorità"; Titì, "Alle Donne: Il Matrimonio"; Ida Merini Catastini, "La Donna nella Famiglia"; and Alba Genisio, "Alle Donne Proletarie."

Chapter 8

Italian Radicals and Union Activists in San Francisco, 1900–1920

Paola A. Sensi-Isolani

"San Francisco may be regarded with pride and hopefulness by every trade-unionist and lover of progress in the country. A year ago the trade unions existed, if not exactly upon sufferance, at least with very little substantial recognition from the government or the public.... Today the city is...a union town."[1] This pride and hopefulness in the union movement that was reported in 1902 in the *Coast Seaman's Journal* did not, however, extend to San Francisco's Italian immigrant workers. Upon first arriving in the city, Italian immigrants got caught between the competing interests of labor unions, tightly controlled by Americans of northern European descent, American businessmen, and Italian immigrant entrepreneurs, or *prominenti*. It was in this environment that between 1900 and 1920 a group of San Francisco's Italian radicals, anarchists, and union activists formed the Latin branch of the International Workers of the World (IWW). In so doing, they forged alliances with other Latin groups—primarily Hispanic and French—and managed to momentarily unite such disparate elements of the Italian community as the conservative immigrant press, anarchists, and syndicalists, in a fight to organize San Francisco's Italian immigrant laborers. Ultimately, the United States' entry into the war in 1917, which ushered in "a period of repression of civil liberties unprecedented in the nation's history,"[2] led to an increasingly hostile political climate that identified socialists, anarchists, and members of the IWW, especially the "foreign element"—and among them the Italians in particular[3]—as seditious enemies of the state. Imprisonments, deportations, and the final raiding and closing of the North Beach office of the Latin branch of the IWW in 1919, ensured an end to organized activity by San Francisco's Italian radicals.

Of the four major immigrant groups in San Francisco (Italian, German, Irish, and Chinese), the Italians were the last to arrive. In 1870 there were 1,600 Italians in San Francisco; by 1890 there were 5,200, and in 1900, 8,000. Then between 1900 and 1924, over 20,000 Italians came to the city; by 1920 they were the largest group among the foreign born.[4] Because of their late arrival, Italian immigrants were disadvantaged in the competition for jobs. Dino Cinel estimates that between 1895 and 1920, more than 40 percent of San Francisco Italians worked in the domestic and personal services sector of the economy. They worked as unskilled workers, including janitors, laborers, servants, bootblacks, bartenders, waiters, and street workers. Most of the rest worked in trade and manufacturing, as bakers, masons, shoemakers, seamstresses, tailors, retailing merchants, peddlers, and packers.[5]

There were three major groups of Italians in San Francisco before the First World War. One was the long-established *prominenti*, who employed a large number of Italians in manufacturing firms. Another group was Italian immigrants and their children, who could speak at least some English and either had marketable skills or owned their own small businesses. San Francisco's Italian community also had a large number of transient Italians. These men, who worked in the agricultural camps for part of the year, "became idle for months, going into debt, moving in and out of the city in search of work, fighting local unions, and causing concern among local officials."[6]

The Employers' Association's use of Italians to break strikes and depress wages threatened San Francisco's unions. Using the language barrier and their belief that unions were intended for skilled craftsmen—not for unskilled immigrant workers—most unions were openly hostile to Italians and did little to recruit them. The Italian-language newspapers *L'Italia, La Voce del Popolo*, and *La Protesta Umana* advised the immigrants to "cercare di entrare nelle unioni del rispettivo mestiere" [try to join the union of your respective craft wherever possible].[7] However, although advocating the benefits of unions, *L'Italia*, San Francisco's Italian-language paper with the largest distribution, was closely tied to the interests of the colony's *prominenti*. Although encouraging Italian immigrants to join unions and exposing the reluctance of unions in the city to admit them, *L'Italia*'s owners did not hire unionized workers. Moreover, it spoke against unions: "Assai spesso esorbitano nelle loro pretese, specialmente quella di voler limitare la libertà dei padroni nel diritto d'impiegare la gente che a loro fa più comodo, come esorbitano nelle pretese dei salari." [They often have extreme demands, especially that of wanting to limit the freedom of the owners in their right to hire those who are most convenient for them, they also are excessive in their demand for wages.][8]

The San Francisco Italian press made constant reference to problems immigrants were having with unions. Immigrants wrote complaining that they were denied jobs in the city because they did not belong to unions. Warnings were issued about abuses, especially concerning city jobs for which native-born men had priority, and which were often denied to Italians born in the United States, in favor of Irish citizens. Antiunion forces in the Italian immigrant community publicized these barriers in order to convince immigrants that they owed nothing to organized labor and were perfectly justified in scabbing against striking union workers. This in turn increased resentment against Italian immigrants. During the summer of 1911, in the Contra Costa County city of Crockett, across the bay from San Francisco, a strike at the C & H Sugar Refinery's warehouse caused work to stop at the refinery itself. Consequently, the company recruited Italian strikebreakers from the East Coast, who were brought in by train and housed— virtually imprisoned—in the town's company hotel. Resentment against them was so strong that mass demonstrations were organized, and two strikebreakers were murdered.[9]

These two factors—the importation of Italians to break strikes and the refusal of the unions to organize Italian workers—served to perpetuate what was often described in the local press as "the Italian problem," that is, the perception of Italians in San Francisco as unskilled workers and union busters. Their limited work choices, coupled with the hostility and discrimination (which in 1909 some likened to the persecution of the Chinese by the Workingmen's Party in the 1870s),[10] meant that by 1910, many Italians who worked in the city did so for other Italians. Some worked in small enterprises in the service sector—especially, in bakeries and groceries—others worked in larger semi-industrialized factories owned by Italian entrepreneurs, such as Marco Fontana, whose North Beach cannery in 1910 hired more than one thousand Italians. These Italian entrepreneurs were the greatest exploiters of workers; for example, the women in the Fontana canneries in 1910 earned 60–70 cents for a 13-hour day, compared with the $1.75 for a 9-hour day earned by Italian women working in industrialized bakeries owned by Americans.[11]

Within this context of discrimination and of control of the job market by the Italian colony's *prominenti,* radical labor activity and organization appear to have been difficult for San Francisco's Italians. Unlike the mines and the lumber and agricultural camps, conservative unions were already in place when Italian immigrants arrived. Moreover, the Italian community itself discouraged any type of radical labor activity. Afraid of replicating the urban ghettos of the East Coast, state authorities and Italian *prominenti* shunted Italian workers outside the community.[12] They did this by encouraging labor contractors to place newly arrived Italians outside the city and by advertising the opportunities afforded outside of San Francisco.[13] What is more important, they blacklisted those Italians who were perceived as radicals or labor organizers. This was evident, for example, in the case of a young Italian anarchist who declared that he had been denied work by "the sigarai di San Francisco perchè posto all'indice dai padroni e costretto a cercare pane altrove . . . boicottato dai padroni per le mie idee sovversive" [the cigar makers of San Francisco because placed on the index by the owners and forced to find work elsewhere . . . boycotted by the owners because of my subversive ideas].[14]

Although the radicalism and labor activism of San Francisco's Italian immigrants was more muted than in the West's logging, mining, and agricultural labor camps, from the earliest times Italian immigrants were advocates of the local labor movement "organizing a series of quasi-labor and benevolent societies."[15] In 1864, when the board of supervisors imposed a license fee on Chinese fishermen and peddlers, this in turn affected Italian fishermen, from whom the Chinese purchased the bulk of their catch. This led to a strike by 305 Italian fishermen, who formed their own union, the Fishermen's Association. By the spring of 1883, through the growing power of the San Francisco Trades Assembly, the first official Italian Fishermen's Union was renting a wharf from the state as their headquarters and marketplace.[16] In 1874, Italian immigrants formed the San Francisco and San Mateo Gardeners' and Ranchers' Association, and in 1879 they formed the Scavengers' Protective Union, protective associations whose membership was passed on to others in the same family, town, or region.

Following in the wake of the movement for Italy's unification, in the late 1800s and early 1900s, political radicalism in San Francisco took the forms of anticlericalism and anarchism. When the Salesian fathers arrived to serve the Italian community in 1897, they were harassed. Copies of *L'Asino (The Donkey)*, an anticlerical sheet, were posted on the church doors, and liberal and radical intellectuals spoke against the priests.[17] The anarchist movement in San Francisco was dominated by Italians at this time, who provided not only the majority of the rank and file but such leaders as Giuseppe Ciancabilla and Eugene Travaglio, who served as editors of *La Protesta Umana* in the city in 1903 and 1904.[18] The Italian anarchists did not work in isolation. Italian and Spanish anarchists worked together to educate workers, organizing plays and *feste liberatarie* (anarchist festivals), about which the paper declared, "È ormai opinione generalmente accettata fra gl'italiani di San Francisco che le sole feste ove ci si possa divertire famigliarmente e ritrarne insieme un insegnamento educativo e di propaganda, sono le feste anarchiche." [It is now common opinion accepted among the Italians of San Francisco that the only feste where one can have a good time with the family and also receive teaching as well as political education, are the anarchist parties].[19] Besides anarchists, there was also a strong Italian socialist presence in the city, which held regular weekly outdoor meetings in North Beach.

These anticlericals, anarchists, and socialists were components of a divided San Francisco Italian immigrant community. Ciancabilla's *Protesta Umana* criticized both the *Voce del Popolo* and *L'Italia*, but especially the latter, accusing it of being more concerned with money than with ideals: "Il suo pattriottismo è il business. La sua patria la pagnotta" [Its patriotism is business, its homeland the loaf of bread].[20] Its plays and *feste* often drew hundreds of spectators, yet the *Protesta Umana* could barely survive financially, wavering between trying to make the monthly paper a weekly one, and continuously issuing pleas for the renewal of subscriptions. Meanwhile, *L'Italia*, largely expressing the political ideals of the *prominenti* and wanting to maintain the image of San Francisco as the model Italian colony, denounced the anarchist paper to American authorities for infractions of the federal postal code[21] and tried to sway its readership away from anarchist and radical sympathies.[22]

A letter from a San Francisco anarchist reader, published in *La Questione Sociale* in 1906, provides a good description of the state of affairs among many Italian immigrants in the city:

In questo paese pazzia religiosa è al suo apice. L'elemento italiano—senza distinzione di meridionali o settentrionali—ci da uno spettacolo sconfortante di servilismo e idiotismo. Quelli del settentrione si atteggiano a socialisti e anarchici, ma quando hanno qualche bambino che viene ad accrescere la famiglia proletaria, tutti questi sovversivi mangiapreti, si affrettano a chiamare il chiercuto nemico per farlo battezzare. I meridionali poi fanno disperare. Il propagandista più forte rinunzierebbe ad ogni proposito fra questa gente. È inutile perciò parlare della schiavitù e miseria in cui si vive. Ognuno accetta rassegnato la sorte che dio ha decretato. Se ai loro lagni mostro le cause della miseria, mi piantano in asso e fuggono. Non posso che augurarmi un risveglio di queste masse.

[In this country religious fervor is at its apex. The Italian element—without distinction between southern and northern—gives us an unsettling spectacle, which is both servile and idiotic. The northerners pretend to be socialists and anarchists, but the moment they have a baby, which comes to increase the proletarian family, all these subversive devourers of priests hurry to call the priestly enemy to have the child baptized. The southerners only make us despair. The strongest propagandist would give everything up when faced with these people. It is therefore useless to speak to them about the slavery and misery in which one lives. Each one accepts resigned the fate that god has decreed. If I confront them with the causes of their misery when they complain, they just abandon me and flee. I can only hope for an awakening of these masses.][23]

In early 1910, a group of Italian socialists who had split from the Socialist Party formed the Latin branch of the IWW. They had allied themselves with the anarchists of San Francisco and with members of the IWW's antipolitical wing to form the branch, whose object it was to spread the anarcho-syndicalist message among the city's Latin workers, which included Spanish, a small number of French, and a much larger number of Italians. The branch distributed two newspapers, *Il Proletario* and *Il Lavoratore Industriale*; it also carried out a tremendous amount of propaganda and propelled a series of labor agitations in the city. As it tried to recruit new members, often from the unions themselves, clashes—either overt or covert—occurred between the Latin branch and a wide array of forces, including the American Federation of Labor (AFL), law enforcement agencies, the Salesian fathers of San Francisco's Saints Peter and Paul Italian Church, and the *prominenti*. These clashes continued until 1919, when the Palmer raids closed down the Latin branch's North Beach office.

The Latin branch's activities among Italian workers in San Francisco took place in a climate that reflected an increasing conflict between the conservative craft union emphasis of the AFL and the industrial union movement advocated by the IWW. Its activities brought to the surface the frustration many Italians felt toward the AFL, as well as the increasingly syndicalist sympathies of many of San Francisco's poorest Italian immigrants. The work of the Latin branch among San Francisco's Italian immigrants combined political education with radical labor activism. Its propaganda threatened established unions and was sharply critical of the rich Italian businessmen within the community.

Unlike San Francisco's AFL, the IWW welcomed all, regardless of their country of origin. It provided for leadership positions within the labor movement to Italian immigrants who, unlike their AFL counterparts, also spoke Italian. In San Francisco, as well as in other parts of the United States, the IWW managed to unite Italian immigrants who had anticlerical, anarchist, and syndicalist sympathies.[24]

Beginning in 1907, when the Unione dei Panettieri (Baker's Union) was granted a charter, the IWW focused its recruitment efforts on the many Latin bakeries, which since 1900 the AFL had unsuccessfully tried to organize. Most workers in the Latin bakeries, whether drivers or bakers, worked in small enterprises owned by fellow Italians, under a quasi-feudal arrangement in which food and a bed were exchanged for low wages and a seven-day work week. Working conditions for these bakers, helpers, and deliverymen, were described as the worst possible: hygiene was nonexistent, and workers slept in lofts that one investigator described as filthy and revolting. [25]

By 1910, roughly 40 percent of San Francisco's Italian men and women worked in the manufacturing sector, most of which—unlike the East Coast's major manufacturing interests—consisted of small enterprises that processed and exported the products of its rich agricultural hinterland for export or produced goods for local and regional consumption.[26] The baking industry reflected the two levels of economic organization that by 1910 had developed within the city's manufacturing sector.[27] At one level, San Francisco had a few industrialized factories that mass-produced baked goods; at the other, there existed a multitude of ethnic enterprises, each of which hired a few bakers and workers. Three industrialized factories in the city produced crackers, cakes, pies, and bread. Then there were innumerable smaller nonindustrialized, quasi-family-run bakeries that hired a few bakers, helpers, and deliverymen.[28]

Although the AFL systematically erected barriers to the entrance of immigrant workers into the labor movement, the Baker's Union appears to have been an exception. By 1900, the AFL's Bakers Union had managed to unionize the predominantly American male workers in San Francisco's three industrialized bakeries. The union began to organize the smaller ethnic bakeries in order to extend the six-day week throughout the industry and equalize competitive conditions for the employers. It was partially successful in 1900, when the German and American bakers merged into a union, thus giving one local of the national union jurisdiction over most bakery and confectionery workers in the city. Then in 1901, the union tried to set up a separate local with jurisdiction over workers at French and Italian bakeries. However, the campaign to organize Latin bakeries—the first of several such efforts to be launched by the union during a dozen years—made little headway. Latin bakeries would continue for years to work exceptionally long hours, thus maintaining a competitive threat disturbing both the Bakers' Union and unionized firms.[29]

The recruitment effort was driven largely by Fred Rovaldi, a member of the Latin Chapter of the IWW and secretary of the Union of Latin Bakers. Appeals were made through pamphlets, the IWW Italian-language paper, and even the conservative *L'Italia* to "tutti quei panettieri che sono consci della loro condizione e che devono sentire il bisogno di unirsi per migliorare le condizioni ed elevarsi moralmente da questo abbietto sfruttamento padronale, e così uniti potremo marciare verso la nostra completa emancipazione" [all those bakers who are conscious of their condition and who feel the need to unite to improve their condition and to elevate themselves from that exploitation of the owners, and thus united we will be able to march toward our complete emancipation].[30]

The effort to recruit Italian bakers, which pitted the AFL against the Industrial Workers of the World, united the conservative *L'Italia,* Italian socialists, and anarchists, with the IWW's Latin branch. This disparate group's battle for free speech and the right to organize aroused opposition from the city's political and police establishment, the AFL, the community's *prominenti,* and the Italian and Irish Catholic priests of North Beach.

It was not until the so-called San Francisco Free Speech Fight—in which anarchists, socialists, and IWW members confronted the San Francisco police, the Italian community priests, and members of the AFL—that Italian bakery workers were recruited to the syndicalist cause in large numbers. The fight took place in mid-August of 1911, between the outbreak of the Fresno Free Speech Fight (in which many of the Italian men arrested in San Francisco had also participated) and the San Diego Free Speech Fight. Although it did not have the level of violence of the other two struggles, the San Francisco Free Speech Fight received vast coverage in the local American and Italian press and proved to be a watershed for Italian radical activity and labor organization in the Bay Area.

Members of the IWW's Latin branch followed the custom of other Italian radicals in the Bay Area, meeting and speaking in public every Sunday.[31] At these meetings, they spoke against the Church, urged workers to organize under the IWW, and expounded on anarchist and syndicalist ideals. It is not a coincidence that the San Francisco meetings were held near Saints Peter and Paul Italian Catholic Church, "quel sacro pastribolo delle coscienze dal quale covo infame l'uomo nero, la bestia malefica, il prete, ordì una fosca congiura" [That sacred gallows of the conscience, from which lair the infamous black man—the evil beast—the priest, plotted a shady conspiracy].[32] This *fosca congiura* (shady conspiracy) began on August 6 (the Sunday before the Free Speech Fight), when one of the priests of the *sacro pastribolo* (sacred gallows) denounced the agitators to the police, calling them anarchists and heretics. This was followed by the arrest of two of the anarchist speakers for disturbing the peace.

The next Sunday, the men returned to their soapboxes, and what ensued became known in the local press as the San Francisco Free Speech Fight. Coverage in the local press presented all the stereotypes of Italians. They were depicted as radicals. One headline read "Police in Street Battle with I.W.W., "Police Guns Quell Riot of Reds." They were described in terms that made them seem out of control and animal-like. A headline in the *San Francisco News Call* announced: "Wild Agitator Hurls Stiletto at Police."[33] Another article, published the same day in the *Daily News*, called the Italians "a hooting howling mob" and claimed, "Italian bites detective's thumb until blood flows." The *News Call's* article ridiculed the Italian demonstrators' behavior. This headline was accompanied by a pencil drawing of the described action: "Angry demonstrator before hurling his stiletto jumps upon his hat as it lies on the ground, and tears his hair in a maddened frenzy."[34] The city's established Italian immigrant press presented a more objective picture. *L'Italia* reported on "Un Vergognoso Sopruso dei Polizziotti di San Francisco" [A shameful abuse by San Francisco's Police].[35] The anarchist paper *Cronaca Sovversiva* expressed shock at the events: "Un fatto mostruoso, inconcepibile, è avvenuto domenica scorsa in questa bigotta città . . . un vergognoso sopruso dei polizziotti di San Francisco: Un gruppo di giovani propagandisti italiani arrestati illegalment e brutalmente malmenati dai cosidetti tutori dell'ordine. Siamo in Russia o in America?" [A monstrous, inconceivable event took place last Sunday in this bigoted city . . . a shameful abuse by San Francisco police: a group of young Italian propagandists illegally arrested and brutally beaten by the so-called guardians of law and order. Are we in America or in Russia?][36] One can arrive at some conclusions despite the differences in the accounts of what actually happened, depending on whether they appeared in articles and letters in the anarchist press or the local Italian- and English-language commercial press.

At the usual Sunday open-air meetings held by Italian socialists and radicals, speakers denounced the Catholic clergy and tried to recruit members for the Union of Latin Bakers and the Latin branch of the IWW. While the anarchist Filippo Perrone[37] was standing on his soapbox, speaking (as one San Francisco paper reported) "disparagingly about the American flag, condemning law and order, and denouncing all form of government, and ending with a tirade against the Pope,"[38] three detectives arrived and placed him under arrest. In the pattern followed by other free speech fights, Perrone was immediately replaced by the syndicalist Fred Rovaldi—the organizer of the Latin bakers—who was in turn arrested, to be replaced by the socialist Centrone, who was in turn arrested. In all, nine men took their turn on the soap box after Perrone, and all were arrested by the San Francisco police who at this point, fearing a riot because more than one thousand sympathizers were gathered around the arrested men, had called in for help from reserves. Fighting broke out during the arrests. The police beat several speakers and charged the bystanders with clubs. Finally, after drawing their pistols, the police retreated with the arrested men into a nearby firehouse, waiting for reinforcements to arrive. By this time, Broadway, for a distance of two blocks, was said to have been filled with a mass of humanity. The police were jeered, and threats such as "Lynch the police!" were howled against the officers. The police stated that they intended to make a report to the proper Federal officials and that since the arrested men were foreigners, if convicted for inciting a riot, they would be deported.

One of the arrested men, Nazareno Parella, who was interviewed by the *San Francisco Call*, admitted, "I belong to the Industrial Workers of the World, and so does Perrone. The others do also, I have been a member of that organization, but have not taken part in many of its affairs. Some of the men arrested were in the campaign for free speech in Fresno, but not all of them. We have our political opinions, and think we have a right to express them."[39] With the exception of the socialist paper, the English-language press emphasized the violence of the rioters, one paper noting, "The lack of firearms among the anarchists is believed to have been the only reason that they were not used yesterday, and scenes repeated following the Haymarket riot in Chicago in 1886, when a number of patrolmen were killed and several injured."[40]

This incident triggered a series of remarkable events. It placed the largest-circulation Italian-language paper, the conservative *L'Italia*, in the unprecedented position of siding with the radicals against Father Piperni, the Salesian pastor of Saints Peter and Paul Church, who in an impassioned letter to the paper accused it of radical sympathies. Anarchist, socialist, and syndicalist speakers addressed meetings, held in the packed Washington Theater. Letters in the Italian-language papers voiced discontent with the role of the Church in this matter. Pressure was brought to bear in order to release the arrested men, and a commitment was made to continue the Sunday meetings. While the AFL's Baker's Union had been trying to organize the French and Italian bakers since 1900, as a result of the San Francisco Free Speech Fight it was the IWW's Latin branch that succeeded in enrolling close to two hundred bakers.

One must situate this particular struggle within the context of the wider labor struggle in San Francisco and the Bay Area, because although it was a fight about free speech it was also a fight about unions. The *International Socialist Review*, in an analysis by Austin Lewis, titled "The Drift in California," pointed out that the labor movement in San Francisco by 1911 could be described as " rich conservative unionism; militaristic in the sense of being organized from above."[41] Italian workers in the city were frustrated by a labor movement which by and large excluded them and which they viewed as discriminatory and corrupt.

The San Francisco Free Speech Fight, coupled with the frustration many Italians felt toward the AFL, with the exception of the Salesian fathers, momentarily united the entire Italian community. The Italian press—from Left to Right—focused on the free speech and union issues of the fight. *L'Italia* actually advocated that Italians join the Industrial Workers of the World. Under its banner headline, "Unionismo, Socialismo, Fratellanza," its editorial was quick to point out that the Free Speech Fight showed that Italian workers should not put their hopes in the AFL: "Se volete divenire forti e riuscire a farvi valere, una sola e l'associazione alla quale dovete iscriveri, quella degli Industrial Workers of the World, che senza far distinzione di razza e di nazionalità apre il suo seno a tutti i lavoratori del mondo, rappresenta la sola e vera alleanza internazionale del proletariato." [If you want to become strong and to make yourselves heard, there is only one association that you should join, that of the Industrial Workers of the

World, which without distinction of race or nationality opens its breast to all the workers of the world and represents the only true alliance of the proletariat.][42] *L'Italia* noted that the unions did nothing to help the Italians who were arrested and brutally beaten by the police while expressing their political views and trying to organize workers: "Chi fra gli unionisti di San Francisco si mosse per dar loro aiuto e conforto? Le unioni assistettero allo svolgersi dei noti episodi colla più olimpica indifferenza, chiuse nei ristretti confini di interessi egoistici che ne fanno altrettante chiesuole, sdegnose di stender la mano ai lavoratori nelle cui vene non scorre sangue anglo-sassone [*sic*]." [Who, among the unionists of San Francisco lifted a finger to help and comfort them? The unions watched these events take place with the greatest of Olympian indifference, closed in their narrow self-interest, and disdaining to give a hand to workers in whose veins Anglo-Saxon blood does not run.][43]

Many saw the noninvolvement of the San Francisco unions in this conflict as a clear sign that the AFL was behind much of the violence. One paper reported: "Those interested in the affair say that the meeting at which the riot took place was called to make conversions among the Italian and French bakers and others to the cause of the IWW. It was charged yesterday that the trouble had been caused by other labor leaders who were anxious to prevent the Industrial Workers from obtaining the membership of the men."[44] The socialist Austin Lewis also believed that the activities promoting industrial organization provoked the San Francisco Free Speech Fight: "Recently Italians who were employed in propagating IWW views in San Francisco and in organizing the French and Italian bakers as industrialists were beaten by the police. Some reason must have existed for an act so unusual in San Francisco. . . . Industrial organization was probably the source of the trouble and with the advance of this form of organization among the Latin peoples there will probably arise a series of clashes between the two forms of organization . . . as far as this state is concerned this event indicates that the AFL will not welcome any other organization and a sulky acquiescence of its existence is the best that can be expected."[45]

The IWW continued its work among the Latin bakers, a few months later helping to organize a strike of drivers and bakers across the bay in Oakland, which tied up 15 Latin bakeries in three transbay cities.[46] However, in subsequent years, it found it difficult to maintain its original membership of close to two hundred. In 1916, working conditions among Italian bakery workers in North Beach were still reported to be bad, and with help from the Latin branch, they threatened to strike for better conditions and one day of rest per week.[47] The owners of five North Beach bakeries, however, retaliated by organizing the Italian-French Baking Company, in order, they claimed, to keep the price of bread down.[48]

The conflict between the AFL and the IWW again erupted when the Latin branch recruited members of the Alaska Fishermen's Union. In 1917, an informant for the State Commission for Immigration and Housing reported that: "There is a Latin branch of the IWW at 403 Broadway, conducted by Secretary

Gioffa. The propaganda and literature are the same as in other branches, only with the language of printed matter translated. Your investigator mixed with several of the men, some of whom are also Alaska Fishermen."[49] The Alaska Fisherman's Union—affiliated with the AFL—numbered 3,100 fishermen, most of them of Sicilian descent. The IWW was successful enough among these San Francisco fishermen that in 1917, without the sanction of the Fishermen's Union, they voted to repudiate their contracts with the Alaska Packers' Association. They adopted resolutions demanding increased wages and regulating the conditions (including their right to take at least five gallons of whisky per man) under which they would agree to work. Their declaration concluded with the statement "If every one and all of the above requests are not granted, the Italian fishermen will refuse to go to Alaska and will declare a strike."[50] After negotiations, a strike was averted and the fishermen ultimately decided to fulfill their agreement, which expired that year.

Conflict with the AFL was also evident when the Latin branch recruited members among the Italian cannery workers in the city and the surrounding area, most of whom worked for Del Monte Corporation, owned by the Italian immigrant Marco Fontana. Whether they worked in agriculture or manufacturing, Italians who worked for other Italians earned the lowest wages of all.[51] In the Bay Area Cannery Workers' Strike of 1917, Italian members of the IWW were said to have pushed the Federal Labor Union—affiliated with the AFL—to organize a more widespread strike. According to the statements of an observer, "it was the intention of the leaders of the Federal Labor Union to call out two canneries only, and if successful to follow up with more. Agitation amongst the Italians however, got them into a frame of mind where they demanded action and as soon as one cannery was pulled they went to another and the strike situation got away from them. . . . They had made the situation impossible of being handled successfully by any AFL official. As previously reported, agitation has been carried on amongst the Italians and Spanish by syndicalists and the IWW for months."[52]

The Latin branch was behind continued conflict between Italian workers and their more powerful employers who often organized themselves into associations to present a united front against their demands. This also had happened in 1916, when the owners of five North Beach bakeries formed an association in order to fight demands from their workers who had threatened a strike. In order to fight the stranglehold of these employers' associations, the Latin branch encouraged Italian workers to adopt new tactics sometimes inspired by those used by their employers. Thus in April 1919, Italian *salumieri,* or sausage makers, formed their own association and threatened the Italian Sausage Manufacturing Association with a strike unless their demands for better working conditions and hours were satisfied.[53]

In spite of these actions, by and large, the presence of a strong AFL in San Francisco severely hindered the Latin branch's activity. Thompson, an informant for the state's Immigration and Housing Commission, declared: "The IWW complain bitterly against the friction between themselves and the AFL unionists, admitting that the strength of the latter around San Francisco hampers the activities of the Wobblies, they being kept too busy fighting the AFL."[54]

The radical Left, including the IWW, opposed U.S. preparation to enter the First World War. This caused the membership of the IWW to become increasingly suspect by the government and subject to hostility within the general society. San Francisco District Attorney Charles M. Flickert campaigned for the Republican nomination for governor of California on a platform that promised to "root out the anarchists and the IWW." In April 1919, California's governor signed the Criminal Syndicalist Law, which criminalized any doctrine advocating changes in the industrial or political system. Under the drastic and sweeping provisions of this new act, persecution of individual members of the IWW greatly increased, and the office of the Latin branch was raided and closed.[55] Coupled with this political repression, radicalism was discouraged by an improved postwar economic climate in the city, as opportunities for work multiplied. An Italian immigrant, Salvatore Reina, described San Francisco in the 1920s as being very different from the San Francisco of the pre–WWI period for Italian immigrants: "There was work for everybody. Newcomers were offered jobs on arrival that immigrants in previous decades had had to wait months and years for, if they were able to get them at all."[56]

Upon arrival in San Francisco after 1900, Italian immigrants found an established and powerful Italian community, as well as strong and entrenched labor unions. While the city's *prominenti* used these new arrivals as a source of cheap labor, the AFL closed its doors to them, thus depriving them of good jobs. Within San Francisco's Italian immigrant community between 1900 and 1920, socialists, radicals, syndicalists, and anticlericals forged an alliance against organized religion, Italian employers and the established labor union movement. Working with other Latin groups, they formed the Latin branch of the IWW, of which they provided the leadership and most of the membership. As can be seen in the organization and threatened strike of the Latin bakers, in the cannery workers' strike and the sausage makers' strike, the Latin branch of the IWW—in its 10 years of existence—gave San Francisco's most exploited Italian immigrants an avenue in which to organize to demand better working conditions. It was the Latin branch of the IWW, with its Italian immigrant leaders, that challenged, among others, the rich Italian businessmen within the community who took advantage of their compatriots by providing worse working conditions and paying even lower wages than American employers.

By 1900, the San Francisco Italian colony had developed to such an extent that it contained competing class and ideological interests. At times, when the entire community was seen as threatened, as during the San Francisco Free Speech Fight, even *L'Italia* rallied behind the IWW and the radicals' cause. Through the IWW, and especially its Latin branch, San Francisco's Italian radicals could direct the battle for recognition of immigrant workers' rights to the larger American society as well as within the Italian community itself. If, as Paul

Avrich claims, Italian immigrants did not "play a notable part in the organized labor movement," in San Francisco, this was due to their exclusion from it rather than from "their suspicion of formal organizations." (This exclusion changed in the post–World War I period when Italian immigrants began to be accepted as union members in the city and to assume leadership roles.) After all, San Francisco's Italian immigrants had organized themselves into trade associations as early as 1864.[57]

In 1919, political repression led to the persecution of individual members and to the forcible closing of San Francisco's IWW office and its Latin branch. This spelled doom for organized Italian radical activity in San Francisco. However, other changes in the Italian immigrant community after World War I also brought about decreased interest in radicalism. Greater economic opportunities opened labor union membership to Italians, and the Catholic Church—which by and large managed to make good (nonradical) American Catholics out of Italian immigrants and their children—also contributed to decreased interest in radicalism, anarchism, and anticlericalism among San Francisco's Italian immigrants.

NOTES

1. "Association and Union," *Coast Seamen's Journal*, 1 April 1902, 1.

2. Paul Avrich, *Sacco and Vanzetti: The Anarchist Background* (Princeton, N.J.: Princeton University Press, 1991), 93.

3. Ibid., 97.

4. Dino Cinel, *From Italy to San Francisco: The Immigrant Experience* (Stanford, Calif.: Stanford University Press, 1982), 18.

5. Ibid., 139–41.

6. Ibid., 243.

7. "Consigli ai Lavoratori Italiani di San Francisco," *L'Italia*, 8 August 1910, 1.

8. "È Commovente," *La Protesta Umana*, 23 April 1903, 1.

9. "The First Violence: Italian Was Attacked," *Contra Costa Gazette*, 17 June 1911, 1.

10. Eugenio Bonardelli, "L'Emigrazione Italiana in California," *Italica Gens*, 2 November 1911.

11. Amy Bernardy, "Sulle Condizioni delle Donne e dei Fanciulli Italiani negli Stati del Centro e dell'Ovest della Confederazione del Nord degli Stati Uniti," *Bollettino dell'Emigrazione* 10, no. 1 (1911): 140–44; Lillian R. Matthews, *Women in Trade Unions in San Francisco*, University of California Publications in Economics, vol. 3, no. 1 (Berkeley: University of California Press, 1911), 66–94.

12. Paola A. Sensi-Isolani and Phylis C. Martinelli, *Struggle and Success: An Anthology of the Italian Immigrant Experience* (New York: Center for Migration Studies, 1993), 13.

13. See, for example, Andrea Sbarboro, "California, La Vera Italia D'America," in *Il Monitore Californiano* 11–12 (1914): 5–10.

14. Francesco Perrone, "Corrispondenza," *Cronaca Sovversiva*, 4 November 1911, 4.

15. "The Fishermen of the Bay of San Francisco Papers," Proceedings of the National Conference of Charities and Corrections, San Francisco, 1906. Bancroft Library, University of California, Berkeley.

16. Ira B. Cross, *A History of the Labor Movement in California* (Berkeley: University of California Press, 1935), 325.

17. Deanna Paoli Gumina, *The Italians of San Francisco* (New York: Center for Migration Studies, 1978), 175.

18. Ralph E. Shaffer, "Radicalism in California, 1869–1929" (Ph.D. diss., University of California, Berkeley, 1962), 247.

19. "La Festa Libertaria," *La Protesta Umana*, 25 June 1903, 1.

20. "Copie di Saggio," *La Protesta Umana*, 2 April 1903, 1.

21. Ibid.

22. "La Forca," *La Protesta Umana*, 4 June 1903, 1.

23. Luigi Rovaldi, "Nostre Corrispondenze," *La Questione Sociale*, 3 November 1906, 3.

24. Besides Rovaldi, who was secretary of the IWW's Union of Latin Bakers, there was Gioffa, secretary of the Latin Branch, and Dan Lavori, who headed the very busy IWW Modesto office.

25. "Transbay Bakers on Strike," *San Francisco Bulletin*, 3 November 1911, 1.

26. Hans C. Palmer, "Italian Immigration and the Development of California Agriculture" (Ph.D. diss., University of California, 1965), 153.

27. In 1911, roughly 40 percent of Italian men and women worked in this sector. Cinel, *Italy to San Francisco*, 135–39.

28. Robert E. L. Knight, *Industrial Relations in the Bay Area* (Berkeley: University of California Press, 1960), 64.

29. Ibid. Unlike the IWW organization effort, Bakery Union organizers spoke neither Italian nor French.

30. "Ai Panettieri," *L'Italia*, 22 August 1911, 1.

31. The IWW Latin branch was formed after a split with the Socialist Party, which ousted a large number of Wobblies during this period. Knight, 235.

32. "San Francisco, Cal," *Cronaca Sovversiva*, 23 September 1911, 1.

33. "Police in Street Battle with I.W.W.," *San Francisco News Call*, 14 August 1911, 1.

34. Ibid.

35. *L'Italia*, 23 September 1911.

36. "San Francisco, Cal," *Cronaca Sovversiva*, 23 September 1911, 1.

37. Perrone, with other Italian anarchists, had returned disillusioned from Baja California and Los Angeles, where they had been involved in revolutionary activity with Ricardo Flores Magón. "Cravello Sputacchiato da Perrone," *Cronaca Sovversiva*, 4 November 1911, 3.

38. "Alleged Rioters in Court," *The Daily News*, 14 August 1911, 1.

39. "Guns Quell Riot of Reds," *San Francisco Call*, 14 August 1911, 1.

40. "I.W.W. Complain of Police Action," *San Francisco Call*, 15 August 1911, 1.

41. Ausin Lewis, "The Drift of California," *International Socialist Review* 12 (October 1911): 273.

42. "Unionismo, Socialismo, Fratellanza," *L'Italia*, 25 August 1911, 1.

43. Ibid.

44. "I.W.W. Complain of Police Action," *San Francisco Call*, 15 August 1911, 1.

45. *International Socialist Review* 12 (October 1911): 273.

46. "Transbay Bakers Go on Strike," *The Bulletin*, 3 November 1911, 1.

47. "Condizioni Pietose, Minacciano Sciopero," *Il Corriere del Popolo*, 18 August 1916, 2.

48. "Bakers Merge As Flour Rises," *San Francisco Examiner*, 22 August 1916, 1.

49. California Commission on Immigration and Housing (CCIH), J. Vance Thompson to George Bell, 26 March 1917, Lubin Papers, Bancroft Library. Also, "Strike Threat in Demands of Fishermen," *San Francisco Bulletin*, 24 March 1917, 3.

50. "Strike Threat in Demands of Fishermen," *San Francisco Bulletin*, 24 March 1917, 3.

51. Palmer, "Italian Immigration," 150–51.

52. CCIH, J. Vance Thompson to George Bell, 24 July 1917, Lubin Papers, 2–3, Bancroft Library.

53. "Salumieri si Organizzano," *Il Corriere del Popolo*, 11 April 1919, 3.

54. CCIH, J. Vance Thompson to George Bell, 26 March 1917, Lubin Papers, Bancroft Library.

55. Howard De Witt, *Images of Ethnic and Radical Violence in California Politics: A Survey* (San Francisco: R & E Associates, 1975), 60.

56. Cinel, *From Italy to San Francisco*, 140.

57. Paul Avrich, *Anarchist Voices* (Princeton, N.J.: Princeton University Press, 1995), 174.

Italian Americans and the American Communist Party

Gerald Meyer

The most neglected aspect of the slowly emerging history of Italian American radicalism has been the relationship between Italian Americans and the American Communist Party (CPUSA).[1] The very existence of a small but vital community of Communists within the Italian American community has gone unreported. This work shows that from its founding in 1919 until the 1950s, when the CPUSA's existence as a mass phenomenon was curtailed in a firestorm of political and cultural repression, the Communist Party maintained a constant presence within the larger Italian American community, which was manifested by an Italian-language newspaper, lodges of a fraternal organization, and units of various political and labor organizations. This occurred because the Communist Party advanced goals of value to many, perhaps a majority, of this community, including the expansion of trade unionism, the fight against discrimination, and the advancement of an alternate view of the American nationality that honored the immigrants' cultures. To many, the Communists also appeared to be the most effective and determined anti-Fascists.[2] At the same time, the Italian American contingent of the Party helped to build its strength and influence by providing leaders and contingents that helped to build the Party's various campaigns and organizations.

The extensive literature on Italian Americans and the vast literature on the Communist Party make only passing mention of one another.[3] Indeed, based on the published scholarship, even a conscientious student would have to conclude that no such relationship in fact ever existed. One recent study of Italian American radicalism erroneously describes the execution of Sacco and Vanzetti as "the end of a road [of Italian American radicalism] rather than the beginning of one." What the execution of "the good shoemaker and the poor fish peddler" does mark is the shift away from anarchism toward an increased influence of the Communist Party in those parts of the Italian American community susceptible to radicalism.[4] This shift was epitomized by the decision of 16-year-old Pietro di Donato to join the Communist Party on August 3, 1927, while taking part in a mass demonstration in New York City's Union Square that demanded a stay of execution for the two avowed anarchists (the demonstrators were attacked by squads of police on horseback).[5]

The statistics on the membership of Italian Americans within the CPUSA reveal a modest yet steady contingent. During the years 1922 to 1925, membership in the Party's Italian Bureau, which consisted of first-generation Americans and other members specifically working with the foreign born, ranged from a low of 138 to a high of 581. In 1938, when the Party's "registered" membership reached 51,000, the Italian Bureau claimed between 500 and 800 members. This placed it far below the Jewish Bureau, which boasted 4,000 members, but within the range of the Germans, Hungarians, Ukrainians, Lithuanians, Russians, Finns, and Greeks, and ahead of the Poles, Slovaks, Croats, and Armenians. A much larger number of second- and third-generation Italian Americans were integrated with Party members of various nationalities and races working in trade union and other Party work.[6] Tabulations based on surnames (which undercount Italian Americans) show that Italian Americans comprised a modest 2.8 percent of the Central Committee, 1.6 percent of the Party cadre, and 3.8 percent of the Party's foreign-born leaders. In 1938, the New York State Committee included 44 Italian Americans, that is, 5.5 percent of its membership.[7] In 1948, Italian Americans represented 300 of New York County's (that is, Manhattan's) 10,000 members.[8]

The circulation of the Party's Italian-language press and membership in the Italian American section of the International Workers Order (IWO), the Party-affiliated fraternal organization, provide two rough measures for quantifying the Communist Party's presence in the Italian American community. The Italian American section of the American Party sponsored *Il Lavoratore* (1924–1931), *L'Unità Operaia* (1932–1938), *L'Unità del Popolo* (1938–1951), and lastly, *Unity* (1954–1961), which appeared weekly, except for the early 1940s, when *L'Unità del Popolo* was issued semiweekly.[9]

The circulation of *L'Unità del Popolo* may have reached its apogee of approximately ten thousand shortly after its founding, in 1940. Vito Magli, a frequent contributor, related how its circulation depended almost entirely on first-generation readers, who gradually died off, and were neither replaced by new immigrants nor by the second generation.[10] The circulation of the *L'Unità del Popolo* represented a smaller readership compared to representative Communist-affiliated foreign-language newspapers and to the commercial press published in these languages. For example, in 1948:

Circulation

Communist Papers	Commercial Press
L'Unità del Popolo, 5,800	*Il Progresso*, 70,000
Freiheit, 21,000	*Jewish Daily Forward*, 89,000
Russkie Golos, 31,000	*Ruskoe Novoe Slovo*, 31,000[11]

These figures show that although the circulation of the Russian-language daily sympathetic to the Communist Party equaled that of the commercial Russian-language newspaper and the Yiddish Communist daily attained almost 25 percent of the circulation of *Jewish Daily Forward*, the largest circulated Yiddish daily, *L'Unità del Popolo's* circulation reached less than 10 percent of *Il Progresso's*. Although Greek Americans were only one-twelfth as numerous as the Italians, in 1940 the 8,500 circulation of the Communist Party-sponsored Greek-language weekly, *Vema*, exceeded *L'Unità's* by almost 40 percent.[12]

The Garibaldi-American Fraternal Society, the Italian-language Section of the International Workers Order, in 1947 recruited nearly eleven thousand members, which represented the sixth largest of its 15 nationality sections and 6 percent of the IWO's total membership.[13] The members were organized into 130 lodges, which were concentrated in New York, Buffalo, Philadelphia, Detroit, the anthracite-mining and western regions of Pennsylvania, New Jersey, Ohio, and Illinois. In 1941, 16 lodges were located in New York City; at one point, 5 functioned in Rochester, New York.[14]

The IWO's monthly publication, *Fraternal Outlook*, reported on the organization's activities as well as presenting the Party's general perspective. Until 1940, it was published in English with one- to three-page supplements in the 14 other languages of the nationality sections. Thereafter, it published in English and issued separate issues in each language. The primary medium of communication between the IWO and its membership was the Communist Party's Italian-language press. Luigi Candela, the national secretary of the Italian Section reported that at its second conference, the delegates endorsed *L'Unità Operaia* as "the best defender of the Italian workers in America and best defender of and agitator for the principles and aims of the I.W.O." The conference then adopted the weekly as its official organ and pledged the financial support of the membership.[15] Without fail, every issue of *L'Unità del Popolo* reported on IWO activities. Its July 6, 1940, issue, for example, announced that the IWO Progressive Lodge in Italian Harlem was sponsoring a group of "juniors" who would dance at the upcoming Garibaldi festival in Washington Square Park. It also published an IWO manifesto that urged the progressive community to focus on demanding an extension of Social Security to those occupations not yet covered. Lastly it reported on a picnic held in Maspeth, Queens, that was jointly sponsored by *L'Unità* and the Italian section of the IWO, which attracted one thousand attendees.[16]

Communist-led organizations, devoted to issues of specific interest to Italian Americans, amplified the Party's influence within this community. For example, after the triumph of Fascism, a coalition of Socialists and activists affiliated with various trade unions organized the Anti-Fascist Alliance of North America (AFANA) to unite Italian immigrants and exiles opposed to the regime. In 1925, Vittorio Vidali and another important Italian Communist, Francesco Coco, became part of its secretariat. The fragility of this coalition, however, was revealed when the internecine warfare of Communist- and Socialist-led factions in the International Ladies' Garment Workers' Union (ILGWU) spilled over into the work of the Anti-Fascist Alliance. Ultimately, the Socialists exited, leaving the Communists to inherit a moribund entity.[17]

The American Committee for Protection of the Foreign Born (ACFPFB)—a Communist-led organization founded in 1933 to provide advocacy, legal assistance to prevent deportations, and help with naturalization—played an important role in this community. In 1936, the ACFPFB established the Italian Committee to Defend the Immigrants, whose advisory board included Edward Corsi (liberal Republican and director of Haarlem House in Italian Harlem), James Mangano (sheriff of Kings County, New York), as well as East Harlem's congressman Vito Marcantonio. The Italian Committee represented an effort to reach out beyond the ACFPFB's relatively narrow range of political influence.[18]

In 1943 the Party joined with others on the Left (especially the Amalgamated Clothing Workers of America) to create the Free Italy Labor Council to mobilize public opinion in the Italian American community in support of a postwar Italian republic that would include the participation of all anti-Fascist forces, including its largest component, the Communist Party of Italy.[19] This organization competed with the fiercely anti-Communist Italian American Labor Council, led by Luigi Antonini, the leader of the Italian Local 89 of the ILGWU. *Fraternal Outlook* warned its members to oppose the latter group because the "Antonini gang ... like Hitler hates the Soviet Union with a consuming venom." The article also warned that the policy of excluding the Communist Party of Italy from the postwar coalition government threatened to "turn the liberated areas of Italy into a bloody battleground of civil war and would smash the anti-fascist unity of the six parties who are fighting Hitler in the underground in the occupied territories of North Italy."[20]

The Communist Party's political work in the Italian American community was based on a nationality policy that envisioned the indefinite maintenance of the immigrant cultures. A 1939 article by Irene Browder, published in *The Communist*, the Party's political journal, contains the clearest and most extended explanation of this singular view. Here she lists "Italians" as second (following Germans) among the "strategic [that is, largest] national groups." After noting that after the invasion of Ethiopia, Mussolini's "demagogy captivated for a time great masses of Italians here [who] thought that their own importance within the U.S. would grow with the expansion of his power abroad," Browder insists that this "fascist influence could have been combated had we been better prepared politically and organizationally, with adequate spokesmen ... leading people who are loved and trusted by the masses." This article signaled the Party's commitment to prioritize political work in the Italian American and other immigrant communities. The strategy for fulfilling this goal was to "draw [the immigrants and their children] fully into the national life while at the same time utilizing and *preserving* [my emphasis] all their healthy national characteristics, traditions, and culture."[21]

Articles in *The Communist* periodically reevaluated the Party's interactions with the Italian American community, now refracted through this newly refined cultural prism. A 1936 article, reporting on the Party's work among Italian American longshoremen in the Red Hook section of Brooklyn, had bewailed the

Party's inability to make clear its position on Ethiopia.[22] However, by 1938 another article applauded the Party's progress in Rochester because its branch's "correct approach to the Italian people" had helped build the American Labor Party (ALP) and had initiated a conference representing 14 Italian American organizations "around the program of the ACFPFB, [which] received favorable comment from leaders of the Italian Civic League."[23] In this same vein, a 1941 article noted that "the large [Fiorello] LaGuardia vote in the Italian assembly districts [in the 1941 mayoral election] resulted from a proper approach to the national aspirations of the Italian people, a correct and patient explanation of the effects in Italy of Nazi domination."[24]

The Party press revealed its strong base in Italian Harlem, the country's largest Little Italy, which was also the bastion of Marcantonio, who maintained an open alliance with the Party. "Party Building Drive in New York," a 1937 article published in *The Communist*, noted that the East Harlem branch had increased from 32 to 62 members. Its activities included "selling from twenty to twenty-five copies of the *Daily Worker* daily," distributing literature on election day, and helping launch the East Harlem Tenants' League, "composed mainly of Italian families."[25] The following year, *The Party Organizer*, its internal journal, noted the increase of East Harlem's Italian membership to 120 and that: "The Italian [language] branch registered fifty-two out of fifty-five."[26]

The Party's influence in this community was enlarged by the IWO lodge, La Progressiva, which was located in the heart of the community, on East 116th Street and Second Avenue. Its activities included providing assistance to those wishing to become American citizens and conducting a series of weekly political lectures. In 1940, it sponsored a cultural program that included an Italian chorus and a young people's dance group, attended by some seven hundred people, in a theater in East Harlem, at which Marcantonio spoke. On a number of occasions, the lodge organized Italian-language classes taught by *L'Unità*'s co-editor, Gino Bardi, but the response was weak and they could not be sustained. Unlike other lodges in the city, which concentrated on cultural and social activities, the Progressiva Lodge focused more on political work, especially by supporting Marcantonio's reelection. The lodge averaged around eighty-five members, but its social and political events attracted as many as two hundred.

The Progressiva Lodge's successes depended in part on excellent local leadership. For many years, Vito Magli, who had immigrated to the United States in 1935 at the age of 14, led the Progressiva Lodge. He had become politically active in the Left even before 1941, when he graduated from Benjamin Franklin High School, which was located in East Harlem. He spoke in Italian and English on street corners on behalf of the American Labor Party, frequently contributed to *L'Unità*, and in 1948 cochaired Marcantonio's election-eve rally, which attracted some ten thousand people to his so-called Lucky Corner, that is the northeast corner of East 116th Street and Lexington Avenue. In 1952, the election after Marcantonio's defeat, he ran as the American Labor Party candidate for Congress.[27]

On rare occasions, the Party's press revealed some of the behind-the-scenes dynamics of the Party's Italian Bureau. In 1935, the *Daily Worker* announced that

five Italians had been "expelled from the ranks as counter-revolutionary elements [who had been] conducting a factional struggle against the Italian Bureau
of the Central Committee and *L'Unità Operaia.*" The leader of the "faction,"
Giovanni Lago, was accused of "having ambitions of becoming the editor of
L'Unità for the expressed purpose of . . . dedicating itself to the publication of historical and scientific material and not the every-day struggles of the working class.
[Furthermore,] one of the major causes of the factional struggle that went on in
the Italian Workers' Center in [Italian] Harlem was Lago's selfish, petty bourgeois
careerist ambition to occupy the most influential position in the [Italian section]
of the Party."[28] This article illustrates the Party's ceaseless fight against what it
termed "sectarianism," that is, the tendency of Left groups to evolve over time
into a means for satisfying the social and cultural needs of their members and
cease relating to, and therefore recruiting among, the wider community. Indeed,
this became the fate of numerous anarchist and socialist organizations.

The Communist Party rarely operated directly under its own name. There was
a constant danger of reprisal for Communist Party affiliation, which was especially
great for the foreign born. Beyond this prudential motive, however, lay an even
more compelling consideration—the Communists could gain much wider audiences for their views when they presented them under the aegis of other organizations. The secrecy of the Party makes it difficult to assess the nature and scope of
its activities. However, interviews with Communist Party functionaries from this
period reveal considerable activity in addition to what was published in the
Party's press. For example, at least as late as 1956, there existed an Antonio Gramsci Club of the Communist Party, comprised of Italian-speaking members of the
ILGWU.[29] In the Bronx, into the 1950s, the Party established a separate Italian
section that consisted of 75–80 members, organized into a number of different
clubs based on "congeniality or confluence of interest." Within the Bronx's largest
Italian American community, Belmont (which is sometimes called Arthur
Avenue), the mostly Italian-born members of the CP club (which included a
number of anarchists) were widely accepted. Indeed, Gabriel Filipi, who sold
copies of *L'Unità del Popolo* in front of Our Lady of Mount Carmel Church after
Sunday mass, was widely known as "the mayor of Belmont." They tended to be
politically active in both their trade unions and the communities. One the activities of this section was the creation of a 300-page history of the Italian community. Marcantonio frequently spoke in Italian and English at outdoor rallies there,
which attracted larger crowds than did the candidates of the major parties.[30]

For one brief moment, however, the Party substantially operated above
ground. In 1946, after leading the campaign to depose Earl Browder as the General Secretary of the Party because, among other things, he had converted the
Communist Party into the Communist Political Association, its new general secretary, William Z. Foster, demanded that the Party act more independently.
Advertisements placed in *L'Unità del Popolo* reveal this new modus operandi. For
example, one ad from an April issue reported that the Sacco and Vanzetti Club
of the Communist Party in Greenwich Village was holding a meeting at which

Peter Cacchione, the city councilperson elected from Brooklyn on the Communist Party ticket, and Michele Salerno, the editor of *L'Unità del Popolo*, would speak on "a lively and topical subject." In June, Cacchione, Salerno, Bella Dodd, and others were scheduled to speak at a meeting, which took place in downtown Brooklyn, on the "situation in Italy." In September, on the seventh anniversary of the founding of the paper, the Gramsci Club of the Communist Party published greetings: "In recognition of your valiant fight for the right of labor, for your noble effort to print the truth for the benefit of the Italian people, and for your unstinting support to the cause of progress, international cooperation, and peace."[31] The growing repression directed against the Communist Party, however, made these forays into openness too risky, and once again evidence of the activities of the Communist Party per se disappeared from the pages of *L'Unità del Popolo*. Henceforth, Communist Party involvement in the activities of organizations must be inferred.

The Communist Party's presence in the Italian American community attracted prominent attention in New York City's mass circulation press for the first and only time in 1935, when it mobilized opposition to Italy's invasion of Ethiopia. Under the auspices of the League Against War and Fascism, it organized two parades that terminated on the western edge of Harlem, where a mass, open-air, antiwar rally was addressed by, among others, Tito Nunzio, the editor of *L'Unità Operaia*. The *New York Times* reported that the estimated twenty thousand participants, who had marched from the east, passed through Italian Harlem, shouting "Italian and Negro people unite in a common front against the war," and "Death to Fascism! . . . with few exceptions those sentiments were cheered by those on the sidewalk and by those leaning out of windows."[32] The African American weekly, the *New York Age*, noted that the "fifty to seventy-five thousand" marchers, who frequently shouted "Down with Mussolini" and "Hands off Ethiopia," included "several large Italian delegations."[33] The *Daily Worker's* coverage showed that the Communist Party had insisted that "the two divisions of the marches will pass through the Negro and Italian sections of Harlem," and that they "will be led by Harlem Negro and Italian groups." Other articles revealed that the Party had achieved this huge turnout by organizing meetings throughout the Italian American communities to promote the march. For example, two days before the march, the *Worker* reported that "Italian and other workers on the Lower East Side pledged to march in the parade today at two enthusiastic meetings [held] at Thompkins Square." The *Worker* also reported on other antiwar meetings that brought together African Americans and Italian Americans. In Boston, Richard Moore, African American leader of the International Labor Defense, and Tom de Fazio, an editor of *L'Unità*, were reported to have "stood with clenched fists upraised on the platform on Boston Common." In Cleveland, "hands clasped in hands . . . Negroes and Italians led a mass parade here following a spirited anti-war demonstration in the heart of the Negro and Italian communities," where "twelve hundred persons at a the park pledged active resistance to war and Fascism and support for the Ethiopian people in their struggle against Italian Fascism."[34]

This spectacular manifestation of Italian American–African American soli-darity challenges the accuracy of Gaetano Salvemini's endlessly quoted state-ment in 1940 that "5 percent of the Italian Americans were true Fascists, another 35 percent philo-Fascists, and 10 percent anti-Fascists," and the rest apolitical.[35] Although no other event would ever again draw the Italian American contin-gent of the CPUSA onto center stage, the detailed day-by-day history of the Communist Party's activities within the Italian American communities has been preserved on the pages of its Italian-language newspapers.[36]

L'Unità del Popolo was founded on March 25, 1939, in New York City, with a long list of sponsors headed by Vito Marcantonio. Co-edited by Gino Bardi and Maria (Mary) Testa, it published eight pages (including one, and after 1940 two, in English), at a cost of $2.00 for a one-year subscription and five cents per copy. Its masthead defined *L'Unità* as "The Italian American Progressive Weekly." Here, "progressive" associated *L'Unità* with the outlook of the Popular Front, which among other things attempted to meld the Communist movement with "progressive" aspects of the American political tradition.[37] Out of the word *del* in the title emerged the Statue of Liberty, and on its masthead Thomas Jefferson is quoted to the effect that: "The most secure protection of the rights of the people is the massed strength of its citizens." The masthead also quoted Giuseppe Garibaldi: "Be United, O People, be united, and you shall be free!" The juxtapo-sition of these quotes underscored the paper's ongoing effort to interrelate the democratic traditions of both countries instead of opposing a democratic United States to a fascistic Italy.[38]

Although *L'Unità*'s Communist Party affiliation was nowhere stated, to even the most casual reader, it was unmistakable. However, *L'Unità* was not an Italian-language clone of the *Daily Worker*. It published relatively little news about the CPUSA, aside from its activities within the Italian American communities.[39] However the radical weekly did defend the civil rights of the Communist Party. An editorial published prior to the 1940 election reminded its readers that: "The experience of other countries has taught us time and again that an onslaught against the Communists is but the first step in a far flung onslaught against the trade unions and other liberties of the whole people."[40] Although in every case they were favorable, it published far fewer articles about the Soviet Union than the *Daily Worker*. Although clearly operating within the parameters of the Com-munist Party's general political positions, *L'Unità* calibrated its responses to the prevailing political sentiments of the Italian American communities. During this period, when the *Daily Worker* unreservedly attacked individuals and organiza-tions that supported U.S. participation in World War II, including La Guardia, *L'Unità* published only one article critical of the Little Flower. In 1940, both the *Worker* and *L'Unità* denounced Franklin Delano Roosevelt and Wendell Wilkie; however, unlike the *Worker*, *L'Unità* failed to directly endorse Browder, the Com-munist nominee for President.

Almost weekly, *L'Unità* published articles inviting Italian Americans to view anti-Semitism as inimical to their interests as a nationality and as members of the working class.[41] Here the paper was responding to the dramatically contrasting sentiments in the Italian American and Jewish American communities regarding U.S. participation in the war, which threatened to disrupt organizations—and especially, the ALP—in which Jewish and Italian Americans provided the base for the Party's hegemony.

L'Unità lambasted Antonini far more frequently than it denounced Mussolini. For example, after Marcantonio won the 1940 Republican and ALP primaries, the paper quoted this excerpt from his victory speech: "The shark of Local 89, Luigi Antonini, who speaks against dictatorship, makes a dictatorship in Local 89 over the sardines." An article relating events at the state committee meeting of the ALP noted that "Antonini tried to transfer his typical gangster methods of trade unionism to the political arena."[42] *Fraternal Outlook* also regularly castigated Antonini. In 1944, for example, they asserted that his "antagonism toward our great Ally, the Soviet Union, has led him into statements and actions of direct aid to Hitler's fifth column in the country."[43] *L'Unità's* unending invective toward Antonini reflected the day-to-day struggle between the Communists and the anti-Communist Socialists for the leadership of the ILGWU and the ALP. In a more general way, however, this hostility was engendered because Antonini's advocacy of socialism directly competed with the Party for their identical core constituency, that is, the radicalized first- and second-generation workers.[44]

Generoso Pope, the publisher of *Il Progresso* and Democratic Party chieftain, also was minutely criticized on *L'Unità's* pages. After characterizing him as "the most authoritative spokesman for Italian fascism in America," one editorial compared his support for conscription to Mussolini's maxim "War is magnificent." Another editorial, which protested his nomination to the Draft Board of Appeals, branded him as "a notorious fascist propagandist, whose sole idea of democracy has consisted of Tammany Hall."[45] Attacking Pope's political ideas and activities became a central task for *L'Unità* because its readers often read *Il Progresso* and lived in communities where the Democratic Party dominated.

Italy's invasion of Greece in November 1940 made front-page news in *L'Unità*. Its headlines, in contrast with other Italian-language newspapers, blared: "A Victory of the Italian People: The Fascist Defeat in Greece" and "There Exists No Greater Courage than the Struggle against the War." An accompanying article concluded its descriptions of the defeats of the Italian armies as a "terrible blow for Italian imperialism." An English-language article's headline averred: "Greek and Italian People Share Common Heritage of Liberty and Culture."[46] *L'Unità's* position on Italy's invasion of Greece was entirely consistent with its general outlook. Earlier that year, for example, Gino Bardi assured an audience of two hundred Italian Americans in Rochester that "Every victory of Italian imperialism constitutes a defeat for the Italian people and a danger for the Italian American people."[47]

In addition to informing its readership about its point of view on Italy's invasion of Greece, *L'Unità del Popolo* strove to help preserve the unity between Italian American and Greek American progressives. *L'Unità*, together with *Eleft-*

heria, the Greek-language weekly associated with the CPUSA, organized a series of meetings featuring speeches by the editors of these newspapers. Its articles and advertisements first encouraged its readers to attend these meetings, and then subsequent articles amplified the meetings' impact by reporting the content of the speeches and the reactions of the audiences. The advertisement for the first of these meetings, which was held on Manhattan's Lower East Side, urged attendance "[Because] it is in our interests to know the truth about the origins of the military and naval conflict in Greece and in the Mediterranean and about the struggle of the Italian people against the war." Other joint meetings were held in Corona Queens, Detroit, Chicago, and on the Lower East Side. The Chicago meeting, which was held at the Congress of Industrial Organizations (CIO) Hall, reported that the audience of "Greeks and Italians . . . pledged ourselves to promote unity and fraternity of the Greek and Italian Peoples in Chicago, and to expose and fight against those who are interested in dividing and disrupting the Greek and Italian peoples for their own selfish and reactionary policies."[48]

At every point, the radical weekly advocated the needs of the foreign born in general and placed the specific needs of the Italian American community within that context. On June 28, 1940, after Roosevelt signed into law the Smith Act, which instituted the registration and fingerprinting of resident aliens (including 600,000 Italian Americans) and raised the specter of deportation for those foreign born—legal aliens and naturalized citizens alike—who had previously held membership in the Communist Party. *L'Unità* rallied its readers to oppose the act on the grounds that it threatened both the general interests of immigrants and their families and the civil liberties of Communists. Speaking at a conference in Buffalo, Bardi emphasized the special danger of the Smith Act to the Italian American community because "it could be used against Fascists or Communists."[49]

It was clear, however, that the small community of Italian American Communists, or for that matter the wider Italian American community, could not reverse a law that had passed the House with only four negative votes. The radical weekly repeatedly encouraged its readership to participate in the activities of the ACFPFB, which had assumed the task of mobilizing the immigrant communities and their supporters to this cause. For example, the paper invited all organizations to join in an ACFPFB-sponsored conference held in New York City and organized for the purpose of mobilizing activities directed toward rescinding the Smith Act.[50] *L'Unità* quoted the president of the organization, Carey McWilliams, that in New York City more than five of its seven million residents were either immigrants or the children of immigrants. He described New York City as "A monument erected by the labor of the immigrants. [However,] today, the increasing war hysteria has intensified the discrimination against these people, who have dedicated all of their lives to the creation of our city."[51]

Without exception, each issue of *L'Unità* contained one, and sometimes more, article that in minute detail reported on the activities of Marcantonio, who was the leading figure not only of the Italian American Left, but also the defacto national spokesperson for the Left. For example, the same issue that announced an ACFPFB-sponsored national radio broadcast of a speech by Marcantonio against the Smith Act contained an article informing its readers that "[On a typical evening,] Marc stops at his favorite pastry shop [in Italian Harlem] for a cup of *caffé espresso* with a group of district captains and friends. He still enjoys most of all the time he spends with his 'boys' analyzing the political situation, listening to their opinions."[52]

L'Unità served as the coordinating organ for all of the organizations related to the Communist Party that operated in the Italian American communities. In addition to reporting on the activities of the Garibaldi Federation in great detail, *L'Unità* publicized the activities of the Workers Alliance (an organization of the unemployed and WPA workers), the ALP, and various Communist-led unions, which had large Italian American memberships. Bardi's nomination in 1940 as the ALP candidate for Congress from a district that included the Italian American community in Greenwich Village underscored the relationship of *L'Unità* with these organizations. Without fail, the paper published articles that prominently related the names of Italian Americans who were running for office under the ALP banner or who held office in these organizations.[53]

Working in a coordinated way, the newsweekly and these organizations regularly sponsored public meetings, dinners, and picnics, which attracted 200–1,000 attendees. These events took place in many towns and cities, including Trenton, Providence, Rochester, Buffalo, Philadelphia, and many New York City communities, including Italian Harlem, Corona, Red Hook in Brooklyn, and Belmont in the Bronx. In 1940, over two thousand gathered to hear Marcantonio, the editors of the paper, and Luigi Candela at a Fourth of July Celebration at the foot of the statue of Giuseppe Garibaldi in Manhattan's Washington Square Park, which was an annual event that simultaneously celebrated Garibaldi's birthday and the birthday of the United States. Clearly, the influence of the Communist Party varied within the Little Italies. For example, during the period examined here, there is little mention of activities in the Lower East Side's Little Italy and in Boston's North Side.[54]

Peter Cacchione, a leader of the unemployment movement, was the CPUSA's most electorally successful officeholder. Under the system of proportional representation that governed the elections of the New York City Council from 1937 until 1949, Cacchione was elected from Brooklyn for three consecutive terms, in 1941, 1943, and 1945. From this position, he strengthened the Party's prestige and association with segments of the Italian American community by vocally and effectively protesting the Italian Americans' second-class status within the city and the country. In 1940, *L'Unità* published this excerpt from one of his radio broadcasts: "Italian Americans suffer from this propaganda against the foreign born. Discrimination has always impeded them from obtaining better employment and this has created obstacles to their participation in politics. In New York City, Italian Americans comprise 15 percent of the population [however] in New York State there is only one Italian American congressman, Vito Marcantonio. Only 4 percent of New York City's school teachers are Italian

American."[55] His personal popularity and the prestige of the Communist Party was evidenced by the outpouring of expressions of sympathy at his funeral in 1947 from masses of ordinary people as well as public officials. Marcantonio eulogized him as "a people's leader and a champion of progress, [whom] so many small people will mourn [because he was] an integral part of their living flesh and blood . . . his heart beat with them." He joined his death to "those of other [recently fallen] people's fighters—Roosevelt, LaGuardia, and Sidney Hillman." Mayor William O'Dwyer's written condolences stated: "I respected him as a man." The president of the city council, Vincent Impellitteri, leading a delegation of 10 councilmen, spoke at the funeral on behalf of the mayor declaring, "The Council has suffered a loss and his wise counsel will be missed. [He was an] able, conscientious, diligent, and courteous member of that body."[56]

Within the Italian American community, the Communist Party benefited greatly from its close alliance with Marcantonio. He had achieved an extraordinary status within Italian Harlem and enormous popularity throughout New York City's Little Italies and to some extent among the larger population of Italian Americans throughout the United States. In his nine elections, he had never failed to achieve a majority of Italian Harlem's vote; in 1949, when he ran for mayor as the ALP's candidate, he garnered 30 percent of New York City's Italian American vote.[57] To some lesser extent, La Guardia's association with the Left, and especially his continued registration in the ALP and support for Marcantonio, served to create a favorable image of the Left in the Italian American community.

Louis Fraina (Lewis Corey), who arrived in 1898 at the age of six from Galdo (Salerno) Italy to live in the Lower East Side's Little Italy, played a large role in the development and propagation of Marxism in the United States and in the founding of the CPUSA. However, in the words of Paul Buhle: "Italian-language radicals belonged to a world too small for Fraina. He identified himself as an American." Indeed, his prominence rested on his acting as a broker between the wider American society and various communities of pro-Communist immigrant leftists—Latvians, Finns, Russians. However, nowhere does his variegated career intersect with the Italian American Left. Fraina found intolerable his own marginalization in the movement that had resulted from a Comintern assignment to help develop the Communist movement in Mexico. After pocketing much of the money with which the Comintern had entrusted him for this purpose, in 1923 Fraina reemerged in the United States with a new name and new identity. By 1926 he began submitting articles on political economy under the name Lewis Corey, ultimately achieving considerable fame as the author of *The Decline of American Capitalism* (1934) and *The Crisis of the Middle Class* (1935). In the postwar period, he became increasingly anti-Communist, going so far as to denounce Henry Wallace as a foreign agent of Stalin when he ran for the presidency on the Progressive Party ticket in 1948, and to demand that the U.S. government launch a preemptive military attack against the Soviet Union. Nonetheless, based on his family's entrance into the United States without papers, his illegal reentrance from Mexico, and his prior Communist affiliation, the government issued an order of deportation to return Fraina to Italy. On Christmas Day, 1952, he received an announcement of the impending deportation order. In part because he had lost his job and in part because of the stress of preparing his legal defense, on September 15, 1953, he suffered a cerebral hemorrhage and died the next day.[58]

Ralph Fasanella, the painter and incomparable self-taught social realist, grew up in Belmont, where he helped his mother publish a small anti-Fascist newsletter in Italian. He joined the Abraham Lincoln Brigade in 1938 and served as an organizer for the Teamsters Union; the Hospital Workers Union; the Communication Workers of America; and the United Electrical, Radio, and Machine Workers of America. In 1949, Fasanella garnered 9 percent of the vote running as the ALP candidate for city council from the Yorkville section of Manhattan. Completely blacklisted during the McCarthy era, he became co-owner, with his brother-in-law, of a gas station in the Bronx. In 1972, a 17-page *New York* article "discovered" Fasanella. More than any other known post–World War II painter, his work had been almost exclusively dedicated to social and political concerns—the execution of the Rosenbergs, the Lawrence general strike, the Triangle Shirtwaist fire, May Day parades, as well as the everyday life of working people, and especially Italian American people. Fasanella's lifelong hero was Marcantonio, after whom he named his son and who was the subject of three of his most-important canvases.[59]

Carl Marzani—whose family emigrated in 1924 from Rome to settle near Scranton, Pennsylvania, when he was 12—is a neglected figure within both the history of the Italian American experience and the American Left. After graduating from Williams College and Oxford University, he traveled to Spain to defend the Republic. On returning to the United States, he became educational director of the Party's Lower East Side Section, which boasted over three thousand members organized into more than forty branches, including a number of Italian-speaking branches.[60] Marzani served in the Office of Strategic Services during the war; however, in 1946 the government disputed his assertion that he had resigned from the Party before he had enlisted and indicted him for perjury. Both the 1948 Supreme Court decision and a 1949 rehearing (only the eighth in the history of the Supreme Court) resulted in a 4–4 vote (Justice William Douglas abstained) and upheld the lower court's conviction. In 1949, Marzani entered jail to serve 32 months, which caused Marzani to claim to be "the first victim of McCarthyism."[61] In the postwar period, he produced a number of documentary films for left-wing unions and to aid the political campaigns of Henry Wallace and Marcantonio. In 1951, he wrote what may have been the first revisionist account of the cold war, *We Can Be Friends: The Origins of the Cold War*, which sold 10,000 hardcover and 50,000 paperback copies. His translations and annotated excerpts of the writings of Antonio Gramsci (which in 1957 was published under the title *The Open Marxism of Antonio Gramsci*) represented the first major presentation in the United States of the most influential Marxist thinker since Lenin. In 1958, there appeared *The Survivor,* one of the first novels about the McCarthy period, whose protagonist, Marc Ferranti, was perhaps Marzani recast as a leftist liberal. He performed another major service for the Left when, in 1954, together with Angus Cameron, he launched a book club (later known as Marzani and Munsell), which published books by blacklisted writers—such as Ring Lardner, Alvah Bessie, Abe Polonsky, and Albert Maltz—as well as books on blacklisted topics such as *Labor's Untold Story,* by Richard Boyer and Herbert Morais, and *Gideon's Army,* a three-volume study of the Progressive Party, by Curtis MacDougall. In his later years until his death on December 11, 1994, he devoted an increasing amount of time to writing a five-volume autobiography, *The Education of a Reluctant Radical.*[62]

General circumstances within the Italian American communities ensured that the Communist Party would attract some of its residents. First, the Party offered its adherents the opportunity of simultaneously becoming part of a worldwide movement attached to a larger culture without having to renounce their ties to their communities and their cultures. Membership in the Party reconciled the conflict for Italian Americans and other "ethnics," who chafed at the narrowness of lives evolving around their families and local communities yet feared losing these attachments. It offered a way for working-class people to become worldly without ever venturing out into the world.[63] This dichotomous situation was reflected in *L'Unità del Popolo's* "bifocal" perspective: an exceedingly sophisticated treatment of international news, and a narrowly parochial approach to local matters.[64] Within the same issue, the defeat of the Italian army in Greece would receive nearly equal coverage as a community meeting with three hundred attendees. The cosmopolitan yet parochial milieu that typified the Party culture held some special value to a community still dominated by fierce family loyalty and *campanilismo.*

Italian Americans constituted America's largest ethnic group, numbering as many as six million in 1940—600,000 of whom were resident aliens.[65] The majority consisted of working-class people who lived in ghettos and experienced discrimination. The Great Depression had struck Italian Americans especially hard, because they were concentrated in those sectors of the economy—such as construction—that had registered the largest percentages of unemployment.[66] The Catholic Church, which immunized the Irish American community from Communism, did not play this role in the Italian American community. There, widespread anticlericalism joined to the widespread view of the Church as primarily a focus of ritual observance diluted its influence in the political realm.

The CPUSA effectively related to the language and cultural needs of the Italian American community. Starting in 1944, for example, the monthly journal of the most openly Communist large union in the United States, the Fur and Leather Workers Union, began publishing "Italian Pages," a short section with articles in English and Italian of special interest to its Italian American members. The November 1944 issue, for example, announced that at a meeting of its Italian American membership, Marcantonio, speaking in Italian, averred that Thomas Dewey, if elected, would "transform Italy into a colony of the most imperialist elements of Wall Street." This article also reported that the union would immediately contribute $10,000 from its treasury toward a $50,000 pledge for Italian war relief and endorse Marcantonio's congressional resolution demanding that Italy be extended lend-lease aid.[67]

The social and economic bases for the Italian American Communist community began to erode during World War II and even more rapidly in the post–World War II era. The Italian Americans' dispersal reduced the size and vitality of the Little Italies. These communities provided an almost-ideal milieu for Communism, a place where those subject to class exploitation and discrimination based on national origin could sense their own strength and develop their own institutions and culture. The mass migration of African Americans and Puerto Ricans into the large cities deflected the discrimination Italian Americans had previously endured. The G.I. Bill helped create for the first time a large middle class within this community.

The Communist Party in the Italian American community was based in the first and second generations. As late as 1947, *Fraternal Outlook* reported that of the 44 delegates to the Garibaldi Association's convention only one-third were American born.[68] It is likely that over the next two decades or so, this organization and *L'Unità del Popolo* would have died a peaceful and natural death. What would have replaced it and how this legacy would have been passed on, however, can only remain in the realm of speculation.

The destruction of this community, however, was sudden, and the cause can be directly tied to the domestic political repression attendant to the cold war. In 1947, the IWO and the ACFPFB, along with almost every other Communist Party–related organization, were placed on the attorney general's list of subversive organizations. Under the Federal Loyalty Program, membership in these organizations—past or present—constituted sufficient cause for dismissal from any government job or any job that accepted government contracts, which in total amounted to some fifteen million persons. Membership in these organizations also provided cause for deportation.[69] Communist-led unions came under a comprehensive and determined attack from the government, the AFL-CIO, and organizations such as the Association of Catholic Trade Unionists. In 1949, 15 CIO unions, including some with large Italian American membership, were expelled from the CIO.

Subscribing to Communist publications, including *L'Unità del Popolo*, represented evidence of disloyalty. The penalties of dismissal from employment and deportation were carried out with no due-process protections other than the rights to a hearing, to legal counsel, and to remain silent. In 1951, *L'Unità* ceased publishing. Its editor, Michael Salerno, and other Italian American Communist Party members and sympathizers, including naturalized citizens with American-born spouses and children, were deported.[70] In 1954, the State of New York seized the insurance funds of the IWO.[71] The most damaging blow, however, had already been dealt. In 1950, despite a 60 percent majority in Italian Harlem, Vito Marcantonio, running solely on the ALP line, was defeated by a coalition candidate of the Democratic, Republican, and Liberal parties. The ALP, which had gained a large influence in New York's Italian American communities, was extruded from the political system by a series of extraordinary measures.

Those who eradicated this community have had no reason to remind anyone of these events, and those who fell victim to this political repression could never be sure what other penalties awaited them or members of their families if they sought rectification. As a result, subsequent generations have been denied any possibility of assessing this chapter in the history of the Italian American experience. However, even this preliminary study demonstrates that within the Italian American community, there existed a small, but influential, Communist contingent. Collectively, *L'Unità del Popolo*, the Garibaldi-American section of the IWO, the predominantly Italian American ALP clubs, and an array of left-wing union locals with large Italian American membership comprised an organic world whose existence challenges a number of widely circulated truisms.[72] The first is that Italian Americans had been absent, indifferent, and/or universally hostile to the Left. Another canard is the reduction of the history of the Communist movement to a conspiracy without ties to specific American realities. Nonetheless, it seems evident that the Italian American Communist community represents a piece of the Italian American experience that has been gouged out and hidden away. Placing it back into the picture will enrich the history of both the Italian American experience and American radicalism.

NOTES

1. In addition to those works cited, prominent contributions to the history of Italian American radicalism include: Rudolph J. Vecoli, "Italian Immigrants in the United States Labor Movement from 1880 to 1929," in *Gli italiani fuori d'Italia. Gli emigrati italiani nei movimenti operai dei paesi d'adozione 1880–1940*, ed. Bruno Bezza (Milan: Angeli, 1983), 257–306; Vecoli, "Italian Immigrants and Working Class Movements in the United States: A Personal Reflection on Class and Ethnicity," *Journal of the Canadian Historical Association* (1993): 193–205; Nunzio Pernicone, "Carlo Tresca: Life and Death of a Revolutionary," in *Italians in Search of a Usable Past*, ed. Richard Juliani and Philip V. Cannistraro (Staten Island, N.Y.: American Italian Historical Association, 1989), 216–35; Bruno Ramirez, "Immigration, Ethnicity, and Political Militancy: Patterns of Radicalism in the Italian-American Left, 1880–1930," in *From Melting Pot to Multi-Culturalism: The Evolution of Ethnic Relations in the United States and Canada*, ed. Valeria Gennaro Lerda (Rome, 1990), 115–42; and Paul Avrich, *Sacco and Vanzetti: The Anarchist Background* (Princeton, N.J.: Princeton University Press, 1991).

2. Mark Naison, "Remaking America: Communists and Liberals in the Popular Front," in *New Studies in the Politics and Culture of U.S. Communism*, ed. Michael Brown et al. (New York: Monthly Review Press, 1993), 47.

3. Harvey Klehr and John Haynes, *The American Communist Movement: Storming Heaven Itself* (New York: Twayne, 1992) contains two references to Italian Americans;

Irving Howe and Lewis Coser, *The American Communist Party: A Critical History* (New York: Praeger, 1962) contains none. In *La Storia: Five Centuries of the Italian Experience* (New York: HarperCollins, 1992), Jerre Mangione identifies himself as a "fellow traveler," who did not join the Communist Party due to some sort of "Sicilian wariness that had developed through centuries." He describes his participation in the John Reed Clubs as well as writing book reviews for the *New Masses* and the *Daily Worker* (pp. 119–21). He fails to mention his membership on the editorial board of *Labor Defender*, the publication of the International Labor Defense. *Labor Defender* (February 1937), 3. Maurice Isserman, in *Which Side Were You On?: The American Communist Party during the Second World War* (Urbana: University of Illinois Press, 1993) relates at some length the often conflictive relationship between the Communist exiles from Italy and Italian American Communists during World War II (pp. 171–72, 225, 251). This subject found its way into Isserman's book because the exiled leaders disagreed with Earl Browder's decision in 1944 to dissolve the American Communist Party and replace it with the Communist Political Association. This incident is also recorded in Joseph Starobin, *American Communism in Crisis, 1943–1957* (Berkeley: University of California Press, 1972), 260, 270.

4. Michael Topp, "The Italian-American Left: Trans-nationalism and the Quest for Unity," in *The Immigrant Left in the United States*, ed. Paul Buhle and Dan Georgakas (Albany: State University of New York Press, 1996), 142. Other works excise every variety of radicalism from the Italian American experience. Richard Gambino in *Blood of My Blood: The Dilemma of the Italian-Americans* (New York: Anchor Books 1975) relegates radicalism in this community to "some Italian labor militants who were socialists or anarchists, [however] the vast majority of the transplanted *contadini* cared nothing for ideologies" (p. 117). Gambino's review of Mangione's *La Storia* states that "the masses of Italian immigrants . . . had little use for politics and almost none for abstract ideologies" (*Italian Americana* [fall/winter 1993]: 115–21).

5. Michael Esposito, "The Evolution of Pietro di Donoto's Perception of Italian Americans," in *The Italian Americans through the Generations*, ed. Rocco Caporale (New York: American Italian Historical Association, 1986), 174–84.

6. Nathan Glazer, *The Social Basis of American Communism* (New York: Harcourt, Brace, and World, 1961), 42, 220; Harvey Klehr, *The Heyday of American Communism: The Depression Decade* (New York: Basic Books, 1984), 370.

7. Harvey Klehr, *Communist Cadre: The Social Background of the American Communist Party Elite* (Stanford, Calif.: Hoover Institute Press, 1978), 105, 220.

8. Glazer, *Social Basis*, 221. In the 1920s, when fully 90 percent of its membership was foreign born, the Communist cadre often adopted Anglo-Saxon surnames as part of an ongoing effort to recruit native-born and Anglo-Saxon workers. For example, in 1930, when Mario Alpi, the editor of *Lavoratore*, was elevated to administering the national headquarters' organization department, he changed his name to F. Brown. In the late 1930s, when more than one-half of its membership was American born, the Party reversed its policy and made a conscious effort to organize among first- and second-generation ethnics—Jews, Slavs, Italians, and others—among whom it already possessed a base and had obtained a positive response. Theodore Draper, *The Roots of American Communism* (Chicago: Elephant Paperbacks, 1985), 392; Klehr, *Heyday*, 25–26; Irene Browder, "Problems of the National Groups in the United States," *The Communist* (May 29, 1939): 456–66.

9. Dirk Hoerder, ed., *The Immigrant Labor Press in North America, 1840s–1970s: An Annotated Bibliography* (Westport, Conn.: Greenwood Press, 1987), 3:75–76,121–22. Vit-

torio Vidali, who edited *Il Lavoratore*, also served as secretary of the Italian section of the Party. Dorothy Gallagher, *All the Right Enemies: The Life and Murder of Carlo Tresca* (New York: Penguin Books, 1989), 137. The Party sponsored daily newspapers for those among whom it had the greatest influence—Jews, Finns, Russians, South Slavs, Ukrainians, Lithuanians, Hungarians, and Slovaks. Indeed, the Finnish-American Communists for some time actually published three daily newspapers. Glazer, *Social Basis*, 80.

10. Vito Magli, telephone interview by author, 6 December 1998. Magli recalled that his readers frequently called him *gioventù* (young man) when he made home visits soliciting subscriptions or donations for the paper.

11. *Ayers and Sons Newspaper Annual* (Philadelphia, 1947, 1948). Ayers did not consistently list *L'Unità* or its predecessors; therefore, this work cites available statistics.

12. Georgakas, "Greek American Radicalism," in Buhle and Georgakas, *Immigrant Left*, 216.

13. Thomas Walker, *Pluralistic Fraternity: The History of the International Workers Order* (New York: Garland Publishing, 1991), 96–97. Membership was counted as policyholders, which caused an undercounting of the IWO's actual membership. As late as 1949, New York City still had 14 Italian lodges. "A Tribute to Congressman Vito Marcantonio" (30 April 1949) (unpaginated, souvenir booklet in author's personal holdings). At one point, provision was made for "social members," especially family members of policyholders, who did not subscribe to IWO insurance.

14. "Bollettino della Conferenza Cittadina di New York del IWO," *L'Unità del Popolo*, 8 February 1941, 5.

15. "Our Italian Section," copy of three-page article (pp. 89–91), no other identification, International Workers Order Collection, Cornell University. See, for example: "La Festa Campestre delle Logge Italiane dell'IWO [has pledged] 400 nuovi abbonati promesi," *L'Unità del Popolo*, 13 July 1940, 4.

16. *L'Unità del Popolo*, 3 August 1940, 3, 5.

17. Klehr and Haynes, *American Communist Movement*, 53; Gallagher, *Al the Right Enemies*, 138. Vidali, who had entered the United States illegally from Italy, where he had been imprisoned and tortured, was deported in 1927. In 1937, under the name Carlos Contreras, he organized the Fifth Regiment of the International Brigade, which became legendary for its discipline and training. It had major responsibility for the defense of Madrid and spawned two generals, Juan Modesto and Enrique Lister. Vidali worked in the Italian underground during the war; in 1958 he served as a Communist deputy from Trieste, and from 1963 to 1968 he served as a senator. Carl Marzani, *The Education of a Reluctant Radical: Spain, Munich, and Dying Empires* (New York: Topical Books, 1994), 3:30–32, 34; Gallagher, 265.

18. Louise Pettibone Smith, *The Torch of Liberty: Twenty-five Years in the Life of the Foreign Born in the U.S.* (New York: Dwight-King, 1959), 11, 63. The IWO was also committed to support the ACFPFB. After quoting the general counsel of the ACFPFB, Joseph Brodsky, that this organization "readily joined with me in helping our members to be admitted to citizenship," the General Executive Board called on IWO members and lodges "to demonstrate our support through an annual contribution to sustain this worthy work" ("Equal Rights," *Fraternal Outlook* [July–August 1943]: 119).

19. John Diggins, *Mussolini and Fascism: The View from America* (Princeton, N.J.: Princeton University Press, 1972), 406–9.

20. John Middleton, "Political Action: Forces for FDR Gain Victory in New York State ALP Primaries in Major Test of Strength," *Fraternal Outlook* (May 1944): 27.

21. Irene Browder, "National Groups," 456–65. In 1945, *The Communist*, the Party's theoretical journal, was renamed *Political Affairs*.

22. Max Steinberg, "Problems of Party Growth in the New York District," *The Communist* (July 1936): 649.

23. Max Steinberg, "Rooting the Party among the Masses in New York," *The Communist* (August 1938): 835–36.

24. Bill Lawrence and Isidore Begun, "The New York City Elections and the Struggle against Hitlerism," *The Communist* (December 1941): 1069; see also Steinberg, "Rooting the Party."

25. Max Steinberg, "The Party Building Drive in New York State," *The Communist* (December 1937): 1140–41.

26. George Charney [George Blake], "The Party in Harlem, New York," *Party Organizer* (June 1938): 15.

27. "Attività della loggia 'La Progressiva,' " *L'Unità del Popolo*, 21 August 1940, 7; "Grand Comizio e Varietà," *L'Unità del Popolo*, 26 October 1940, 1. See also, issue of 21 September 1940, p. 3. Following the tradition initiated by Fiorello La Guardia, who served as congressman from East Harlem from 1922 to 1932, "Marcantonio always concluded his electioneering with a rally on the Lucky Corner" (Vito Magli, telephone interview).

28. "Counter-Revolutionary Group Expelled from the C.P.U.S.A.," *L'Unità Operaia*, 7 August 1935, 2.

29. Fay Leviton, interview by author, New York City, 27 September 1993.

30. Gene Perlstein, interview by author, New York City, 31 October 1994. Perlstein, who had fought in Italy for three years in the infantry, spoke fluent Italian. He recalled that in 1948 the Communist Party in the Bronx enrolled some five thousand members organized into six sections: four organized according to district and two based on nationality—one Italian and one Puerto Rican. The last editor of *L'Unità del Popolo*, Michael Salerno, lived in Belmont until he was deported in 1950. David Caute, *The Great Fear: The Anti-Communist Purge under Truman and Eisenhower* (New York: Touchstone Books, 1978), 588.

31. "Conferenza Cacchione e Salerno," *L'Unità del Popolo*, 6 April 1946, 3; "Reunione Speciale," *L'Unità del Popolo*, 15 July 1946, 6; "Greetings," *L'Unità del Popolo*, 28 September 1946, 5.

32. "White and Negro Join Peace Rally: Separate Parades of 20,000 in Harlem Unite in Anti-War Meeting: Ethiopia Is Cheered; Cry of 'Down with Mussolini!' Brings Approval from Sidewalk Crowds," *New York Times*, 4 August 1935, 28.

33. "Settlement of Italo-Ethiopian 'War' by League of Nations Council Held Improbable: Hostilities Continue," *New York Age*, 3 August 1935, 4; see also "The August Third March against War," *New York Age*, 3 August 1935, 2. In addition, see "Will March Today Protesting War," *New York Amsterdam News*, 3 August 1935, 5.

34. The following *Daily Worker* articles reported other antiwar meetings—which did not explicitly mention the participation of Italian Americans—that took place in cities and towns with large Italian American populations, such as Chicago and Union City, New Jersey: "Anti-War March Rankles Mussolini," 2 August 1935, 1; "Unite against War: 100,000 March in Harlem Today," 3 August 1935, 1; "Unite to Smash Fascism: 'Hands off Ethiopia!' Is Demand of 100,000," 5 August 1935, 1; "New York Parade Shows Growing Unity of People against War," 5 August 1935, 6. Richard Moore is not to be confused with

Fred Moore, a white man who was involved in several cases for the IWW, including the defense of the Lawrence strike leaders, Joe Ettor and Arturo Giovannitti.

35. Gaetano Salvemini, "Mussolini's Empire in the United States," in *Neither Liberty Nor Bread: The Meaning and Tragedy of Fascism*, ed. Francis Keene (New York: Harper & Brothers, 1940), 345–46. It also illustrates the interracialism that became the trademark, and one of the greatest strengths, of the Communist Left..

36. For example, in 1940 Marcantonio (whose campaign slogan, "The United States needs overalls not uniforms," epitomized the antiwar stance) garnered 65 percent of East Harlem's vote—72 percent on the Republican and 28 percent on the ALP lines. This contrasted with the 60 percent of the vote he garnered in 1938—53 percent of which was registered on the Republican and 47 percent on the ALP lines. Gerald Meyer, *Vito Marcantonio: Radical Politician, 1902–1954* (Albany: State University of New York Press, 1989), 6.

37. The Popular Front was dedicated to the organization of a broad political movement of workers, farmers, minorities, and some sectors of the middle class to fight simultaneously against the Right and advance the program of the Left New Deal. Progressivism in this sense also meant the replacement of socialism from the political agenda with demands for the broadening of the social sector and the strict regulation of the private sector, viz., a type of diluted social democracy. This movement, under ideal circumstances, was expected to include the Communist Party, or at the very least not to attack the Communist Party. This explains the omission from *L'Unità's* title of *operaio* (working class), which in its predecessor's title had been joined to *Unità*.

38. This analysis of the content and approach of *L'Unità del Popolo* is limited to the period from July 6, 1940, to March 1, 1941, that is, a nine-month span during the period of the German-Soviet Non-Intervention Pact (August 24, 1939—June 22, 1941). During this period of confusion and conflict, the Communist Party experienced major losses of membership among Jewish Americans and the resignation of some intellectuals. However, among Italian Americans, where antiwar sentiment predominated, the Party's new— albeit short-lived—position met with enthusiasm. A general analysis of *L'Unità* can be found in Gerald Meyer, "*L'Unità del Popolo*: The Voice of Italian American Communism, 1939–1951," *Italian American Review* (spring/summer 2001): 121–56.

39. "Un Discorso di Earl Browder a Boston," *L'Unità del Popolo*, 12 October 1940, 1.

40. "Defend Free Elections," *L'Unità del Popolo*, 26 October 1940, 1.

41. Ronald Bayor, *Neighbors in Conflict: The Irish, Germans, Jews, and Italians of New York City, 1929–1941* (Urbana: University of Illinois Press, 1988), 174; "La Cosa e l'antisemitismo," *L'Unità del Popolo*, 14 September 1940, 7. On November 20, 1938, *L'Unità* sponsored, "Gli Italiani Non Odiano gli Ebrei (The Italians Don't Hate Jews)!," a "protest meeting" against the Italian government's imposition of the anti-Semitic laws; it was held at the Manhattan Opera House. The keynote speaker was Marcantonio; other speakers included Giovannitti and the ALP city councilman, Salvatore Ninfo. Author's personal holdings.

42. "Il popolo di East Harlem rieleggerà Marcantonio," *L'Unità del Popolo*, 28 September 1940, 3; "Il Convengo de Comitato dell ALP a Utica," *L'Unità del Popolo*, 21 September 1940, 1.

43. Mario D'Inzillo, "The Italians Are Important," *Fraternal Outlook*, August 1944, 14.

44. Luigi Antonini was affiliated with the Social Democratic Federation, which was founded by anti-Communist Socialists who had exited the Socialist Party in 1936 when it adopted a policy of collaborating with the Communist Party. Almost entirely limited to

the Jewish American community, this peculiarly right-wing variety of social democracy was able to enormously amplify its influence through a set of interlocking institutions such as the International Ladies' Garment Workers' Union, the Workmen's Circle, *The Jewish Daily Forward*, and WEVD Radio.

45. "Generoso Pope difende la coscrizione," *L'Unità del Popolo*, 7 September 1940, 4; "Un affronto agli Italo Americani," *L'Unità del Popolo*, 9 November 1940, 9.

46. "Una vittoria del popolo italiano: La Sconfitta militiare fascista in Grecia," *L'Unità del Popolo*, 30 November 1940, 1; "L'imperialismo anglo-americano e la lotta per la liberazione della Grecia," *L'Unità del Popolo*, 30 November 1940, 1, 5.

47. "La Conferenza del Prof. Gino Bardi," *L'Unità del Popolo*, 20 July 1940, 3.

48. "La Guerra in Grecia: Conferenza pubblica sotto gli auspici dell *Unità del Popolo* e del settimanale greco *Eleftheria*," *L'Unità del Popolo*, 30 November 1940, 1; "Comizio Italo-Greco a Corono," *L'Unità del Popolo*, 7 December 1940, 3; "Comizio Italo-Greco a New York," *L'Unità del Popolo*, 14 December 1940, 2; "Comizio Italo-Greco," *L'Unità del Popolo*, 22 February 1941, 2; "Comizio di Solidarietà Italo-Greco," *L'Unità del Popolo*, 25 January 1941, 2; "Greeks and Italians Hold Mass Meeting in Chicago," *L'Unità del Popolo*, 22 February 1941, 1; and, "Greeks and Italians Hold Mass Meeting Detroit," *L'Unità del Popolo*, 8 March 1940, 8.

49. "Smith Bill Recalls Sacco and Vanzetti," *L'Unità del Popolo*, 6 July 1940, 5; "I Italiani di Buffalo," *L'Unità del Popolo*, 13 July 1940, 2.

50. Smith, *Torch of Liberty*, 82; "The Struggle for the Peace and for the Civil Rights of the People: For the Defense of the Immigrants," *L'Unità del Popolo*, 28 March 1940, 1. Marcantonio, of course, cast one of the four votes.

51. "Una Conferenza cittadina in difensa dei nati all'estero," *L'Unità del Popolo*, 28 September 1940, 1.

52. "An Evening in East Harlem," *L'Unità del Popolo*, 20 July 1940, 5, 47. The entire third page of *L'Unità's* July 6, 1940, edition was devoted to the IWO. The articles included: "L'Ordine Operaio Internazionale e la Assicurazioni Sociali" and "I membri e simpatizzanti dell' IWO riguardo alla commemorazione el 4 Luglio." There was also an advertisement that announced that the IWO had (1) paid out $794,000 in benefits to holders of insurance; (2) enrolled 161,000 members; and (3) recruited 14,000 new members in 1939.

53. "Altri candidati italo-americani dell ALP," *L'Unità del Popolo*, 24 August 1940, 1.

54. La Manifestazione del Quattro Lugio Oltre 2,000 persone celebrano L'Independenza americana e la nascità di Garibaldi," *L'Unità del Popolo*, 7 July 1940, 1. Routinely the newspaper and the fraternal organization cosponsored picnics. See, for example, "Verso un altro successo: Il Picnic dell' 11 Agosto," 3 August 1940, 5.

55. "Un Discorso di Peter Cacchione," *L'Unità del Popolo*, 5 October 1940, 4.

56. *Daily Worker* articles: "Peter V. Cacchione Dies," 7 November 1947, 1; "He Was the People's Councilman," 7 November 1947, 4; "Notables to Attend Cacchione Rites," 9 November 1947, 3; "12,000 Bid Farewell to Peter V. Cacchione" 10 November 1947, 3. See also, Simon Gerson, *Pete: The Story of Peter Cacchione, New York's First Communist Councilman* (New York: International Press, 1976).

57. Gerald Meyer, "The American Labor Party and New York City's Italian-American Communities: 1936–1950," in *Industry, Technology, Labor, and the Italian American Communities*, ed. Mario Aste et al. (New York: American Italian Historical Association, 1997), 38.

58. Paul Buhle, *A Dreamer's Paradise Lost: Louis Fraina/Lewis Corey (1892–1953) and the Decline of Radicalism in the United States* (New Jersey: Humanities Press, 1995), 1–2, 65–77, 93, 95–96, 104, 175–77.

59. Dan Georgakas, "Fasanella, Ralph," in *The Encyclopedia of the American Left* (New York: Garland, 1990). Fraser Ottanelli, who is currently researching Italian American anti-Fascist volunteers in the Spanish Civil War, has identified almost three hundred Italian Americans who fought in Spain—some in the Lincoln Brigade, others in the Garibaldi Brigade. Ottanelli, telephone interview by author, 1 September 1998.

60. Marzani, *Reluctant Radical*, 3:47–50; 4:22, 26, 30, 34–36, 62. In his memoirs, he relates an example of his troubleshooting activities while serving as a Party leader. A branch organizer, Maria, an Italian member who was the leader of the Workers Alliance, demanded that Marzani expel Paolo, another member, because he had collected one dollar from each member so that he could buy a new suit, which he insisted would help him get results from social workers at the relief center on behalf of the unemployed (4:35).

61. Marzani, *Reluctant Radical*, Book Four, 208, 254, 258–59, 261. In his autobiography, he describes the Lower East Side of this period as a community where "New Deal Democrats were the right wing of the political spectrum, and Republicans . . . an endangered species." It was also a place where the Party—working through the ALP, the National Negro Congress, the International Workers Order, and many other organizations—attained great influence. Marzani described the Party in this community as a "humane, democratic force. . . . We eased suffering, nourished hope, and organized our neighbors to defend their rights and needs. . . . Ninety percent of Communist activities dealt with the people's daily needs and daily problems. . . . It took janitors and educated them to the level of professors. . . . If you saw a truck driver reading the *New York Times,* you were probably looking at a Communist."

62. Gary Crowdus and Lenny Rubinstein, "Union Films: An Interview with Carl Marzani," *Cineaste* (spring 1978): 34. *We Can Be Friends* was published in New York by Topical Books Publishers, 1952. *The Survivor* and *The Open Marxism of Antonio Gramsci* were published in New York by Cameron Associates. Prior to this, the only other notice of Gramsci appeared in *Science & Society*, which in 1949 published a translation by Lewis Marks of Gramsci's writings on Benedetto Croce and in 1949 and 1952 published reviews by Henry Mins of volumes of his *Prison Notebooks*. Also in 1953, Eric Bently enthusiastically commented on Gramsci's early theater criticism in *The New Republic* (October 5, 1953). See John Cammett, "Antonio Gramsci (1819–1937) and the American Left," in Marzani, *Reluctant Radical*, 3:271–75.

63. Ilene Philipson, *Ethel Rosenberg: Beyond the Myths* (New Brunswick, N.J.: Rutgers University Press, 1993), 124.

64. Nadia Venturini, "African American Riots during World War II: Reactions in the Italian-American Communist Press" (paper presented at the American Italian Historical Association Conference, Cleveland, Ohio, 15 November 1997).

65. William Beyer, "Creating *Common Ground* on the Home Front: Race, Class, and Ethnicity in a 1940s Quarterly Magazine," in *The Home-Front War: World War II and American Society*, ed. Kenneth O'Brian and Lynn Parsons Hudson (Westport, Conn.: Greenwood Press, 1995), 64–65.

66. Bayor, *Neighbors in Conflict*, 10–11.

67. *The Fur and Leather Worker* (November 1944): 5. This union's secretary-treasurer was Pietro Lucchi; other Communist-led unions also had Italian American leadership. The extent of this phenomenon, however, requires additional research.

68. Vito Magli, "L'Unità del Popolo," *Fraternal Outlook* (August–September 1944), 21.

69. Caute, *The Great Fear*, 169–72.

70. Caute, *The Great Fear*, 239, 588 n; Smith, *Torch of Liberty*, 353–54.

71. Roger Keeran, "National Groups and the Popular Front: The Case of the International Workers Order," *Journal of American Ethnic History* (spring 1995): 23–51; Arthur Sabin, *Red Scare in Court: New York versus the International Workers Order* (Philadelphia: University of Pennsylvania Press, 1993).

72. Meyer, "The American Labor Party," in *The Encyclopedia of Third Parties in America*, Vol. III, ed., Immanuel Ness and John Ciment (Armonk, N.Y.: M. E. Sharpe, 2000), 682–90.

Chapter 10

Father James E. Groppi (1930–1985): The Militant Humility of a Civil Rights Activist

Jackie DiSalvo

Few of the demonstrations I have joined in my life are more memorable than the tense march into the white sector of Milwaukee led by Father James Groppi and his contingent of African American youth, rhythmically chanting to bolster our spirits, "Sock it to me Black Power, Oooh Ahh! Sock it to me Black Power, Oooh Ahh!" The extraordinary relationship between this passionate white priest and his mostly young black followers inspired in him a radical form of Christianity, a lifelong commitment to struggles for justice, and a kind of leadership in the Civil Rights movement unique among white activists.

Despite his great notice in the press at the time, Groppi has not been the focus of any larger study. His activities have been most extensively treated in journalist Frank Aukofer's *City with a Chance*, a study of Milwaukee in the 1960s. Otherwise, he is mentioned mainly in Wisconsin history, in treatments of the Catholic social-justice tradition, or in memoirs. Yet, the editors of the Associated Press newspapers, radio, and television station member affiliates selected him the most important religious figure in the news in 1967. I have also heard personal testimony from radicals from the Midwest who were inspired by his example. Although he is an extraordinary figure—a conjuncture of 1960s activism, radical Catholicism, and an Italian American sensibility—he has mostly been overlooked until now in Italian American studies, receiving no mention at all, for example, in Jerre Mangione and Ben Morreale's *La Storia*. For this essay I have been able to consult not only the newspapers and Groppi's collected papers, but also people who knew him in Milwaukee.[1] My understanding is also informed by our somewhat parallel experiences and overlapping networks in the 1960s in the Catholic reform movement inspired by Pope John XXIII, in radical Catholic circles in the Midwest, and in the Civil Rights movement, both in the South and in Wisconsin, where Groppi was in the daily press and we activists all felt his influence.

Youth council, NAACP

His activism began in 1965, when he joined clergy mobilized in Selma, Alabama, by Martin Luther King's militant, prophetic Christianity.[2] He returned to Milwaukee in October 1965, all fired up to participate in the battle against school segregation led by the Milwaukee United School Integration Committee (MUSIC). At that time, while a new segregated school was being built in the ghetto, black children were being bused from overcrowded inner-city schools to all-white schools, where they were segregated in classes, recreation, and even at lunch. Joining a human chain to block school buses, Groppi began his political history of militant direct action and civil disobedience. These actions, which then Mayor Henry Maier branded "Ku Klux Klanism in reverse," led to his being repeatedly arrested. MUSIC eventually succeeded in getting a federal court order to desegregate the schools, but only after Groppi led a massive boycott in which as many as 10 percent of the city's 122,000 students participated. Most stayed home, but some attended alternate freedom schools he helped to organize and taught in, until ordered by the bishop to desist. Later, he would not always obey.[3]

Father Groppi was then assistant pastor at St. Boniface, a black inner-city Catholic church, which he made the headquarters of Milwaukee's Civil Rights struggle. As adviser to the National Association for the Advancement of Colored People's (NAACP's) multiracial Youth Council, his slogan was "Agitate, agitate, agitate!"[4] To do so, he organized the controversial Commandos, a cadre of young black men who served as his personal bodyguard and security guard for demonstrators. Uniformed in black sweatshirts and black berets (they could not afford jackets, let alone the leather ones that would later identify the Black Panthers) and marching in militant formation, completely independent of any establishment liaisons, the Commandos evoked furious resentment among whites, who branded them dangerous thugs and projected upon them white fears of violent black revenge. Groppi set up Freedom House as a headquarters and home for the Commandos, and for a time not only worked but ate and lived with them as well. For the next few years, they would give the segregationist establishment of Milwaukee no respite. In retrospect, the highly disciplined group has been acknowledged as peacemakers who channeled into constructive political action the black rage that was to burn down other American cities.[5] Consequently, when much of the nation exploded in riots after King's assassination, Milwaukee did not erupt, but witnessed an integrated memorial march of fifteen thousand people.

The Youth Council's first campaign targeted public officials who belonged to the segregated club of the Fraternal Order of Eagles. In August 1966, while picketing the suburban Wauwawtosa home of liberal judge Robert C. Cannon, they chanted: "Get off the bench or get out of the club."[6] For 11 days, the nightly protests drew more and more violent counterdemonstrators, hurling racial slurs, along with bottles, bricks, and firecrackers, until 500 National Guard members had to be brought in to protect the Youth Council demonstrators.[7]

It was, however, their open-housing campaign in 1967 that would bring Groppi national prominence. Thwarted by racist violence, Martin Luther King himself had failed to desegregate housing in nearby Cicero, Illinois. Groppi was determined, however, to break through such resistance. Led by Groppi and sur-rounded by the Commandos, African American youth and civil rights activists of all races and ages marched from the North Side ghetto across the 16th Street Bridge, which marked Milwaukee's racial divide into the segregated South Side where Groppi himself had grown up in a nearby neighborhood.[8]

The second night, marchers faced a jeering mob of nearly two thousand white segregationists brandishing Confederate flags and an effigy of Groppi, painted with swastikas and swinging from a rope and a coffin lettered "God is White" and "Father Groppi Rest in Hell."[9] Groppi describes how the 250 mostly young pro-testers walked bravely through a crowd that rained on them rocks, bottles, obscenities, and racial epithets:

The crowd [was] like a football game being let out. . . . It started to corner us and a few of the Youth Council members broke down and began to cry. . . . We got to the park. . . . I told everybody to sit down[.] I wanted to talk to them because I didn't know whether we were going to make it back or not. . . . When they all sat down, someone threw a bomb . . . that landed right next to a white girl from the south side. . . . It burned her quite severely. . . . I said . . . when we sing "We Shall Overcome," we sing "We are not afraid, black and white together," Black and white are out here and we are not afraid. . . . Why? God is on our side. . . . Are you afraid to die? No. . . . I said, "Alright, let's march." . . . So we got in the road and we marched back . . . and the bottles and bricks began to fly again. . . . We got to Freedom House on the northside. . . . about twenty miles away. . . . a little ruckus occurred and the police. . . . threw tear gas in our Freedom House and shot their rifles off in the air and scattered us. . . . This tear gas bomb in that old house got so hot it started the house on fire. . . . The policemen held the fire truck back. . . . they let the house burn.[10]

Yet, despite curfews, arrests, and a crescendo of attacks on Groppi—who waged a war of words and wills with then mayor Henry Maier—for 200 nights the Youth Council never did back down, and eventually they succeeded in pressuring the city council to pass an open-housing ordinance. Fifteen Wisconsin suburbs would eventually follow suit.[11]

Groppi's militancy would lead to more than a dozen arrests (two of which were appealed all the way to the Supreme Court) for breaking curfews, disorderly con-duct, obstructing police, resisting arrest, and so forth. He was subject to constant threats and continual surveillance, even by army intelligence. He told the Kerner Commission on Civil Disorders of one three-month period in which he was followed every night by detectives from the police department, even into restaurants, where they watched him eat. Threats on his life and in 1966 the bombing of another NAACP office caused him to post armed guards around Freedom House.[12] A suspicious fire destroyed the station wagon in which, according to journalist Frank Aukofer, he could constantly be seen "ferrying his allies, ready to go, to race to a picket, to a demonstration . . . to picket or sit in, to be arrested or do whatever seemed necessary, even when cooler heads cautioned restraint and planning."[13]

Aukofer wrote that he "combined in one personality the extremes of the two most fundamental human passions: love and hate. He loved the oppressed of society—the black poor. . . . He hated racism and injustice with a rage that was all-consuming. . . . He also had the revolutionary leader's instinctive feel for what would provoke responses from those who followed him as if he were a pied piper and those who would have hanged him from the nearest tree."[14] At one time, he was both the most hated and the most loved man in Milwaukee, around whom the city was completely polarized. His activities were debated daily in let-ters to the editor, in which he was alternately compared to Christ before Pilate or denounced as a traitor to Christianity and the priesthood. At a tribute to Groppi in August 1967, attended by almost one thousand mostly white supporters, the Reverend Lucius Walker, an African American activist, would say: "It isn't often you see a saint in the flesh, and I literally consider Jim one of the saints of the church."[15] Meanwhile, conservative Catholics in white parishes boycotted the offerings plate and cancelled subscriptions to the Archdiocesan newspaper as part of an unsuccessful campaign to pressure Archbishop Cousins to ban Groppi's activities. They demanded he "be defrocked," "have his collar torn off," and "be sent back to Africa." A "Milwaukee Citizen's Committee for Closed Housing" formed around Father Russell Witon, who fumed, "We are not going to let those savages—those black beasts—take our rights away."[16] One of the largest files in the Groppi archives is labeled "Hate Mail." Even after his death, his enemies were still clamoring to deny him a church burial.[17]

But as Aukofer has noted, "His bond with the children was surreal . . . a bois-terous and cheerful group, honed by life in the black ghetto, seemingly immune to most authority figures." Aukofer recounts an incident when police threatened to arrest youthful picketers, who were whooping it up particularly noisily, for dis-turbing the peace. They offered Groppi a microphone, and he simply raised his hand and said, "'This is Father Groppi. Can you hear me?' In seconds, the street was so quiet you could hear whispers from across the street."[18] At mass after com-munion, Groppi would gather the children around the altar for informal ser-mons, described by his pastor, as follows:

He asked "Did you know that black is beautiful?" Their faces looked like question marks. . . . "God loves differences," he said. "Look at the animals; they're all different. The flowers are all different, and they are all beautiful. God makes beautiful things. Look at human beings. . . . They are all so different. Some are big, some are fat, some are tall, some are not. . . . Wouldn't it be monotonous if everything God made was the same? . . . He didn't do that. He made you and he made me, and he made us in His likeness and His beauty. That's why I said black is beautiful. You are black and you are beautiful." . . . I saw their faces light up and their eyes shine. . . . They were excited . . . and they felt good about themselves. They were different people with a new self-image.[19]

Aukofer continues, "had they been asked, they probably would have walked into gunfire with Groppi, arms linked and laughing with youthful excitement. But, the relationship was affectionate, playful and often irreverent. They never treated him as a cult figure. But they responded with astounding courage and discipline."[20]

He had formed his Commandos from a group of tough ghetto youths, some with police records, others scarred by a life of neglect. Their participation in this organization gave them a sense of unity, pride, importance, and accomplishment. Many remained his friends until he died. Paul Crawford recalled how it changed their lives: "At that time people called us thugs and crooks. But that's not what was going on at all. We felt a part of something and responsible." He said Groppi had given him self-esteem and hope for better things in life. Another former Commando told Nancy Cooney, "We would have died for him."[21] The strength of those bonds, based on the totality of Groppi's commitment, created the anomaly of a white leader in a black movement. Although the Youth Council advocated Black Power and frequently spouted antiwhite rhetoric, they remained committed to integration and welcomed white supporters. When black nationalists at a Methodist social action conference in Washington, D.C., in 1967 urged the Commandos to repudiate Groppi's leadership, they stood by him and their integrationist agenda.[22]

Groppi's relationship as a white man to a black constituency was indeed extraordinary, in both the intensity of his immersion and the strength of their loyalty to him. He never spoke of blacks as "you" or "them" but always "we" or "us." Among all the obscenities flung at him by the bigots, the epithet "white nigger" was one he considered a great compliment, for although he insisted no white person could ever fully do so, he strove to see the world from an African American point of view.[23] "In this struggle," he said, "I believe there are white men who are black and there are black middle class men who are white. I think I'm black."[24] When rioting broke out in Milwaukee's black community in July 1967, he refused to either condemn or try to defuse the disorders, but sat in St. Boniface rectory and read a book as he said he would, insisting that oppression made violence inevitable.[25] Unlike many white liberals, he never seemed to look over his shoulder to court the approval of the respectable and powerful or to present himself as a mediator between them and his grassroots followers. More threateningly, he was an enthusiastic participant in their spontaneous militancy, dedicated to creating in his Youth Council an independent, self-determining cadre of young working-class black leaders whose moral legitimacy he defended to the wider community.

Some of the greatest animosity toward Groppi arose as his cause broadened from racial justice to economic justice. On September 29, 1969, after his 83-mile march to Madison, about one thousand protesters took over the Assembly chambers for eleven hours to oppose welfare cuts by the Republican legislature. His rhetoric showed a growing class consciousness as he charged the legislators with placing the tax breaks of the rich over the needs of the poor and defended marches and civil disobedience as the only form of lobbying available to the dispossessed. Amid charges of anarchy, thievery, and disorder, the Senate hastily adjourned and called in the National Guard.[26] I remember it as a moment of utopian exaltation, in which Students for a Democratic Society activists, black militants, and black and white welfare mothers imagined for a few hours what it might be like to have a government of, by, and for the people. The significance of an interracial group of poor people taking over the Capitol was not lost on the legislators, who jailed Groppi for 10 days without bail for contempt of the Legislature under a hitherto-never-used 1848 statute, an action that would be eventually declared illegal by the U.S. Supreme Court. Like Martin Luther King, Jr., he was moving toward a perception that the fundamental problem was economic. After King's assassination, Groppi had become a passionate organizer for his Poor People's Campaign, giving speeches around the Midwest to drum up support and taking the Youth Council to Resurrection City in Washington, D.C.

His political commitments continued to broaden. He met with Bernadette Devlin in northern Ireland and was arrested for demonstrating against the Vietnam War. He picketed with striking clerical workers at Yale, and supported local laundry workers. He even toyed with the idea of forming a union of priests. In June 1975, with Marlon Brando, he joined an occupation of a vacant Alexian Brothers seminary in Shawano County, Wisconsin, by armed Indian activists of the Menominee Warrior Society to help negotiate a settlement. He lost his integral relationship to the community, however, when he passed on leadership of the Youth Council to African Americans and, hoping to be replaced by a black priest, was transferred from St. Boniface to St. Michael's, a predominantly white parish. Frustrated in his desire for a black parish of his own, after a few years he withdrew from parish work entirely to seek new ways to serve. He studied at Antioch Law School in Washington, D.C., in 1972, and then directed a program for Volunteers in Service to America (VISTA) in Racine, Wisconsin. In 1973, he drove a cab, but quit, he said, because he did not like competing with other workers for money.[27] Then in 1976, he was forced out of the priesthood altogether when he married Margaret (Peggy) Rozga, former church secretary at St. Boniface, a college English teacher and fellow activist for many years. He considered becoming an Episcopal priest and spent 1978 at the Virginia Theological Seminary, but his loyalties to his city and church were too visceral. Although his head might have been closer to Canterbury, his heart, he said, was still with Rome; he could not make the change. According to his friend Don Richards, another former priest, Groppi never ceased to think of himself as a priest. He would always miss parish work, wishing for a reconciliation with the Church which could not be, and up until their last conversation before he died was protesting the injustice and the waste of the Church's rejection of married priests.[28]

Nevertheless, he had three children to support and in 1979 finally settled down as a Milwaukee bus driver. Always modest in his personal ambitions, he seemed to revel in the human contact afforded by his new proletarian role, which allowed him to still be out in the streets, extending his empathy and compassion to whomever needed it. He commented that: "In a lot of ways I think of the bus as being my church. I miss the opportunity for preaching, teaching, and counseling but this job gives me chances to carry out my ministry in some smaller ways."[29] His instinctual solidarity ensured, however, that his leadership would be sought again, and in 1983 he was elected president of the Amalgamated Transit Union, where he fought against a two-tier wage system. His successor, Bruce Colburn, would later say, "A lot of members became involved in the union out of seeing his commitment to it and to people in society in general. He had a strong sense of the dignity of workers and their right to be represented."[30]

Looking back at this extraordinary political career, one wonders what inspired it and whether Father Groppi's Italian American heritage played any role in his developing into an activist priest. He was born in 1930, the ninth of 10 children, into the family of Giocondo and Georgina Groppi. His father, an immigrant from Lucca, near Florence, owned a small grocery store in the southern Italian community of Bayview on Milwaukee's South Side. The children all worked in the store and still run it today. In an unpublished autobiography begun but never completed, Father Groppi recalled growing up as an oppressed minority. In the 1920s, Italians, unwelcomed by the Irish pastor at Immaculate Conception Church, had to worship in a shoemaker's shop across the street with an Italian priest they brought in from Our Lady of Pompeii, an Italian church across town, where the Groppis had taken their children to be baptized. Groppi would attend the Catholic school that had once barred Italians and would be stung by the "humorous contempt" evoked by his father's broken English. "Some of us suffered from outright self-hatred," he wrote, and "were apologetic for our Italian characteristics; some Southern Italians . . . became extremely touchy about their dark complexions." He added, "I attribute to my mother and father the best course that I have ever taken in inter-group relations. My father had a deep sense of the dignity of man. Wherever my father was . . . if he was in the *bocce* alley, and someone used a term like 'Pollack' or 'Nigger' he would voice his disapproval. I remember him doing this a number of times in the grocery store. 'That is like calling an Italian a 'Dago,' he would say."

Groppi embraced his Italian identity: "Even today I feel a little kinship when I meet a man with an Italian name," he wrote, "It brings me back to my days as a kid in the streets. It reminds me of the *bocce* alleys, the mandolins and accordions, the Garibaldi picnics, the crap games and the unlawful swimming off the docks."[31] He remarked that he learned civil disobedience delivering grapes to basement wineries in violation of the Prohibition laws. However, while he acknowledged the influence of his own experience as a minority, saying, "I came from an Italian ghetto. I am committed to working in a Negro ghetto," he did not like to make too much of the analogy.[32] When his father arrived in Milwaukee around 1913, Father Groppi said, "The Italian was in pretty bad shape. But nothing as far as the black man is concerned. . . . An Italian is white, and that's everything. . . . Some of the worst bigots in this country are Italians who had gone through terrible suffering in the past."[33] When he led open-housing marches just a few blocks from his father's store, some of his old Italian buddies threw rocks and shouted racist remarks, although some, he was glad to see, defended him courageously.

Groppi himself traces his empathy with the black poor to the summers he spent as a seminarian working at Blessed Martin's Youth Center, an inner-city day camp, where he formed strong bonds with these ghetto youth, visiting their families in the housing projects. Much of his revulsion against racism is expressed in stories about the humiliation of children at the playgrounds:

I remember one of the first evenings that our teen-age girls were playing softball in a white neighborhood. . . . One of the girls had some special leadership ability. . . . She was one of those beautifully sensitive persons who was constantly looking out for others. She loved the white kids and the Black kids on that playground that night, and she wanted to be loved. . . . Then, some white male teenager, who had most likely been taught to hate by some sick parents, walked past Loretta and called her "nigger." It hurt her very badly. . . . She lost her smile, her enthusiasm and just sighed, "Oh, Father Jim."

"I saw the social suffering and ostracism," he said. "I suffered with them, and I have never stopped suffering." When he returned to seminary he smarted at the racism expressed by his fellow seminarians, "I nearly threw away my collar in disgust. Every time I heard a racist remark, a Black child's face came to mind."[34] At St. Boniface, he gave the children black and brown paint and told them to change all the white plaster statues of saints and Christ to something they could identify with.[35] One can wonder what part his own childhood might have played in his becoming one of the rare Italian priests, or in his identifying so passionately with blacks as he led them into those bitter confrontations with bigotry in the mostly Polish neighborhoods of the South Side where he grew up in an Italian enclave in an Irish enclave.

If the style of Groppi's activism bears a distinctly Italian American character—passionate, gregarious, working class—the sources of his radicalization must be traced to the conjuncture of the 1960s protest movements with the Risorgimento, the "renewal" launched by Pope John XXIII that was turning Roman Catholicism upside down. The religion in which we both had been educated had sought to barricade us in a Catholic ghetto from the heresies and temptations of modernism with its Index of Forbidden Books, its total priestly authority, the absolute truths of its catechism and its panoply of rituals—the Latin masses, rosaries, novenas, and so forth—through which we would earn good time in purgatory. John XXIII blew the trumpet on this insular counter-Reformation religion with all its comfortable insignias of belonging when, in his two encyclicals, *Mater et Magistra* (Mother and Teacher) and *Pacem in Terris* (Peace on Earth), he called on the Church to end its war on humanism and become its main proponent. The Catholic ideal would no longer be characterized by its purity from the world but by its vocation to bring about peace and justice within it.

The Civil Rights movement's call for white support in biblical language directed especially at religious groups provided an exemplary arena for U.S. Catholics, liberated and commissioned by the Second Vatican Council, to unveil their new faith, and, like Jim Groppi, they headed South. This involved a radical ideological conversion. For, before the meeting of Marxist insurgents and Chris-

link btw CR movement, white society & religious groups

tians in Latin America had given birth to Liberation Theology, the African American redefinition of Christianity as a freedom movement had offered Catholic activists an alternative to the medievalisms we had been forced to memorize by the nuns. More of an activist than either a theologian, a political theorist, or a writer, Groppi would rouse the movement with angry sermons based on a radical biblical rhetoric, attacking government and Church officials as Pharisees who preached pie in the sky to the oppressed and arguing in contrast:

The Gospels celebrate the good news of Christ's concern for suffering humanity. He fed the hungry—the story of the loaves and fishes. . . . Instead of spreading this good word, we have reduced it to a list of do's and don'ts. . . . The Church has narrowly confined itself to the supernatural realm and closed its eyes to the needs of suffering humanity. The Christian . . . is to go to Church on Sunday and conform to Church legalisms.[36]

The trappings and rituals of his Church had no appeal for him, but he responded to the liturgical reform movement, which sought to redefine the Mass as a participatory experience for laity that would encompass, rather than substitute for, their secular activities.[37] Although undoubtedly influenced by such trends, Groppi, who drew his own theological insights mostly from experience, typically went beyond them in envisioning the Mass as a ritual of solidarity:

We can offer Mass with emphasis on this being the source of strength for us to go out into the community and to feed the poor, clothe the naked, to get involved in social action. . . . We talk about the sufferings of black people and the injustices of society, the meaning behind black spirituals. . . . When we start praying for individuals who have been arrested or have been beaten by the police, they listen and the Mass suddenly has meaning for them.[38]

The Jesus whose example he followed into the streets was above all a militant rebel: "Christ was not a peaceful, meek type of individual. This was a radical man when he picked up a whip and drove the money changers from the temple," said Groppi.[39]

Unlike much of the 1960s white Left, segregated in university towns and counterculture ghettos, Groppi, as a Catholic parish priest, staged his blunt confrontation within the most mainstream of communities. Part of the intense public hatred directed at him reflected the threat he represented to one of the bastions of conservatives who feared and resented any radical appropriation of the tremendous outreach, resources, and legitimizing function of a mass institution like the Church, which for years had managed to elicit polite submission from its poor and working-class constituencies. Thus, a group of "Catholic Laymen" would write to the archbishop, "It is regrettable that Catholic clergy should encourage contempt for the law by urging children . . . to aid and abet this school boycott. . . . Children should be taught discipline in accord with the fourth commandment. Rebellion is a primary tenet of communism."[40] Groppi had no tolerance for either such authoritarianism or for Puritan moralism and blasted the Church for conveniently exonerating poverty by condemning the ethics of the poor with the story of an unmarried woman with five children living in terrible destitution:

> She came from Mississippi . . . never learned how to read and write because the white man in the South told her that she had no time for that. All her life she had been called a nigger. Early in life she had been taught that her proper function in life was to pick the White man's cotton and satisfy his lust. So she came to Milwaukee looking for a better life. . . . She and her children knew what it was like to be hungry, what it was to live with the presence of rats. . . . She could not get any welfare money because she was not in Milwaukee for a year. . . . Finally, she found a job, picking chicken feathers for less than fifty cents an hour. But she got tired of begging to supplement her inadequate wages in order to feed her children. . . . She became a so-called prostitute. . . . The tragedy is not her prostitution but the judgment of White Christians who call her an adulteress. This reminds me of one of the Gospel incidents: the weeping woman crouching at the feet of Jesus. . . . Listen to his words, "Let him who is without sin among you cast the first stone." How many White Christians have had the audacity to throw the first stone?[41]

In contrast, arguing that "Christ preferred the morality of the poor," Groppi found sanctity in the maligned young men, whom he often had to rescue from the law, living together at Freedom House. He insisted, "I see a kind of Christianity there that is unbelievable. One of the guys has a pack of cigarettes. . . . It's everybody's pack. A guy has two bits. It's everybody's two bits."[42]

While I have uncovered no direct links between Groppi and earlier immigrant radicalism, he replicates the language of the kind of popular Christian socialist tradition studied by Anthony Mansueto in ways that suggest, at least, some common cultural matrix. He describes, for example, in the immigrant lay confraternities that served as mutual-aid societies "a radical laicization of the liturgy and a transposition of the symbolic solidarity of the Eucharist into a real solidarity among friends, a solidarity mobilized on a day to day basis . . . in the community's struggle for survival" which "could not help but begin to take on political functions." Likewise, Groppi adopts an image of Jesus similar to the Gesù Socialista who appeared in radical interpretations of the Gospels, which appeared in *La Parola del Populo*, the newspaper of the Italian Socialist Federation.[43] Thus, he would state, "[Jesus] didn't say that he came to bring peace to the earth—that's part of the white lie—but rather to cast a sword upon the earth. You must be revolutionaries. Christ was a revolutionary. That's why he ended up on a cross."[44] Groppi seems not to have inherited, but rediscovered, the radical Bible of a popular Christianity that had inspired insurgents from the peasant revolts of the fifteenth century to the Sandinistas in the twentieth, inventing his own version of their Christian-based communities.

It also seems to me that one of the ideological and psychological resources that infused his radical Christianity was a kind of solidarity rooted in an Italian American sense of family and community. Jim Groppi began his life in a large,

Italian family whose interdependence was probably reinforced by their daily cooperation in the family store, and it is not surprising that he finally sacrificed his passionately committed ministry for what appears to have been a deeply bonded marriage and a devotion to fatherhood.

Scholars of Italian American urban culture have noted that the intense family emphasis did not always tend to apolitical exclusiveness but could extend into communal bonds and wider political identifications. Robert Orsi describes how in East Harlem "the lines between neighborhood and domus were not sharply defined": life was lived in public, spilling out onto the stoops and streets in an intense neighborhood intimacy.[45] The boundaries between family and community life would have been very fluid in the grocery store where Groppi's large family mingled with their neighbors and, during the Depression, was intimately involved with their day-to-day survival. Groppi had little of the middle-class Anglo-Saxon instinct for protecting his private life; he was in his element in the streets, surrounded by people, especially children. Serving in his parish almost literally as a surrogate "Father" would only intensify the merger of family and community he had learned in the Groppi grocery store. Those informal conversations with children around the altar brought the Mass as close as one might imagine to an intimate family dinner, and his favorite metaphor for both Christianity and politics was the injunction to feed the hungry. He once envisioned the church tearing out the pews to literally replace them with beds and tables to house the tired and feed the needy. When he left parish work, he tried to set up the St. Joseph's Young Christian Worker Center as a storefront church of action in the streets, but his dream was frustrated when the city denied him a permit.[46] His embrace of the children was always gently paternal, and for a time he lived with the Commandos. One of them, Richard Green, remarked, "There was always a close, family kind of feeling between us. He'll always be the father to us." Groppi adopted the movement as a surrogate family: "as we were marching and singing together, we were growing in our relationship as brothers. White people and Black people. . . . And the more we grow in brotherhood, the more we grow in the Spirit, for brotherhood and life in the Spirit . . . are inseparable."[47]

Thus, Groppi consciously transmuted familial values into political rhetoric in a way that commentators have found in other Italians, such as Leonard Covello ("Let us strive to live on a family basis with all our neighbors") or more recently in Mario Cuomo's social democratic communitarian rhetoric: "We believe in a single fundamental idea that describes . . . what a proper government should be. The idea of a family. Mutuality. The sharing of benefits and burdens for the good of all. . . . We believe that we should be the family of America, recognizing that at the heart of the matter we are bound to one another."[48] Groppi said, "I believe that all sin is social. Most basically it is separating oneself from the family of men." As a denial of the unity of the human family, racism was the greatest sin and heresy, which he came to feel as a family wound. "A family reunion," he preached, "is essential, for herein lies our salvation." This was the gospel he both lived and taught with the children gathered around his altar, where he asked one day, "What did Dick Gregory mean when he went down to jail and the police officer asked, 'You got any brothers or sisters?' And he replied, 'You take all the people in the world and subtract myself, they're all my brothers and sisters.' What'd he mean by that?" They repeated, "Everybody in the world is his brother and sister!" And Groppi added, "All right so that's what we talk about and that's what we sing about."[49] Christianity was simply the practice of fraternity and the extension of its bonds to the ostracized.

Finally, Groppi's priestly position as well as his working-class identifications enabled him to exert an organic form of leadership rising directly from the ardor of his involvement with the community in which he found himself. Seeing them as his family, their needs became his own. Although he was a central figure in Milwaukee politics at one time, he never became a politician or even a major figure on a wider national stage. In an era of self-promoting leaders sucked into the "celebrityitis" of the media circus, he did little to seek the fame that came to him and nothing to capitalize on it. He seemed utterly unself-conscious about his role. He never formed any organization strictly his own but served in a local NAACP group, through which he was unlikely to ever achieve broader power; he never sought to put his patent on anything he said or did or to market himself in his notoriety. He seemed to have no personal goals beyond those of his community but happily allowed it to define his identity. Immersing himself in its struggle, he lent his voice to urging on its action in ephemeral impromptu speeches that had a powerful effect on fellow activists but found little record beyond a few echoes in the newspapers.

One observer, Brother Leo Ryan, once described his stance as "militant humility," a quality that identifies him with a pattern that has characterized other Italian American activists, such as Mario Savio who, after having been synonymous with the revival of student radicalism in the Free Speech movement at the University of California, Berkeley, fell back into anonymity.[50] Like Savio, moreover, Groppi never abandoned his commitments, but remained content to quietly work in the vineyards. But, when his new community of local bus drivers called forth his natural feelings of solidarity, they would compel him to take up leadership once more. It seems somehow appropriate that Groppi, the working-class Christian collectivist, should in the end find his place at the head of such an interracial association of workers. We can only speculate on where this role might have led him in the new phase of struggle faced by trade unionism in America today or how he might have contributed to the crucial task of linking it to the struggle of the black community.

But as with Martin Luther King's dream of transforming the civil rights struggle into a class-based movement of working and poor people, it was not to be. Jim Groppi developed cancer, and after a painful year was to die of a brain tumor in 1985. His death, as his life, testified to a life lived in community. Even after he was defrocked, Groppi had continued to practice his radical communalist Catholicism, celebrating unofficial masses, weddings, and baptisms with a close network of friends and supporters in Milwaukee's "underground church." The depth of this solidarity is movingly exemplified in their mobilization to personally provide round-the-clock care for him, so he could spend the last, difficult days of his illness at home with his beloved wife and family.[51]

Now he has also gained a permanent place in the memory of a wider community, as the City of Milwaukee finally resolved, in honoring him, to honor its finest history and its best hope for itself. In 1988, after much community pressure and debate, the 16th Street Bridge, where he led civil rights marchers across the racial divide, was officially renamed the James Groppi Unity Bridge. Today, there is a bridge to the twenty-first century one might be willing to cross! Groppi may not be just an icon of a lost era of radicalism, however, but something more prophetic: something seen in the new generation of "wiggers," self-proclaimed "white niggers" among alienated white youth identifying, as he did, with rebellious black culture; something in his marriage of the Left's vision of material improvement, the 1960s utopian imagination, and the poetic and psychological resonance and communal celebration found in religion; something in his fusion of an embracing Italian sensibility with African American militancy, foreshadowing perhaps the possibility of a revolutionary culture of greater depth and wholeness, warmth and passion, intimacy and solidarity than we have yet seen— but maybe could see if and when the people start making history again.

NOTES

1. Frank A. Aukofer, *City with a Chance* (Milwaukee: Bruce, 1968). The best chronicle of James Groppi's activities is a summary of news articles, principally from the *Milwaukee Journal* (*MJ*) and the *Milwaukee Sentinel* (*MS*) from June 9, 1965, to April 20, 1976, compiled by college students in the Milwaukee Urban Semester Program (MUSP) of the Open Door Foundation, fall 1985, and available in the Milwaukee Public Library. I cite publication dates of articles. Important articles reviewing Groppi's activities appeared in the *New York Times* (*NYT*) July 25, 1971; *MJ*, November 17, 1968, October 24, 1969; July 12, December 13, 1970; and April 25, 1976. The struggles against segregation in the schools and the Eagle Club are described by Eugene F. Bleidorn, his pastor at St. Boniface Roman Catholic Church, 1965–1967, in his self-published autobiography, *In My Time* (Milwaukee, 1994). There is a short chapter on Groppi in *Wisconsin Heroes* by Marv Balousek (Wisconsin: Waubesa Press, 1995) and a brief discussion in *Parish Boundaries: The Catholic Encounter with Race in the Twentieth Century Urban North*, by John T. McGreevy (Chicago: University of Chicago Press, 1996). A play about Groppi, *Judgement of a Priest*, by Louis Miller, was performed in Milwaukee in the late 1960s. Groppi's papers have been preserved in the Milwaukee Urban Archives at the University of Milwaukee Library. I also benefited from conversations with Nancy Hennessy Cooney. Cooney was a friend of Groppi and his wife, Peggy, and had participated in his civil rights activities.

2. *MJ*, 9 June 1965; Aukofer, *City*, 60–61. His return to the South in 1966 is described in Thomas Blackburn, "Mississippi Heat," in *Big Book of Italian American Culture*, ed. Lawrence De Stasi (New York: Harper, 1989).

3. Quoted in Aukofer, *City*, 68; see also pp. 50–79; Bleidorn, *In My Time*, 65–78; *MS*, 19 October 1965, 29. Acting Bishop Atkielksi issued the order when Archbishop Cousins was out of town. Catholic opinion on Groppi remained polarized, but Cousins resisted

pressures to censure him in 1967 and was supported by the Priests' Senate in a 21 to 28 vote. MS, 16 September 1967.

4. *NYT*, 4 November 1985.

5. McGreevy, *Parish Boundaries*, 200–1; *MJ*, 4, 5 November 1985, December 1987.

6. Balousek, *Wisconsin Heroes*, chapter excerpted as "James Groppi: Radical Priest and Unpopular Hero," *Wisconsin State Journal (WSJ)*, 18 January 1996, 1C.

7. Aukofer, *City*, 97–104; Bleidorn, *In My Time*, 81–85; *MJ*, 29 August, 28 September 1966.

8. Aukofer, *City*, 105–36; Bleidorn, *In My Time*, 91–102; Balousek, *Wisconsin Heroes*, 1C; *MS*, 29 August 1967, 4, 11, 20, 29 September, 6, 31 October, 30 November; *MJ*, 16, 21 September, 7 October, 30 November, 13 December 1967.

9. *MS*, 29 August 1967.

10. Pages 7–8 in untitled and undated manuscript, listed as a speech by Groppi in the Groppi Papers, Milwaukee Urban Archives, 15:5.

11. *NYT*, 7 November 1985; Balousek, "James Groppi," 1C.

12. *Transcript, Hearings, National Advisory Commission on Civil Disorder*, September 1967 (Groppi testimony, pp. 1518–32).

13. *MJ*, 9 September 1969, 4 November 1985.

14. *MJ*, 4 November 1985.

15. Aukofer, *City*, 80.

16. Aukofer, *City*, 127; *MJ*, 3 September 1967, 10 October 1968, 30 June, 4, 17, 22, 30 October 1969; *MS*, 19 October 1967; *Catholic Herald Citizen*, 16 September 1967.

17. *MJ*, 7 November 1985.

18. Aukofer, "A Classic Revolutionary," *MJ*, 4 November 1985; *City*, 73.

19. Bleidorn, *In My Time*, 66–67; *MJ*, 27 January 1967; Aukofer, "Revolutionary."

20. Aukofer, "Revolutionary."

21. *MJ*, November 1985; *MS*, 6 November 1985; personal conversation, 1997; see also Warren Hinckle, "Left Wing Catholics," *Ramparts* 6 (November 1967): 19.

22. *MJ*, 4 November 1985; *MS*, 30 September 1967.

23. Aukofer, *City*, 81; Balousek, "James Groppi," 1C; see also Groppi speech, Milwaukee Urban Archives, 15:5.

24. Quoted by Hinckle, "Left Wing Catholics," 18.

25. *MJ*, November 4, 1985, Balousek, 1C.

26. *MS*, 3, 9, May, 22, 23, September, 2, 3, 6 October 1969; *MJ*, 10, 15 May, 28, 29 September, 1, 2, 5, 17, 28 October 1969.

27. *MJ*, 4 November 1985.

28. Letter from Richards, also an ex-priest, to Groppi's friends, Christmas 1985; see also, comments by his wife, Peggy Rozga, in Meg Kissinger, "A Legacy Lives On," *Milwaukee Journal Sentinel* (*MJS*), 31 October 1995.

29. *MJ*, 5 November 1985.

30. *MS*, 5 November 1985; see also *MJS*, 31 October 1995.

31. Unpublished autobiography (20 pages) in Milwaukee Urban Archives, begun by Groppi but never completed. Chapter 1 covers his growing up to his deciding to become a priest; chapter 2, seminary, work in inner-city summer camp, and first assignment at St. Veronica's, a white parish.

32. Balousek, "James Groppi," 1C.

33. Aukofer, *City*, 90.

34. Groppi, "Autobiography," 14–16.

35. Hinckle, "Left Wing Catholics," 18.

36. Aukofer, *City*, 70–71.

37. Groppi's followers included students from the first "Lay Theology" program in U.S. Catholicism, founded by Fr. Bernard Cooke at Marquette, a Jesuit University in Milwaukee and a center for much of the rethinking of Catholicism in response to Vatican II. There may well have been mutual influence between his parish-based politics and the new thinking at Marquette.

38. Aukofer, *City*, 84.

39. *MJ*, 4 November 1985.

40. McGreevy, *Parish Boundaries*, 201.

41. Groppi, "The Church and Civil Rights," in *The Underground Church*, ed. Malcolm Boyd (New York: Sheed and Ward, 1968), 81.

42. Groppi, "Civil Rights," 77; Hinckle, "Left Wing Catholics," 18.

43. Mansueto, "Blessed Are the Meek . . . Religion and Socialism in Italian American History," in *The Melting Pot and Beyond: Italian Americans in the Year 2000*, ed. Jerome Krase and William Engelman (Staten Island, N.Y.: American Italian Historical Association, 1987), 127–29.

44. Aukofer, *City*, 83–84.

45. Orsi, *The Madonna of 115th Street: Faith and Community in Italian Harlem, 1880–1950* (New Haven, Conn.: Yale University Press, 1985), 83.

46. Aukofer, *City*, 82; *MJ*, 25 July, 2 August 1974.

47. *MJ*, 5 November 1985; Groppi, "Civil Rights," 74.

48. Quoted in Orsi, 89; Cuomo, "Keynote Speech," 1984 Democratic Convention, *NYT*, 17 July 1984.

49. Groppi, "Civil Rights," 75; Aukofer, *City*, 83.

50. *MJ*, 7 November 1967.

51. Described to me by Nancy Cooney, whose husband, Chuck, organized this informal hospice.

Chapter 11

Mario Savio: Resurrecting an Italian American Radical

Gil Fagiani

The linkages between Mario Savio's radicalism and his Italian American background have gone unacknowledged. The one time I heard him speak in person, in 1985, he opened with, "I'm Mario Savio and I'm from a Sicilian American background."[1] Those words echoed in my mind after his death. They gave me a sense that Savio did indeed value his ethnic identity. They helped me press on with this hunch in face of the strong resistance I met among those who insisted he had no ethnic identity and was merely an American homegrown product.[2]

Source materials on Savio's life are scarce. He rarely put his thoughts into print. He was a modest man who rejected the idea of being a political leader and avoided interviews. Understandably, his family, which is still mourning his death, is reluctant to speak about his life to outsiders.

Savio was born December 8, 1942, on the Feast of the Immaculate Conception and in the Italian tradition was named Mario.[3] He spent his childhood in Floral Park, Queens. He referred to himself as the son of immigrants; his father, and maybe also his mother, was born in Italy, making him a second-generation Italian American. As best as I can determine, one half of his family came from northern Italy and the other from Sicily.[4]

Savio has described his family as working class "on both sides." His father was a mechanic and a machine-punch operator. His parents were New Deal Democrats. He once confided that he had one relative in Italy who had been a Fascist official. A bit of history, he said, best left undiscussed.[5]

One story claims that as a young child, Mario was teased about his first name. His mother reacted by legally changing his name from Mario Robert Savio to Robert Mario Savio.[6] Until his enrollment at Berkeley, he was known as Bob Savio. Having spent my own childhood in a similar community as Savio, it is probable that his name change to Bob was related to the pressure on immigrants to Americanize.

Savio's family was devoutly Catholic and proud that two aunts were nuns. He was an altar boy, and for his first 10 years, he was convinced that he would grow up, enter a seminary, and become a priest known as Father Bob.[7] He was powerfully influenced by the dramatic changes emanating from Vatican II, and while attending Queens College presided over the Confraternity of Christian Doctrine, an organization dedicated to teaching young people the basic principles of Catholicism.

Although he later became famous for his brilliant oratory, Savio grew up with a severe stutter. His wife, Lynne Hollander, says that he liked to refer to the name "Free Speech movement" as a "pun," because for him it referred, among other things, to the free movement of his own speech.[8]

From an early age, Savio showed great academic promise. He finished first in his class at Martin Van Buren High School, where, in spite of his stutter, he was elected president of his class and delivered the valedictorian speech. A finalist for the Westinghouse Talent search, he attended Manhattan College, run by the Christian Brothers, for a year on scholarship, transferred to Queens College, and was later accepted to the University of California at Berkeley.

To my knowledge, the first political demonstration Savio took part in was in 1963, while a student at Queens College. Together with other classmates, he traveled to Albany to join protests against the first imposition of tuition on the City University of New York. Later in the spring of the same year, he joined a contingent of the Queens College Mexico Volunteers in Taxco, a city in the state of Guerrero. The sharp class divisions of Mexican society, and the unwillingness of the Mexican government to ameliorate conditions for the poor, further strengthened Mario's social consciousness.[9]

While a student at Berkeley, Savio was first arrested in the spring of 1964 at a sit-in at the San Francisco Palace Hotel that had been organized to demand that blacks be hired for positions other than maids.[10] In 1964, he was among the many Americans who left their homes and colleges to go to Mississippi and register black voters. Three members of that group—James Chaney, Michael Schwerner, and Andrew Goodman—were murdered.

When Savio returned to the University of California, he led the Berkeley chapter of the Friends of the Student Nonviolent Coordinating Committee. The chapter brought the Civil Rights movement north by organizing demonstrations against San Francisco area businesses that discriminated against African Americans. This angered business executives and their allies on the University of California Board of Regents, who pressured the Berkeley administration to enforce its policy against on-campus political activity.

It was unrealistic to expect that students who had been shot at in Mississippi would shut up. "For us," Savio recalled, "it was a question: Whose side are you on? Are we on the side of the Civil Rights Movement? Or have we now gotten back to the comfort and security of Berkeley, and can forget about the sharecroppers whom we worked with just a few weeks before? Well, we couldn't forget."[11]

The key moment came on December 2, 1964. Students marched into Sproul Hall on Berkeley's campus and took part in a sit-in that led to 800 arrests, the largest number in California history. Savio stood on top of a police car engulfed in a sea of thousands of students and said in a speech that articulated the moral tone of a political era:

There is a time when the operation of the machine becomes so odious, makes you so sick at heart, that you can't take part; you can't even take part tacitly, and you've got to put your bodies upon the gears and upon the wheels, upon the levers, upon all the apparatus and you've got to make it stop. And you've got to indicate to the people that run it, to the people who own it, that unless you're free, the machine will be prevented from working at all. [12]

A massive student strike, supported overwhelmingly by the Berkeley faculty, erupted. The administration was forced to back down, and on January 4, 1965, the Free Speech movement held its first legal rally on Sproul Plaza.

The size and militancy of the Free Speech movement startled observers who were sure that America's white college students were politically conservative and apathetic. By linking the civil rights protests of the early 1960s to the antiwar demonstrations of the later years, the Free Speech movement served as a catalyst for the explosive growth of the New Left in America and throughout the world.[13]

In a movement that publicly rejected leaders—and none more so than Savio himself—he emerged as its principal spokesman and the first of the New Left media personalities of the 1960s. Savio paid a price for his celebrity: a four-month prison sentence, expulsion from the university, and an education delayed for some twenty years.

After running unsuccessfully for California state senator in 1968 on the Peace and Freedom ticket, he dropped out of the limelight, shunning requests for interviews. In the 1970s, he worked at a variety of jobs, including bartender, bookstore clerk, and private math tutor. This was a period of personal anguish for him. His first marriage ended in divorce, and he struggled with a developmentally impaired son and his own severe depression. In 1980, he married former Free Speech movement comrade, Lynn Hollander, and returned to grassroots politics, helping to create the Citizens Party with Barry Commoner. In 1984, he spoke out nationally against U.S. military intervention in Nicaragua, and in 1985 he took part in protests against apartheid in South Africa.[14]

Savio taught remedial math and physics at Sonoma State. While there, in 1994 he organized to defeat anti-immigrant Proposition 187 and fought to prevent increases in student fees. In 1996, he was working against Proposition 209 to save affirmative action on state campuses when at the age of 53 his heart failed.

In my discussions with people about Savio's sense of *italianità*, his attachment to his Italian roots, I have encountered a disturbing phenomenon. Apparently, it is important to many of those around him to deny the possibility that he identified with or was in any way shaped by his Italian American background. Their comments in support of this attitude included: "He was tall, blue-eyed, and blonde"; "He had no identity with Europe—strictly a home-grown product"; "It would be more fruitful to explore the Jewish influence on his politics."

It appears at least publicly, that until the 1970s Savio had little conscious ethnic identity. But the impact of ethnicity cannot be reduced to a simple matter of self-awareness. I agree with many commentators that an essential part of his politics was his faith in the American town-hall tradition, the Jeffersonian idea of participatory democracy. I do *not* believe this tells the whole story. The wellspring of Savio's radicalism can also be found in his strongly held spiritual beliefs, rooted in his Italian Catholic background.

Although highly critical of institutional Catholicism, Savio summed up the positive moral aspects of his religious education as: "Resist evil." What he observed and experienced in Mississippi the summer of 1964 sealed his commitment to radical politics. There his sense of justice was so outraged by the evil of a violent caste system that he felt compelled—even at the point of risking death—to fight it. In a 1995 interview, he described the perspective he brought to the Free Speech movement after his stay in Mississippi as "secularized liberation theology."[15]

As a child, it is likely Savio spoke Italian, and almost certainly he understood it. He later studied Italian and learned to speak it fluently.[16] While traveling to Italy for the first time in the mid-1970s, he visited distant relatives in Sicily. That is when he encountered the Italian Left and Antonio Gramsci. While in Italy, he reportedly marched in a parade celebrating the Italian Resistance. Friends have commented on his enthusiasm about reconnecting to his Italian roots. Savio was coming out of a very low period in his life, and it appears that the rediscovery of his Italian heritage was part of a healing process.[17]

In a trip that he made with his wife in the 1980s, he spoke out against apartheid at Italian Communist party *feste* in Ferrara and Torino. He also spoke on Italian radio. Savio's attachment to Italy became so strong that he inquired about applying for Italian citizenship. However, it does not appear that he ever joined any Italian American organizations. He may have felt negatively about, if not ashamed of, the Italian American community because he perceived it as dominated by right-wing political interests.[18]

In summary, Mario's Italian background strongly influenced him. Its influences included his taste in food and travel, his fluency in Italian, the spiritual values of solidarity and justice prevalent among workers and peasants, and his identification and participation in the Italian Left. Despite his alienation from the Italian American community, his relationship to his Italian roots served as a reaffirmation of his connection to his family and a wide range of Italian values.

Savio suffered a form of ethnic alienation very common to Italian Americans who have been involved in progressive politics. Right-wing politicians inside and outside the Italian American community have directed Italian American resentment at falling wages, failing services and deteriorating neighborhoods toward people of color, immigrants, gays, and others at the margins of society—a margin many Italian Americans have just left. In league with the mass media, right-wingers perpetuate an image of the Italian American community as being universally conservative.[19]

When I was growing up in the 1960s, it wasn't so much Don Corleone and a bunch of celluloid Mafia characters that alienated me from my ethnic background, but real-life characters like Mayor Frank Rizzo of Philadelphia, a man the mass media promoted as the highest exponent of Italian American politics, perhaps even the first Italian American president. It was Rizzo who boasted that his approach to law and order would make Attila the Hun look like a "faggot," and whose notorious antiblack harassment included stripping Black Panthers in the street.[20] Another 1960s Italian American media darling, Anthony Imperiale, an organizer of 1,500 white vigilantes with armored cars called "Jungle Bunnies," positioned himself as the defender of the Italian American community of Newark.[21]

And then there was the Italian American Civil Rights League, ostensibly created to counter the stereotype of Italian American affiliation with the Mafia. Fifty thousand people attended the founding rally in 1970, with big-name entertainers like Frank Sinatra raising up to $500,000 at fund-raising benefits. But as was obvious from the beginning, the League was controlled by mob boss Joe Colombo, who in 1971 was shot down at a rally at New York's Columbus Circle by Joey Gallo's hired gun.[22]

I would be remiss if I didn't mention the role the Left itself has played in this ethnic alienation. The New Left was a white, predominantly middle-class, student-based movement that tended to denigrate the cultures and economic interests of white ethnics, particularly those groups from Catholic backgrounds. In its most extreme form, elements of the New Left simply condemned the entire white working class as hopelessly racist and reactionary. This pervasive attitude alienated and distanced from the Left Italian and Polish Americans, who were the most proletarian of all the major white ethnic groups. [23]

The amnesia about Italian American radical legacy made it easier for Savio and others who came of political age in the '60s and early '70s to view the Italian American community as an obstacle to the progressive agenda and, at worst, to be part of the enemy camp. In thinking of the current crop of high-profile Italian American politicians in the state of New York (D'Amato, Bruno, Vacco, and Giuliani), I am reminded of a line from the great Italian novel *Il Gattopardo* (The leopard), by Giuseppe di Lampedusa, "*Se vogliamo che tutto rimanga come è, bisogna che tutto cambi*" [The more things change the more they stay the same].

When I heard Mario Savio speak that night in 1985, he said, "My name is Mario Savio, and I'm from a Sicilian-Italian background." He paused for a moment and looked at the crowd, "You know I never would have said that in the old days." Those words hit me like a revelation. Finally, I thought, it could be possible to join the love of my ethnic background—my *italianità*—with my progressive politics. Maybe I could stop warring within myself and feel good about what I really was—an Italian American progressive. I owe Mario Savio a lot for his candor and courage.

NOTES

1. To my best recollection, Savio said this at a rally at Columbia University in the fall of 1985, when he joined Abbey Hoffman in speaking out against U.S. military intervention in Nicaragua.

2. For an example of this resistance, see Lucia Chiavola Birnbaum's "Mario Savio— Sicilian American Radical" (paper presented at the conference "The Lost World of Italian American Radicalism," New York, 15 May 1997), in which she discusses the views of Reginald Zelnik, professor of history at the University of California, Berkeley.

3. Art Gatti, "Mario Savio's Religious Influences and Origins" (paper presented at the conference "The Lost World of Italian American Radicalism," New York, 15 May 1997), 4.

4. Lynne Hollander, letter to the author, 3 May 1997.

5. Mario Savio, "Two Anniversary Speeches," *The Three Penny Review* (summer, 1995): 34.

6. Art Gatti, interview by author, 4 April 1997.

7. Gatti, "Mario Savio's Religious Influences," 4.

8. Lynne Hollander, "Speaking Freely," *New York Times*, 5 January 1997, sec. 7, p. 4.

9. Gatti, "Mario Savio's Religious Influences," 15.

10. Larry Hatfield, "Mario Savio Dies: Free Speech Activist, Berkeley Student Helped Kick off the '60s Protest," *San Francisco Examiner*, 7 November 1996, A1.

11. Karlyn Baker, "Rebel with a Cause," *Washington Post*, 8 November 1996, D1. See also Mario Savio, "An End of History," *Humanity* (December 1964).

12. Paul Jacobs and Saul Lindau, *The New Radicals: A Report with Documents* (New York: Vintage Books, 1966), 61.

13. Bret Eynon, "Free Speech Movement," in *Encyclopedia of the American Left*, ed. Mari Jo Buhle, Paul Buhle, and Dan Georgakas (Chicago: University of Illinois Press, 1990), 242.

14. Michael Taylor, "Stirring up a Generation," *San Francisco Chronicle*, Sunday, 8 December 1996, 1, Z3.

15. Savio, "Two Anniversary Speeches," 34.

16. Mario Savio, "Organizing the Movement," *North Coast Xpress* (April–May 1995). In this article, Savio uses the Italian saying, *Fra il dire e il fare, c'è il mezzo della mare* [It's easier said than done].

17. Samuel Farber, telephone interview by author, 4 April 1997.

18. Lynne Hollander, letter to author, 3 May 1997.

19. See Gil Fagiani, "An Italian American on the Left: Drugs, Revolution, and Ethnicity in the 1970s," in *Italian Americans in a Multicultural Society*, ed. Jerome Krase and Judith N. DeSena (Staten Island, N.Y.: American Italian Historical Association, 1994).

20. Michael de Courey Hinds, "Frank Rizzo of Philadelphia Dies at 70," *New York Times*, 17 July 1991, D23.

21. Tom Hayden, *Reunion: A Memoir* (Collier Books, 1988), 160.

22. Mark R. Levy and Michael S. Kramer, *The Ethnic Factor: How America's Minorities Decide Elections* (New York: Simon and Schuster, 1973), 159–61.

23. Gil Fagiani, "White Ethnics, Racism, and the Left: The Italian American Experience," *Art and Academe* 7 (fall 1994): 31–52.

Part III

Culture

Chapter 12

The Radical World of
Ybor City, Florida

Gary R. Mormino and George E. Pozzetta (1941–1994)

In 1965, Angelo Massari set out to write his autobiography. Born in 1888 in
Santo Stefano, Sicily, Massari left his village for the cigar factories of Tampa,
Florida. "When in 1902 I landed in Tampa," he recollected, "I found myself in a
world of radicals for which I was prepared. . . . In those days in Tampa, anarchists
and socialists were many."[1] Angelo Massari was part of the greatest migration in
recorded history, the movement of millions of southern and eastern Europeans to
the Americas between the 1880s and the 1920s. He also represented a small part
of that migration to Tampa, Florida.

In 1886, the Spanish *patron*, Vicente Martínez Ybor, created an industrial complex called Ybor City. Spaniards and Cubans comprised the original workforce,
highly skilled and highly paid artisans organized around the cigar industry. Cigar
making reflected many preindustrial vestiges, since it was an industry without
machinery. A radical culture grafted onto the frontier settlement from the very
beginning, as Spaniards and Cubans brought to Ybor City Old World resentments
against the Catholic Church and entrenched power.[2] In the early 1890s, a handful of Sicilians first encountered Ybor City. They represented a vanguard of a large
Sicilian workforce seasonally employed in the sugar plantations of St. Cloud,
Florida. Sicilians clustered in quarters soon called "Little Italy."

A remarkable community, or set of communities, evolved in Ybor City. By
1900, Cuban, Spaniard, and Italian working-class immigrants had established
distinct colonies. A familiar network of social institutions evolved, ministering
to the needs of cigar makers and families. Yet what was most extraordinary, a
"Latin" identity also evolved, a culture that bonded Italians, Cubans (white and
black), and Spaniards around commonly held values: working class solidarity,
international brotherhood, and distrust of institutions, chiefly the Catholic
Church.

Ybor City (and later a sister industrial community, West Tampa), attracted impressive numbers of Latin immigrants to its cigar factories. By 1910, over 2,500 Italian immigrants had settled in Tampa, complemented by approximately 6,200 Cuban and Spanish immigrants.

The reader, *el lector,* stood at the epicenter of Ybor City's radical culture. *La lectura* (the reading) had begun in Cuba in the 1850s, and by the 1880s *los lectores* read to cigar workers in Cuba and in Key West and Tampa, Florida. In Tampa, *el lector* loomed large in social, intellectual, and political circles. For four hours a day, *lectores* read—always in Spanish—novels, newspapers, and political tracts. Readings in political economy and history included Henry George, Karl Marx, and Giuseppe Garibaldi. Several Italians, including Onofrio Palermo, became readers, as did several women.[3]

For Italians in Ybor City, the reader invited entry into a newfound world of ideas and opportunities. The *lectura* provided a crash course in Spanish and offered an inspired incentive to learn the language, since it was the vehicle to participate in a shared experience. For Italians, the least educated and least equipped to compete in the urban industrial market, the reader represented a pivotal, revered figure who granted access to a wider world.

For Latin women, the reader presented a world of ideas and international sisterhood. Spain, Cuba, and Italy tendered few opportunities for formal education to working-class women. Italian women, who worked in greatest numbers at the stripping rooms and tobacco benches, typically had little formal education on arrival in the United States. In 1910, only 45 percent of Italian women—and

Year	Native white-native percentage	Native white-foreign percentage	Foreign-born white	Black	Foreign-born Cubans	Foreign-born Spaniards	Foreign-born Italians
1890	2,473	742	1,427	1,632	2,424	233	56
1900	4,557	2,497	4,371	4,382	3,533	963	1,315
1910	12,037	6,857	9,896	8,951	3,859	2,337	2,519
1920	17,542	11,837	10,666	11,531	3,459	2,726	2,817
1930[a]	43,096	22,296	14,521	21,172	5,112	3,457	2,817
1940	50,201	23,760	11,082	23,331	3,317	2,600	2,684

[a]Includes West Tampa, incorporated into Tampa in 1925.
Source: Eleventh Census: Population, I, Table 23; *Twelfth Census: Population,* II, Table 27; *Thirteenth Census: Population,* II, Table 21; *Fourteenth Census: Population,* III, Table 10; *Fifteenth Census: Population,* III, pt. 1, Table 15; *Sixteenth Census: Population,* Table C-40.

men—could read and write, compared to nearly 100 percent of Hispanic women. Italian women learned Spanish quickly, however, advancing rapidly in the factories while appreciating the *novellas* and classics. Only one city in the United States, Tampa, attracted more Italian immigrant women than men. These reasons underscore the importance of cigar work and solidarity.[4]

Italian women joined the ranks of radicals struggling for social and political equality in Tampa. On November 15, 1910, the *Tampa Tribune* observed: "At the factory of Arguelles, Lopez and Bros., nine Italian women gave an entertainment that was about as ludicrous as any that has been inflicted upon the local public since the strike. The misguided ones, armed with clubs, paraded the streets about the factory. Their weapons they brandished and their tongues they did wag, giving vent to threats that they would beat all to death who would work."[5]

In the cigar factories, Italians listened to the daily readings, with their stinging criticisms of capitalism. On the closely packed streets and corners of Ybor City and the open-windowed meeting halls of the clubs, they debated anarchism and socialism; in the newspapers they read the point and counterpoints of radical speakers. They filtered all of this through their own encounter with leftist philosophies in the Old World.

Ybor City and West Tampa attracted an extraordinary array of left- and right-wing socialists, centrists, revolutionary and Industrial Workers of the World (IWW) syndicalists, pacifistic and "propaganda of the deed" anarchists, and a number of others as well. In both communities, they organized various socialist *circoli* (discussion groups) and *sezioni* (sections), anarchist *gruppi* (groups), debating clubs, speaking societies, and political organizations. The majority were small entities formed for the purposes of self-education and debate. The small anarchist club that attracted Angelo Massari shortly after he arrived in 1902 typified these groups. "In our community, socialism and anarchism were in vogue," Massari observed of the early years. "I associated with a group of friends who had organized a club for social studies. At the club, I read pamphlets, newspapers, books, and all kinds of sociological literature. I also attended all the lectures and debates that the two groups, socialist and anarchist, organized, inviting to Tampa the greatest exponents of the two theories who were living in the North."[6]

Club libraries stocked their shelves with an impressive collection of literature. These collections typically featured a wide assortment of reading matter, ranging from simple spelling and grammar texts to Italian-language editions of the great radical masters. Invariably included among the latter were the works of Mikhail Bakunin, Peter Kropotkin, and Errico Malatesta. Most items in these club libraries were small, inexpensive pamphlets offering polemical essays on various topics or excerpts from larger works.[7]

Socialists also supported a variety of *circoli*, which regularly advertised their meetings and agendas in the local newspapers. The most popular socialist group was Gruppo Lorenzo Panepinto (named for a Sicilian martyr) begun by Giovanni Vaccaro in 1911, after Panepinto's assassination. The organization quickly counted more than two hundred members. The club often held joint meetings with other radical groups in the area to raise money for worthy causes, hold debates, and plot strategy. It also pledged a yearly stipend of 1,200 lire to the socialist section of Santo Stefano to assist in its work among the peasantry.[8]

Alfonso Coniglio epitomized the radical world of Ybor. Just as Italians rapidly integrated themselves into Ybor City's radical structure, so too did they quickly become part of the worldwide community of Italian radicals. Born in Alessandria della Rocco in 1884, Coniglio immigrated to Tampa in 1896, following the brutal suppression of the *fasci* (agricultural workers) in Sicily. He soon found work at the cigar benches, where he was attracted by the messages of the readers. "It was at La Rosa Español [factory] that I first heard the readers," he later reminisced. "Oh, I cannot tell you how important they were. . . . To hear them, we owe particularly our sense of the class struggle." Coniglio rose to the rank of a leader in radical circles, communicating with fellow immigrants in Paterson, New Jersey, and Barre, Vermont. He also operated as a distributor for the anarchist newspaper *Cronaca Sovversiva*.[9]

Aside from the printed word, Ybor City's Italian radicals accessed this wider universe in many other ways. Club resources financed radical speakers and authors who participated in the *giro di propaganda* (propaganda tour), a vigorous network that carried personalities and ideas along well-worn routes connecting the various hubs of the radical immigrant world. Again, young Angelo Massari remembered the dynamics of the process as it worked in Ybor City. Socialists and anarchists "vied with each other, and brought in well-known speakers. There were well-attended lectures and debates." Ybor City became a regular stop for radical luminaries as they circulated throughout the world, visiting the far-flung outposts that immigrants had populated. Between the years 1890 and 1919, virtually every radical of distinction came to Florida to spend time with their Ybor City *campanieri*. Panepinto, the Sicilian agrarian leader, visited Ybor City prior to his assassination in 1911. Malatesta, anarchist veteran of revolutionary activities in a dozen different countries, visited in February 1900, lecturing and debating for several days while enjoying the warm Florida winter. His talks, delivered in both Spanish and Italian, filled lecture halls to capacity.[10]

Socialists Arturo Caroti and Vincenzo Vacirca, as well as anarchist Luigi Galleani, responded to invitations and made journeys to Tampa. Giuseppe Bertelli, socialist editor of Chicago's *La Parola dei Socialiste*, who made a 10-day visit in May 1910, published several lengthy reports of his stay in his newspaper. He commented on, among other things, the amicable relationships existing in the Tampa area among Italian socialists and anarchists, the nature of the cigar industry and its unions, his public debates with the Spanish anarchist Pedro Esteve, and the status of religion among the city's immigrants. As a parting gift, cigar makers presented Bertelli with a bundle of Havana tobacco marked "tobacco anarchico per la pipa di Bertelli."[11]

The practice of working-class solidarity lent Ybor City a leftist orientation. That the level of acceptance was more than merely superficial or confined to a tiny segment of the community can be seen in the character of Ybor City's unions, its shared club programs, its pattern of consumer cooperatives, its press, and, of course, the profound impact of the *lector*. One can also chart the reaction of the community to events outside its borders. Ybor City residents were forever taking up collections and demonstrating to aid one leftist cause after another. The endorsers of one mass rally in 1913 included the Italian local of the Social-ist Party, Gruppo Panepinto, Gruppo Risveglio (Italian anarchist), Grupo La Luz (Spanish anarchist), the IWW local, and all of the Cigar Makers International Union (CMIU) locals. Funds flowed out of Ybor City in a steady stream to sup-port the 1905 Russian Revolution, the Mexican Revolution, the defense of arrested comrades around the world, and the establishment of various leftist groups and newspapers elsewhere. Reports of collection committees often included block-by-block itemizations of contributions, revealing the breadth and depth of community support.[12]

At no time were Ybor City's radicals and the Italians among them more on the defensive than during the World War I era. The federal government monitored community activities with scrupulous attention, as it honeycombed Ybor City with agents and informants. The file drawers of the Bureau of Investigation brimmed with alarming reports, including allegations of plots to kill President Woodrow Wilson and President Victoriano Huerta of Mexico. Documents reveal an unmistakable pattern of government espionage, establishment violence, and deep paranoia over the "Ybor City problem." One agent alleged that "the entire Ybor City, with all its Spaniards, Cubans, Italians . . . are [not] in harmony with this government. This is evidenced by the large number of this class who attempted and in fact did avoid the draft law." Another agent insisted, "I can state that the Italian-Spanish colonies of West Tampa and Ybor City, Florida are the most advanced towards the 'Social Revolution.' I could say that they have established here a Soviet on a small scale . . . [one has] the impression of being in Russia." In November 1919, undercover operative A. V. French noted a sore point in community relations: there "has always been a certain amount of ani-mosity between the American and the Latin American element in this city, due to the fact that public opinion is aroused against the foreign population here on account of their alleged disregard of the selective service regulations."[13]

No lockstep march to Americanization characterized Ybor City's immigrants during World War I. The war was not popular there, especially among the radical elements. Editorials critical of the lack of enthusiasm in Ybor City for the war effort dotted the English-language press. The *Morning Tribune,* for example, chided the county registration board for not recording the names and addresses of individuals who had denied their American citizenship to avoid the draft. "These husky young aliens are fattening off the wages of the products of the United States and are walking about in pompous indifference, not to say defi-ance, of the government's pleas. . . . While the American boy is off to camp of training [sic] or in the trenches facing the enemy. . . . The calls for aid to the Lib-erty Bond fund, the Red Cross, the Y.M.C.A. War Council, and every other demand for money and loyal self-sacrifice have brought no responsive contribu-tion from thousands of these. . . . They should be interned in prison camps and there sent to work for the common good. . . . Many of these alien exempts have fled from the country until after the war is over." Particularly galling to many natives was the rising curve of strike activity. In 1918, one city lawyer claimed, "The man who quits his job at the present time without just and proper cause is a traitor." More common were complaints about the *lectores*, who allegedly were "reading books condemned by the government" and encouraging disloyalty. Authorities arrested several readers for persisting in such activities.[14]

Italians represented the only major immigrant group whose homeland fought in the struggle, but this hardly translated into greater enthusiasm for the war. Indeed the Italian government viewed Ybor City as a center of opposition to its participation in the war. Unlike some other enclaves, which greeted Italy's entry into the war on May 23, 1915, with wild cerebrations and parades, Ybor City experienced no public manifestation of any kind. Nor did Italians rush home-ward to enlist in the Italian military. Rather, they and their Latin neighbors responded to the war by studied indifference, open hostility, or temporary migra-tion to Cuba.[15]

The bilingual labor paper *El Internacional*, Ybor City's most popular newssheet, provides an insight into the community reaction to the war. During the period 1914–1918, the paper contained only three articles reporting on war events in Europe, and these merely transmitted information on important military devel-opments. Chest-thumping jingoism and 100 percent Americanism were com-pletely absent. The great battles in France and Italy failed to change the paper's editorial policies, which continued to stress reports on labor-related news and discussions of strategies to organize the working class.[16]

Since Ybor City possessed no Italian-language commercial press (the usual source of progovernment, pro-war campaigns), there were no public efforts to whip up enthusiasm for the war. Italian government officials struck a near solid wall of indifference when they arrived to sell Italian bonds, both during and after the war, finding success only among a handful of prosperous Italians, most notably Val Antuono, a cigar factory owner who had earned a reputation as the most determined open-shop advocate in the city. In 1919, Antuono stumped the community in an effort to sell Italian government bonds, explaining that this was an excellent way to show the community's "patriotism." Ultimately he purchased nearly £500,000 worth of bonds himself, in a bid to receive an appointment as Italian consul in Tampa, but he was only able to sell a small amount to several other businessmen. His close identification with the Italian government, his position as a factory owner, and particularly his antilabor reputation, from the start doomed his campaign.[17]

Fund-raising in Ybor City typically went toward very different ends from those desired by Antuono. The activities of Domenico Lodato, secretary of the Italian Socialist Federation of Tampa, revealed the nature of the community's responses. Acting on a complaint from Carlo Papini, Italian vice-consul of New Orleans, federal agents investigated (and confirmed) reports that Lodato had collected money in Tampa by popular subscription "for the purposes of overthrowing the Italian government." Lodato was "spreading bolshevikism in that community," the vice-consul added, urging that this "dangerous menace" be silenced.[18]

Latin radicals were not content simply to ignore the war. According to the *Morning Tribune*, one tangible result of antiwar sentiment was a "considerable exodus of conscription age men [twenty-one to thirty years old] to Havana," and within a week Governor Sidney Catts felt compelled to order deputies to inspect all boats leaving Tampa for foreign countries. One irate citizen detailed the vigorous responses of the Tampa Left in a letter to the Bureau of Investigation:

[Radicals have] discouraged enlistments in our Army and Navy and aided those who wanted to evade the draft by giving them money to leave the country. After the Armistice, these men affiliated themselves with anarchists from Spain, Cuba, and New York, also with Bolsheviki of Russia. These men were interested in doing bodily harm to our President. They also tried to bring about a race riot by inciting the negroes [sic] against the whites. They are also responsible for various strikes.[19]

Radicals paid a heavy price for their opposition to the war. Not only did the government greatly increase its surveillance and control, but the native community's hostility rose to new heights. The socialist locals in particular, perhaps because of their greater visibility and size, increasingly felt the pressure of public opinion. The Red Scare scoured and scarred Ybor City's radical community. Agents seized presses, and scores of radicals were deported.

Although radical influence diminished in the cigar factories after 1921 and the Red Scare repression diluted its impact in the wider community, leftists did not wholly abandon Ybor City. The scattered elements of the Left rallied around two causes that gave their presence purpose and commitment. Throughout the seven-year life of the affair, the celebrated case of Sacco and Vanzetti galvanized the Ybor City radical community, and particularly the Italian element within it, with an almost missionary zeal. Ybor City's leftists scrutinized with intense interest the events surrounding the arrests, trial, conviction, appeals, and eventual executions in 1927. They collected money for defense funds, held rallies, sent telegrams and petitions, and staged protest strikes in support of the two anarchists in Massachusetts.[20]

As in Italian American communities elsewhere, passions mounted as the date for execution neared. One manifesto of July 1, 1926, explained that the "bourgeoisie is trying to kill two comrades. . . . Their only crime was to be opposed to the war." The document summarized the details of the case, claiming, among other things, that the two men had been tortured by the police. CMIU Local 464, the Italian local, now headed by Alfonso Coniglio, coordinated the Pro-Prisoner Committee to raise money for the Sacco and Vanzetti defense fund. More-militant radicals scoffed at the CMIU's use of peaceful protests, suggesting that the unionists were in fact on the side of the capitalist oppressors. In their view, "only a general strike" could help free the men. Despite differences over tactics, wide community support greeted efforts to raise money and organize protests. On April 27, 1927, cigar workers overwhelmingly approved a strike resolution and left the workbenches en masse for a one-day walkout. Three months later, a joint committee headed by Alfonso Coniglio, Vincente Antinori, José Esposito, and Francisco Alonzo organized another one-day strike involving some twelve thousand workers. When Massachusetts Governor Alvan T. Fuller announced on August 5 that he would not intervene in the case, cigar workers again struck, this time sending fifteen thousand people to the streets.[21]

Characteristically the *Morning Tribune* only saw evidence of radical excesses in these disruptions. One editorial on August 6 explained that Sacco and Vanzetti were "defiant of law, hostile to government, murderers at heart," concluding, "We know of no convicted, condemned men who have enjoyed such exceptional indulgence at the hands of the law." An August 10 walkout again emptied the cigar factories. More than five thousand cigar workers, including several hundred women and children, jammed into the Labor Temple to hear speeches in Italian, English, and Spanish. Time after time, frenzied applause swept the audience as speakers lionized the condemned men. Ybor City's main thoroughfare, Seventh Avenue, was virtually deserted as every store fronting the street closed for the day after gracing the windows with crudely painted signs—"Save Sacco and Vanzetti," "Help the Innocents," and so on. The last and largest strike, on August 23, ended with a memorial to "bid farewell to our noble comrades." On this sad occasion, some five thousand Italians gathered at the Italian Club for speeches and memorializing. All of Ybor City's businesses closed, with *La Traducción* suspending publication.[22]

The onset of the Great Depression devastated Ybor City's vaunted cigar industries. Ironically, this great challenge to capitalism also challenged radical cigar makers' source of membership and income. "Pure Havana" cigars made in Tampa had always been considered a luxury—a badge of identification for the successful middle classes—but the Depression capsized the consumer market for handrolled cigars. Cigarettes largely replaced expensive cigars, just as machines were replacing cigar makers. In a larger sense, the successes achieved by cigar workers since the 1890s also undermined the radicals' message in the 1930s. Former Tabaqueros had opened grocery stores and businesses, giving rise to a class less receptive to strikes and appeals to challenge capitalism.

In times of tumult, societies seek out scapegoats. In 1931, the last great strike engulfed Ybor City's cigar factories, as Latins fought to hold onto their revered readings. Tampa's businessmen and politicians blamed the decline of the cigar industry on the reader, always a convenient lightning rod. Latins lost, and the readers' tribunes came tumbling down. "It was an extraordinarily radical strike," remembered José Yglesias. "The cigar makers tried to march to City Hall with red flags, singing the old Italian anarchist song, 'Avanti popolo.'"[23]

Throughout the 1930s and World War II, Ybor City served as a sanctuary and cockpit for leftist causes. Latins enthusiastically supported the Republican cause during the Spanish Civil War and Italy's anti-Fascists. The last public gasp of Ybor City's radical past occurred in November 1948. Henry Wallace found enthusiastic support among Tampa's aging Latins, and in the election, the Progressive Party candidate won eight precincts. Paul Robeson campaigned for Wallace, also finding cheering crowds in Tampa. At least one Latin, Henry Wallace Lavendara, was named for the progressive. McCarthyism and mortality eroded the last vestiges of Ybor's radical heritage.[24]

Overall, the size of the radical element in Ybor City was disproportionate to its influence. Clearly, radicals never comprised more than a minority of residents, but they served important functions as intellectual critics and as leaders of working-class organizations. On the union front, they supplied a class ideology that helped to create a labor consciousness of such a broad and flexible nature that members of disparate immigrant groups were able to find common ground. That immigrant workers could strike for protracted periods of time and still maintain their solidarity despite determined manufacturer opposition, vigilantism, and economic deprivation attests in part to the effectiveness of this message. Radicals gave voice to the "class obligations" existing among workers; the dynamics of unionism in Tampa cannot be understood without reference to their presence.

Through their clubs, newspapers, educational work, cooperatives, and debating forums, radicals articulated a leftist orientation to the social problems of the day. They dramatized issues of work and life and often instilled a spirit of pride and class consciousness in their fellow residents. Through these actions, they reached not only to the immigrant generation but to the children of immigrants as well. José Yglesias, Tampa's greatest native-born writer, was only one of many second-generation Latins profoundly affected by the radical climate existing during his youth. In this sense, the radical influence extended beyond the years of community building and migration.

Unlike the Labor Temple, which still stands proudly in the heart of Ybor City, little remains today of the radical presence, in part because the causes championed by radicals so often failed to meet with success and because the legacy of repression directed against them still leaves a bitter taste in the mouths of many. Although absent from Tampa now, radicals nonetheless did force the host society to cope with their presence. Tampa's political values, nativist sentiments, and propensities toward vigilantism all owe a heavy debt to the reactions radicals generated. To look only at the contemporary terrain without reference to this earlier experience is to miss an important formative aspect of Tampa's past.

The fires of labor conflict tempered working-class activism into simple reductions: "Bread and Work" and "Class War." The heady solidarity generated by militant trade unionism and leftist ideology engendered ethnic cooperation and economic interdependence. But cigar makers lost nearly every labor battle and radical groups declined. It remained to be seen whether Cubans, Spaniards, and Italians could organize themselves in other ways.

NOTES

The authors wish to express appreciation to the University Press of Florida for the rights to print substantial excerpts from *The Immigrant World of Ybor City*.

1. Angelo Massari, *The Wonderful Life of Angelo Massari*, trans. Arthur D. Massolo (New York, 1965), 56.

2. For an overview of Ybor City, see Gary R. Mormino and George E. Pozzetta, *The Immigrant World of Ybor City* (Urbana, Ill., 1987), and new edition, (Gainesville, Fla., 1998).

3. Gary R. Mormino and George E. Pozzetta, "The Reader Lights the Candle: Cuban and Florida Cigar Workers' Oral Tradition," *Labor Heritage* 4 (spring 1993): 4–27.

4. *Reports of the Immigration Commission, Immigrants in Industries*, pt. 14, tables 172–74, 192 (Washington, 1911).

5. "Our Alien Burden," *Tampa Tribune*, 15 November 1917, 6; "Patriotism," *Tampa Tribune*, 12 August 1918, 3.

6. Massari, *Wonderful Life*, 91.

7. George E. Pozzetta, "An Immigrant Library: The Tampa Italian Club Collection," *Ex Libris* [University of South Florida journal] 1 (1978): 10–12.

8. *El Internacional*, 14, 21 April, 8 December 1911; 5 February, 9 March, 27 August 1915; *Il Proletario*, 15 September 1911; *La Voce della Colonia*, 10 June 1911. *El Internacional* served as the newspaper for the Cigar Makers International Union (CMIU).

9. Department of Justice, Investigative Case Files (ICF), "Untitled Report," no. 194147, 17 May 1918; Yglesias, *Truth about Them* (New York, 1971), 209. Radical newspapers often carried a column titled "Piccola Posta" (Little Post Office), which reported on events occurring in other radical centers. Tampa soon began to appear with frequency in these listings.

10. Massari, *Wonderful Life*, 68, 106.

11. *La Parola dei Socialisti*, 14, 21 May, 2 July 1910 (Bertelli), 2 July 1910 (Galleani); *El Internacional*, 10, 17 November 1905 (Caroti), 14 May and 17 October 1915 (Vacirca).

12. *El Internacional*, 14, 28 April 1911 (calling for a general strike to support the Mexican Revolution); *La Voce della Colonia*, 17 June 1911 (collection for Panepinto family); *La Parola dei Socialisti*, 17 July 1909 (collections for a defense league for political refugees); *Tampa Morning Tribune*, 20 January 1906 (Russian Revolution), 27 September 1918 (Tom Mooney defense fund), 28 September 1912 (Ettor and Giovannitti defense fund). Department of Justice records relating to Alfredo Rubio Rodríguez (alias Jack Rubio), a Spanish anarchist, give evidence of the immigrant groups' mixing in radical Ybor City. Rubio's career intersected with Cubans and Italians on many different levels. See especially "Jack Rubio File," ICF, no. 374384, 6, 14 November 1919.

13. "Investigation of Spanish Press in Tampa," ICF, no. 342696, 6 February 1919; reports, 25 March 1919, 7 January 1920; "Report of A. V. French," ICF, no. 382470, 18 November 1919.

14. *Tampa Morning Tribune*, 15 November 1917, 12 August 1918.

15. Ibid., 23–30 May 1915; John Massaro, interview by author, 1 August 1983.

16. This assessment is based on a close reading of the labor newspaper *El Internacional* for the war years.

17. Massari, *Wonderful Life*, 196. When the bonds failed to mature, Antuono lost heavily. No greater success attended efforts to sell American war bonds among Latins. See *Tampa Morning Tribune*, 15 November 1917.

18. "Report on D. Lodato," ICF, no. 366198, 29 May 1919.

19. *Tampa Morning Tribune*, 23, 31 May 1917; "Report of Byrd Douglas," ICF, no. 362112, 14 July 1919, includes a letter from mayor D. B. McKay complaining of the number of men leaving for Cuba and Spain to evade the draft; "Letter from 'A Citizen,' " ICF, no. 362112, 15 October 1919; *Tampa Morning Tribune*, 24 April 1919.

20. *El Internacional*, 11 April 1919; 12 March 1920; 10 June, 12 August 1921; 18, 21, 27 April 1927.

21. "Pro-Sacco and Vanzetti Protest Organizing Committee," *Manifesto*, 1 July 1926; "Torcedor Bulletin," *Manifesto*, 6 August 1927, P. K. Yonge Library, University of South Florida.

22. *Tampa Morning Tribune*, July–August 1927. The Central Trades and Labor Assembly of Tampa had voted against the protest strike, but the cigar workers acted independently.

23. Mormino and Pozzetta, "The Reader," 12–14; Robert P. Ingalls, *Urban Vigilantes in the New South: Tampa 1882–1936* (Knoxville, Tenn., 1988), 150–58; Yglesias quoted in Studs Terkel, *Hard Times* (New York, 1970), 110–111.

24. *Tampa Morning Tribune*, 11, 23 September, 5 October 1948; *Tampa Daily Times*, 30 September, 5 October 1948; Ana M. Varela-Lago, " 'No Pasarán!' The Spanish Civil War's Impact on Tampa's Latin Community, 1936–1939," *Tampa Bay History* 19 (fall/winter 1997): 5–36.

Chapter 13

Follow the Red Brick Road: Recovering Radical Traditions of Italian American Writers

Fred Gardaphè

> If the Euro-American ethnic culture were reintroduced in a way that centers on the class-conscious, antichauvinist, antiparticularist, and antiracist traditions of Farrell, di Donato, and Gold, such a cultural revival might have a salutary and unifying, rather than retrograde and divisive, impact on the general drive toward cultural democracy that we are witnessing in scholarship today. White ethnic literary studies will never be legitimate until radical pasts are reclaimed.
>
> Alan Wald, "The 1930s Left in U.S. Literature Reconsidered"

> In those hag-ridden and race conscious times we wanted to be known as anti-fascists, and thus get over our Italian names.
>
> Felix Stefanile, "The Dance at Saint Gabriel's"

Michael Miller Topp's recent essay on the Italian American Left concludes with the pronouncement that the deaths of Sacco and Vanzetti "was a radicalizing moment that would redefine their [American intellectuals'] political mindset for at least the next decade," but that for "Italian American radicals the executions marked the end of a road rather than a beginning of one,"[1] What Topp was referring to was the presence of Italian Americans as a recognizable force within the American Communist and socialist organizations. This essay picks up where Topp left off by surveying the radical tradition that can be found in the writing of Italian Americans that has emerged since the Sacco and Vanzetti executions. A major theme of this writing is that you don't have to be a "commie" to be a radical. This radical tradition in Italian American writing is working-class based; shaped by the experience of Italian immigrant workers. This tradition is built solid as a red brick road by such writers as Luigi Fraina, Arturo Giovannitti,

Frances (Vinciguerra) Winwar, Pietro di Donato, Angelo Pellegrini, Carl Marzani, Vincent Ferrini, Diane di Prima, and many others.

This essay argues that the traditions of Italian American radical writers have been covered by the asphalt of critical cultural histories that have left Italian American writers out of American history. Documentation and close reading of Italian participation in American culture rarely earns more than a footnote in most studies of American radical culture. For example, there is not a single reference to Italians as minorities in a 1937 research memorandum on minority peoples during the Great Depression by Donald Young—referred to as a substantial contribution to "our knowledge of the period through his examination of the influence of radicalism, crime, education and religion as they affected minority group behavior."[2] This, in fact, is quite characteristic of scholarship even today, which lumps Italian immigrants and Italian Americans with whites, a practice that, although pleasing to those who wish to erase the immigrant past and thus pass as whites, not only distorts the social and political problems encountered by Italian Americans, but also shadows the contributions they have made to American culture. What follows is a brief survey of the contributions that a few American writers of Italian descent have made to radical thought in the United States.

The earliest voices of Italian Americans heard publicly were those of political and labor activists such as poet–organizer Arturo Giovannitti, biographer and novelist Frances Winwar, journalist–organizer Carlo Tresca, and organizer Louis Fraina. In the early 1900s, Fraina, who later changed his name to Lewis Corey, was one of the earliest to publish Marxist literary and cultural criticism in America.[3]

Fraina was born in Galdo, Italy, in 1892 and came to America with his mother at the age of three to join his father, a republican exile. An early participant in both the Socialist Labor Party and the Industrial Workers of the World, Fraina was involved in the founding of the American Communist Party. However, by the age of 30, he had disconnected himself from any political group, changed his name, and eventually became a leader of the anti-Communist liberal movement. Working as a proofreader and editor by day as Charles Skala, Fraina began writing under the name Lewis Corey. During this period, he was a union activist and a prolific Marxist critic and journalist. Despite never having been formally educated beyond grammar school, he wrote *The House of Morgan* (1932), *The Decline of American Capitalism* (1934), and *The Crisis of the Middle Class* (1935), which helped fuel the radical movement of the 1930s.[4]

Fraina dedicated his entire life to theoretical analysis of the impact of capitalism on American democratic culture and to the search for a new social order that would respect and reward human labor. In light of the decline in the middle class we are witnessing today, what he wrote in the 1930s was prophetic:

We must learn to appreciate the underlying unity of events, the logic of historical development. The threat of fascism, of new world wars and a new barbarism, arises out of the class necessity of entrenched interests which cling, at all costs, to the old order. This menace to all other classes can be met only by a struggle for a new social order capable of creating a new and higher civilization, for capitalism in decay is now capable only of creating reaction and death.[5]

Corey believed that the struggle would require education, especially of the middle class, as to its historical role in the propagation of the traditions of the ruling class. Only through education, he believed, could "the dispossessed elements of the middle class" understand their role in creating a new society.[6] But Fraina was not one to advocate revolution from an office. He also worked on the front lines.

During the Depression, he worked as an economist for the Works Progress Administration (WPA), and from 1937 to 1939, he served as educational director of Local 22 of the International Ladies' Garment Workers' Union. In one of his few directly anti-Fascist articles, "Human Values in Literature and Revolution," Corey argues that the only good literature is that which concerns "itself primarily with consciousness and values, with attitudes toward life." Of the literature of his time that does this, Fraina notes three types: (1) "the literature of capitalist disintegration," (2) "the literature of fundamental human values and defense of those values," and (3) "the literature of conscious revolutionary aspiration and struggle." Fraina saw Fascism as "the final proof [that] in any period of fundamental social change, particularly as the old order decays, there is an increasing degradation of human values." Fraina points to the writing of Ignazio Silone as truly revolutionary:

In one of his short stories, Silone (whose *Fontamara* combines the understanding of theory and the sweep of life into a magnificent symphony) tells of a group of radical workers who are destroyed by a fascist spy because of their sense of decency. The moral is: you cannot be decent against the indecent. But Silone conveys more: that it is terrible to abandon decency, even necessarily and temporarily, because our fight is to make life decent.[7]

In the early 1940s, as a result of the German-Soviet Pact of 1939, Corey broke from his belief in Marxism and struggled to find ways of creating a more democratic economy. His thoughts on this subject were first expressed in *The Unfinished Task* (1940). He went on to teach from 1942 to 1951 at Antioch College, and from there he held the position of educational director of the Amalgamated Butcher Workmen, American Federation of Labor, in Chicago. This experience generated *Meat and Man: A Study of Monopoly, Unionism, and Food Policy* (1950). Despite his long-professed anti-Communism, the U.S. government attempted to deport him for being in the country illegally and for having once been a Communist. Two days after Fraina's death in 1953, the U.S. Department of Justice issued him a certificate of lawful entry.

Quite a different experience belonged to the next generation of writers. In his essay on the late Pietro di Donato's contribution to the Third American Writers' Congress, Art Casciato helps us to understand why writers like di Donato have been ignored by the established critics and scholars of the period. As Casciato points out, di Donato, in his brief speech—which Malcolm Cowley asked to be rewritten so that it would conform to Cowley's expectations—refused to adopt "the prescribed literary posture of the day in which the writer would efface his or her own class or ethnic identity in order to speak in the sonorous voice of 'the people.' " Casciato explains that di Donato's style resisted the modern and "thus supposedly proper ways of building his various structures." The result is that he is "less the bricklayer, than a *bricoleur* who works not according to plans but with materials at hand."[8] At the age of 16, on the night that Sacco and Vanzetti were executed, di Donato joined the Communist Party. The following excerpt from his contribution to the Third American Writers' Congress reflects di Donato's attitude, which Malcolm Cowley found troublesome: "I am not interested in writing for class-conscious people. I consider that a class-conscious person is something of a genius—I would say that he is sane, whereas the person who is not class-conscious is insane. . . . In writing *Christ in Concrete* I was trying to use this idea of Christianity, to get an 'in' there, using the idea of Christ."[9] Needless to say, di Donato's use of "comrade-worker Christ" as a metaphor for the working-class man would prove to be quite problematic when viewed from a Marxist perspective.[10]

Although sympathetic to the Communist Party in America, Jerre Mangione never formally joined it because he recognized in it a constraining dogmatism that reminded him of Catholicism. His memoirs *Mount Allegro* (1943) and *An Ethnic at Large* (1978), along with *The Dream and the Deal* (1972)—a study of the Federal Writers' Project—present the 1930s from an ethnic perspective. His interest in writing and his encounters with American avant-garde artists of the 1930s led him to dismiss the "art-for-art's-sake" cult and to realize that "no writer worth his salt could turn his back on social injustice."[11] For a brief time, he attended meetings of the New York John Reed Club and taught literary criticism at the New School in New York. Though uncomfortable with party-line politics, he became a dedicated anti-Fascist and contributed to the anti-Fascist cause through news articles and book reviews, as well as social and political satire published in the *New Republic*, the *New Masses*, the *Partisan Review*, and, under the pen names Mario Michele and Jay Gerlando, in the *Daily Worker*. Nonetheless, his left-wing activity and his strong anti-Fascist beliefs, Mangione's work has never been adequately acknowledged in histories of this period.

In 1937, Mangione left a New York publishing job to work for the New Deal. In the course of this period of politicization, he came to understand the terrible threat that European Fascism presented to the world. As he worked to understand it better, he befriended Carlo Tresca, an Italian anti-Fascist and anarchist who came to America in the early 1900s to aid the exploited Italian immigrant laborers. The material for Mangione's second novel, *Night Search* (1965), evolved from his interactions with Tresca. *Night Search* dramatizes the experience of Michael Mallory, the illegitimate son of an anti-Fascist labor organizer and newspaper publisher who searches for the murderer of his father, Paolo Polizzi, a character based on Carlo Tresca who in 1943 was murdered in New York City.

Mallory is an apolitical public relations writer inclined toward liberalism who, through an investigation of his father's death, learns to take action, and in doing so, comes to an understanding of where he stands in relation to contemporary politics. Mallory very much resembles Stiano Argento, the Catholic protagonist in Mangione's earlier and more strongly anti-Fascist novel, *The Ship and the Flame* (1948).

During this same period, Mangione also read Sicilian writers, interviewed Luigi Pirandello, and convinced the publishing firm that employed him to accept the translation of Ignazio Silone's now classic anti-Fascist novel, *Bread and Wine*. Mangione explored in greater depth the effects of Fascism on his relatives in "Fontamara Revisited," in which he describes a visit to Realmonte, his ancestors' homeland in southern Italy. In a later publication, based on his European experiences of the late 1930s, Mangione presents a more sophisticated overview of the effects of Fascism. In *The Ship and the Flame*, he creates an allegory for the sorry state of political affairs in Europe before America's entry into the Second World War. Aware of the dilemma of the liberal and the fate of the revolutionary in the world, Mangione created a microcosm of the larger world of his time, suggesting that the struggle against Fascism could be won through heroic action that would not compromise one's Catholic beliefs.

Another strong Italian American public voice of anti-Fascism was Frances Winwar—who Anglicized her Italian name, Vinciguerra, at her publisher's suggestion so that it would fit on the spine of her first book. Winwar was the only Italian American writer besides di Donato to speak at an American Writers' Congress. At the Second American Writers' Congress, in 1937, she presented a paper titled "Literature under Fascism," in which she described the effects of Fascist repression on Italian literature. She suggested that unless Fascism was fought, similar consequences would face the writers of other countries. Winwar concluded her survey of contemporary Italian literature by announcing that "The dark *Seicento* has come again over intellectual Italy. Fortunately, there are exiles. Wandering from land to land, from country to country, they and their works are the living proof that the best of Italy cannot be destroyed."[12] Winwar echoed these sentiments a few weeks later in her review of a translation of Alberto Moravia's *Wheel of Fortune*, in which she berated the novel and most of contemporary Italian literature, aside from those works of Fascist exiles, for seeming to "have been written in a vacuum . . . in some Never Never Land" or "far removed from the Italy of dictatorships and Ethiopian conquests."[13]

Although Winwar unabashedly displayed her anti-Fascist beliefs in her critical articles, she displaced those direct attacks by devoting her time to literary biographies: *Poor Splendid Wings: The Rosettis and Their Circle* (1933) concerned Italian expatriate artists, and *The Romantic Rebels* (1935) focused on the revolutionary spirit found in the life and works of Englishmen in Italy—Byron, Shelley, and Keats. In *Farewell the Banner: Coleridge, Wordsworth, and Dorothy* (1938), she created, as in her other books, an allegory for the contemporary period. In essence, with these books, Winwar, kept alive the belief of better times in Italy while reinforcing the idea that great writers can indeed affect history.

Carl Marzani—author of a novel titled *The Survivor*, a number of studies of American cold war policy and Eurocommunism, and a five-volume memoir—suffered a persecution quite similar to Fraina's. Born in Italy in 1912, he was just 10 years old when he published parodies of Fascist songs. He wrote six books, dozens of pamphlets, and produced a number of film documentaries. In each case, his goal had been to make America a better place to live by keeping a vigilance over corporate capitalism's Fascist tendencies. In *The Open Marxism of Antonio Gramsci* (1957), Marzani translated and annotated excerpts from Gramsci's prison notebooks, including "Preliminaries to a Study of Philosophy," "Base and Superstructure," "What Is Man," "Marxism and Modern Culture," and "Translation of Philosophic and Scientific Idioms."

Late in his life, the writer whom Italo Calvino called "The only man truthfully and completely in love with the United States,"[14] shifted his focus to recount the story of his life in *The Education of a Reluctant Radical*. Marzani had used some of this material in *The Survivor*, his only novel, published in 1958, seven years after he was convicted of "defrauding" the government by concealing a reluctant, one-year membership in the Communist Party. In the novel, Marc Ferranti, a Marzani-like character, is acquitted—a verdict achieved through the help of a senator who reads Ferranti's unpublished autobiography. It is this story within a story that depicts Marzani's response to Fascism and his family's flight from Mussolini's Fascism to American democracy. During a scene of a bitter coal miners' strike, Giordano Aurelius, Ferranti's father, explains the miners' situation to his son: "A man doesn't crawl, that's what he means. Mussolini and Fascism are like all the companies and all the Sor Panunzios [a *padrone*] sitting on top of the Peppones [a strike leader]. By fraud and by force, and a man can't speak, only to say yes sir and thank you sir. They trick and force the people into slavery, beat them into submission so that we bend our backs, walk on four legs, until we are sick with fear and sick with shame and rage."[15] It is this strong sense of what happened in Italy to his father, that leads Ferranti to stand strong against injustice, even if his actions are seen as un-American. This is a theme that replays itself consistently throughout the critical writings of Marzani.

Marzani worked his way through an education that earned him a scholarship to Oxford University. He was planning for a career as a dramatist when, in 1939, he left Oxford for Spain. In the third volume of his memoir, *Spain, Munich, and Dying Empires*, Marzani recalls his student days in 1936 at Oxford University. Out of curiosity and strong anti-Fascist beliefs, the young scholar visited Spain and found himself fighting Fascism alongside the anarchists in the Spanish Civil War. The experience became one in which his "life was altered forever."

When he returned to Oxford, he met actress Edith Eisner—a member of the American Communist Party, and the woman he would marry. Because of her, he reluctantly joined the Communist Party, an action to which he had not given much thought at the time. "[I]t never crossed my mind that joining the party might embarrass or harm me by jeopardizing my future or making me an outlaw in American society," Marzani wrote. "Given Spain and the CIO, most Communists and Communist sympathizers were accepted and even respected."[16] An honored veteran of World War II for his work in the Office of Strategic Services, Marzani was indicted as a former Communist under the Smith Act and spent over a year in jail as a political prisoner. It was during this time that he wrote a history of the cold war. In *We Can Be Friends* (1952), introduced by W. E. B. Du Bois, Marzani's study argues that the Truman Doctrine and the Korean War were nothing more than "a plan for cold-blooded aggression."[17] The last volume of his memoirs to be published before his death, *From the Pentagon to the Penitentiary* (1995) deals with his persecution by the American government. In the 1970s, Marzani continued his study of European communism and wrote *The Promise of Eurocommunism* (1980), a detailed and critical analysis of western European communism in the 1960s and 1970s.

Another radical writer of this period was Angelo Pellegrini, who in his memoir *American Dream* (1986) documented his coming-of-age in the 1930s, which included a stint as a Communist Party member. Radical thought in poetry can be found in the writing of Vincent Ferrini, Lawrence Ferlinghetti, and Diane di Prima. In fiction, Mari Tomasi's *Like Lesser Gods*; Michael DeCapite's *No Bright Banner*; Chuck Wachtel's *Joe the Engineer*; Daniela Gioseffi's stories in *In Bed with the Exotic Enemy* and her edited anthologies, *On Prejudice* and *Women on War*; and the works of many other Italian American artists reveal similar themes. Similar radical thinking can be found in the paintings of Ralph Fasanella, Lawrence Ferlinghetti, Robert Cimballo, and Vincent Ferrini, and in the plays of Albert Innaurato, Michelle Linfante, and Teresa Carilli.

These writers and artists are just a few of the many Italian American intellectuals whose Americanization included both a critical examination of the consequences of class in America and the development of a radical mode of thinking that encourages us to join them in challenging the social and economic status quo. Rather than abandon their working-class origins, they focused their life energies on understanding their own class origins and working for change. Unlike the few Italian immigrant writers who preceded them, whose work essentially argued for acceptance as human beings and pleas for recognition as Americans, these children and grandchildren of Italian immigrants used their writing to document and explore the conditions under which they were born and raised. Recovery and consideration of their works will aid us in re-creating a literary history that is sensitive to the process by which they created radical American identities brick by brick on the road of American radicalism.

NOTES

1. Michael Topp, "The Italian-American Left: Transnationalism and the Quest for Unity," in *The Immigrant Left in the United States*, ed. Paul Buhle and Dan Georgakas (Albany: State University of New York Press, 1996), 142.

2. Donald Young, *Research Memorandum on Minority Peoples in the Depression*, preface (New York: Social Science Research Council, 1972), i.

3. Paul Buhle master's thesis on Fraina was the basis for his book, *A Dreamer's Paradise Lost* (Amherst, N.Y.: Prometheus Books, 1995). I deal with Fraina's writing, especially his anti-Fascist writing, in "Fascism and Italian/American Writers," *Romance Languages Annual*, ed. Anthony Tamburri et al. (West LaFayette, Ind.: Purdue University Press, 1993), 254–59. See Fraina's obituary, "Lewis Corey, 1894–1953," *Antioch Review* 13 (December 1953): 538–45.

4. The information in this section was taken from an article by Fraina's wife, Esther Corey, "Lewis Corey (Louis C. Fraina), 1892–1953: A Bibliography with Autobiographical Notes," *Labor History* 4 (spring 1963): 103–31.

5. Luigi Fraina, *The Crisis of the Middle Class* (New York: Covici-Friede, 1935), 12–13.

6. Ibid., 19.

7. Luigi Fraina, "Human Values in Literature and Revolution," *Story* 8 (May 1936): 8.

8. Arthur Casciato, "The Brick Layer as Bricoleur: Pietro di Donato and the Cultural Politics of the Popular Front," *Voices in Italian Americana* (fall 1991): 70, 75–76.

9. Ibid., 69.

10. Pietro di Donato, *Christ in Concrete* (Indianapolis, Ind.: Bobbs-Merrill, 1966), 173.

11. Jerre Mangione, *An Ethnic at Large* (Philadelphia: University of Pennsylvania Press, 1983), 49.

12. Frances Winwar [Vinciguerra], "Literature under Fascism," in *The Writer in a Changing World*, ed. Henry Hart (New York: Equinox Cooperative Press, 1937), 91.

13. See Frances Winwar, review of *Wheel of Fortune*, by Alberto Moravia, *New Republic*, 16 June 1937, 165.

14. Italo Calvino, "Carl Marzani: An Appreciation," in *The Education of a Reluctant Radical: Roman Childhood, Book 1*, by Carl Marzani (New York: Topical Books, 1992), xi.

15. Carl Marzani, *The Survivor* (New York: Cameron Associates, 1958), 135.

16. Carl Marzani, *The Education of a Reluctant Radical, Spain, Munich, and Dying Empires, Book 3* (New York: Topical Books, 1993), 49–50.

17. Carl Marzani, *We Can Be Friends* (New York: Topical Books, 1952), 14.

Chapter 14

Behind the Mask: Signs of Radicalism in the Work of Rosa Zagnoni Marinoni

Julia Lisella

This essay takes its title from Rosa Zagnoni Marinoni's first book of poems, *Behind the Mask*, published in 1927. Marinoni often posed as a neutral or innocent observer whose short lyrics and epigrams could unmask or expose what was—for good or ill—genuine in people. It could be said that she herself wore a series of masks, from suffragist to genteel Southern lady intellectual to ambitious, hard-working Italian immigrant. What I aim to show, however, is that such cultural roles were not necessarily mutually exclusive. Many of Marinoni's poems iconoclastically criticize "proper society"; they often analyze the system of racial oppression in the South where she was a popular literary voice, and many feature women and women's labor as their main subjects. Nonetheless, Marinoni was reluctant to view herself as a political writer—she claimed always to be responding to racism, economic hardship, or sexism, as a moralist rather than as an ideologue.

   Much of Marinoni's work engages and struggles with a politicized aesthetic that developed in particular among women writers during the 1930s: a documentary style that combined elements of "proletarian" writing—realism, public discourse, narrative—with a personal, individualized lyric voice. Such an aesthetic enabled women writers to make certain heretofore private or "sentimental" experiences present, such as maternity and domestic labor, and indeed to demonstrate their relationship and importance to a wider context of social concerns, such as unemployment, racism, and economic struggle. In this essay I would like to argue for inclusion of Marinoni's voice within the tradition of women's literary radicalism, despite the fact that Marinoni herself might have been surprised to be included in such politically charged company as other willing spokeswomen of the American Left, such as Tillie Olsen, Meridel LeSueur, Genevieve Taggard, or Muriel Rukeyser. However reluctantly Marioni may have been to define herself

politically, by portraying women's lives and their work in her poems, and by publishing in a variety of progressive and mainstream journals and newspapers, she
made her voice known to an audience of readers during the 1930s who were
eager for progressive messages.

Marinoni emerged outside of any organized political or cultural group. She was
not a self-proclaimed Communist, socialist, or anarchist. She did not consider
herself a modernist, or for that matter, an antimodernist. Yet, this Italian-born
American writer produced poetry between the late 1920s and the early 1940s
that challenged American concepts of race and gender; called attention to the
lives of both urban and farm workers, particularly women; condemned the middle and upper-middle class, often characterizing them as shallow, silly, or unfeel-
ing; and highlighted the plight of working-class, as well as more-assimilated
middle-class, Italian immigrants. Perhaps because of her own unwillingness to be
labeled or classified, her career has suffered from a lack of critical attention. Yet
in her lifetime she achieved a high degree of popularity, garnering the titles of
Poet Laureate of the Ozarks in 1936 and Poet Laureate of the state of Arkansas in
1953. In the 1960s, when so many critics were beginning to reexamine radical
writing of the 1930s,[1] the literary critic Guy Owen wrote confidently of Southern
poetry "we did not produce a Lola Ridge or Kenneth Fearing or much of anything
that would fit into the proletarian anthology *We Gather Strength* (1933)."[2]
Though Owen could find no evidence of a progressive 1930s voice, Marinoni
had published in two of the leading proletarian journals of the early '30s: *The
Rebel Poet* and *The Anvil*. By 1938 she had published five volumes of poetry. And
though she did not publish another collection until well after World War II, in
1954,[3] she continued to print many of her socially conscious poems of the 1930s
in her later five volumes, including a bilingual edition of her poems called *Radici
Al Vento* (Roots to the Sky) published in Milan.

Born in Bologna, Italy, around 1890, had Marinoni continued living in New
York, where she first settled with her parents (Antero Zagnoni, a journalist and
author, and Maria Marzocchi Zagnoni, a poet and artist) the radical energy of
Greenwich Village may have drawn her to a meeting with Arturo Giovannitti or to
a lecture in the Great Hall of Cooper Union by Emma Goldman.[4] She may have
written about Italian factory workers rather than Ozark farmers, thus making her
connection to a leftist literary tradition more obvious. But she did not stay long
enough to imbibe the potential radicalizing effect of New York City. Instead of
meeting a fellow comrade at a Communist Party meeting, she met Antonio Marinoni, a young Italian-born, Yale-educated academic who was on his way to his post
as professor of Romance languages at the University of Arkansas, Fayetteville. They
married in Brooklyn in 1908 and moved to Fayetteville, where she lived for the rest
of her life. Despite Marinoni's lack of formal education (she had been tutored at
home by her parents), she did some course work at the University of Arkansas in
drama and art. She campaigned for woman suffrage and served as the chairwoman of
the movement's Arkansas chapter from 1913 to 1915. After that, there is no indica-
tion that she involved herself in any organized political struggles. She died in 1970.[5]

Perhaps because of this denial of political affiliations, she felt free to publish widely. In addition to leftist journals, she appeared in mainstream literary journals, such as *The Greenwich Village Quill* and *American Poetry Magazine*, as well as in an anthology edited by Stanley Braithwaite, then a leading critic of contemporary poetry. She also published in such newspapers as the *Chicago Tribune* and in ladies' magazines as well as in such Catholic venues as the Paulist Press. She was a great democratizer of poetry. She read poetry over the radio and issued her poems in pamphlet form as though they were travelogues for tourists. In the early 1960s she established a poetry day in Arkansas, now nationally commonplace, but rare then. She did not regard poems in a precious light but churned them out by the hundreds. Helen Barolini makes mention of Marinoni in the introduction to her groundbreaking anthology of Italian American women writers, *The Dream Book,* as "an indefatigable poetaster of some years ago."[6] Indefatigable, yes. She wrote with the fury of a newcomer eager to make a name for herself in the literary world. Though she began writing poems when she was in her mid-thirties, a late bloomer by her own generation's standards, she also published stories for adults and children, and she had edited several anthologies promoting poetry of the American South.

If it is difficult to place Marinoni politically, it is even more difficult to place her in terms of modernist categories, especially as the critical field shifts in its view of what was truly "modernist." She wrote in both tight metric forms and in free verse, and her poetic temperament ran the gamut from sentimental to caustic and cynical. As Michael Tratner has noted in his work on modernism and mass politics, "Emerging together in the early twentieth century were modernist literary forms, collectivist political theories, new intellectual disciplines such as sociology and anthropology, mass movements such as socialism, feminism, and Fascism, and new collective or corporate structures of mass society such as unions, welfare systems, corporations, and modern political parties. The lines of influence went in all directions."[7] Marinoni's poems demonstrate this cross-current of political and literary forces in a powerful way. One has only to look at Marinoni's complicated publishing history to see the surprising and ironic ways in which the movements of the Left and the Right coexisted. In 1930, Marinoni published an anti-lynching poem called "Man Hunt" in *Unrest: The Rebel Poets Anthology for 1930,* edited by Jack Conroy and Ralph Cheyney, leading proponents of leftist literature at the time.[8] That poem was in no way an anomaly for Marinoni. Other anti-lynching poems followed. "Man in a Tree," for example, first published in the early 1930s in *Unity,* a periodical of "social vision verse" edited by Ralph Cheyney and Lucia Trent, parodies the Joyce Kilmer poem "Trees" by using singsong rhyming couplets, but rather than describing a "lovely" tree, Marinoni describes a figure of a man hanging beside a tree.[9]

Around this same time, in May 1931, Marinoni also published a short story in *Atlantica,* "The Weed Addict," about a young woman smuggler who almost outwits the federal authorities. The contrast between the heartfelt humanism and urgency to witness of the anti-lynching poems and the more cynical modernist minimalism of the story are not the only inconsistencies present. *Unrest* and *Unity* were confirmed leftist publications. *Atlantica* was an American-based literary and cultural journal sponsored by the Italian Fascist government. Publishing in these extremely divergent magazines may reveal more about the times in which Marinoni wrote than it does about her political persuasion.

Indeed, *Atlantica* itself shows evidence of these cross-currents of Left and Right politics. Geared toward Italian and Italian American intellectuals, *Atlantica* began in 1923 as a bilingual journal published in Rome as *Rivista d'Italia e d'America*, with its stated goal of "stimulat[ing] interest and understanding of Italy" by Americans, and vice versa. Its first article, written in English, was called "America and Fascist Italy." In 1929 it began publication in New York and most of its articles began to be published in English. Its editorial objective was described in Italian: "vuol essere, in questo grande centro, una rivista moderna" (what is needed in this great city is a modern journal). In its transformation it continued to proudly tout Mussolini as Italy's great leader and most of all, its great modernizer. In an article titled "L'Aeroporto del Littorio" (The superb things accomplished by the new Italy), about the newly built airport in Rome, for example, the writer unabashedly applauds Mussolini as "the savior of Italian aeronautics [whose presence] at this inauguration is evidence enough of the interest that the National Government and Fascist Italy have taken and are taking in this courageous enterprise."[10] Yet *Atlantica* may not have been perceived as exclusively a Fascist publication but rather a cosmopolitan journal. Italian intellectuals from a variety of political persuasions, including such anti-Fascists as Leonard Covello, found a publishing outlet there.[11] Its pages also contained favorable book reviews of *Jews without Money*, by Michael Gold, a leading leftist critic who made no apologies for his Communism. It also sympathetically reviewed the novel *Il Vecchio e I Fanciulli* by Nobel Prize winner Grazia Deledda, whose portrayals of women clearly challenged Fascism's ideal of woman.[12] In a sympathetic review of *The Letters of Sacco and Vanzetti*, edited by Marion Denman Frankfurter and Gardner Jackson, Sacco and Vanzetti are revered as "two social martyrs."[13] In that same issue, an article appears about Margaret Fuller, the American transcendentalist, called "An American Disciple of Manzini." In the essay she is cast as "a martyr for Italian liberation." In the early days of Fascism, *Atlantica* positioned itself as part of a noble tradition of rebellion.

There is really no way to discern whether it was the journal's progressive socialist interests or its promotion of Italian Fascism that interested Marinoni, or whether she was an ambitious writer eager to increase her readership, to reach her fellow Italians as well as her fellow Southerners in Arkansas, or even whether we can use publication history as an indicator of political or aesthetic persuasion, especially in the late 1920s and early 1930s when so many venues espoused a particularly socialist viewpoint. But her publication in *Atlantica* certainly points to her pride in her native country. And the fact that *Atlantica* offered the United States an intellectual vision of Italians to dispel the image of the illiterate immigrant *Wop* (a term Marinoni was not afraid to use in several of her poems to demonstrate the cruelty and danger of cultural stereotypes) must also have meant a great deal to Marinoni who wrestled very specifically with this issue in her poetry. She knew both first-hand and as a Depression-era witness the effects of social displacement caused by immigration, exploitation, and poverty. In "Tony the Ragman," in which she describes the desperate times of the Depression, identified as a desperate wop, even the ragman can't convince anyone to give up the few goods they have to keep him in business. In the final stanza, she refers to her act of witnessing hardship as she often did, by characterizing herself as a fool. For Marinoni, playing the fool meant being willing to witness and report injustices suffered by the unknown and marginalized.[14]

"Spasmodic Equality,"[15] in its startling simplicity and political astuteness, stands out as one of the most revealing poems in terms of her American progressivism. It very clearly questions what constitutes national identity, at least American national identity. The poem is unique in this period for the way in which Marinoni groups the plight of Italians, African Americans, and Chinese Americans together, describing their struggle as a common one against an institutionalized form of racism, a notion much more sympathetic to a socialist argument rather than a Fascist vision. Published just one year after the publication of her short story in *Atlantica,* this poem uses a comic form, the ethnic joke, "Once there were three men," and turns on that joke very quickly through the use of racial epithets to make her point. "Spasmodic Equality" points to the hypocrisy of the American government's use of ethnic and racial minorities, inviting them into the American project during times of war as cannon fodder, and then returning them to their oppressed positions once peace is declared.

In "Who Are My People?"[16] which first appeared in *Behind the Mask,* Marinoni posed a question that was central to her, and that remained pressing enough for her to reprint the poem in two of her collections from the 1940s and 1950s. This poem points to Marinoni's desire to lift the mask, to use poetry as a way to humanize and be humanized. Though Marinoni often did not identify directly with the immigrant experience, and specifically with Italian Americans, she did often articulate the loss of being unable to assimilate, as well as its concomitant benefits—namely, being able to identify with "the folk," whether they were Depression-era Ozark farmers or the urban poor. In this poem as in many others, the speaker identifies with the struggling rather than with the comfortable and achieved of America. The poem explores the difficulty of finding true kinship with people of her class, her religion, or even her nationality. Indirectly, she also identifies her own loss as an immigrant living in America. She is no longer Italian—she is a stranger there—nor is she completely welcomed in her adopted country. At the end of the poem the speaker meets an old man who does not speak her language but who offers her his patched umbrella. Finally, the community Marinoni comes to define is one marked by a shared experience of suffering, loss, and poverty, rather than a shared language, nationality, or organized religion. She identifies with the poor man in the street.

Despite her allegiance to the down-and-out, Marinoni was herself a woman of means. She was a landlady in Fayetteville, Arkansas, an active member of several society groups, and wife of the Yale-educated, Italian-born professor of Romance languages at the University of Arkansas, Fayetteville, Antonio Marinoni.[17] Jonathan Wilson has argued that a common trait among middle-class leftist writers was self-contempt for their lack of authenticity, for their not being factory workers or farmers themselves.[18] Marinoni never seems caught in this self-doubt. She never berates herself for her class position, or apologizes. Indeed, she often uses her class position as a vantage point from which to observe the hypocrisies of middle-class life.

In "From Three to Six," another poem from her first collection, the speaker describes an excruciating women's tea, focusing all the anxiety of the women's feelings of belonging or not belonging in terms of their dresses and physical attributes.[19] The poem itself turns on the hypocrisy of the educated, polite, middle class who prefer their women not to hide behind ostentatious dresses that require the help of other women to don, and who also frown on women revealing their own physicality in any way. The poem focuses on one young woman in particular who cannot hide her body, her large hands and a flashy hat. Marinoni identifies with this outsider, the woman who wants to leave the party. Marinoni was a large, masculine-looking woman herself, who wore her hair dramatically short at times. She was often described in newspapers and magazines of her day in terms of her Italian or sometimes more generically Latin heritage, as "a strikingly handsome woman with flashing dark eyes," "La Rosita," or "Donna Rosita."[20] Although the detailed descriptions may seem complimentary at first glance, Raffaele Cocchi notes "it seems she was not accepted by the academic environment, because of her 'illiteracy' and her strange behavior: those academic 'cherubic gentlewomen' did not like her fancy European way of dressing and her energetic attitude."[21] It is odd to think about this prolific poet feeling "illiterate." But her "energetic attitude" must have come into direct conflict with the Southern ideal of female gentility.

"Painted Feathers" and "Steerage-Swallow," both of which appeared in *Red Kites and Wooden Crosses* (1929), deal more specifically with the inner class conflicts, as well as the internalized shame, of the newly arrived immigrant who struggles to assimilate, or at the least, survive. Like much of the cultural production of ethnic Americans, both poems do in some part promote ethnic stereotypes just as they attempt to dispel their negative connotations. In "Painted Feathers," after the children have taught Mrs. Repetti how to fit in by smiling silently, wearing pointed shoes, and greeting her neighbors with the correct English salutations, the mother still cannot stop singing. The Italian woman is passionate, emotional, and primitive here, barely able to fit her feet into the constricting American shoes and the demure American role of quiet middle-class neighbor. Mrs. Repetti recalls for us all the other women who do not fit the American mainstream's notion of femininity.

And like the girl in the hat Marinoni describes in "From Three to Six," the character Giovannina in "Steerage-Swallow" dreams of escape. Despite her husband's rise to the upper middle class, by the end of this poem Giovannina longs to return to her native city of Naples so that she can return to her true identity and wear her old brown immigrant-identified shawl. These poems of ethnic displacement and discomfort are the closest Marinoni comes to autobiographical lyric making. They are instead really story-poems, small narratives not unlike the many stories of her contemporary, Anzia Yezierska. Both writers focused on the sense of alienation these unnamed women experienced as they rose to the middle class—distanced from both their own (Americanized) children and their ethnic kin.

Though Marinoni's lyrics speak to the difficulties of maintaining one's culture—and for the Italian woman that included a particular type of strength and power, at least within the home—her brand of feminism was not without its own contradictions. By the 1930s, the feminism born out of the suffragist movement (with which Marinoni had been deeply involved), based on an ideal of female moral superiority, was already considered somewhat old-fashioned. And the less-moral, "new woman" of the 1920s had already been "subsumed by anxiety over the unemployed man, and competition for a limited number of jobs reinforced cultural assumptions about the proper sexual division of labor."[22] So although she may have been considered a radical feminist in the early 1900s, Marinoni's attitude toward gender roles was also in keeping with a less-challenging, patriarchal vision of women's social place that was often shared by the Left and the Right.

"I Am a Woman" speaks to this cultural tendency of both camps to identify women's strength with their ability to mother.[23] Read as Helen Barolini directs us to in *The Dream Book*, "I Am a Woman" essentializes and reduces women's worth to their role as mother. But read within the context of the emerging ideologies of women's sources of strength, the poem might be seen as an enormously liberating poem in which, in a few brief lines, Marinoni ably releases women from other traditional narratives that rely on male power and male knowledge. Ultimately what distinguishes women from other human beings in this poem is their potential to bring forth life. On a basic level she underscores woman's traditional role. But her forthrightness also opens up another channel of interpretation that values woman's creative force.

Fred Gardaphè argues that "If an ethnographic critic is to be successful, he or she must be able to read the culturally specific signs generated in the multicultural text."[24] Marinoni's work reflected both her cultural and political influences: egalitarianism and patriarchalism, liberal humanitarianism and Catholic fatalism, Southern American wit and Italian *bella figura*, nineteenth-century European romanticism and twentieth-century American realism, an Arkansas folklore tradition and Bolognese '*zdoura*.[25] Marinoni's poems that feature women, especially mothers, are rich in moments that bridge these various opposites. So although Barolini offers "I Am a Woman" as proof that Marinoni was a bad but popular poet, she also raises an essential critical consideration about the role of the mother in Italian culture that may go a long way in explaining both the more-radical content of some of Marinoni's work as well as her stingingly acerbic and judgmental poems about women. As Barolini explains, Italian and Italian American women have historically been tragically wedded to a patriarchal view of the world "in which her life was always dependent upon a male—

her father, brother, husband, and, eventually, if widowed, her sons. Family was the focal point of her duty and concern, and, by the same token, the source of her self-esteem and power, the means by which she measured her worth and was in turn measured, the reason for her being."[26] Barolini points out the major paradox for many Italian American women. Although they are inculturated by a patriarchal system in which boys are valued over girls and male leadership is accepted, they have also participated in a private, homebound matriarchy in which the mothers set the standard: "Within Italian culture," Barolini writes, "reinforcement of the woman's role and definition in the family was gained through the strong cult of the Madonna—the Holy Mother who prefigured all other mothers and symbolized them."[27] Italian immigrant women found no such equivalent in the Anglo-American culture they confronted. Mrs. Repetti is still the mother of the house, but in American culture such status means little. Indeed, as Barolini suggests, women of Italian ethnic origin often have, or at least up until the last generation or so, found a "source of power" in their roles within the family as opposed to their roles in public life, and in the symbolic representations of such power. Eve, for Marinoni, always renders Mary, the Madonna because the Madonna figure rises above and beyond Eve's curse. However problematic that configuration may seem, Mary is a crucial figure for Catholics as well as for many other 1930s women writers. Lola Ridge, Genevieve Taggard, Lucia Trent, and many others were quite fascinated with Mary as representative of maternal power. Perhaps this is because her sole biblical role as mother of Jesus reverberates both privately in the life of the man, Jesus, and publicly in the spiritual life of Christians as a source of inspiration. She is important to the life of the community *and* she survives Christ. The silent, long-suffering women of the Ozarks who Marinoni praises in her poems might not necessarily seem like agents of change, but, like Mary the Madonna, they interrupt other conventional narratives of traditional womanhood in interesting ways.

During the 1930s, there was another ideological reason why women were portrayed as modern Madonnas. Wendy Kozol notes the reasons for such a trend in the New Deal's photography project which produced 270,000 photos between 1935 and 1942: "Pictures often depict women as mothers, including secularized portraits of the Madonna and Child. The female ideal of motherhood was loudly praised during the Depression as *the* symbol of that most fundamental of traditional institutions, the family. Although there were social struggles and tensions over gender identities in the 1930s, the majority of RA/FSA photographs of mothers do not show this conflict. Rather, these pictures construct reassuring depictions of who suffered and who survived the Depression."[28] As Kozol explains, Madonna-like figures were more able to drum up public sympathy for "the deserving poor." Marinoni, like many artists of her day, also produced her share of idealized, secular versions of the Madonna and child that did not disturb or challenge gender roles. Or at least seemingly did not. But her work reverberated on so many social registers that if the image did not disturb one image of poor, oppressed women, it certainly disturbed some other vision.

In "Women Are They" for example, poor women are depicted as patient survivors. And in the tradition of idealized versions of the good, they make their mark only through their death.[29] Marinoni describes their smiles and demeanor as brave, but clearly they are also passive. If they have any power, they are unaware of it. And certainly their power, as described by Marinoni, is not in the conventional form it took in more-radical 1930s literature. These women do not complain or fight or organize. Their worth and their power, instead, is in their ability to wait, even unto death, and to be remembered by their men. Marinoni had a tendency to shut her poems down in the final two lines with sentimental closures that distanced both writer and her readers from the subject material. There is love and admiration in this poem to be sure, but there is also a far-distant stance that tells Marinoni's readers that they are not implicated in the poem. There is one haunting element of this poem, however, a kind of moralism presented as an answer to an unheard question. As in "I Am a Woman," which answers a "why" or a "how" (how are you able to call yourself a woman?), "Women Are They" seems to answer an onlooker's question: could those dust-encrusted, hard-working, thin-faced people really be Southern *women*? Here Marinoni answers an emphatic "yes" by attempting to silence questions of what is feminine with questions more closely akin to Alice Walker's notion of what is "womanist."[30] Marinoni's version is still patriarchally inflected; these women are only fully women in the eyes of their men. But Marinoni qualifies such "patriarchy" by reminding her readers that the men in this story are as equally unfortunate and invisible to the mainstream culture as their women. Though it seems like a highly sentimentalized vision of women, the poem boldly insists on granting these waiting figures, class-bound and to a large degree powerless, the status of "women," a tactic that went far beyond "humanizing" women.

The more political version of Marinoni's sentimental "Women Are They" might be found in the poem "Unemployed."[31] The title is ironic because it features women's domestic work. As Marinoni explains, the Depression may have put men out of work, but women are, for better or worse, never unemployed, and indeed, no one is clamoring to take their jobs of drudgery away from them. In this poem, Marinoni loses her patience with unemployed men; in the light of the park benches, breadlines, and closed factories she describes men as drowsing, muttering, or sulking, while women continue to work: washing, scrubbing, mending, cooking, rocking babies, nursing babies, soothing babies. As in "Women Are They," the poem neatly shuts down with its final conceit, that motherhood is itself both job and vocation. So, although the poem reads as a potentially radical message about women's unpaid work, it cannot seem to stay open to its own power. For better or worse, the poem also illustrates Marinoni's independence from leftist politics. Its view of unemployed men slouching on park benches would hardly make it a candidate for publication in journals that had readily accepted her poems against lynching or hunger in the South. In this poem, gender wins out over class solidarity. It reads very differently from a poem like Genevieve Taggard's "Feeding the Children,"[32] in which Taggard admonishes women for putting their private "conservative" desires of feeding their children before the more pressing global issue of supporting the strike, even if it means there will be no food on the table.

More-militant images of maternity emerge in Marinoni's poems that feature a battle with nature rather than a battle with capitalism as in "Go Away Spring"[33] in which the poet admonishes nature for its inability to provide food and sustenance while it is able to produce useless blossoms and other forms of beauty. And in *The Ozarks and Some of Its People*, published in pamphlet form, one untitled poem describes a mother fighting starved wild wolves and wielding an ax to fend off the beast. If this is a Madonna figure, it is a kind of liberation theology version, ready to fight for her young at any moment.

"Drought," a poem published in *The Rebel Poet* in 1928 and later in her 1938 volume *Side Show*, displays one of the most important characteristics of radical women's writing: an insistence on combining the private lyric with public narrative. In this poem the speaker describes the effect of a long drought on a poor Arkansas family. What distinguishes this poem from other poems of witness, however, is its strong narrative thread, its persistent speaker-witness, its long full lines, and its inclusion of wisdom figures, such as the old woman who appears at the end of the poem to explain "drought" as a figure for death and destruction. The lone poet in "Drought" closely aligns herself with her subject matter rather than standing at the edge of the scene. The poem also differs from "Women Are They" and the more conventional use of first person of "I Am a Woman" in its combination of narrative and lyrical elements. In "Drought," Marinoni chooses a flatter line that resists romanticizing motherhood. Description and imagery are less robust and overdone than in other poems on the subject of poverty and women. It is as though Marinoni trusts the English language and its cadence to do the work for her. She even ventures a personal pronoun, underscoring this poem as one of personal witness rather than of objective reportage, and favors free-verse lines that come to full stops.

Marinoni's interest in folk wisdom is also used well in "Drought." Here an older woman, a female folk figure, provides the speaker with insight. Her observations allow the speaker to abandon her observer's tone and instead to connect personally with the experience of poverty and injustice personified by the quasi-Madonna figure at the end of the poem, who is depicted rocking in a chair on her porch and holding a starving child, perhaps a dead child, on her lap. This poem is particularly poignant because of the way Marinoni resists a theatrical tendency in her poems to address her audience. She moves instead from narrative and observation to interiority, releasing a prayer or plea that she might not see, not know, or forget that she has witnessed. It is a genuine moment of despair, not presented as a lesson to other listeners, finally, but as a private lyric moment between the speaker and God. The mother's rocking motion and the speaker's repetitive prayer for rain join together, as does the lyric and narrative strain of the poem. The safe distance between the "I" of the speaker-witness and the "they" of her listeners returns briefly near the final section of the poem. But finally, Marinoni ends the poem with a more-militant assertion in which she willingly indicts a system that cannot provide for its people. This poem does not argue for the battle between humans and nature but places the natural elements, starvation, and death in a political context: pennies, ash cans, all symbols of the economic oppression that was destroying people's lives in the South and around the country.

The long critical silence around Marinoni has to do with critics' inability to find a place for her: she was too socially conservative and upper middle class to be considered either leftist or "proletarian"; too scathing and analytical, and perhaps too ethnically identified, to be considered a traditional Southern writer; and too linguistically conservative to be considered a modernist. Marinoni's more-progressive poems suggest a story about the 1930s that was perhaps more common for the ethnically identified American writer. Marinoni was not a curious spectator of the events of the Depression. She was certainly never neutral. Nor was she on the front lines. Marinoni's cultural popularity and her unwillingness, or inability, to declare (in the words of Florence Reece's strike song of that era) "which side" she was on have overshadowed the power of much of her work. Michael Denning argues that the Depression era "marked the first time in the history of the United States that the left—the tradition of radical democratic movements for social transformation—had a central, indeed shaping, impact on American culture."[34] That Marinoni, an upper-class, socially conservative landlady in the southern United States, enthusiastically participated in a leftist-inspired transformation of American poetry perhaps speaks more to the power of the Left at that time on American culture than it does to some odd quirk of Marinoni's nature.

In 1963, Marinoni republished many of her older poems in the collection *The Green Sea Horse*, including "Who Are My People?" and "Go Away Spring." A former student of hers, Edsel Ford, wrote of the volume, "This is mankind looking at his unadmirable self in 1963." But, he goes on to say, "Mrs. Marinoni doesn't dismiss man as a hopeless case. Indeed, her compassion through the years of writing has grown in proportion to her awareness of a large and increasingly complex world."[35] It is true that Marinoni's refusal to commit to any specific political movement or to allow her most-radical political tendencies to take hold of her work appear in some of her poems as linguistic conservatism. Still, into the 1960s she remained convinced that her importance as a poet was in her ability to empathize with the haves and have nots. She understood her position as both insider and outsider in the culture and in her own life, and her poems speak to the poignancy of that knowledge. In "Sea Wall,"[36] which appeared in *The Green Sea Horse*, she described herself as a woman on a border between, never belong-

ing specifically to one side or the other. The sea wall in this poem separates tenements on one side from yachts, sailboats, and the leisure class playing in the
ocean. The power of the speaker is in her ability to span the length of that sea
wall, to know and to understand both the poverty of tenement row and the privilege just peaking over the other side of the wall. This was the place of poetry
itself for Marinoni, literally between the two worlds, between the rich and the
poor, the privileged and the destitute. She may not have believed that poetry
could change the world, or that it could even point blame at one political party
or another. But she did believe it could, like the natural world of the gulls, the
wind, and the waves, create the constant movement, sound, and even beauty,
that could draw our attention to the social, economic, and cultural barriers that
exist between each of us.

NOTES

1. See, for example, Daniel Aaron, *Writers on the Left: Episodes in American Literary
Communism* (1961; New York: Columbia UP, 1992), and James Gilbert, *Writers and Partisans: A History of Literary Radicalism in America* (1968; New York: Columbia UP, 1992).

2. Guy Owen, "Southern Poetry during the 30s" in *The Thirties: Fiction, Poetry, Drama*,
ed. Warren French (Deland, FL: Everett Edwards, 1967) 167.

3. Olga Peragallo, *Italian-American Authors and Their Contribution to American Literature* (New York: S.F. Vanni, 1949), 149.

4. Marinoni's birth year is listed variously as 1888 [*Contemporary Authors—Permanent
Series* (Detroit: Gale Research, 1975–78)] or 1891 [Peragallo, 1248–49].

5. Biographical information has been drawn from the following sources: Raffaele Cocchi, "Rosa Zagnoni Marinoni: From the Bolognese Hills to the Ozarks," *Bologna: La Cultura Italiana e Le Letterature Straniere Moderne*, ed. Vita Fortunati, vol. 1 (Bologna: U of
Bologna P, 1988) 312–321; Myra Miles Moran, "Rosa Zagnoni Marinoni," unpublished
paper, Arkansas Writers-Arkansas Regional Studies, spring 1982, collected by Arkansas
State Library, Little Rock; and Olga Peragallo, *Italian-American Authors and Their Contribution to American Literature* (New York: S. F. Vanni, 1949).

6. Helen Barolini, *The Dream Book* (New York: Schocken Books, 1985) 9.

7. Michael Tratner, *Modernism and Mass Politics: Joyce, Woolf, Eliot, Yeats* (Stanford:
Stanford UP, 1995) 6.

8. Ralph Cheyney and Jack Conroy, eds., *Unrest: The Rebel Poets Anthology for 1930*
(London: "Studies" Publications, Braithwaite and Miller, 1930). Marinoni later collected
this poem in *North of Laughter* (Atlanta: Oglethorpe UP, 1931) 69.

9. Marinoni, *North of Laughter*, 6. Permission from the estate of Rosa Zagnoni Marinoni could not be obtained to quote directly from the poems discussed in this essay. While
all Marinoni's books are now out of print, most can be found in large university libraries
and in many of the local libraries of Arkansas.

10. "L'Aeroporto del Littorio," *Atlantica, Rivista D'Italia e d'America* (June–July 1928): 270

11. Thanks to Gerald Meyer for pointing out Leonard Covello's article, "Language
Usage in Italian Families," *Atlantica* (October 1934): 327.

12. For more on Italian women writers and Fascism, see Robin Pickering-Iazzi, introduction, *Unspeakable Women: Selected Short Stories Written by Italian Women during Fascism*
(New York: Feminist Press, 1993).

13. *Atlantica* (Feb. 1929). The letters themselves are described as having "passages that are sublime in their assertion of principle at the expense of life; there are others whose human touch brings tears to the eyes of the most callous anti-radical."

14. Rosa Z. Marinoni, *Side Show* (Philadelphia: David McKay, 1938) 62.

15. Rosa Z. Marinoni, *Red Kites and Wooden Crosses,* intro. Stanley Braithwaite (Chicago: Robert Packard, 1929) 80.

16. Marinoni, *Behind the Mask*, 40. The poem also appeared in Marinoni, *North of Laughter*, 16, and Marinoni, *Radici al Vento* (Milan: Mario Bazzi, 1956) 12–13.

17. Her obituary notes that "The Marnoni's built up sizable real estate holdings in the city of Fayetteville during their lives together and during her later years, Mrs. Marinoni handled more than 100 apartments." From "State Poet Laureate Dies; Verses Flowed During Long Career," *Arkansas Gazette,* 27 March 1970, 1–2A. Reproduced from the Holdings of Special Collections Division, University of Arkansas Libraries, Fayetteville, Arkansas.

18. Jonathan Wilson, "On Radical Writing in the 1930s," *The Literary Review* 27 (fall 1983): 44.

19. Marinoni, *Behind the Mask,* 13–14.

20. From various newspaper articles reproduced from the Special Collections Holdings of the University of Arkansas Libraries, Fayetteville. I must acknowledge Ms. Andrea E. Cantrell, director of the Research Services Department, for responding so promptly and so extensively to my request for information about Marinoni.

21. Cocchi, "Rosa Marinoni," 317.

22. Constance Coiner, *Better Red: The Writing and Resistance of Tillie Olsen and Meridel Le Sueur* (New York: Oxford UP, 1995) 38.

23. Barolini, *Dream Book,* 10.

24. Fred Gardaphè, *Italian Signs, American Street: The Evolution of Italian American Narrative* (Durham and London: Duke UP, 1996) 20.

25. This last quality, *'zdoura,* was suggested by Raffaele Cocchi's biographical essay. He describes *'zdoura* as "common sense sayings," "grandma sayings," or the sayings of "the woman of experience in everyday life" (318). Like *bella figura, 'zdoura* has its roots in folkloric traditions.

26. Barolini, *Dream Book,* 9.

27. Ibid.

28. Wendy Kozol, "Madonnas of the Fields: Photography, Gender, and 1930s Farm Relief," *Genders* 2 (summer 1988): 1–2.

29. Marinoni, *Behind the Mask,* 11.

30. Ethnically identified women have traditionally had to seek alternative ways to envision and represent female power and agency that may stand as much outside patriarchal models as they do Anglo feminist models. In the opening pages of her early collection of essays, *In Search of Our Mother's Gardens: Womanist Prose* (New York: Harcourt Brace Jovanovich, 1983), Alice Walker presents the term *womanist* as having an "official" dictionary definition, which begins: "Womanist 1. From *womanish*. (Opp. of "girlish," i.e., frivolous, irresponsible, not serious.) A black feminist or feminist of color. From the black folk expression of mothers to female children, 'You acting womanish,' i.e., like a woman. Usually referring to outrageous, audacious, courageous or *willful* behavior." Although Marinoni's women lack the agency Walker describes, her impulse to work outside the proscribed definitions of culturally accepted femininity lead me to the comparison.

31. Marinoni, *Side Show,* 101.

32. Genevieve Taggard, *Calling Western Union* (New York and London: Harper & Brother, 1936) 54.

33. Marinoni, *Radici al Vento*, and Marinoni, *The Green Sea Horse* (Francestown, NH: Golden Quill Press, 1963).

34. Michael Denning, *The Cultural Front: The Laboring of American Culture in the Twentieth Century* (New York: Verso, 1997) 1.

35. Edsel Ford, "Salty Sea Horse from the Ozark Mts.," *New Arkansas*, 18 Oct. 1963, 3.

36. Marinoni, *Green Sea Horse*, 39.

Chapter 15

Rooted to Family: Italian American Women's Radical Novels

Mary Jo Bona

My definition of radicalism has less to do with the social realism of the working classes[1] (as fascinating as that topic is) and more to do with the etymological significance of the word *radical* itself, which comes from the Latin word *radix*, meaning root.[2] The root of Italian American radicalism in the literature of the late twentieth century goes back to the family, is unceasingly about the family, as it struggles with the complexities of its own ethnicity and the divergent paths that children of families take regarding how they are going to live and whom they are going to love. For example, two lesbian novels—Dodici Azpadu's *Saturday Night in the Prime of Life* and Rachel deVries's *Tender Warriors*—examine how the Italian American family struggles with the sexual identity of its determined, gay daughters. Coming out to the family as gay or lesbian threatens these families, who have struggled so many years to gain acceptance as Italian-descended immigrants in America. Both Azpadu and deVries suggest that the families' refusal to accept their gay daughters is deeply rooted in a desire to bury any discussion of sexuality itself—as though to examine sexual identity would be potentially to unearth secrets too private (or too shameful) to discuss.[3]

Alongside issues surrounding sexual orientation, writers such as Dorothy Bryant (*A Day in San Francisco*) and Carole Maso (*The Art Lover*) openly examine gay sexual practices in their novels in order to remember those who are HIV infected and are deeply suffering. Unlike Azpadu and deVries, who are more traditional in their narrative structures, Bryant and Maso utilize the aesthetic orderings of modernism and postmodernism to examine the fundamental issues of family, gayness, and illness in their novels. What may be considered too private or too shameful to portray in Azpadu's and deVries's Italian American families becomes the obsessive focus of female protagonists in Bryant's and Maso's texts.

In an attempt to control their overwhelming grief over the suffering of their loved ones, the women narrators in Bryant's and Maso's novels immerse themselves in the literature of illness, from the pamphlets disseminated about STDs (sexually transmitted diseases) to the complicated (and toxic) medicines taken during the final stages of dying. These narrators (or multiple narrators in Maso's novel) function as "wounded" storytellers, listening to narratives told by agonized patients. Illness provides those suffering the means by which not only to tell stories about their wounds, but to encourage the healing of their listeners.[4] Bryant and Maso in fact de-emphasize the issue of their characters' sexual identity in their novels in order to portray the pain resulting from contracting virulent illnesses that ultimately kill young people.

All four novels puncture the illusion of the ideal nuclear American family: the idea that all family members are and will be heterosexual, married with children, healthy, happy, and upwardly mobile. By fictionalizing the gay experience in the twentieth century, the writers also analyze how other features of identity, such as ethnic background, social class, and gender profoundly affect the development of characters passionately devoted to family, however modified it is from an original (and impossible) ideal. Both Azpadu and deVries suggest that when families abide by customs that do more to destroy than uphold family unity, they invariably lose the devotion of children who identify themselves as gay. For Maso and Bryant, the fictionalized families have already undergone radical modification from the original ideal; in disrupting the idea/ideal of family, both authors focus on one-on-one relationships that develop as a result of life-threatening illnesses.

In her introduction to *Inside/Out: Lesbian Theories, Gay Theories*, Diana Fuss explains that sexual identity is "less a matter of final discovery than perpetual reinvention" (7), an explanation that parallels the porous nature of ethnicity itself.[5] Italian American writers at times characterize family members as incapable of accepting the changing nature of their positions as Italians in America, imposing inhibitive rules on their children that only serve to alienate them further. Nontraditional behavior potentially isolates family members, especially when a particular member of the family is gay. Azpadu and, earlier, Octavia Waldo,[6] portray the family's tacit decision to ignore the character who has deviated from the standards of *la famiglia*. When this happens, the family symbolically "kills" the character. According to ethnologist Maureen J. Giovannini, such a symbolic death is "often a more effective deterrent to deviance than is violence" ("A Structural Analysis" 329).

To announce publicly to the family that one is gay not only potentially places one outside the perimeters of the conventional, heterosexual model, but it can effectually lock one out. For gays and lesbians, however, "coming out" has become "conventionalized as a personal rite of passage" and as such has become a process of recovery and discovery of their sexual selves (Gever 195). Like other gay persons, Italian American lesbians experience the ongoing intersection between two images of gay life in Western culture: the image of coming out and the image of the closet. In "Epistemology of the Closet," Eve Sedgwick explains that the process of coming out is not unidirectional; the revelation has the potential for "serious injury," to both parties involved—gay and straight.[7] Aware of the fact that coming out of the closet is never purely a "hermetic" act (Sedgwick, 80), the writer's decision to depict this social process is a profoundly courageous and necessary declaration of independence.

For the lesbian characters in Azpadu's *Saturday Night in the Prime of Life* (1983) and deVries's *Tender Warriors* (1986), coming out to the family means the emergence of further alienation: the adult gay characters are excluded from family matters, and a veil of silence shrouds their existence. In both novels, the characters hope to recover a space in which they are allowed to be visible as lesbian *and* Italian American. By attempting to place their characters as sexualized beings inside the houses of Italian Americans, Azpadu and deVries reinforce Diana Fuss's claim that "to be out is really to be in—inside the realm of the visible, the speakable, the culturally intelligible" (4).

Saturday Night in the Prime of Life is Azpadu's fine first novel. Azpadu's protagonist, Neddie Zingaro, never returns home, although her family, especially her mother, haunts her life. The novel revolves around the 26-year estrangement between mother and daughter. Neddie and her longtime partner, Lindy, painstakingly compose a letter of invitation to Neddie's mother, who had expressed feelings of loneliness in old age in one of the rare letters written to her daughter. Fifty years old herself, Neddie recognizes the fear of aging and invites her mother to come live with them. Neddie's mother, Concetta, responds by phoning several weeks later, only to repeat all the invectives of the earlier days, reducing the conversation to a one-way string of epithets thrown at her only daughter and eldest child. The novel ends with Neddie and Lindy pondering the course of their own uncharted aging.

As much as the novel revolves around the lesbian history between Neddie and Lindy, it is a history that is highly informed by Neddie's Sicilian widowed mother. Azpadu does not suggest that Neddie revitalizes her Sicilian American heritage through an engagement with culinary traditions and holidays. In contrast, deVries and several writers of Italian American experience, such as Rose Romano, Helen Barolini, Louise DeSalvo, Rita Ciresi, and Lynn Vannucci, to name just a few, invoke memories of meals and recall the concentrated efforts made by families (especially women) to celebrate their culture through culinary rituals.[8] Evident in Azpadu's novel is the *absence* of such nurturing traditions. Instead, the presence of Concetta looms ubiquitously over the couple's lives, even though the mother herself has practiced a "studious and long-standing avoidance" of her daughter (16).

Saturday Night in the Prime of Life examines how lesbian identity interpenetrates with Sicilian family culture, highlighting the marginalization of both mother and daughter. Barolini's description of the Italian immigrant woman's diminishment of power in America parallels Concetta's position in Azpadu's novel: "In America [the Italian woman] was quickly dethroned into the image of the old woman in the kitchen, stirring the sauce, . . . a figure of ridicule, a caricature" (*Dream Book* 12). Although she is no longer the vibrant figure that she was as a young mother, Concetta continues to wield power in manipulative and effective ways. Poignantly aware of her mother's circumscribed life and the limited means by which she can still use power, Neddie explains: "I can't ignore my mother. Regardless of her tricks. Scheming is the only way for her to take care of herself" (87). The novel portrays Concetta's life as a widowed grandmother whose two sons perform their filial duties without complaint or enjoyment. Never challenging her outmoded beliefs, they ignore their sister's decades-long illness. As a result, their silence reinforces the will of the mother and symbolically annihilates their sister.

Incapable of admitting, in any sustained manner, that the only person left in her life who reaffirms her Sicilian cultural identity is her daughter, Neddie, Concetta limits her life by adhering to beliefs and behaviors (about family, sexuality, gender, and power) that are either ineffectual or damaging. The mother's denial of the daughter at the novel's conclusion injures both of them, reinforcing Sedgwick's assertion that confessing one's gayness, especially to parents, can cause injury "that is likely to go in both directions" (80). Both women, sadly, enter old age without the comfort of a shared cultural identity.

When the family of origin ostracizes members because of their deviation from prescribed sexual norms, those persons may suffer a crisis of cultural identity, a suffering that may continue throughout their life. Rachel deVries's *Tender Warriors* treats the issue of gayness from the vantage point of a woman reintegrated into her Italian American family. Unlike Azpadu's novel, *Tender Warriors* revolves around a non-gay member of the family, whose illness serves to reunite the other members, who have been estranged since their mother's death. The death of Josephine DeMarco brings on a quest for each member of the family: Rose, the eldest child and a lesbian; Lorraine, a reformed drug addict, now married; and Sonny, the youngest and only son, whose brain seizures have partially blocked the memory of his mother's death. The novel revolves around each family member's returning home, where Dominic DeMarco, a violent and angry father, still lives. Together, Rose, Lorraine, and Dominic search for Sonny.

That Rose DeMarco is neither the center of the novel nor its narrative consciousness suggests deVries's interest in the interdependence of the Italian American family. Despite her brother's illness and her sister's drug habit, Rose, at age 37, still tortures herself with the knowledge "that everything about her was different from them" (71). On her own journey to locate her brother, Rose returns to the parental home, where she and her father eat *fusilli* and meatballs, feeling "as though the meal had given them back something familiar" (106). "Mangiando, ricordo," Barolini writes in her book *Festa:* "by eating, I remember" (13). Rose's response to sharing a meal with her father recalls a sense of comfort felt when Josephine, the undisputed center of the family, was alive.

Tender Warriors functions more like an ethnic or communal bildungsroman along the lines of Mari Tomasi's *Like Lesser Gods* or Marion Benasutti's *No SteadyJob for Papa* than it does a traditional lesbian text.[9] In *The Safe Sea of*

Women, Bonnie Zimmerman identifies four germane characteristics that high-light lesbian writing: female characters identify themselves with the lesbian com-munity; the novel primarily revolves around lesbian histories; lesbian love and passion are at the center of the story; and finally, the lesbian text places men at the margins of the story (15).

Although such features are represented in Azpadu's *Saturday Night in the Prime of Life*, they are entirely absent from the focus of deVries's first novel, *Tender Warriors*.[10] Instead, deVries develops one of the predominant themes in the writ-ing by critics and novelists on southern Italian culture: the elevation of the maternal role.[11] Josephine DeMarco's maternal function in the family parallels many immigrant mothers, who often mediated between the demands of the Ital-ian father and the differing needs of the children. Social historian Elizabeth Ewen describes how the transformation of traditional values created particular problems for women, especially for mothers: "Caught between the desires of their children and devotion (and obedience) to their husbands, called on to reinforce the patriarchal wishes of their husbands, the women found themselves in the middle of emotionally explosive family situations" (190).

Mediating between Dominic's tyrannical need to control his children and the children's fear and misunderstanding of their father, Josephine functions as a "guiding light," helping each of the family members understand their lives more clearly (119). The mother's untimely death brings each family member to a crisis of ethnic identity. In order to revitalize their relationship to the family, each DeMarco member prays to Josephine, as though she were the Madonna or the treasured Santa Lucia, symbolizing light and vision. For Rose, the lesbian daugh-ter, caring for her mother's grave and involving herself in Sonny's return to the family brings her back to the parental home. In fact, like her mother, Rose assumes the role of mediator between her father and Sonny, but without relin-quishing her relationship to her female lover.

The narrative structures of both Azpadu's and deVries's novels reveal the kinds of stories they will tell. For example, *Saturday Night in the Prime of Life* incorpo-rates the cluster of features germane to lesbian texts and therefore dictates against reunion with the Italian mother at the end of the novel. In contrast, deVries's narrative structure—following more closely a communal focus on fam-ily—encourages reconciliation between father and children throughout the novel's development. As a result of such structures, Azpadu remains firmly tied to a woman-centered locus, whereas deVries's depiction of lesbian love remains important, but not central, to the narrative focus. In fact, male desire (of both father and son) is paramount in deVries's text, underscoring the mother's power-less status outside "the world beyond her home" (54). Both mothers in Azpadu's and deVries's novels abide by destructive familial customs, and as a result, sacri-fice themselves in the process. By locking her daughter outside the Italian Amer-ican house, Concetta denies her Sicilian cultural heritage, sacrificing daughter for patriarchal customs that no longer apply to her own life or her two sons' lives. In contrast, but equally problematic, Josephine "gets out the only way she can"—

by sacrificing herself and dying; however, her daughter, Rose, is reintegrated into the Italian American family as a sexualized person (21). Yet, such reunion ultimately results from her mother's death and her brother's severe illness.

Just as the image of the closet remains a shaping presence for the lesbians depicted in *Saturday Night in the Prime of Life* and *Tender Warriors*, Italian American households—whether the women are inside or outside of them—also forcefully continue to influence their lives. Both families—Italian American and homosexual—intersect, reinforcing the fact that cultural and sexual identities are subject to persistent and undeniable change.

Unlike Azpadu and deVries, Dorothy Bryant and Carole Maso do not focus on lesbian characters, but their interests in sexual identity and the aesthetic orderings used to portray that identity, run deeply along their pulses. Both *A Day in San Francisco* (1982) and *The Art Lover* (1990) are radical novels in two major ways. First, both authors utilize a nonlinear, nonrepresentational mode of writing, in which standard flow of language is replaced by fragmented utterances and narrative continuity is interrupted by other modes of representation, such as details of art, advertisements, newspaper articles, pamphlets, and posters. The authors also depart from traditional ways of representing characters in their use of stream of consciousness—in particular, interior monologue—to record the movement of thought precisely as it occurs in the character's mind.

The second way in which these novels are radical is in their thematic focus on nonmonogamy as both a celebrated and problematized way of being sexual. Even though gay male characters might be engaging in sexual practices unacceptable to their families, the authors nonetheless closely align these characters to families. Bryant and Maso examine how the traditional family collapses for a variety of reasons but is reconstituted by the commitment members have to remaining part of the fold.

A Day in San Francisco, Bryant's seventh novel, is closely affiliated thematically with Azpadu's and DeVries's novels in its careful delineation of one family's struggle with the relationships between gay lifestyle, illness, and ideology. Bryant immediately overturns the myth of the model nuclear family by introducing two nontraditional family members: a divorced Italian American mother and a homosexual son, Frank. The novel takes place during the 1980 Gay Freedom Day Parade, after the assassinations two years earlier of George Moscone, mayor of San Francisco, and Harvey Milk, board supervisor. It is no coincidence that Bryant chooses this day to frame her novel, for it dramatizes the fragility of a freedom that can be obliterated by violent hatred and by serious, heretofore unidentified illnesses. Bryant's inclusion of advertisements promoting gay lifestyles (including sexual practices) alongside an interview with a virulently antigay spokesman reinforces the profoundly polarized views of the city and foreshadows the dissension between mother and son.[12]

Antigay attitudes also partially fueled the violence against Moscone and Milk—both males, both the same age, one Italian American, one homosexual—who were brutally shot down in their offices by a man 18 years their junior, by the name—of all names—Dan White. Within this highly charged political atmosphere—including the aftermath of the assassinations, the inflammatory verdict of voluntary manslaughter (and a maximum sentence of seven years), and the ensuing riots near City Hall—Bryant diminishes the differences between gay and straight, mainstream and marginalized, through the voice of her middle-age narrator, who realizes that she, like her son, has lived as a "thinly disguised alien, . . . in constant fear of exposure to ridicule or hatred" (46). At the same time, Bryant heightens the tensions between mother and son, whose confrontation at the end of the novel exposes the unresolved nature of their relationship.

A divorced Italian American woman—a history professor, a close friend of an older gay man, and the mother of a gay son—Clara Lontana, persuasively appeals to an audience at The Old Wives' Bookstore, when she reads her autobiographical article about the political underpinnings that caused a man like Dan White to assassinate men like Moscone and Milk. In doing so, Clara makes a connection between her experience of the mediocre, inefficient, often corrupt men of the forties and fifties—who questioned her ability to be a teacher because she was a mother—to the same enemies of the seventies, who "created" Dan White, "a living embodiment of their casually voiced pride in stupidity, cruelty, and fear" (47, 49).

Even though Clara makes credible and moving connections between her situation and her son's, she cannot adequately articulate to the audience (or to herself) the fact that her divorce "from her family's expectations and values, from the family itself," was just as unacceptable to them as is her son's wholesale rejection of his mother's beliefs in monogamy and nonsexual relationships with friends and acquaintances. Frank has instead opted for a life of promiscuity: "multiple sex contacts—yes, hundreds, . . . maintaining that razor edge of heightened life" (132). *A Day in San Francisco* concludes with Clara's struggle to accept her 30-year-old gay son's criticism of heterosexual monogamy, along with the constraints of marriage and children.

As her surname suggests, Clara Lontana has carefully repressed her feelings about her son's sexuality in the same way that she has deliberately avoided returning to the Mission District, the neighborhood where her Italian American parents raised her during the Great Depression, which becomes a metaphor for her parents' joyless lives. Clara's distance from her own true feelings about her immigrant past and her present life as the mother of a son whose sexual practices literally make him sick, make her incapable of fully hearing what may be described as the early drafts of Frank's illness narrative.[13] Clara theorizes about the connections between her childhood as an Italian American; her fear of exposure by her community for being intellectual, a reader of books; and her son's life as a gay man in the 1970s, his fear of exposure and rejection by family, friends, and coworkers. Unfortunately, Clara's actual feelings are ultimately unresolved and filled with anguished emotion about his present illness (hepatitis contracted from having sex in the bathhouses).

Bryant's penultimate section of the novel highlights the painful confrontation between Clara and Frank. Before locating the house in which Frank is renting a room, Clara walks down Castro Street through a dense fog, a metaphorical image that anticipates the fact that their conversation will not achieve clarity. In fact, when the mother-son talk focuses on Frank's lifestyle, Bryant drops the dialogue marks, separating mother and son visually by italicizing only Clara's comments. The story that Frank tells his mother is influenced by his belief that he is only temporarily ill; that cruising provides a "joyous freedom society hasn't ever known," an activity that calls for "dedication like a religious vocation" (132). Unaware that he is only at the beginning of his illness journey, Frank avoids discussing the implications of his frequent illnesses and instead displaces his anger onto his mother. Dismissing Clara's concern for him as *only* a reflection of her own unresolved feelings about reentering the Mission District earlier that day, Frank effectually locks Clara out of his (rented) house.

Clara plods on, weeping uncontrollably on the dark streets of the Castro District, reduced in the final section of the novel to a grief-stricken *mater dolorosa*, muttering, like Mary before her, "my son, my son." Such words recall the religious art works of the Garden of Gethsemane and Calvary displayed in the house of Frank's landlord, further testimonial to the elegiac tone of the narrative, and, perhaps, to its not new but nonetheless radical suggestion that the outsider son is being crucified again.

The suffering son, the grieving mother, and the artist as re-creator of family unity haunt the pages of Carole Maso's second novel, *The Art Lover*. Three concurrent fictional narratives about families make up this multidimensional text. The first two narratives introduce putatively traditional families—that is, nuclear families in which heterosexual couples marry and have children. But Maso immediately disrupts the family narrative by suggesting that such families are plagued by the conditions of modern life (for example, alienation, psychic struggle, and instability). The Maggie-Henry (parents), Candace and Alison (daughters) family story is disrupted by Henry's abandonment of the family, although he intensely loves them. The Max-Veronica (parents), Caroline, David, and Grey (children) family is suffering a long grief from the early death of the mother and the recent death of the father.[14]

Interwoven within these two narratives is Steven's story—another family narrative—the story of a friendship between a gay man dying of illnesses related to AIDS and a female narrator remembering and mourning his loss and her loss. By aligning Steven's story alongside the other family narratives, Maso expresses what Rachel Blau DuPlessis describes as a "critical dissent from dominant narrative. . . . Writing beyond the ending . . . produces a narrative that denies or reconstructs seductive patterns of feeling that are culturally mandated" (5). Maso's postmodern strategy in *The Art Lover* is to reconstruct seductive narrative patterns (that is, the family romance) that are nontraditional in themselves, thus delegitimating any one primary or quintessential family story.

In the fourth narrative of the penultimate section, Maso shifts to first person; all fictional stories momentarily collapse as Maso includes an autobiographical fragment describing the illness and death (from AIDS-related illnesses) of her close friend, Gary. As horrifying and impossible as this death is—"I can't believe this happened to you"—Maso seeks the story of it, re-creates the story of it through the fictionalized Caroline-Steven narrative, never realizing that "living could be this dangerous" (197). Nevertheless, as a wounded storyteller hearing stories from her dying friend, Maso recalls "intricate, marvelous stories," about desire, about art, about living. As Arthur Frank explains in his analysis of illness narratives, "the good story ends in wonder, and the capacity for wonder is reclaimed from the bureaucratic rationalizations of institutional medicine" (68). Before he was too weak to speak, Gary and Carole "walked around the fourteenth floor, you dragging your bag of blood," telling stories. Suffering from blindness and dementia, Gary, with "his wonderful and perfect sight" (243) saw "hoops of gold" at death, a circular image that winds itself around the other narratives in the novel, and an image that leaves the communal protagonist and the reader in wonder.

Within the several narratives, Maso inserts miniature commentaries on paintings of Giotto, da Vinci, Vermeer, Matisse; on stars—their motions and composition; and on the suffering and crucifixion of Jesus. In the vignette called "Jesus with Palm and Thistle," the narrator imagines Jesus in the late twentieth century, "dragging his bag of tricks—his basket of fragments, his fish and thistle. . . . A star blooms on his forehead like some dark horse. He looks to his brothers, anorectic and dying. 'Stay a little.' . . . He can't save anyone" (176). Just as the narrator Caroline, of the Max-Veronica narrative, mourns the loss of dying individuals in her Greenwich Village neighborhood; just as Alison in the Maggie-Henry narrative places her lost father in the sky, Ursa Major, the family bear, in order to channel her loss and protect her life, just as Caroline/Carole watches Steven/Gary remember what the light looked like: a "flared starlike" light that flashed in them for a "fraction of a second in the history of the planet," they can't save anyone, but they can learn something about the consoling, indeed, transcendent, nature of art and storytelling.

The Art Lover, a novel perpetually interrupting itself with images and words, self-reflexively dramatizes the life of the ill—a life that is unpredictable, interrupted, and uncontrolled. Maso's novel bears witness to the agony of AIDS in the twentieth century and the necessity of finding the words to tell the story of wounding. For Azpadu, deVries, Bryant, and Maso, at the heart of the novel lies the romance of the family—divided, suffering, confused, and dying. One of the salient features undergirding Italian American novels is the unceasing devotion to the crisis of family, as it is reconstituted by different life choices, by illness, and by death.

In Rose Romano's "Final Stages," a poem recalling the death of the speaker's ex-husband from the ravages of full-blown AIDS, the gay speaker and the dying man are faithfully connected to their cultural heritages—she, Italian American; he, African American. Both feel out of place in mainstream America; and, most essentially, both value their flawed families. Romano's lines encapsulate the thematic focus of this essay—the radical nature of families, our rootedness to families in the midst of our alienation and confusion. Her words appropriately close this essay: "It all comes back to family, / starts with family, / lives with family, / goes on and on and on with family. / I'm not going to call you / my ex-husband anymore. From / now on, I'm going to call you / my daughter's father. / But I have to stop and think / before I say it because if I just / let it come out of my mouth, / smooth and natural, / I get confused and I call you / my father's daughter" (*The Wop Factor* 34).

BIBLIOGRAPHY

Azpadu, Dodici. *Saturday Night in the Prime of Life*. Iowa City, Iowa: Aunt Lute, 1983.

Barolini, Helen. *The Dream Book: An Anthology of Writings by Italian American Women*. New York: Schocken, 1985.

———. *Festa: Recipes and Recollections of Italian Holidays*. New York: Harcourt, 1988.

Benasutti, Marion. *No Steady Job for Papa*. New York: Vanguard, 1966.

Bona, Mary Jo. *The Voices We Carry: Recent Italian/American Women's Fiction*. Montreal: Guernica, 1994.

Bryant, Dorothy. *A Day in San Francisco*. Berkeley, CA: Ata Books, 1982.

Cappello, Mary. "Nothing to Confess: A Lesbian in Italian America." *Fuori: Essays by Italian/American Lesbians and Gays*. Ed. Anthony J. Tamburri. West Lafayette, IN: Bordighera, 1996. 89–108.

Ciresi, Rita. *Blue Italian*. Hopewell, NJ: Ecco, 1996.

DeSalvo, Louise. *Vertigo: A Memoir*. New York: Dutton, 1996.

deVries, Rachel Guido. *Tender Warriors*. Ithaca, NY: Firebrand, 1986.

DuPlessis, Rachel Blau. *Writing beyond the Ending: Narrative Strategies of Twentieth-Century Women Writers*. Bloomington: Indiana University P, 1985.

Ewen, Elizabeth. *Immigrant Women in the Land of Dollars: Life and Culture on the Lower East Side, 1890–1925*. New York: Monthly Review P, 1985.

Frank, Arthur W. *The Wounded Storyteller: Body, Illness, and Ethics*. Chicago: U of Chicago P, 1995.

Fuss, Diana, ed. *Inside/Out: Lesbian Theories, Gay Theories*. New York: Routledge, 1991.

Gambone, Philip. "Learning and Unlearning and Learning Again the Language of *Signori*." *Fuori*. 60–80.

Gever, Martha. "The Names We Give Ourselves." *Out There: Marginalization and Contemporary Cultures*. Ed. Russell Ferguson et al. New York: Museum of Contemporary Art, 1990. 191–202.

Giovannini, Maureen J. "A Structural Analysis of Proverbs in a Sicilian Village." *American Ethnologist* 5 (1978): 322–33.

Klein, Marcus. *Foreigners: The Making of American Literature, 1900–1940*. Chicago: U of Chicago P, 1981.

Maso, Carole. *The Art Lover*. Hopewell, NJ: Ecco P, 1990.

Romano, Rose. *Vendetta*. San Francisco: malafemmina p, 1990.

———. *The Wop Factor*. Brooklyn: malafemmina p, 1994.

Sedgwick, Eve Kosofsky. *Epistemology of the Closet*. Berkeley: University of California P, 1990.

Tamburri, Anthony J. *Fuori: Essays by Italian/American Lesbians and Gays*. Intro. by Mary Jo Bona. West Lafayette, IN: Bordighera, 1996.

Tomasi, Mari. *Like Lesser Gods*. Milwaukee: Bruce, 1949. Shelburne, VT: New England P, 1988.

Vannucci, Lynn. "An Accidental Murder." *The Voices We Carry*. 371–76.

Waldo, Octavia. *A Cup of the Sun*. New York: Harcourt, 1961.

Zimmerman, Bonnie. *The Safe Sea of Women: Lesbian Fiction, 1969–1989*. Boston: Beacon P, 1990.

NOTES

1. Radicalism in literature traditionally applies to novels that embody or reflect characters and events that accord with the idea that the struggle between economic classes is the essential dynamic of society. Although he does not mention Pietro di Donato's classic proletarian novel, *Christ in Concrete*, Marcus Klein, in *Foreigners: The Making of American Literature, 1900–1940* (Chicago: U of Chicago P, 1981), offers a useful distinction between "traditionalism" and "barbarism" in his analysis of immigrant writers who managed to exist "despite the predominance of the modern movement and . . . many other considerable odds" (18).

2. The etymological significance of the word *radical* has a long history, going back to the fifteenth and sixteenth centuries. The *Oxford English Dictionary* (*OED*) cites several writers who use the word to mean "forming the root, basis, or foundation," as in W. Whateley, "The grace of faith is the radicall grace, that upon which all other graces grow as on their roote" (*OED* 1639). For the Italian Americans about whom I write, the family is the locus of such faith, upon which other graces grow.

3. Mary Cappello brilliantly explores the intersection between lesbianism, Catholicism, and Italian American ethnicity when she writes, " 'Italian' [the language] is the route to the elders, who, the family assumes, are better off *not* knowing what they cannot understand about their third-generation Italian/American offspring. . . . Is the lesbian in an Italian/American family the *embodiment* of the family secret?. . . . In 'becoming queer,' I was becoming what my Italian/American forebears denied about themselves even as they provided the example." In "Nothing to Confess: A Lesbian in Italian America," *Fuori: Essays by Italian/American Lesbians and Gays*, ed. Anthony J. Tamburri (Lafayette, IN.: Bordighera, 1996) 93, 97.

4. I take the descriptive "wounded storyteller" from the title of Arthur Frank's critical study of ill people. Frank writes, "As wounded, people may be cared for, but as storytellers, they care for others. The ill, and all those who suffer, can also be healers." *The Wounded Storyteller: Body, Illness, and Ethics* (Chicago: U of Chicago P, 1995) xii. Although he mentions AIDS narratives in an informational note, Frank excludes using examples from this group of wounded storytellers in his analysis—which seems to be an oversight on his part. For further information on illness narratives and on the ways in which illness is interpreted by culture, see Arthur Kleinman, *The Illness Narratives: Suffering, Healing & the Human Condition* (New York: Basic Books, 1988), and Susan Sontag's *Illness as Metaphor* (New York: Farrar, Straus and Giroux, 1978) and *AIDS and Its Metaphors* (New York: Farrar, Straus and Giroux, 1988).

5. See Diana Fuss, ed., *Inside/Out: Lesbian Theories, Gay Theories* (New York: Routledge, 1991); Estelle B. Freedman et al., eds., *The Lesbian Issue: Essays from SIGNS*

(Chicago: U of Chicago P, 1982); Sally Munt, ed., *New Lesbian Criticism: Literary and Cultural Readings* (New York: Columbia UP, 1992); Henry Abelove, et al., eds., *The Lesbian and Gay Studies Reader* (New York: Routledge, 1993); and Eve Kosofsky Sedgwick, *Epistemology of the Closet* (Berkeley: U of California P, 1990).

6. Octavia Waldo's *A Cup of the Sun* (1961) examines the Italian American community's disapproval of unconventional sexuality, that is, practices that do not fit the heterosexual model of marriage and motherhood. Illegitimate children, parental abandonment of children, premarital sex, birth control, and abortion are anathematized in this novel about Italian American families living near Philadelphia in the World War II era. Characters failing to exemplify rigid familial standards are branded and ostracized.

7. Philip Gambone writes, "And we both are . . . still too concerned about doing the right thing. . . . In my mother's case, that means, among other things, that she still worries about what her friends will think if they find out her son is gay." "Learning and Unlearning and Learning Again the Language of *Signore*," *Fuori: Essays by Italian/American Lesbians and Gays,* 79.

8. Rose Romano's poems "Confirmation," "Italian Bread," "To Show Respect," and "That We Eat" explore the connections between food, sexuality, and love, in *Vendetta* (San Francisco: malafemmina press, 1990). Lynn Vannucci's short story, "An Accidental Murder," suggests the potential for violence in the reputed sanctuary of Italian American homes: the kitchen. See Mary Jo Bona, ed., *The Voices We Carry: Recent Italian/American Women's Fiction* (Montreal: Guernica, 1994). For a humorous fictional portrayal of the dinner table as both appealing and appalling, see Rita Ciresi, *Blue Italian* (Hopewell, NJ: Ecco P, 1996). An autobiographical listing of foods the author found repugnant (and inedible) is depicted in Louise DeSalvo, *Vertigo* (New York: Dutton, 1996). Finally, Helen Barolini writes a combination memoir and recipe collection to celebrate her ties to Italy and to Italian foods as a source of spiritual energy in *Festa* (New York: Harcourt Brace Jovanovitch, 1988).

9. For more-detailed information on how Mari Tomasi and Marion Benasutti's novels function as communal bildungsroman, see my critical study *Claiming a Tradition: Italian American Women Writers* (Carbondale: Southern Illinois University Press, 1999). On lesbian novels, see Bonnie Zimmerman's chapter, " 'It Makes a Great Story': Lesbian Culture and the Lesbian Novel," in *The Safe Sea of Women: Lesbian Fiction, 1969–1989* (Boston: Beacon Press, 1990) 1–32.

10. Zimmerman lists both Azpadu's and DeVries's novels in her selected bibliography but only gives a couple of sentences to Azpadu's novel in her analysis.

11. For critical readings of the Italian American woman's centrality to the family, see the following: Colleen Johnson, "The Maternal Role in the Contemporary Italian-American Family," in *The Italian Immigrant Woman in North America* (Toronto: Multicultural History Society of Ontario, 1978) 234–44; Micaela di Leonardo, *The Varieties of Ethnic Experience: Kinship, Class, and Gender among California Italian-Americans* (Ithaca: Cornell UP, 1984); and Robert Orsi, *The Madonna of 115th Street: Faith and Community in Italian Harlem, 1880–1950* (New Haven: Yale UP, 1985).

12. Bryant commented that publishing a book like *A Day in San Francisco* in 1982 was "an act of marketplace suicide with the audience I had built up." Personal communication with the author, 22 April 1997.

13. Because HIV infection was not yet identified in 1980 as the virus that causes Acquired Immune Deficiency Syndrome (AIDS), Bryant instead incorporated into her narrative a recent pamphlet on socially transmitted diseases (syphilis, gonorrhea, gay

bowel syndrome, and trauma-related injuries, such as anal fissures due to fisting). The narrative is deliberately and forcefully interrupted by this overwhelming information, which in retrospect (in the age of AIDS), characterizes the HIV virus without naming it. Likewise, both Frank and Clara are entering the "early stages" of their illness narratives, unable to name the thing that is hurting them.

14. The Max-Veronica family narrative is reminiscent of the Christine-Michael family narrative of Maso's first novel, *Ghost Dance*. Just as the narratives within *The Art Lover* spill into each other, Maso's six novels speak to each other; all of them, Maso would claim, are books about desire.

Chapter 16

Where They Come From: Italian American Women Writers As Public Intellectuals

Edvige Giunta

And of course I am afraid, because the transformation of silence into language and action is an act of self-revelation, and that always seems fraught
with danger.

Audre Lorde
"The Transformation of Silence into Language and Action"

Maria Mazziotti Gillan's *Where I Come From: New and Selected Poems* (1994)
foregrounds the importance of origins in the poet's self-definition, her subject
matter, her poetics, and her politics. Recovery and reinvention are instrumental
to the formation of Italian American public intellectuals. For such individuals,
situating themselves in relation to ethnic origins represents a potentially radical
act, radical in the sense of going back to the roots: roots of identity, roots of culture, roots of oppression—the roots where transformation can and must begin.

Over the last two decades, Italian American women writers have begun to
transform "silence" into "language and action." In breaching the boundary
between traditionally private and public spaces, authors such as Louise DeSalvo,
Mary Cappello, Nancy Caronia, Rosette Capotorto, Maria Mazziotti Gillan,
Rose Romano, and Sandra M. Gilbert, to mention just a few, have given form to
untold stories and utterance to unspoken words.[1] Their words have shattered the
quasi-mythological status of the Italian family as a locus of nurturance and safety.
At the same time, these authors also question American narratives of individual
emergence and success. Thus, an exploration and a reworking of the significance
of community are central to the work of contemporary Italian American women

authors, who are intent on remaking the very communities they have defied and escaped. As Audre Lorde knew so well, there is danger involved in this act: danger of becoming unpopular, the betrayer, the outcast, the exile within both the culture of descent and the culture of assent.[2] And yet, as Lorde puts it, "what is important . . . must be spoken, made verbal and shared, even at the risk of having it bruised or misunderstood" (Sister 40).

While not all writers—and not all Italian American women writers—are public intellectuals, in making certain words (and worlds) public, some writers pursue the kind of social and political transformation that is at the heart of the task of the public intellectual. In doing so, these writers call into question commonsense understandings of the disjunction between public and private. The radicalism of writers such as DeSalvo and Mazziotti Gillan, for example, lies both in their deeply personal work and in their public response to the lack of a supporting context for their work.[3] Such work demonstrates that the function of the public intellectual is to be a spokesperson for the community—and especially for the silenced and disenfranchised who, paradoxically, are often marginalized by the same community on whose behalf these women speak. Italian American authors recognize the cultural marginalization of their ethnic group;[4] at the same time, they strongly and painfully recognize that they cannot fully embrace their community, that they must understand the ways in which it constrains and silences its members, and that they must act on such an understanding. The relationship with the community is, for these women, as problematic as the definition of this politically ambivalent concept.[5] The community of origins often represents the very space they must evade, even as they confront, challenge, and reinvent it in their works and lives.

From Maria Mazziotti Gillan's Where I Come From to Louise DeSalvo's Vertigo (1996) and Breathless: An Asthma Journal (1997), to Mary Cappello's Night Bloom (1998) and Maria Laurino's Were You Always an Italian? (2000), the literature produced by Italian American women grapples with specific manifestations of issues relating to their Italian American experiences, which also concern other communities. These issues—like ethnic stereotyping; cultural assimilation; gender, race, sex and class oppression; domestic violence; mental illness; sexual and environmental abuse; and public health—are central to the life narratives of these Italian American women.[6] For them, becoming a public intellectual defies historical definitions and perceptions of both their gender and ethnicity, both within and outside the Italian American community—even as, I would argue, there is no such thing as "Italian America" understood as some homogenous or unified social reality or monolithic community.

The very nature of their work puts these Italian American women in a position that makes the recognition of their status as public figures difficult, if not questionable. Helen Barolini claims that Italian American voices have been excluded from national public forums. The New York Times, she notes, has been indifferent to Italian American authors, with the exception of those, such as Mario Puzo, Gay Talese, and Francis Ford Coppola, who cater to conventional and stultifying images of Italian Americans (Barolini, *Chiaroscuro* 98–101). Authors who challenge such prevailing views—and women fall in great numbers into this category, Barolini argues—get neither their books reviewed nor their letters published in prominent national venues. As Rose Romano reminds us, censorship "doesn't always have to be censorship in order to be effective" ("Nella Sorellanza" 152). But then, as Edward Said has pointed out, to be a public intellectual one must be ready to be on the outside, to be an exile, both literally and metaphorically: "The exile . . . exists in a median state, neither completely at one with the new setting nor fully disencumbered of the old. Beset with half-involvements and half-detachments, nostalgic and sentimental on one level, an adept mimic or a secret outcast on another" (49). Said's description aptly illustrates the predicament of authors who constantly negotiate ambivalent relationships to the community of origins as well as the communities they are involved with through marriage, as in Joanna Clapps Herman's essay; through sexual and political identification, as discussed in writings by Cappello, Romano, and Saracino; or through multiple ethnic or racial origins, as in Caronia's, Ragusa's, and Savoca's works. Existing in a median state means traveling back and forth between different communities and identities, juggling a self-conscious mimicry and a sense of outsidership that is simultaneously feared and proudly asserted.

The work of many Italian American women writers wavers between the desire for home and the necessity to reject it. These authors can be described in terms of Said's definition of the exile, as "constantly being unsettled, and unsettling others." As Said puts it, "You cannot go back to some earlier and perhaps more stable condition of being at home; and, alas, you can never fully arrive, be at one with your new home or situation"(53). For these writers, specifically those who engage in the kind of radical work that questions the cultural dictates of familial culture, a state of permanent homelessness becomes a choice and necessity.

Gay and lesbian writers experience the ambivalence of home in an especially acute manner. "Eating dinner alone feels like a symbol of my capitulation to American culture and my complete assimilation as an Italian American" (Tamburri 31), writes Giovanna (Janet) Capone, one of the contributors to *Fuori: Essays by Italian/American Lesbians and Gays*. Capone writes of the pain of craving home in the social isolation that she experiences as an Italian American lesbian, particularly when home is associated with the "homophobia and ignorance" within her family (Tamburri 39). Permanent homelessness is the condition that Rosette Capotorto describes in her poem "Red Wagon": "I have no party / affiliation I am / a one woman band / see my red wagon. / I pull / it along piled with / paper and pasta." It is a condition that is not in any way easy or conflict free, for it does not imply a disregard for home, but rather a troubled and constant longing for a place that can still be evoked in writing and re-created in communities that selectively incorporate elements of the home of origins.[7] For these authors, a safe home is always—and only—a process, never a place of arrival.

To become a public intellectual requires, at times, erasing the markers of ethnicity. This erasure can be a necessary stage in the negotiation between one's own understanding of one's ever-changing ethnic and cultural roots, and the uncomfortable position one comes to occupy as an Italian American intellectual in an American culture that stigmatizes Italian Americans—especially women—as anti-intellectual. One example of this attempt to come to terms with the contradictions inherent in such a negotiation is DeSalvo's 1984 essay, "A Portrait of the Puttana as a Middle-Aged Woolf Scholar," in which she reveals how she is constantly at odds with her ethnic origins. The clash between "Italian" and "intellectual" is articulated through the seemingly paradoxical juxtaposition of the title words *puttana*—Italian for *whore*—and *Woolf scholar*. In this essay, DeSalvo expresses her ambivalence about identifying herself as an Italian American. She views that identification as encumbering the process of that intellectual growth she has pursued as a scholar of Virginia Woolf. A decade later, DeSalvo includes that essay, significantly revised, in *Vertigo*, a memoir in which, far from shying away from her Italian roots, she claims and embraces those roots, even as she relentlessly indicts the patriarchal modes of oppression within Italian American familial and cultural structures. Understanding the repercussions of cultural isolation, DeSalvo places herself within a large and ever-growing movement of Italian American women authors in a gesture that enables her to gain access to other unspoken personal narratives.[8]

Vertigo (1996) delves deep into DeSalvo's working-class origins and the history of the Italian American neighborhood where she grew up, in Hoboken, New Jersey. *Breathless: An Asthma Journal,* an autobiographical, literary, cultural, and political meditation on asthma, articulates, like *Vertigo,* with remarkable clarity DeSalvo's commitment to being an Italian American intellectual. The publication of *Vertigo* has broken the historical silence enveloping the relationship of Italian American women to the family—and to their culture—and has transported the primarily private and domestic discourse of Italian American women into a politicized realm. *Vertigo* has been followed by another groundbreaking memoir, Mary Cappello's *Night Bloom* (1998) and by the anthology *Curaggia: Writing by Women of Italian Descent* (1998), edited by Nzula Angelina Ciatu, Domenica DiLeo, and Gabriella Micallef, a melange of daring, political and culturally self-aware voices that question the cultural heritage they courageously flaunt.[9] By writing of incest, physical abuse, and mental illness, not only does DeSalvo—as do Cappello and the contributors to *Curaggia*—violate the taboos surrounding these subjects, but she also demonstrates the complicated ways in which these forms of violence are interwoven with class and ethnic oppression. *Vertigo,* like Dorothy Allison's *Bastard out of Carolina* and Michael Ryan's *My Secret Life,* makes it clear that the sexual oppression and exploitation of children is linked to the failure of the family to protect them, even when family members are not directly implicated in the abuse. The family, we discover, is not an inviolate space, but rather one deeply implicated in the politics of gender and sexual oppression.

In a polemic fashion, *Breathless* brings to the forefront of literary discussion a burning political issue: the asthma crisis that has struck particularly the inner city, victimizing primarily those who live in conditions of economic deprivation, many of them children. DeSalvo paints a frightening picture of a society that has given up the right to free and clean water and is progressively surrendering the right to free, clean air: "How long will it be," she asks, "until those of us who can afford it will hook ourselves up to portable air purifiers to go outside?" (148–49). This poignant question foregrounds the connection between class privilege and the ability to protect oneself from environmental abuse. *Breathless* describes a power game that the poor are doomed to lose.

It comes as no surprise that the mainstream press has not given *Vertigo* or *Breathless* their fair share of praise. This neglect is coupled with the current back-lash against memoir (a phenomenon that leads some columnists to deride the genre and its practitioners as trendy) illustrates the co-optation of the memoir as a politically radical genre. Such co-optation is illustrated by the popularization of what DeSalvo calls, in *Breathless*, "the recovery narrative":

I see the perniciousness of the word recovery, for it suggests that the illness or the condi-tion (asthma, whatever) is over, though it isn't. It suggests, too, that people are personally responsible for curing their illnesses. I realize that I am against the neatness and the lie of what I suddenly recognize as the comforting arc of the recovery narrative. The narrative that says, in essence, I was sick, I suffered, I did this and that and the other thing, I figured it out, I made changes, I am now much better, don't worry, there is nothing urgent we really need to do as people to help prevent asthma. (150–51)

Neither *Vertigo* nor *Breathless* subscribes to the recovery narrative; in fact, they radically upset the expectations of its "arc." Going against what she calls the "true American tradition of Benjamin Franklin," in *Breathless* DeSalvo proclaims herself "the imperfect asthmatic," who refuses to be blamed for her "imperfec-tion" (151), and instead indicts those who are polluting the air and causing human and environmental trauma at all levels.

The story DeSalvo tells in *Breathless* is one that will not make people feel bet-ter; it does not allow us to feel comfortable about the way we have surrendered responsibility for our lives and the lives of others. DeSalvo thus joins authors such as Audre Lorde, Sandra Gilbert, and Nancy Mairs, who have all written elo-quently of the politics of illness. Mairs highlights the correlation between popu-lar success and the "feel-good" book—which she does *not* write. Mairs calls her memoir *Waist-High in the World: A Life among the Non-Disabled*, "a feel-real book"—"and reality," which she points out, "has never been high on any popular list" (18). *Breathless* takes on an almost prophetic tone as DeSalvo comes to view her illness as that which has opened her eyes to the frightful question of environ-mental abuse:

I sometimes wonder who is the more highly evolved. The person who responds adversely to chemical fumes, exhaust fumes, cigarette smoke, noxious odors, trauma, or the person who doesn't. Maybe, I tell myself, I'm like the canary [ken-air-ee] in the mine shaft. Maybe my gasping for air is information that other, less sensitive people should heed.

Maybe the fate of the planet depends upon people like me whose responsive bodies are telling us all that there is something very wrong around here. (149)

The power of DeSalvo's narrative lies in its insistence that there are communities of people out there who will recognize and respond to the urgency of her words—and of the situation that they describe.[10]

The encounter between writers and readers who listen to each other's words and, in doing so, begin to listen to their own, represents an important first step toward understanding what it takes to transform "silence" into "language and action." The labors of Maria Mazziotti Gillan are directed at an exploration of ethnic identity that is always biographical and historical, personal and political. Recognition of the radical potential of personal power, of the ways in which we can organize ourselves—as students, teachers, parents, writers, and readers—shapes all aspects of her work.[11] In her poem "Coming of Age: Paterson," published in the 1996 anthology *In Defense of Mumia*, edited by Anderson and Medina, Maria Mazziotti Gillan writes:[12]

In the streets of our cities
the poor rise again like dough,
no matter how we push them down. (70)

This poem relies on a familiar Italian American trope, making bread, as it addresses problems that transcend the Italian American community, on whose behalf she has so eloquently spoken elsewhere. Yet the grief expressed in this elegy for the children of Paterson, "beaten to death," the children of Micronesia, "born without bones / as the result of nuclear testing," and "the young men on street corners, / blown like refuse against Black Bear Liquors" (69), is connected to the grief that pervades her more overtly Italian American poems such as "Growing up Italian," "Public School No. 18, Paterson, New Jersey," and "Arturo." These poems are rooted in the search for, and reclaiming of, cultural and ethnic origins.

Where I Come From continues the work of recovery and reinvention that Mazziotti Gillan had initiated with *Taking Back My Name* (1991), a chapbook that captures the vital place of memory for the poet. It is through memory that she can trace the painful but important experience of discrimination suffered by Italian Americans. She describes such an experience in linguistic terms: "English words" fall "thick and sharp as hail" on the immigrant child. She is silenced as a result:

I grew silent,
the Italian word balanced on the edge
of my tongue and the English word, lost
during the first moment
of every question. (1)

The poet must trace the story of the silencing that occurred in her past in order to reach a present in which she can proudly claim, as she does at the end of the poem:

today, I take back my name
and wave it in their faces
like a bright, red flag. (3)

Mazziotti Gillan's well-known activities as a poet and radical cultural worker thus appear grounded in the intimate connection between her cultural activities and her Italian American working class roots.

* * *

In the edited collection *Selections from the Prison Notebooks*, Antonio Gramsci writes that "All men are intellectuals . . . but not all men have in society the function of intellectuals" (9). Gramsci's statement sheds light on the work of Italian American women authors as public intellectuals. His concept of the "intellectual function" underscores the relatively obvious point that intellectuals are not, at least inherently, all that different from non-intellectuals: everyone has "got it" to some extent; what counts is what one does with it. It is this intellectual potential that books such as *Where I Come From*, *Vertigo*, and *Breathless* not only recognize, but also nurture—in their authors and in their readers.

My experience as a teacher of working-class and minority students makes me value the radical possibilities that books like *Vertigo*, *Breathless*, and *Where I Come From* offer for multiply marginalized students—regardless of whether they are Italian American. These texts can trigger a process of understanding their lives and the world in which they live as intensely political: an insight fundamental to the possibility of critical social agency and transformation on any level. As I was reading my students' papers while working on this essay, I was struck by the irony of the literary world's reception of the works of Italian American women. Although a few reviewers have not failed to recognize the importance of *Vertigo*, for example, this memoir has not received the kind of mainstream recognition given to less original, less provocative, less daring, and less radical memoirs. My "nonintellectual" students, on the other hand, have consistently found *Vertigo* profoundly important and inspiring. Annalisa Ronquillo, a Filipina student, wrote: "*Vertigo* has taught me . . . lesson[s] . . . that I will take with me to my dying day. Some of these are: the importance of writing; the control I must gain over my asthma; and the lesson of dealing with the things and people in [my] life." Until she read *Vertigo*, this student did not know, as she puts it in her final exam essay, that she, herself, "had been writing for survival." "Tears formed in my eyes," she continues, "as I began to piece together the meaning of my life. I felt as if [DeSalvo] was speaking for me: for my disturbances, my shame, my failures, my efforts and my will to survive." Similarly, an African American male student was moved by "Growing up Italian"; the stark simplicity with which Mazziotti Gillan portrays her experience of cultural marginalization spoke powerfully to him. And another student, Bart Babinski, wrote in response to *Where I Come From:* "As I write my memoir, and relive as well as re-evaluate my experience, Maria Mazziotti Gillan's work shines like a guiding light. . . . The poems are sweet and short and somewhat quiet. But I can sense the rage and anger and frustration and mounting explosion boiling just beneath the surface. The fury that she wants to unleash on every person and thing that ever walked all over her, all over her mother and father. All over her heritage. I am touched by each regret and mourning, as I remember my own faults and mistakes. The times I disregarded my mother or father as foreign and dumb. The time I changed my name, and made fun of other odd, exotic, beautiful foreign names. The times I mocked customs of Indians or Chinese, or South Americans, or my fellow Polish companions because they did not find it necessary to hide and become American the way I had." Reading *Breathless* prompted yet another student to investigate the high incidence of asthma among African American poor. Consistently, the diverse student population at New Jersey City University felt that their experiences of marginalization and oppression were validated by these Italian American authors.

The work of Italian American women writers who embrace the position of public intellectuals, opens up important cultural spaces. These authors argue for the necessity of such spaces as the forums in which words can be spoken and change can begin. In doing so, they politicize their ethnic identity as one of the means that makes it possible to rid communities of the insidious power of silence. Writing, then, makes it possible to pursue the kind of work that is at the center of the public intellectual's life: to build community even as one seems engaged in dismantling community. The question of origins becomes a question of direction. The act of looking back to the past, then—while "beset with half-involvements and half-detachments, nostalgic and sentimental on one level, an adept mimic or secret outcast on another" (Said 49)—paves the way for a future in which the voiceless can learn to transform their silence into language and action.

BIBLIOGRAPHY

Alaya, Flavia. *Under the Rose: A Confession.* New York: The Feminist Press, 1999.

Anderson, S. E., and Tony Medina, eds. *In Defense of Mumia.* New York: Writers and Readers, 1996.

Baker, Aaron, and Juliann Vitullo. "Mysticism and the *Household Saints* of Everyday Life." *Voices in Italian Americana* (special issue on women authors) 7.2 (1996): 55–68.

Barolini, Helen. "Becoming a Literary Person out of Context." *Massachusetts Review* 27.2 (1986): 262–74.

———. *Chiaroscuro: Essays of Identity.* West Lafayette, IN: Bordighera, 1997.

———, ed. *The Dream Book: An Anthology of Writings by Italian American Women.* 1985. New York: Shocken, 1987.

———. *Umbertina.* Afterword by Edvige Giunta. 1979. New York: The Feminist Press, 1999.

Capotorto, Rosette. *Bronx Italian*. Unpublished manuscript.

Cappello, Mary. *Night Bloom*. Boston: Beacon Press, 1998.

Caronia, Nancy. "Go to Hell." *Curaggia: Writing by Women of Italian Descent*. Ed. Nzula Angelina Ciatu, Domenica DiLeo, and Gabriella Micallef. Toronto: Women's Press, 1998. 216–25.

Ciatu, Nzula Angelina, Domenica DiLeo, and Gabriella Micallef, eds. *Curaggia: Writing by Women of Italian Descent*. Toronto: Women's Press, 1998.

Ciresi, Rita. "Paradise below the Stairs." *Italian Americana* 12.1 (1993): 17–22.

DeSalvo, Louise. *Breathless: An Asthma Journal*. Boston: Beacon Press, 1997.

———. *"Paper Fish: An Appreciation." Voices in Italian Americana*. 7.2 (1996): 249–55.

———. "A Portrait of the Puttana as a Middle-Aged Woolf Scholar." *Between Women: Biographers, Novelists, Critics, Teachers and Artists Write about Their Work on Women*. Ed. Carol Ascher, Louise DeSalvo, and Sara Ruddick. Boston: Beacon Press, 1984. 35–53.

———. *Vertigo*. New York: Dutton, 1996.

———. *Writing as a Way of Healing: How Telling Our Stories Transforms Our Lives*. New York: Harper San Francisco, 1999.

Gilbert, Sandra M. *Wrongful Death: A Memoir*. New York: Norton, 1995.

Gillan, Maria Mazziotti. *Taking Back My Name*. Franklin Lakes, NJ: Lincoln Springs, 1991.

———. *Where I Come From: Selected and New Poems*. Toronto: Guernica, 1995.

Gillan, Maria Mazziotti, and Jennifer Gillan, eds. *Unsettling America: An Anthology of Contemporary Multicultural Poetry*. New York: Penguin, 1994.

Giunta, Edvige. "Figuring Race: Kym Ragusa's *fuori/outside*." *Shades of Black and White: Conflict and Collaboration between Two Communities*. Ed. Dan Ashyk, Fred L. Gardaphè, and Anthony Julian Tamburri. Staten Island, N.Y.: American Italian Historical Association, 1997.

———. "The Quest for True Love: Nancy Savoca's Domestic Film Comedy." *Melus* (Summer 1997): 75–89.

Gramsci, Antonio. *Selections from the Prison Notebooks*. Ed. and trans. Quintin Hoare and Geoffrey Nowell Smith. New York: International Publishers, 1971.

Gutman, Amy ed. *Multiculturalism: Examining the Politics of Recognition*. Princeton, NJ: Princeton University Press, 1994.

Hendin, Josephine Gattuso. *The Right Thing to Do*. Boston: David R. Godine, 1988.

Herman, Joanna Clapps. "The Discourse of un'Propria Paparone." *Curaggia: Writing by Women of Italian Descent*. Ed. Nzula Angelina Ciatu, Domenica DiLeo, and Gabriella Micallef. Toronto: Women's Press, 1998. 176–79.

Laurino, Maria. *Were You Always an Italian? Ancestors and Other Icons of Italian America*. New York: W. W. Norton, 2000.

Lorde, Audre. *The Cancer Journals*. San Francisco: Aunt Lute, 1980.

———. *Sister Outsider: Essays and Speeches*. Freedom, CA: The Crossing Press, 1984.

Mairs, Nancy. *Waist-High in the World*. Boston: Beacon Press, 1996.

Messina, Elizabeth. "Soul-Food and Psychologically Transcendent Ways of Knowing." *Food, Tradition, and Community among Italian Americans: Proceedings of the 1996 American Italian Historical Association Conference*. Ed. Edvidge Giunta and Samuel J. Patti. Staten Island, N.Y.: American Italian Historical Association, 1998. 68–82.

Ragusa, Kym. *fuori/outside*. Ibla Productions, 1997.

Romano, Rose. *Vendetta*. San Francisco: malafemmina press, 1990.

———. "Where Is Nella Sorellanza When You Really Need Her?" *New Explorations in Italian American Studies: Proceedings of the 25th Annual Conference of the American Italian*

Historical Association. (Washington, DC, 12–14 November 1992). Ed. Richard Juliani and Sandra P. Juliani. Staten Island, N.Y.: American Italian Historical Association, 1994. 147–54.

———. *The Wop Factor*. New York: malafemmina press, 1994.

Said, Edward. *Representations of the Intellectual*. New York: Random House, 1994.

Saracino, Mary. *No Matter What*. Minneapolis: Spinsters Ink, 1993.

———. *Talk It with the Moon*. Unpublished manuscript.

Savoca, Nancy. *Household Saints*. Columbia TriStar, 1993.

———. *True Love*. MGM/USA, 1990.

Sollors, Werner. *Beyond Ethnicity: Consent and Descent in American Culture*. New York: Oxford University Press, 1986.

Tamburri, Anthony, ed. *FUORI: Essays by Italian/American Lesbians and Gays*. Intro. by Mary Jo Bona. West Lafayette, IN: Bordighera, 1996.

Vecoli, Rudolph J. "Italian Immigrants and Working Class Movements in the United States: A Personal Reflection on Class and Ethnicity." *Journal of the Canadian Historical Association* (1993): 293–305.

Weiss, Penny A., and Marilyn Friedman, eds. *Feminism and Community*. Philadelphia: Temple University Press, 1995.

NOTES

1. Filmmakers such as Nancy Savoca and Kym Ragusa have also tackled the conflicted nature of women's relationship to community. See, for example, Savoca's *True Love* and *Household Saints* and Ragusa's *fuori/outside*. On Savoca's *True Love*, see my essay, "The Quest for True Love: Nancy Savoca's Domestic Film Comedy"; on *Household Saints*, see Baker and Vitullo and Messina. On Ragusa, see my essay, "Figuring Race: Kym Ragusa's *fuori/outside*."

2. See Werner Sollors's classic distinction in *Beyond Ethnicity*.

3. See Ciresi, "Paradise below the Stairs," and Barolini, introduction to *The Dream Book;* "*Umbertina* and the Universe," *Chiaroscuro: Essays of Identity*, 129–38; and "Becoming a Literary Person out of Context."

4. On the politics of recognition, see Gutman.

5. For a theoretical discussion of various notions of community, see Weiss and Friedman.

6. On issues of public health, in addition to DeSalvo's *Breathless*, see Sandra M. Gilbert's memoir *Wrongful Death*, and Audre Lorde's *The Cancer Journals*.

7. See the other essays in Tamburri, *Fuori*, the first collection of writings by Italian American gays and lesbians. See also Mary Cappello's exploration of lesbian identity in *Night Bloom*.

8. See DeSalvo, "*Paper Fish*: An Appreciation."

9. *Curaggia* is the feminization of the word *curaggiu*, which in southern Italian dialect means courage.

10. See DeSalvo's 1999 book, *Writing as a Way of Healing*.

11. See Vecoli. Maria Mazziotti Gillan's work as a poet, as coeditor (with her daughter Jennifer) of *Unsettling America: An Anthology of Contemporary Multicultural Poetry*, as the director of the Poetry Center at Passaic County Community College, and as the indefatigable organizer of numerous cultural events, is rooted in her Italian American working-

class origins and in her understanding of the rightful place of Italian Americans in multiculturalism.

12. This multicultural anthology, edited by S. E. Anderson and Tony Medina, includes the artwork and writings of 140 international activists who came together in support of the journalist Mumia Abu-Jamal, who is widely recognized as a political prisoner allegedly accused of the murder of a policeman and currently sitting on death row in eastern Pennsylvania.

Conclusion

Lost and Found: Italian American Radicalism in Global Perspective

Donna R. Gabaccia

Every people deserves its own history, its own historiography, and its own historiographical controversies. This is as true of Italian Americans as of other human groups. The essays in this collection certainly point to some emerging and unresolved controversies in Italian American history, and I both expect and hope that new research will pursue these. Still, my main purpose in writing this concluding essay is to view the lost world of Italian American radicalism not as a world unto itself with its own internal debates—worthy as these are—but rather as one important dimension of a global history of population movements out of Italy. What can we learn about the lost world of Italian American radicalism when we view it as one of many cultural and political products of the migratory *italiani nel mondo*? Comparison to other histories, and other historiographies, allows us to understand what was Italian and transnational about Italian American radicalism, but also what made it unique to the United States. Comparison also allows us to post complex questions about how scholars in the United States differ from those in other countries when they write about ethnicity, radicalism, and their own identities.

The more than four million Italians who lived in the United States in 1920 represented about half the Italians living outside Italy at that time. They were a significant component and an important remnant of a much larger movement of fourteen million migrants who left Italy between 1870 and 1914. Most of the fourteen million went to countries other than the United States, and many of them—perhaps even the majority—returned again to Italy.[1] With significant Italian populations living in Tunisia, France, Germany, Switzerland, Argentina, Brazil, Canada, and Australia in the early twentieth century, opportunities to examine almost any dimension of Italian American life from a global and comparative perspective are rich.[2] Examining Italian American radicalism from this perspective is particularly compelling because the radicals of the modern world have themselves so often embraced internationalism and the possibility, first raised by Marx, that the "workers of the world" could "unite."[3]

Comparative methodologies are useful, however, only if they begin with a careful interrogation of the analytical categories chosen. Without careful definition, we make useless comparisons: as we put it in everyday life, "there is little sense comparing apples with oranges."[4] By far the most complex category evoked in the essays here is that of radicalism. On its meaning, contributors to this volume have differed fundamentally from each other and—as a whole—they have defined radicalism somewhat differently than a comparable group of scholars in Europe or Latin America might have. Not surprisingly, the definition of radicalism that is chosen largely determines whether or not scholars actually find a radical Italian American world to explore. They also influence how central tales of collapse or loss will be in these tales of radicalism.

As Mary Jo Bona points out in "Rooted to Family," (see chapter 15) the word *radical* comes from the Latin word *radix* for "root." For most of the contributors to parts 1 and 2 of this book, radicalism means the well-known counter-ideologies of modern Western political and economic philosophy. Radicalism means anarchism, communism, socialism, syndicalism, and feminism. These radical ideologies view capitalism, the state, or patriarchy—in some combination—as the root of human oppression. Radicals are the militant minority among migrants most dedicated to eradicating those oppressions through collective action or radical "movements" of large groups of people.

Of course, at least since Alex Haley wrote his African family odyssey, the related term *roots* also resonates in very particular ways in studies of ethnicity. "Roots" situate individuals in the histories of families and nations, thereby creating identity. Along with Mary Jo Bona, Fred Gardaphè, Julia Lisella, and Edvige Giunta present Italian American writers as radicals, too. In some cases, the writers have been radicals in the first sense—supporters of mass movements for radical social or economic change. In other cases, however, they have been radicals because they have explored new literary forms, broken with family or ethnic group expectations of silence to write about taboo topics like sexuality or disease, and made public their thoughts about their personal lives. The radicalism of many of the writers discussed in this volume originates in their attention to the ethnic dimensions of their identities—dimensions that American culture for long decades denied or eradicated. To define oneself in writing, these authors suggest, is a radical act in itself.

Of the two meanings of radicalism used in this collection, one could be described, somewhat ideally, as ideological—connected to mass movements and to structural changes. The other could be described as contextual—connected to personal transformation, consciousness, and to what we today call identity politics. The first definition of radicalism is widely used in studies of Italians living and working in other parts of the world, allowing many direct comparisons between the essays presented here and an international historiography on Italian migrants as "workers of the world." The second, by comparison, is a meaning of radicalism used more often in the United States and in the English-speaking world than elsewhere. Both meanings deserve further reflection for what they tell us about Italian American radicalism and for what they tell us about American history and scholarship on radicalism. The first points our attention to what was "Italian" about Italian American radicalism and thus shared by Italians migrating elsewhere, creating a transnational radical world. The second helps us better understand the uniquely American dimensions of that radicalism.

Whereas students of French, Brazilian, and Argentine labor movements early identified Italian immigrants as militants and leaders, their counterparts in North America have labored within a historiography that easily renders radicals generally, and Italian American radicals specifically, marginal when not invisible.[5] Initially, the problem was the cold war era's unquestioned assumption of American exceptionalism—the once vigorous claims that the United States, unlike the rest of the industrialized world, had no self-consciously radical working class worth writing about. A second problem was the shadow of Werner Sombart, who had asked, "Why is there no socialism in America?" and had wondered if divisions within an immigrant-origin working class provided an answer. Finally, when a vigorous historiography on Jewish (and German and some other immigrant) activists effectively countered even Sombart's arguments, American social science had a ready, cultural, explanation for Italians' limited contributions to radicalism. In the 1950s, Edward Banfield argued that southern Italians were "amoral familists" incapable of collective action.[6] His portrait of Italians, as we will see, has proved tenacious, at least in the English-speaking world.

The essays collected in this volume make it possible for us to see just how much Italian radicalism in the United States before World War I shared with Italian radicalism elsewhere in the world in that era. Ideological flexibility was common among Italian immigrants everywhere in the world, as was a marked preference for anarchism and syndicalism and a decided disinterest in socialist party membership and electoral politics. Whether in Tampa, as described by Gary R. Mormino and George E. Pozzetta (see chapter 12), or San Francisco, described by Paola Sensi-Isolani (see chapter 8), immigrant anarchists and syndicalists were numerous, and vociferous, and they worked closely—as they did also in France and Latin America—with other immigrants or "Latin" speakers of Romance languages. In Tampa and New York, anarcho-syndicalists and the Industrial Workers of the World (IWW) more generally accomplished what similar syndicalist movements of Italians did in southern France, Argentina, and Brazil—mounting huge and successful multi-ethnic strikes in which Italian immigrant workers established reputations for workplace militancy and even leadership. Although only occasionally the unchallenged leaders of immigrant communities (as they were in Tampa), radicals usually gave priests and *prominenti* healthy competition for community leadership in the United States. In addition, these radicals were anything but isolated, marginal men. Salvatore Salerno's essay (see chapter 7), in particular, reminds us of the transnational lives and extensive transnational connections of Italian radicals of this era. If their ideas kept them outside the mainstream of American labor, they made them much more central to intellectual currents outside the United States, especially to the histories of anarchism and syndicalism as global movements of considerable influence in such countries as France, Italy, Spain, Argentina, and Brazil.

Together, the essays on the prewar "world" of radicals in this volume add rich detail to a once-hazy North American corner of our global portrait of Italian radicalism. There are few real surprises here, at least for readers familiar with the radical worlds of Italian immigrants elsewhere. Jennifer Guglielmo's study (see chapter 4) of anarchist feminist voices does identify one dimension of radicalism not yet noted or explored extensively in other settings. And Cal Winslow takes up a troubled issue—that of labor racketeering on the docks—without losing sight of the multi-ethnic rank-and-file activism that opposed it. Still, one more often hears in these essays murmured arguments against old stereotypes rather than affirmation or revision of the already-existing historiography on Italian workers' activism worldwide. Charles A. Zappia's essay (see chapter 5) reminds us of the presence of socialists among Italian labor activists in the garment trades, a reminder, perhaps, to Sombart, that there *was*, in fact socialism in the United States. Paul Avrich reminds readers familiar with the legal travesty of Sacco and Vanzetti's execution that the two men were indeed dedicated anarchists who believed in, and may have used, violence as a form of political expression (see chapter 6).

It is not the case that the writers of these essays present their research as completely new, or are unaware that the existence of Italian American radicalism has been fairly well documented (the notes to the essays in parts 1 and 2 show a thorough familiarity with earlier work). The problem seems to be, instead, that this earlier documentation of the radicals' world has not displaced stereotypes of Italian immigrants as familists incapable of collective action. Why this should be the case is too complicated to explore here and may require the tools of postmodernist analysis of discourse. Perhaps the essayists simply understand better than I that the most-pressing historiographical task remains the toppling of old stereotypes unaffected as yet by the accumulation of considerable evidence to the contrary. Still, I remain hopeful that this new collection of essays will make it possible for a new generation of researchers to end their quarrel with old stereotypes and to turn instead to new, interpretive controversies. Not surprisingly, I would urge Americanists to interpret the lost world of Italian American radicalism as part of a transnational world, of which the United States is an important, not marginal, corner.

Taken collectively, these essays also do point the way toward fresh controversies within Italian American history. Where the history of the Italian American radical world diverges from that of Italian workers in other parts of the world is in the subsequent, postwar history of radicalism's collapse in the United States. Rudolph J. Vecoli offers a challenging interpretation of that collapse. Most American historians focus on the "Americanization" (or "working-class Americanism") of immigrants during the interwar years; Vecoli emphasizes instead the formation of anti-radical but national (or ethnic) identities under the sway of Mussolini—what he terms Italian Americans' "fascistization" (see chapter 1). This seems to suggest that radicalism's collapse orginated in the evolving dynamics of Italian American immigrant communities themselves—as first the *prominenti* and then workers' growing sense of ethnic nationalism nudged them toward philo-fascism. Nunzio Pernicone's essay (see chapter 2) on the harsh ideological battles raging among anarchists lends some support to this possibility; divisions among Italian American radicals hindered them from building a coherent counter to Fascist propaganda.

Mass fascistization did not occur among Italian immigrants everywhere in the world, however. In rather sharp contrast—to name just two cases—Italian immigrant workers in Belgium and France became virulent anti-Fascists as part of their integration into the multi-ethnic and anti-Fascist labor movements of those countries.[7] (The more-complex cases of Brazil and Argentina seem to fall intermediately between those of France and the United States.)[8] The fates of the early, transnational radical world in differing nation states in the interwar years were not a straightforward reflection of Mussolini's level of interest. Mussolini was certainly as eager to court the *prominenti* and workers of other countries as he was to have the support of Italian Americans in the United States. Nor was it for lack of internal divisions. It is difficult to imagine more fractious, personalized, and conflict-ridden political environments than the working-class neighborhoods of La Boca in Buenos Aires or the Left Bank of Paris in the 1920s.

As Vecoli's essay shows, intense American hostility to radicalism allowed Americans to tolerate Fascist sympathizers, even after the United States went to war with Italy. This suggests that there may be something distinctively "American" about fascistization, even if calling it "Americanization" seems inaccurate. Radicalism's demise in the United States may have originated not so much from within the worlds of Italian Americans and Italian American radicals as in the repression, anti-Communism, and anti-radical nativism of the interwar years. Is it possible that the United States welcomed ethnic nationalism, and even fascistization of Italian Americans, because it helped make them opponents of radicalism, and thus ultimately good Americans?

The periodization of radicalism's decline is by no means well established, even for the United States. Indeed, other contributors provide us alternative explanations and timetables for the collapse of the prewar radical, and transnational, world Italian Americans shared with immigrant Italian workers elsewhere. Focusing on writers, many of whom remained active in left-wing movements in the 1930s and 1940s, Fred Gardaphè's essay (see chapter 13) makes the clearest argument for continuity and evolution rather than a sudden collapse in the face of fascistized Italian American identities. Perhaps Italian American anarchists, syndicalists, and Communists disappeared; Italian American novelists did not. They continued to raise questions about poverty and Fascism as well as about racial, class, and gender oppression, and they continued to raise them in connection to personal identity and personal, private, life in their fiction, memoirs, and poems. Exploring the modest, but real, influence of Italian American Communists in the inter-war years, Gerald Meyer (see chapter 9) also echoes Charles A. Zappia in seeing the ultimate demise of the radicals' world in the second era of Red Scares, during the cold war (see chapter 5).

In addition, as essays by Jackie DiSalvo (see chapter 10) and Gil Fagiani (see chapter 11) remind readers, one can still find outspoken Italian American radicals—Father Groppi, Mario Savio—working collectively for fundamental change in American political and economic life, even in the era of the so-called working-class "white ethnic" conservative "hard hats" of the 1960s. The connections we see between these later radicals and their predecessors need to be extended, and explored, before we reach any firm conclusions about the "loss" of the prewar world of radicals. The essays of both Guglielmo and of Vecoli suggest that analysis of gender dynamics within families—and the success or failure of radicals in building family-based cultures of resistance—may hold important clues to this kind of cross-generational analysis of radicalism.

Perhaps collapse will ultimately prove too strong a word to describe the fate of the prewar radicals' world. It may very well be that scholars need instead to explore the transformation, and even the Americanization, of radicalism, not its demise. By introducing an alternative definition of radicalism in this collection, scholars in literature and cultural studies force us to ask about the origins and history of a more-American understanding of radicalism, nurtured from within. For these scholars, radicalism is focused on individual identity and originates in Italian American writers' refusal to conform to American culture's expectations that ethnicity disappear in the years after World War II.

Having recently edited a collection of essays on Italian immigrant radicals around the world, I am particularly aware of the extent to which interest in gender, in individual biography, and in the connection of the personal and political distinguishes American studies of radicalism from their counterparts in other nations.[9] Outside the United States, the radicalism of workers continues to mean, and to mean quite firmly, the collective pursuit of a fundamental political, economic, and cultural transformation of capitalism and the state. Recognizing this tension among differing definitions of radicalism has helped me to understand why my Argentine, French, and German colleagues in labor history so often stare blankly when issues of gender and of ethnic or racial identity are raised in discussions of Italian American radicalism. To their eyes, these are issues for psychologists and therapists, not students of radicalism.

By contrast, many contributors to this collection have been drawn to study radicalism defined by culture, character, gender, identity, and by the so-called private or personal worlds of reproduction, family, and character. Whether or not there is something we can call American radicalism, there certainly are definitions of radicalism that seem uniquely American, and approaches to the study of radicalism that are more appealing to scholars in the United States than in the Latin American, French, and Italian-speaking worlds. These more-American understandings of radicalism are part of the story of the evolution of the "lost world," and essays on radical writers in this collection do a particularly good job of demonstrating the benefits of this approach. Their definition of radicalism, too, raises important questions about what makes Italian American history and culture uniquely American.

Whether the topic is the working-class anarchists of the prewar years or the writings of poet Rosa Zagnoni Marinoni, the lives of many of the radicals explored in this collection do not fit easily within the rubrics of American politics and culture. Nunzio Pernicone must explain in some detail the seriousness of personal and ideological conflicts such as that between Carlo Tresca and Luigi Galleani precisely because they can so easily appear as trivial, silly, and inconsequential to American eyes. Tresca, he concludes, remained "always a little outside the favor of all the subversive theologies, always suspect in the community of the faithful." Similarly, Julia Lisella introduces us to Marinoni—who is almost completely unknown, even to students of American literature—and tells us that she was too middle class and well educated to be considered a proletarian writer of the 1940s, yet neither was she a local colorist or Arkansas sentimentalist or "Southern writer" (see chapter 14). Men as diverse as Father Groppi, Carlo Tresca, and Vito Marcantonio also prove hard to categorize ideologically; each seems to have patched together his ideas from the complex strands of unique family histories and a confrontation with issues and pressures unique to his own times. How else to explain a man like Marcantonio (a sometimes Republican with a voting record applauded by the Communist Party) other than biographically?

The lives documented in this collection remind us of the limits of studying radical or literary movements exclusively as groups of people we assume to have lived internally cohesive lives or to have held consistent and uniform ideas. In fact, the radicals we meet in this collection were, with few exceptions, conformist in extremely individual ways. They seemed more concerned with personal integrity, and with personal connection and loyalty to the human beings in their immediate surroundings, than they were with the movements that ostensibly give them historical significance. Most seemed also to qualify as "charismatic" in the manifold and complex meanings of that term. Even radicals deeply committed to collective action and to structural change lived, died, and made their most-important moral choices, as individuals.

Persistence in exploring individual identity and writing about it—without finding an easy response from audiences or from critics—is, Giunta and Bona remind us, the fate of many contemporary Italian American writers too. Their radicalism, Giunta suggests, "lies both in their deeply personal work and in their public response to the lack of a supporting context for their work" (see chapter 16). Perhaps this helps to explain why Italian American radicals have become such attractive objects of scholarly study in the 1990s. Like radicals past and present, intellectuals in American society today often feel they "have no audience," and that they work alone and invisibly in a culture hostile to intellectual work. Some of the contributors to this collection seem consciously to seek moral encouragement and guidance in the present by exploring the radicals of an early age. As Guglielmo notes, modern radicals hoping to overcome their own isolation could learn much from the Italian American anarchist feminists of the turn of the twentieth century. They teach us strategy, she says: "They disrupt stereotypes and they force us to examine and interrogate the way power operates within and between communities to silence and make [us] invisible."

The timing of scholarly interest in the "lost world" of Italian American radicalism seems particularly worthy of comment; so does the fact that scholarly efforts to recover this world in the United States seem to increase as the radical movements rooted in the nineteenth century lose political significance. A conference on Italian American radicalism held in New York in 1997 attracted more than three hundred participants, whereas a similar conference held 25 years earlier, in the aftermath of the activist 1960s, had generated only nine papers.[10] Around the world, by 1997, Communism had collapsed and labor history was in eclipse. In the United States, one could find precious few remnants of the old or new left, and if the American labor movement was not exactly moribund, neither was it the center of moral energy for intellectuals, as it has been in some other eras of the twentieth century. Why then are Italian American scholars— quite unlike those of Italian descent in other parts of the world—so eager to understand the lost world of the radicals only at the present time?

What distinguishes the United States and its historians of radicalism from those in many other countries is their sense of having "lost" the world of the radicals. First, it seems true that—far more than in other countries—the fascistization or Americanization of Italian immigrants in the United States required a sharp break from the radicalism of nineteenth-century Europe. This break most certainly did not also occur in France, where immigrants continued to be seen as providing the core support and leadership for labor and Left movements into the 1940s, and in some cases beyond into the post–World War II period. Not having been lost in quite the same extreme fashion, the world of the radicals is less in need now of being found.

In turn, the fact that Italians in Argentina or France did not become Fascists and anti-radicals in order to become good citizens of their new homelands means that the identities of people of Italian descent elsewhere did not evolve into the exact counterparts of the identities of Italian Americans. Argentines and French men and women of Italian descent frequently know of their origins, and they are as much in contact with their relatives at home as are Italian Americans; they may even belong to an Italian cultural organization or travel regularly in Italy. But only rarely do they claim, or claim to understand, the hyphenated identities, the sense of loss or of celebration or of recovery that we see in discussions of ethnicity in the United States. The Argentine of Italian descent claims to be "just an Argentine"; the Frenchman of Italian descent is comfortable with a national identity unmodified by an ethnic marker—he is firmly French, without hyphens. Ethnic identity did not become an arena of personal resistance to national identities in Argentina and in France, as it did in the United States.

Radicals in the United States, try as they may, could not simultaneously be good leftists and good Americans. If Italian Americans today remain engaged in recovering from their losses and more interested than their counterparts abroad in identity as a form of radicalism and a form of politics, we must seek explanations in the history of radicalism in the United States, which has not followed the trajectory of radical movements in other countries. Immigrants finding incorporation into the United States had to create new identities in a nation which was—and arguably remains—what Italian immigrants often described it to be in the early twentieth century—the heart of, and best expression of, the power of the "capitalist beast." Capitalism, class, politics, and the state were not trivial players in the making of Italian Americans, or in the making of Italian American ethnicity. They determined Italian Americans' losses, restricted their choices, and made them—along with Italian American studies—what they are today.

NOTES

1. Gianfausto Rosoli, ed., *Un secolo di emigrazione italiana, 1876–1976* (Rome: Centro Studi Emigrazione, 1978).

2. There is a modest but growing literature that examines Italian migrations worldwide, from a variety of perspectives. See Robert Foerster, *The Italian Emigration of Our Times* (1919; New York: Russell & Russell, 1968); George E. Pozzetta and Bruno Ramirez, eds., *The Italian Diaspora: Migration across the Globe* (Toronto: Multicultural History Society of Ontario, 1992); Gianfausto Rosoli, "The Global Picture of the Italian Diaspora for the Americas," in *The Columbus People: Perspectives in Italian Immigration to the Americas and Australia*, ed. Lydio F. Tomasi, Piero Gastaldo, and Thomas Row (New York: Center for Migration Studies, and Turin, Italy: Fondazione Giovanni Agnelli, 1994); Donna R. Gabaccia, *Italy's Many Diasporas: Elites, Exiles, and Workers of the World* (London: University College of London Press, 2000).

3. Good starting places for those interested in the global dimensions of Italian radicalism are Ernesto Ragionieri, "Italiani all'estero ed emigrazione di lavoratori italiani: Un tema di storia del movimento operaio," *Belfagor, Rassegna di varia umanità* 17, no. 6 (1962): 640–69; Bruno Bezza, *Gli italiani fuori d'Italia, Gli emigrati italiani nei movimenti operai dei paesi d'adozione 1880–1940* (Milan: Franco Angeli, 1983); Vanni Blengino, Emilio Franzina, and Adolfo Pepe, *La riscoperta delle Americhe; Lavoratori e sindacato nell'emigrazione italiana in America Latina 1870–1970* (Milan: Teti Editore, 1993); Donna R. Gabaccia and Fraser Ottanelli, "Diaspora or International Proletariat?" *Diaspora* 6, no. 1 (1997): 61–83.

4. On the use of comparison in studies of migration, see Nancy Green, "The Comparative Method and Poststructural Structuralism—New Perspective for Migration Studies," *Journal of American Ethnic History* 13 (summer 1994): 3–22.

5. Samuel L. Baily, "The Italians and the Development of Organized Labor in Argentina, Brazil, and the United States, 1880–1914," *Journal of Social History* 3 (winter 1969–1970): 123–34; Baily, "The Italians and Organized Labor in the United States and Argentina," *International Migration Review* 1 (summer 1967): 55–66.

    6. Edward Banfield, *The Moral Basis of a Backward Society* (Glencoe, Ill: The Free Press, 1958).

    7. Anne Morelli, *Fascismo e antifascismo nell'emigrazione italiana in Belgio (1922–1940)* (Rome: Bonacci, 1987); Pierre Guillen, "Le rôle politique de l'immigration italienne en France dans l'entre-deux guerres," in *Les italiens en France del 1914 à 1940*, ed. Pierre Milza (Rome: Collection de l'École Française de Rome, 1986), 337–41.

    8. Angelo Trento, "Il Brasile, gli immigrati e il fenomeno fascista," in Blengino, Franzina, and Pepe, *La riscoperta delle Americhe*, 250–64; Maria de Lujén Leiva, "Il movimento antifascista italiano in Argentina (1922–1945)," in Bezza, *Gli italiani*, 549–82.

    9. Donna R. Gabaccia and Fraser Ottanelli, eds., *Italian Workers of the World: Labor Migration and the Making of Multiethnic Nations* (Urbana and Chicago, University of Illinois Press, 2001).

    10. Rudolph J. Vecoli, ed., *Italian American "Radicalism": Old World Origins and New World Developments* (Staten Island, N.Y.: American Italian Historical Association, 1972).

About the Editors and Contributors

PAUL AVRICH is the author of many books, including *The Haymarket Tragedy: Anarchist Portraits; Sacco and Vanzetti: The Anarchist Background;* and *Anarchist Voices: An Oral History of Anarchism in America,* as well as countless articles in publications ranging from *The New York Times Book Review* to *Encyclopedia Britannica.* He is a professor emeritus at Queens College (City University of New York).

MARY JO BONA is the editor of *The Voices We Carry: Recent Italian/American Women's Fiction,* coeditor (with Anthony J. Tamburri) of *Through the Looking Glass: Italian & Italian/American Images in the Media,* and author of *Claiming a Tradition: Italian-American Women Writers.* She teaches at the State University of New York, Stony Brook, in the Italian American Studies Program.

PHILIP V. CANNISTRARO is Distinguished Professor of Italian American Studies at Queens College and the Graduate School (City University of New York). An authority on the Italian American experience and the history of modern Italy, he has written numerous books, including works on Fascist cultural policy, a biography of *Margherita Sarfatti,* and *Blackshirts in Little Italy.* Cannistraro has also edited *The Italians of New York: Five Centuries of Struggle and Achievement* and is coauthor of *The Western Perspective: A History of Civilization in the West.* He is currently writing a biography of Italian dictator Benito Mussolini.

JACKIE DISALVO is the author of *War of Titans,* has coedited (with George Anthony Rosso and Christopher Hobson) *Blake's Critique of Milton and the Politics of Religion* and *Blake, Politics and History,* and has published numerous Marxist feminist articles on Milton. She is a professor of English at Baruch College and the Graduate Center at the City University of New York.

GIL FAGIANI is a poet, translator, and short-story writer. He is the author of more than a dozen essays published in such journals as *Forum Italicum*, *Voices in Italian Americana*, *Differentia*, and the *Italian American Review*. Most recently, his poems were published in *Off the Cuff*, edited by Jackie Sheeler. A social worker by profession, Gil is the director of Renewal House, a residential treatment program for recovering addicts.

DONNA R. GABACCIA's recent publications include *Italy's Many Diasporas* (University of Chicago Press); *Italian Workers of the World: Labor, Migration, and the Making of Multi-Ethnic States*, coedited with Fraser Ottanelli (University of Illinois Press); and *Women, Gender, and Transnational Lives: Italian Workers of the World*, coedited with Franca Iacovetta (University of Toronto Press). She teaches history at the University of Pittsburgh.

FRED GARDAPHÈ's books include *Italian Signs, American Streets: The Evolution of Italian American Narrative*; *Dagoes Read: Tradition and the Italian/American Writer*; *Moustache Pete Is Dead!: Italian/American Oral Tradition Preserved in Print*; and *Leaving Little Italy: Essaying Italian American Culture*. He is associate editor of *Fra Noi*; editor of the Series in Italian American Studies, State University of New York Press; and cofounding coeditor of *Voices in Italian Americana*, a literary journal and cultural review. He directs the Italian American Studies Program at the State University of New York, Stony Brook.

EDVIGE GIUNTA is the author of *Writing with an Accent: Contemporary Italian American Women Authors* (Palgrave/St. Martin's Press), and *Dire l'indicibile: memoir di autrici italo americane* (University of Siena). She coedited, with Louise DeSalvo, *The Milk of Almonds: Italian American Women Writers on Food and Culture* (Feminist Press), and coedited, with Maria Mazziotti Gillan and Jennifer Gillan, *Italian American Writers on New Jersey* (Rutgers University Press). Her essays, memoirs, and poetry have been published in many journals and anthologies. She is poetry editor of *The Women's Study Quarterly*. She teaches English at New Jersey City University.

JENNIFER GUGLIELMO is coeditor of *Are Italians White?: How Race Is Made in America* (Routledge, 2003). She teaches history at Smith College.

JULIA LISELLA has written extensively on women poets, including Rosa Zagnoni Marinoni, Genevieve Taggard, Lola Ridge, Muriel Rukeyser, Margaret Walker, Lucille Clifton, and Maxine Hong Kingston. Her own poems appear in many journals and anthologies. She is a lecturer in history and literature at Harvard University.

GERALD MEYER is a professor emeritus of history at Hostos Community College (City University of New York). The author of *Vito Marcantonio: Radical Politician, 1902–1954,* he has also written more than forty articles, reviews, and encyclopedia entries on a wide range of Italian American topics including educator Leonard Covello, the history of Little Italies, and aspects of the Italian American encounter with the American Left. Meyer lectures widely and is an editor of *Science & Society and The Italian American Review.*

GARY R. MORMINO has written *Immigrants on the Hill* (University of Illinois Press), and is coauthor, with George E. Pozzetta, of *The Immigrant World of Ybor City.* He has also written many articles and reviews. He teaches at the University of South Florida, St. Petersburg Campus.

NUNZIO PERNICONE is the author of *Italian Anarchism, 1864–1892* (Princeton University Press), and numerous articles on the Italian labor movement and the role of anarchism in the history of the Italian American community. He teaches at Drexel University.

GEORGE E. POZZETTA is the coauthor, with Gary R. Mormino, of *The Immigrant World of Ybor City* (University Presses of Florida). He taught at the University of Florida until his death in 1994.

SALVATORE SALERNO is the author of *Direct Action and Sabotage: Three Classic I.W.W. Pamphlets,* and *Red November, Black November: Culture and Community in the Industrial Workers of the World.* His essays on Italian immigrant radicalism and culture have appeared in several anthologies and journals. He is an independent scholar.

PAOLA A(LESSANDRA) SENSI-ISOLANI has edited several books on Italian Americans, the most recent together with Anthony J. Tamburri, *Italian Americans: A Retrospective on the Twentieth Century* (American Italian Historical Association, 2001). She is the author of articles on Italian migration to California and Central America. She is a professor of anthropology at Saint Mary's College of California.

RUDOLPH J. VECOLI has written many seminal articles on the Italian American experience, including "*Contadini* in Chicago: A Critique of *The Uprooted,*" "The American Centrifuge: Ethnicity at the End of the Century," "Prelates and Peasants: Italian Immigrants and the Catholic Church." He is the director of the Immigration History Research Center at the University of Minnesota.

CALVIN WINSLOW has coedited *Waterfront Workers: New Perspectives on Race and Class* (University of Illinois Press), and many articles and reviews in a wide range of topics. He is currently the director of the Mendocino Institute, a research and education center located in Mendocino, California.

CHARLES A. ZAPPIA has written many articles on race, ethnicity, and gender in relationship to work and trade unionism. He presently teaches at San Diego Mesa College.

INDEX